D0939081

THE VORTEX

THE
VORTEX

A True Story of History's Deadliest Storm,
an Unspeakable War, and Liberation

SCOTT CARNEY
AND JASON MIKLIAN

€€€€
An Imprint of HarperCollins *Publishers*

HarperCollins books may be purchased for educational, business, or sales promotional use. For information, please email the Special Markets Department at SPsales@harpercollins.com.

Ecco® and HarperCollins® are trademarks of HarperCollins Publishers.

FIRST EDITION

Designed by Michelle Crowe

Frontmatter map illustrations by Mike Hall

Background art by APHITHANA / Shutterstock, Inc.

Library of Congress Cataloging-in-Publication Data has been applied for.

ISBN 978-0-06-298541-5

22 23 24 25 26 FB 10 9 8 7 6 5 4 3 2 1

For the Bangladeshis who never saw independence

CONTENTS

ACT II: OPERATION SEARCHLIGHT

ACT III: THE RECKONING

SOUTH ASIA
in 1970

500 miles

⊛ Capital city
○ Other major city
······ International border
-·-·- Disputed borders

CHINA

AFGHANISTAN

WEST PAKISTAN

Islamabad ⊛
Rawalpindi ○

Indus River

Multan ○

New Delhi ⊛

H i m a l a y a s

NEPAL

BHUTAN

Brahmaputra River

Ganges River

EAST PAKISTAN
⊛ Dacca

Karachi ○
Tropic of Cancer

Calcutta ○

I N D I A

BURMA

ARABIAN
SEA

Bombay ○

BAY OF
BENGAL

Andaman
Islands

ANDAMAN
SEA

INDIAN
OCEAN

SRI
LANKA

Nicobar
Islands

EAST PAKISTAN
in 1970

100 miles

⊛ Capital city
○ Other city or town
✕ Battle site
···· International border
→ Path of the Great Bhola Cyclone

Ganges River

Brahmaputra River

Tura

Kamalpur ✕

Chargram ✕

I N D I A

I N D I A

Padma River

⊛ Dacca

Boxanagar

○ Jessore

Calcutta ○
○ Salt Lake
Refugee Camp

Barisal
Lalmohan
Tetulia River
Hatiya
Bhola   Manpura

Chittagong

Gasper
Light

Cox's Bazar

B U R M A

B A Y   O F   B E N G A L

Authors' Note

This book is the product of more than two hundred interviews over four years, multiple trips to Bangladesh, and correspondence with sources in Bangladesh, Pakistan, India, the United States, the United Kingdom, South Africa, and elsewhere. We have spoken with cyclone survivors, freedom fighters, members of the Pakistani military, historians, scientists, policymakers, hotel employees, TV broadcasters, climate experts, and other individuals who all contributed valuable pieces to the puzzle.

Our archival research spans an additional seven hundred and fifty sources, including books, academic articles, reports, newspaper and magazine articles, government statements, and other publications. Some documents, like Yahya Khan's service record, are presented here publicly for the first time. These sources helped contextualize our characters' experiences and validate the stories we collected from eyewitnesses. For ease of reading, we do not employ in-text citations. Instead, we present the reference section in endnotes, noting the relevant text.

This book is a work of narrative nonfiction. While all details herein are true and research-based, the act of putting disparate pieces together in a way that puts the reader in the historical moment required us to make judgments at times about motivations and states of mind that are not preserved in the historical record. In some places, we condensed timelines, dialogues, competing perspectives, and peripheral details for clarity and to better bring out the essence of the events. For example, some scenes combine events that occurred over multiple days into a single narrative moment. In other places, we extrapolate minor pieces of dialogue, mannerisms, and presumable emotional responses in places where the participants themselves did not remember the specific details of a conversation that happened fifty years ago. For transparency, we have referenced all such instances in the notes section. These stylistic edits have no material bearing on the factual events we present, and responsibility for any errors or possible misinterpretations remain ours alone.

Furthermore, we opted to use the spellings of locations, military ranks, and people that were in use in 1970 in order to preserve the flavor of the moment. So cities like Kolkata and Dhaka appear in this text as Calcutta and Dacca. Similarly, we chose the spelling Manpura over Monpura, despite both spellings being in popular usage. We refer to our central sources by their first names instead of their last names to avoid the confusion that would emerge where people share common family names.

THE VORTEX

Blackout

White mist surged across the *Mahajagmitra*'s bridge and the ship's aging frame creaked with each menacing gust. The man in charge, Captain Nesari, watched the pressure fall a bit more on his ship's barometer and paced the length of the control room. With its holds crammed to capacity with jute fiber and steel, the ship rocked ominously as it inched toward the open sea.

Nesari and his ship were leaving the great Hooghly River, the westernmost finger of India's Ganges delta and one of the world's most troublesome waterways. The Hooghly meets the Bay of Bengal at a point about thirty miles south of Calcutta, where incalculable volumes of silt wash down from the Himalayas and form a fan of ever-shifting rivers, tributaries, and temporary islands. A freighter that alights on a sandbar here might never break free.

As if to prove the point, the rusty hulls of abandoned vessels dotted the seascape. Colossal silt deposits alter the map on an almost daily basis, which is why Nesari hired the expert river pilot R. K. Das from the Port of Calcutta to navigate this stretch of water. Das deftly guided the six-thousand-ton ship through the narrow channels as the wind began to pick up.

Nesari darted his eyes back and forth between the barometer and a stack of outdated maps as he tried to estimate the coming storm's strength. The stakes were high. Waiting out the weather system would add at least a day to their two-week trip to Oman. It would mean that the company would have to pay another day's worth of salaries to the crew of forty-eight seamen, deplete another day's worth of fuel, and stretch their already narrow profit margins to the breaking point—all potentially fireable offenses for any captain who signed off on such a cost overrun.

Then again, pushing onward out of the delta would expose the ship to the full power of whatever weather system lay just over the horizon. The worst-case scenario was too terrifying to contemplate. So Nesari had a decision to make: Would he take the risk, or would he power down?

If it was just a squall, then the *Mahajagmitra* would be fine. But what if they were witnessing the edge of a cyclone? Cyclonic storms—called hurricanes in the Americas and typhoons in the Pacific Rim—are especially deadly in the Bay of Bengal. Here storms spin counterclockwise, which means that any ship leaving the Port of Calcutta would have to travel directly into the center of the storm's power—facing potentially devastating wind and waves head-on. Once a ship turned southward, the wind would crash against the port side, which could capsize a vulnerable vessel.

Nesari thought of his family and then considered his first mate. David Machado wore the starched white uniform of the Indian Merchant Navy, complete with three gold stripes and a diamond on his epaulettes. Machado couldn't help cracking into a smile when he thought no one was looking. Last week, he'd married the love of his life. After the ceremony in South India, the newlyweds flew to Calcutta together. Sailors like him didn't always get to pick the location of their honeymoon, yet somehow he'd convinced his bride that a cruise to the Middle East would be a fine way to start their life together.

Machado's wife stowed herself below deck, her heavy wedding jewelry tucked safely away in a trunk in their shared compartment.

The crew knew the ancient Greek warning that women on board were bad luck. Ostensibly, this was because women caused distractions, but more superstitious sailors claimed that they also attracted misfortune and bad weather. Captain Nesari was glad that they lived in more civilized times.

It was November 11, 1970, yet despite thousands of years of seafaring, a sailor's ability to predict the weather hadn't improved much since the nineteenth century. The radio was the biggest breakthrough in the last hundred years and allowed mariners to speak with other ships who were closer to dangerous weather systems. A smart navigator could triangulate a storm's center by matching other ships' weather reports to his ship's current position—a method that wasn't so different from how truckers relayed traffic patterns to their colleagues over CB radios.

The catch was that the radio operator had to actually find another ship's signal. As far as Nesari could tell, there wasn't a single transmission coming from anywhere in the Bay of Bengal. This meant that if the *Mahajagmitra* proceeded onwards it would be the first to brave the swells. It would be their job to report back to other vessels contemplating the journey.

Barring radio contact, Nesari had only one other tool to understand the weather system: Buys Ballot's law. In 1857, the Dutch meteorologist Charles Buys Ballot invented a method for determining the direction of a storm. He wrote that if a sailor in the Northern Hemisphere stood on deck with his back to the wind, he could use his senses like a human compass. The pressure would be low on his right and high on his left, which meant that his right hand would point to the center of the system—the most dangerous part. As long as Nesari could steer clear of that point, they'd avoid the most intense wind and waves. The ship and its crew would be safe, and they'd save valuable days at sea.

The problem was that Buys Ballot's law was really more of a guideline than a law. It was about as accurate as navigating through crowded

Calcutta streets using only the North Star as a guide, which is to say, it was not very accurate at all. Nevertheless, Nesari walked out onto the deck, turned his back to the growing gale, and guessed that the *Mahajagmitra* would make it safely through.

It was his call.

An hour later, the ship reached Gasper Light, a repeating signal tower that marked the last point on the river system before open water. Das recorded in his log that the ship was in fine sailing shape after he handed control back over to the captain. Das also noted that the waves were growing and the weather was "not at all good" but "not so bad as to make boating impossible." With those mixed messages he left out any mention of whether he agreed with Nesari's decision to push out into the bay. His job done, Das disembarked, then watched as the *Mahajagmitra*'s silhouette diminished in the distance, until it was just a dark speck on a sinister orange-green horizon.

The ship moved forward under Nesari's confident hand. He'd worked on oceangoing vessels like this one for most of his career and knew every compartment, bolt, and line of rope on board, but this storm already felt different from any other he'd pushed through. The wheel pulled against his hand, and it became more and more difficult to keep his ship on course. First mate Machado tried to comfort his wife as the ship rocked back and forth on the waves. Perhaps he told her that this was a large ship and they would be fine.

The *Mahajagmitra*'s engines strained as the boat pitched through the churn. Though there was no way for Captain Nesari to know it, he was sailing directly into the center of a cyclone. The vortex cast a wide disk of clouds spanning almost the entirety of the Bay of Bengal, an expanse of water about the same size as Texas. The swirling storm gathered strength from warm waters and conjured winds that screamed across the sea at a hundred and forty miles an hour.

The system whirled around a perfectly still eye. Clouds spun like the hands of a clock turning backward, yet inside the eye, the winds fell to a whisper. Here, an impenetrable cloud wall touched the sky as it rotated slowly. This gyre fed on the power of the earth itself, dragging the ocean along its rotation so that the sea formed a gigantic whirlpool, pulling everything toward one ultimate point.

An hour after Das disembarked, a nearby ship named the *Desh Alok* picked up the dots and dashes of a distress call from the *Mahajagmitra's* transmitter. The radio operator deciphered the line of Morse code inside his damp radio room:

AFRAID OF DRIFTING INTO STORM CENTER.

Captain Nesari didn't know it yet, but his ship had already crossed the point of no return—the storm's event horizon. Its fate was sealed as if it were light entering into a black hole.

As water crashed against its gunwales and poured onto the deck, the *Mahajagmitra* had no way to find its bearings. The forty-eight-member crew secured every hatch and portal to the lower decks, in the hopes that a watertight ship might survive on luck alone after they lost control of the helm. Every eight seconds, the vessel pitched fifty degrees along its axis as it rode up the face of one wave and into the trough of another. Nesari would have tried to keep the bow facing directly into the threat of oncoming waves, but he couldn't do anything when the water came from all directions at once.

Two hours out from Gasper Light, just after noon, the radio operator of the *Majahagmitra* sent out another message. This time, it was a request for bearings. They were lost. If two ships responded with their positions, the navigator could try to ascertain the ship's place on a map by triangulating the signals. Yet any attempt would have been little more than an academic exercise.

By this time, the cyclone's tendrils brushed against the sandy islands that make up the Ganges delta, testing the point where it would eventually meet land. Though the storm was moving northeast, the wind hit the coast from the south as the storm circulated.

One hour later, the *Mahajagmitra* sent out another distress call.

WIND HURRICANE FORCE. ALL ACCOMMODATION AND STOREROOMS FLOODED. ALSO HATCHES MAKING WATER. NOW TRYING TO RUN WITH THE WIND MAKING APPROXIMATELY NORTHEASTERLY COURSE. PRESENT POSITION VERY APPROXIMATE. UNABLE TO GIVE INDICATION AS TO WHERE.

Hurricane force means gusts moving at speeds of at least seventy-four miles an hour, but this ship experienced far stronger. The wind carried almost enough force to take a man airborne. The vessel's prodigious storerooms took on water, making it almost impossible for the ship to maneuver. Their northeast course meant that the storm rode directly up their stern.

In the swells of anxiety and desperation, Machado might have summoned his bride up from the flooding decks below to the bridge, one of the ship's highest and driest parts. The couple would have watched helplessly as waves crashed over the bow. The captain may have tried to keep up morale, perhaps he brought the crew together in a song, or he might have laid out an action plan of how best to survive a sinking vessel.

The irresistible forces of nature dragged the *Mahajagmitra* into the very center of the cyclone, where it started to sink amid mountains of water. Jute bags floated in the storerooms and the wind drowned out the crew's prayers as they neared the cyclone's rear eyewall, beyond any hope of extrication. The old diesel engines could not power them away from their doom.

Ten minutes later, the *Mahajagmitra*'s radio operator transmitted his last signal into the void:

WILL LEAVE SHIP. NO REPLY EXPECTED.

ACT I

THE VORTEX

1

Hafiz Uddin Ahmad

DACCA, EAST PAKISTAN

FALL 1968

Two years before landfall

Thirty thousand fans erupted into cheers the moment that the football hit Hafiz Uddin Ahmad's chest. The ball dropped down to his feet with a featherlight touch. Hafiz raced forward with his precious cargo, commanding both the match and the crowd as he sprinted across the halfway line.

This was Hafiz's home turf: Dacca, the Bengali capital of East Pakistan. Clad in the green-and-white uniform of the Pakistan National Team, his back bore a big number 10 in stark white. He chose the number in honor of the Brazilian football superstar Pelé, who wore that same lucky number half a world away. Hafiz welcomed the comparison between himself and the greatest football player of all time. After all, to millions of East Pakistanis, Pelé was no Hafiz.

Today, Hafiz and his teammates—Pakistan's most talented players—hosted the mighty Soviet Union, one of the world's best teams. Hafiz dribbled around a Soviet midfielder and passed the center circle, paying the opposing player little mind. He kept his eye on the keeper's hands, fifty yards ahead. Hafiz had that rare sixth sense for knowing what opposing players were going to do a split second before even they did. He focused on the little details that everyone else missed. A keeper might twitch a finger and give away which side of the net they thought Hafiz might aim for. Pakistan was down 0–1, they needed an equalizer, and this was their best chance yet.

A burly defender squared off against Hafiz's charge. Without breaking stride, he flicked a sharp cross into the box to his teammate, a striker from Islamabad, while he sprinted toward the goal. The ball arced high and true, over three Soviet midfielders and defenders. Then a strange thing happened. The moment the ball struck his teammate's chest, the crowd fell silent. If the Soviet players had a chance to catch their breath, they would have wondered what it meant.

In truth, Pakistan was a country divided, both geographically and culturally. A simple glance at the map showed how strange it was. Half the country lay to India's west. West Pakistan was the center of political and economic power and home to the capital city of Islamabad. The citizens of West Pakistan spoke mostly Urdu and Punjabi. The other wing, to India's east, had a much larger population but not nearly as much power. Here, in East Pakistan, people spoke Bengali.

West Pakistan and East Pakistan had been locked in a kind of cold war within the Cold War for the last twenty years. Tensions were so high that that no one in Dacca dared to cheer for a West Pakistan player, even one who played for the home team. A few goals from Hafiz's Punjabi teammates weren't going to get the fans to forget that West Pakistan treated East Pakistan like a colonial province.

Hafiz and the striker from Islamabad crisscrossed the ball on Dacca's only perfectly manicured patch of grass. The mood in the stadium alternated between somber moments of silence when the Punjabi had control to thunderous cheers every time Hafiz cradled the ball.

Hafiz didn't care for politics. He relied on his Punjabi teammates and considered them friends. Though sometimes he wondered if he only ran so hard because he wanted to hear the crowd cheer his name.

Seeing his opening, Hafiz dashed toward the goal, as the Punjabi player maneuvered the ball to take advantage of a gap in the defense. Three Soviets pressed down on the Punjabi, but he somehow threaded a miraculous pass through the defenders to Hafiz.

Now Hafiz was living every striker's dream scenario: one on one with the keeper, twenty yards out. Hafiz sprinted forward, eyes lasered in, not on the ball or the net but on the keeper's fidgeting fingers. *Left or right?*

Almost too easy, he thought.

Hafiz planted his left foot into the ground and fired with his right, just a fraction of a second ahead of two defenders sliding in for the tackle.

The Soviet keeper's gloved hands lunged to the right for a split second, as if by instinct. By the time he realized that the ball was sailing directly over him, he was too flat-footed to deflect it. The keeper's outstretched fingertips flickered in vain at the gently spinning ball, which snuck just under the crossbar and into the net.

"Goal!" an announcer shouted over the stadium's speakers. "Gooooaaaalll!"

Hafiz sprinted toward the Punjabi forward. They embraced, raising their hands together as the rest of the national team mobbed the strikers. Already high on their hometown star's performance, the crowd lost it. The Bengalis saluted their champion with full-throated roars. They started chanting *Joi Bangla*—Bengali words that translate to "Victory to Bengal"—in his honor.

Hafiz soaked in the adulation. As he looked out at the cheering throng, his very soul felt full. To them, he was a national hero. But that wasn't the only reason that Hafiz felt a particular sort of wistful exhilaration today. The crowd had no idea that he'd decided that this was the last professional match he'd ever play.

The teams went into the locker room tied at the half. No one expected a small developing nation to have a chance against a global superpower, but the entire Pakistani team tingled with nervous energy. There was an earthquake of an upset in the making. This could be the greatest moment of their careers.

Yet the Punjabi players on the team couldn't shake the sense that something seemed off.

"Why don't they cheer us, Hafiz?" one Punjabi striker whispered into Hafiz's ear while their coach gave his half-time pep talk.

That was *the* question. Hafiz could answer, but he didn't have a spare hour to do so. Instead, he looked around at the ratty wooden benches that he and his teammates sat on and thought of the gleaming locker rooms in the Islamabad stadium. East Pakistan couldn't even afford to give players their own lockers.

Hafiz wasn't about to launch into a generational history lesson about how West Pakistan had suppressed Bengalis at every possible turn. How could he capture all of the inequality, the violence, the injustice in a few whispered words? So he waved his teammate off. He preferred to let his feet do the talking.

Besides, why did they have to talk politics? Couldn't they just stick to football?

A sudden commotion outside the locker room interrupted the coach's flash strategy session. The players heard something crash and someone yell, "Stop!"

Hafiz jumped up and peeked around the corner, bumping headlong into a group of Bengali student activists who had just pushed past security. They demanded the coach show himself.

East Pakistan's biggest political party, the Awami League, liked to insert itself into just about every aspect of life in Hafiz's half of the country. Apparently they wanted to talk game strategy, too.

One student stepped forward, wearing a starched white embroidered kurta that appeared far too dignified for his irate manner. He presented the coach with their sole demand: The National Team must field only Bengali players in the second half. "If you don't, we'll riot."

It wasn't an idle threat. They'd employed similar tactics before.

The coach explained that acquiescing to their demand would mean that they'd have to leave their two best defenders on the bench. They had a chance at a major upset here. Couldn't the students just let the team do its best to win?

The student countered that if the coach refused and the stands turned bloody, the team would have to forfeit to the Soviets anyway.

The coach looked at the floor and shook his head.

Hafiz glanced across the locker room at two Punjabi defenders in their grass-stained jerseys. Despite their different home regions, the three were friends, and the team needed their talent badly. Fighting to a tie, this far, had been lucky. It would take all the team's best players on the field to stand a chance.

Hafiz didn't want to end his career like this. Maybe a little star power would sway the protesters to give up their demands, just this once.

He took a few steps toward the students, but just as he was about to open his mouth, his mind conjured an image of something even more powerful than his desire to win: his father's disapproving face. The corresponding jolt of shame stopped him in his tracks faster than even the most imposing Soviet defender.

Back on Hafiz's home island of Bhola—East Pakistan's biggest island, which hosted a million people in a space about the size of Rhode Island—his father, Dr. Azhar Uddin Ahmad, loomed large. Not only was he the island's most respected doctor but he was also their elected Awami League representative. As a member of Pakistan's parliament, he fought incessantly to reduce discrimination against Bengalis, insisting on equal treatment from the government. These students had the same mission at heart, even if they went about it in a way that was inconvenient to Hafiz. He could never disrespect his father by challenging them over a game, even one as important as this one. Hafiz slunk back to the bench without a word. The coach gave in.

In truth, Hafiz's father was the reason he was retiring from football. While the Bengalis loved Hafiz on the field, he knew he could never truly fill his father's shoes by staying on the pitch. He needed to leave the game behind and, as his father put it, "do something in service to the country." In fact, according to his father, he should have done this years ago.

The problem was that Hafiz avoided politics like the plague, so being a politician like his dad was out of the question. His only other real option was to pursue a desk job in the government's bureaucratic elite. Maybe he would receive an ambassadorship one day if he worked hard enough. So Hafiz spent his time between rigorous team training sessions getting his bachelor's and then master's degree in political science at the prestigious Dacca University. And now he'd reached the educational end of the line. In a few weeks, he was due to sit for the country's annual civil service exam, a test that would determine his career and the rest of his life.

Although he'd tried to study hard so that he could live up to his father's expectations, he hated the exam-prep books. Every time he reached for one of those dry four-hundred-page tomes, filled with finely printed protocols, arcane regulations, and legal theories, his hand always seemed to drift toward the pulp detective novels set in Calcutta on the shelf below instead. It was useless. But it was his path.

When Hafiz jogged back out after halftime, it was not the roar of the crowd echoing in his head but rather his father's scolding voice: "Football is not a career. You can't do this forever. Someday you are going to have to be serious." He took his place on the field, trying to ignore the sullen stares of his benched Punjabi teammates.

In the second half, the Soviets sliced through the Pakistanis with ease, scoring four unanswered goals. Pakistan's best defenders watched helplessly from the sidelines.

We weren't supposed to win anyway, Hafiz told himself as he passed through the midfield handshakes after the 5–1 loss. It was little consolation. If the Awami League hadn't gotten involved maybe the Pelé of Pakistan would have gone out on top.

Despite the loss, Hafiz's fans roared in appreciation when he took center circle for a quick wave. Tears fell down his cheeks as he soaked it all in. Barring a miracle, his boyhood dream of living in the sporting spotlight, traveling the world, and maybe even running his own football club would die when he took off his jersey.

Hafiz left the field and trudged into the locker room. Inside the cramped chamber, an army major who was the head of the Pakistani Football Federation greeted each player with a handshake and a pat on the back, consoling everyone on their hard-fought battle.

"Hafiz!" he said as his eyes landed on his intended target. "Have you thought about my offer?"

"Not here!" Hafiz whispered. The absolute last thing he wanted his football comrades to think was that he was abandoning them for *this* guy. The major had nagged Hafiz for two years now and wouldn't take no for an answer. It was time to set him straight once and for all. "Madhur Café, in an hour."

The major understood. He always appreciated Hafiz's dedication to discretion and patted a few more backs on his way out.

Hafiz changed into street clothes and gathered his belongings one by one. Only someone who'd lived through the feeling of those last moments in a locker room before leaving it behind forever would truly understand.

Hafiz waited for the crowd to thin, then ducked out of the stadium and headed to where he'd parked his light blue Vespa. He was proud of the small Italian scooter. It was an expensive luxury in a country where most people still had trouble scratching enough money together for their daily meal. Zooming through Dacca's lackadaisical streets gave him an odd sense of purpose. It was as if the next adventure was just a curve in the road away.

Today, Hafiz decided, he'd take the long way back to the university. He gunned the engine and expelled a bird's-egg-blue puff of two-stroke smoke behind him. The wind blew his hair back as he cruised down a riverfront that travelers from around the world once hailed as the Venice of Asia. He passed money changers, tea sellers, and hawkers offering roasted nuts and sweetmeats. Occasionally, a sharp youth caught sight of Hafiz and yelled his name, but the baby-blue scooter would be gone before they could catch him for an autograph.

This was freedom.

He crossed a busy intersection and turned onto a tree-lined boulevard with British-era brick buildings and bungalows. When he entered the university gate, he made out the minaret of one of East Pakistan's only Sikh temples: a structure called a gurdwara.

He parked a few feet away from an enormous banyan tree that stood in front of the admissions building. The tree was a sprawling monolith, with an inviting canopy that stretched out for twenty feet in every direction from its dense tangle of trunks and branches. Some people believed it was as old as the Buddha himself—a 2,500-year-old relic that perfectly symbolized the melting pot of religions, politics, and ideas that swirled around the people of the Ganges delta. After a hundred generations of societal upheaval and rebirth, the tree now stood at the epicenter of Dacca University's political scene. Students gathered daily under its branches to make impassioned speeches about whatever political point took their fancy, and today was no exception.

Hafiz caught sight of a rakish young man in front of the crowd. He sported a wispy beard, long white kurta, and Western blue jeans—the de facto uniform of a certain type of political rabble-rouser. He was maybe eighteen years old and fashioned himself something of an orator. He raised his fist in the air and yelled with a passion reserved for people who took too many sociology classes. Hafiz didn't listen. He didn't need to. He was sure it was the same old complaints. It wasn't that Hafiz was against the cause, rather he thought there were better ways to spend his time. The kid had probably read Marx or Lenin and now squawked into the breeze about Bengali independence or how no one wanted Urdu as the national language.

It didn't take a PhD in history to realize that Pakistan was in trouble. For thousands of years, South Asia was the center of religious, philosophical, and artistic movements, as well as wars between kingdoms. It was also one of the richest regions on earth. In 1757, the British took control of those riches and brought the subcontinent's imponderable diversity under one giant territory called India.

What worked out well for the colonizers didn't sit well with the

colonized. The British policy of "divide and rule" set opposing seg-
ments of society against one another, cementing differences between
Hindus and Muslims that would shape their political destiny. While
British India claimed to be secular, nobody was under the illusion
that Hindus and Muslims were treated as equals, especially when it
came to well-connected Hindu landlords and their Muslim subjects.
The wealth disparities were so great that some Hindus built immense
marble palaces while tens of thousands of Muslim subjects on their
land lived on the brink of starvation.

The idea of Pakistan arrived in the early 1930s, taking the political scene by storm. The name wasn't some ancient tribal homage; it
was simply an acronym for the country's biggest provinces and ethnic
groups, all located in the western part of British India: *P* for Punjab
and Pashtuns, *A* for the Afghans, *K* for Kashmir, *S* for Sindh, and *TAN*
for Balochistan. Pakistan's founding father, Muhammad Ali Jinnah,
promised that the new country would be a home for all Muslims—a
land of equality and true democracy.

In 1947, just two years after the end of World War II, during which
Indian troops—Muslims and Hindus together—fought in Europe for
the good guys, an anti-colonial independence movement won freedom from the British. Mahatma Gandhi, the most visible leader of
the movement, favored a united India, while Jinnah believed that the
Muslims should have their own nation. Seeing the writing on the wall
and too broke after the war to do anything about it anyway, the British
split the subcontinent across religious lines and relinquished their colonial Crown Jewel. They called the process "Partition." Hindus made
up the majority in the new country of India, and Muslims claimed
most of Pakistan. The haphazard redrawing of a society divided the
territory in a way that drove tens of millions of panicked migrants
over the new borders in the first week of its existence, triggering riots
and violence that left more than a million people dead. Partition also
cleaved Bengal in two, with the cultural capital of Calcutta going to
India and Dacca parked in Pakistan.

Pakistan gained independence but emerged a divided nation, figuratively and literally. The two sides of the new country were supposed to find common cause in religion, but without a shared culture or language, the connection felt hollow. The *New York Times* described the divisions in broad terms: "It is hard to imagine two races or regions any more different. They speak different languages—Urdu in the West, Bengali in the East—eat different foods—meat and grain in the West, fish and rice in the East—and have almost contradictory cultures, for the Bengalis are volatile and love politics and literature while the Punjabis are more stolid and prefer governing and soldiering."

It didn't help that Pakistan's leaders used the old British governing system as a blueprint for how to deal with their eastern wing a thousand miles away. They treated it like a colony, shipping in thousands of police and administrators and shipping out literal boatloads of cash and goods like tea, jute, and oil, courtesy of the east's rich resources.

The student under the banyan tree, with his partially grown facial hair and elegant shirt, echoed a sentiment that resonated with most Bengalis: A unified Pakistan was a farce. The British and the Hindus had given Pakistan's leaders all the tools they needed to make Bengalis their vassals, and West Pakistan used those tools with gusto, curtailing Bengali culture and language at every available turn. After all, there was no *B* in the acronym of Pakistan.

But recognizing problems and actually fixing them were two very different things. Hafiz had seen his father tilt at the same windmills for decades and what had it ever gotten him? Every few years, the cycle repeated itself: The agitators would get angry that nothing was changing and would riot. The army showed up to put down the unrest. Activists would either go to jail or be killed, and the survivors would go free. Eventually the whole thing would start all over again.

Hafiz walked around the corner to his favorite spot on campus, Madhur Café—the perfect place for a postgame snack. Although it was only a one-minute walk from the protest, he figured that it wouldn't get crowded until after the students grew tired of chanting.

The place was empty when Hafiz walked in. Only the canteen manager, Madhusudan Dey, stood at the heavy wooden counter. He wore a white, buttoned-up kurta and had a mark on his forehead for a Hindu festival of some sort—Hafiz never could keep track of them all. Dey was bent over a neat ledger, accounting for every flaky roti, singara (a savory stuffed potato pastry), and sugary cup of milk tea that students had promised to one day repay. Dey looked up and brandished a wide, warm smile when he saw Hafiz.

"At last, someone who can pay for his own meals!" said Dey, greeting the star. Dey shook his head in mock despair at the vast sums of debt the rest of the student body had managed to rack up.

Dey's food was pretty much the only thing that Hafiz liked about the university, and Dey appreciated that Hafiz's 5,000-rupee-a-year salary as a sporting icon was more than enough to pay for his prodigious appetite. Yet Hafiz knew that Dey wasn't too worried about the deadbeats either. After all, Dacca University was the Oxford of East Pakistan. Dey saw how, time and again, even the brokest Dacca U students would go on to become business moguls, lawyers, politicians, or societal elites, so he extended liberal credit to every student. People all around Dacca had stories about the old canteen manager showing up at their office a decade after they had graduated with a bill for four years of tea and singaras in hand. Almost all of them had such fond memories of the man that they paid him back with interest. Hafiz couldn't help but like Dey.

A few minutes later, the major strolled through the door, exactly on time. He'd changed into a more formal uniform, complete with a beret. Hafiz noticed an uncharacteristic bounce in the man's step.

"Hafiz Uddin Ahmad! My savior!" The major stuck out his hand, and Hafiz reflexively grasped it. "I'd like to get right to the point. What would it take to sign you up with us? I see how you play. The army team would be unstoppable."

"So you keep telling me."

"Listen, you know it's my job to make sure the army has star players.

You're on the national team, of course, but between us, I think you're the best player on it. It would be a shame to see all that talent go to waste. I'm giving you a chance to keep playing for another decade or more. Think about it. We'd bring you in as a junior officer with a steady salary and plenty of room to grow. You'd get to travel the world, keep yourself in the game, and best of all, be of service to your country." The smooth-talking major clearly had years of experience in pampering young men's egos.

Hafiz considered this, then shrugged. "I've already told you. My father wants me to get a real job."

"What could be more real—and respectable—than the army? Is stamping invoices in some stuffy office your idea of a real job?" The major eyed Hafiz knowingly, pausing for a bite of singara to let that visual sink in.

There were definite similarities between life in a military unit and his current morning-till-dusk practice schedule. But while a good fight might quicken his blood on the football field, he didn't see anything worth dying for.

In twenty years, would he be in the major's shoes, pleading with potential recruits while sweating through a wool uniform at a student hangout? Was that the best he could hope for? Would being in the army ever compare to the feeling of thirty thousand people in Dacca Stadium cheering just for you? Could anything?

Yet there was something else to consider—a loophole that could keep his dream of playing on the field at least partially alive—joining the army would be *in service to the country*. The army was an honorable profession. The money was regular enough to start a family. Sure, the national team's pittance made him a rich student but it would never scale up to adult wages. With hard work and dedication he would rise through the ranks. His father might even like that he'd joined. Maybe Hafiz really could have the best of both worlds.

As the soldier and star talked, a boisterous crowd of students made their way into the cramped canteen. Their smiles faded when they saw the uniformed major munching away. West Pakistani soldiers were not welcome in their de facto organizational headquarters.

The major looked at Hafiz pointedly as the students ordered tea and fried snacks on credit. "Here's another thing to consider: The army is the one place in the nation that's above politics. There's no difference between East Pakistan and West Pakistan in our ranks. We're soldiers together. There's none of what you saw at today's game."

The major's words hit their mark. Hafiz thought back to the disappointment on his teammates' faces when the student activists forced them to sit on the bench in the second half.

The major nodded at Hafiz. "Well? Shall we go for it?"

"Thank you, sir, but no. I need to study."

"Think about it, at least. It's a great life." The major stood up and left, passing the banyan on his way to the nearby military barracks.

The major's offer stuck in Hafiz's head long after he'd finished his tea. He thought about it as he walked across campus to his dorm. He thought about it as he climbed up the stairs of his redbrick dorm, Iqbal Hall, with its ornate facade that harkened back to the fragile imperial glory of the British era. He thought about it as he unlatched the door to the austere quarters that only a student could love—a cramped and mildewy room that epitomized Dacca's ever-present lack of resources. He thought about it all night as he lay awake, staring at the damp concrete ceiling. He thought about it every evening in the weeks that followed—each time he grabbed a novel off his shelf instead of his prep book, then guiltily put it back a few hours later, heavy with the knowledge that he was wasting his precious last days of cramming. He thought about it while his father, his family, and the local imam gathered a hundred miles to the south to pray for his success on the civil service exam. And Hafiz thought about it on the morning of the test itself. That's when he finally knew what he had to do.

At the testing hall a hundred ambitious, freshly minted degree holders waited for the signal to start furiously scribbling in their exam booklets. Only Hafiz's seat was empty.

As the proctor gave the order to begin, Hafiz was in a cab on his way to the airport. Pelé would never give up on his dreams for some stupid test, and neither would he. The National Team had already left for Rangoon, but he was sure that they'd let him back on the squad. He was going to keep on playing football no matter what. Hafiz pushed down the nagging twinges of guilt at his father's unanswered prayers, but this was his life and his choice to make.

As the cab pulled up to the airport, Hafiz thought about the major's offer too. After one last season of success and fame, he'd decided to join the army. The major promised Hafiz could have the best of both worlds: being an officer and an athlete.

Hafiz had it all figured out.

2

Agha Muhammad Yahya Khan

Agha Muhammad Yahya Khan, Pakistan's new president, paused for a second with his hand outstretched in midair, considering his options. Then the decorated World War II hero reached for a refill. Weaving past the Johnnie Walker, he picked up a bottle of the Pakistan-distilled Black Dog whiskey. It was a vile, turpentine-like swill. His toxic love affair with the liquor dated back to his military days when Black Dog rations carried liquid gold status with him and his fellow tank drivers.

But by this time of night, it didn't really matter what was in his glass.

Yahya looked over his giant, ornate teak desk, on which sat a few papers, a Mont Blanc pen, an untouched cork coaster, and a black rotary phone. The phone's hold light flashed red.

Yahya methodically filled his tumbler with a pour that would get a bartender fired, then raised the glass to his lips. His once calloused and now pudgy, yellowed fingers dwarfed the tumbler. The booze splashed across his prodigious black mustache.

Yahya sat alone in his dimly lit chamber, which was full of the usual South Asian bureaucratic baubles: red leather chairs with big buttons, sprawling Peshawar wool rugs, and gilded portraits of British grandeur that rose up the walls to the twenty-foot-high ceiling. He liked to take these sorts of calls without anyone else around. Solitude helped him think. Helped him focus. And kept away the second-guessers that hung around like gnats.

Above all else, Yahya was a man of action. He could accomplish just about any given task with the efficiency and unswerving nerve that had been cemented into him from a childhood raised in police stations and then through his decades of military service. Problem was, his instinctual lurch to let someone else set the agenda meant that he often found himself taking on the stance of whatever adviser he had spoken to most recently. So at times of great national importance like this, he knew he had to be alone.

Alone, he could channel the courage he'd displayed on the battlefield—fighting for the British in World War II and then for Pakistan in its ongoing fights against India. It was that courage that earned the respect of his countrymen. It was that courage that helped him kill Nazis and Hindus alike. It was that courage that he needed to draw on if he was going to have the balls to ask the most powerful man in the world to give him some guns. For free.

But Richard Nixon would have to wait another minute.

Let them come to you, Yahya thought, *especially if they think they are more powerful than you are. Can't let them think you're a weak chap.* He learned this lesson the hard way a few years back, when he led his forces to Pakistan's worst ever military defeat.

Since Partition, Pakistan and India fought constantly over Kashmir, a wealthy Muslim-majority region that sat between the two nations. Both countries saw Kashmir as their own. To India, bringing Kashmir into the fold meant uniting Muslims and Hindus under a secular banner. To Pakistan, Kashmir belonged to a shared Muslim homeland. Whoever controlled Kashmir would control South Asia's destiny—or so the thinking went. Each side annexed about half of it and stuffed one of the subcontinent's most beautiful and imposing areas with tanks and troops along the Line of Control.

In 1965, Pakistan saw its first strategic edge in a generation. India had just engaged in an ill-fated skirmish with China over another border dispute and was licking its wounds. Pakistan exploited the chance and invaded Kashmir with a small, quick strike force that smashed through the Indian lines of defense.

General Ayub Khan, a dictator who took power in a coup d'état seven years earlier, led Pakistan at that time. Ayub liked Yahya. He valued Yahya's loyalty. He knew from their time together in the army that Yahya was a paragon of obedience and would carry out orders to the letter. Most of all, he figured that Yahya wasn't smart enough to pull off his own coup if he tried. So he made Yahya a general— Pakistan's youngest ever—and his right-hand man.

Ayub put Yahya in total operational control on the morning of the final attack. The plan was that Yahya would order the decisive blow, then they would revel together in the guaranteed victory. They outnumbered the Indians four to one in troops and six to one in tanks; a child could have looked at the game board and made the winning move.

Instead, Yahya waited. He inexplicably stared at charts while Indian reinforcements rushed up from the plains. The window of opportunity shrank a bit more with each wasted minute. Hours passed.

Yahya's junior officer came to his tent desperate for action. "Sir, my boys are ready to strike."

Yahya'd had a few drinks, and he was sure that somehow what everyone presumed was an advantage was actually a trick by the Indians. The charts looked fuzzy. He swore at the junior officer and kicked him out. So the troops waited some more.

When Yahya finally shook off his paralysis, it was too late. India had rushed enough troops in to easily stave off the belated charge. Instead, Yahya's forces advanced into a massacre. The tactical blunder single-handedly turned the war from a success to a defeat. To cap off the disaster, the American president Lyndon Johnson put harsh military and economic sanctions on both India and Pakistan for starting it.

Yahya's loyalty had bought him a long leash with Ayub. The debacle wasn't his fault, Yahya explained to Ayub, but that of those dastardly Indians. If they just fought like men, Yahya would have crushed them. Ayub bought the excuse. After all, everyone in Pakistan knew in their hearts how devious the Indians could be.

Still, Ayub was confused. The United States was supposed to be a faithful ally, and here they were punishing Pakistan for fighting India, which sympathized with the Soviets. So in the spirit of the global Cold War game of chess, each country started looking for new allies. Pakistan found a friend in China. India got even cozier with the Soviet Union. More friends meant more weapons and more geopolitical fault lines to exploit. Everyone knew that it was only a matter of time before the countries clashed again.

Yet new allies alone weren't enough. The American sanctions tanked Pakistan's economy, and citizens who tolerated authoritarianism when times were good started losing their patience when things turned sour. Ayub staged a referendum to shore up his popularity. He handpicked eighty thousand supporters to be "representative voters," earning a dictator's majority of 95 percent of the vote in the process. His tactics backfired. By 1969, as the economy cratered, riots broke out in every major city over his corrupt rule. Ayub turned to Yahya, the one man he knew wouldn't imprison or execute him for his crimes, and made him president in exchange for amnesty.

Pakistan was just past its twenty-second birthday when Yahya became the country's sixth leader at the age of fifty-two. Every leader before him promised to deliver democracy to the masses in one way or another. Every one failed miserably. So on his way out, Ayub gave Yahya the greatest task of all: a mandate to steward a free and fair election. Yahya never wanted to be president, but he knew a mission when he saw one. He loved the challenge and was determined to be the man who would finally make Pakistan a democracy. It would be good for his legacy, yes, but more important, it was a clear task that everyone could get behind. There wouldn't be any second-guessers when the goal was as lofty as democracy itself.

Yahya said as much in his inaugural speech, on a sweltering March day in 1969. He took a seat before a chrome microphone and broadcast his self-inauguration to the nation over Radio Pakistan. While his appointment as president wasn't democratic, Yahya promised profusely that, after serving a short term, he would hand over power to a truly democratically elected leader. Yahya made this solemn promise to his 125 million subjects:

> My prime duty is to protect this country from utter destruction.
> My sole aim in imposing martial law is to restore life, liberty and property.
> I promise to bring representative, full, free and impartial democracy and that is all.
> Once that is done, I will go.

More surprising, Yahya also promised that the days of Bengali discrimination were over. Bengali-speaking East Pakistan had 60 percent of the population but only got about 10 percent of the country's development aid, lagging far behind West Pakistan in hospitals, doctors, housing, and social services. Yahya said that a free and fair election would finally deliver on the dream upon which the country was built in 1947: one nation, united under a Muslim faith.

The convincing display of humility bowled over the local press. They gushed that Yahya's legacy was already assured and that he'd be remembered as a hero—a selfless servant who brought suffrage to millions. Now all he had to do was hold an election for both wings of the country and form the country's first honest parliament. Then he could welcome in whomever the people elected in a grand display of duty and honor. It would make Yahya something akin to George Washington, who famously gave up the presidency at the end of his second term in order to enshrine the peaceful transition of power into the lifeblood of the United States.

This wasn't to say that Yahya ached in his bones to be remembered as the father of Pakistani democracy. Universal suffrage sounded like a good idea, and he would do his best to organize the infrastructure to pull it off, but to him, it was just another way to prove that he was a man of action, by tackling a mission head-on and delivering results. To Yahya, getting a democracy up and running was a concrete goal, like building a building, growing the economy by 5 percent, or winning a war.

And Yahya saw an intriguing opportunity in America's new president. Richard Nixon took office the year before and had a soft spot for Pakistan that dated back to his first visit there in the 1950s. Yahya wanted to see if he could cajole some state-of-the-art game changers from the planet's biggest weapons manufacturer to help settle the score with India. After all, Nixon was sending hundreds of millions of dollars' worth of arms, not to mention half a million American troops, to stop Soviet sympathizers in Vietnam. Why not send weapons to Pakistan for the same purpose? Nixon had a reputation for bending the rules when it suited him. Maybe he'd have a creative solution to the military sanctions that were crippling Pakistan.

The light on Yahya's phone continued to blink. Nixon waited on hold. Confident that his power play had achieved the desired effect, Yahya picked up the handset and pushed the red button.

Yahya's voice delivered a deep baritone into the receiver as he greeted his guns gatekeeper: the world's most powerful man. Yahya's heavy British accent came courtesy of his military-school upbringing, perfectly fluent and proper but with a halting, dragging cadence that hung on the last syllable of seemingly random words. His critics called it slurring.

The two men exchanged genuine pleasantries. Nixon and Yahya shared a camaraderie built on their mutual struggle to keep a lid on the disrespectful miscreants who refused to respect their authority.

The one big thing that the unlikely pair understood, above all else, was that everyone was always out to get them. So both men had no qualms about getting their hands dirty in pursuit of defending their respective nations.

For his part, Nixon also found the rarest of humans in Yahya: a true friend. Historian Gary Bass wrote that, aside from a certain banker in Florida, Yahya might have even been Nixon's only real friend in the world.

It only took a matter of minutes for the men to reach an agreement: Nixon would come to Pakistan for an official visit in August, at which time they would proclaim their friendship through an arms deal masquerading as a humanitarian aid package. Nixon would find a way around the pesky embargo, and Yahya would ensure that Pakistan would be a loyal American ally for the next fifty years.

Yahya hung up and lit a Chesterfield. As he exhaled, smoke danced over his impossibly bushy eyebrows, which curled skyward above the sides of his eyes. Yahya loved his eyebrows. He felt they were the true source of his strength, just like Samson's hair. So he twisted the center of each brow up to a point, thinking it gave him a distinguished air.

Yahya drained the last of his tumbler, then reached for a celebratory nightcap.

3

Candy Rohde

DACCA, EAST PAKISTAN

MAY 1969

Eighteen months before landfall

Candy Rohde squeezed her way through leaning pillars of fifty-pound rice bags, pivoting past the beat-up stacks of cooking-oil containers that crowded every step of the narrow stone-and-dirt walkway. She backtracked a few times after hitting dead ends piled high with blankets and cooking implements. *It had to be around here somewhere.*

She peered down an alley, confused. Household goods mostly—stacks of stoves and round tin containers. She stared ahead at row after row of sari and lungi sellers. They were packed so tightly that it felt like the alleyway would cave in, drowning them all in fine imported Indian silk.

A few hawkers peeked out from the apertures of their mini-pharmacies, watching the American woman with the long straight brown hair as she continued on her search. It was always fun for the hawkers to watch tourists get lost in Old Dacca's centuries-old labyrinth of a bazaar.

Candy took another wrong turn and somehow found herself back at the entrance. Dacca's punishing summer sun came into view. It shone off the penny-theater movie screens that squatted on street corners to lure in children. The mobile-movie men set up next to the curbside barbers and street dentists. They sold tickets for local Bengali films, pilfering coins from idle children whose fathers were getting a shave or having a molar removed. Most of the men dressed head to toe in long white shirts, per Islamic guidance.

Candy did an about-face, grabbed the folds of sari cloth slipping down off her hips, and pushed back into the maze. It was time to be more systematic. She made a mental map as she passed through the shops this time, asking sellers in broken Bengali at every haphazard junction.

Inside the heart of a labyrinth made out of a thousand shops crammed into just a few city blocks lay a gleaming oasis of brilliance.

Just past a sickly-sweet-smelling opium den was the object of her desire: a row of jewelers who could turn giant conch shells dredged from the Ganges delta into elaborate wedding bangles for Hindu brides. Invariably nearsighted and mustachioed Hindu men oversaw each shop and squinted through their secondhand loupes.

Candy carefully scanned the merchandise as she moved from shop to shop. While gold and silver were just as timeless in Dacca as anywhere else, exquisitely carved conch-shell bangles were the ultimate status symbol for Bengali women. More than even the temples, jewelers' row served as the cultural epicenter of Dacca's Hindu-minority population. With half a million Hindus living in the city, the alleyway was always crammed with customers.

Candy caught sight of an especially intricate piece and asked to see it by pointing and smiling. She accepted the piece carefully, turning it over slowly in her palm and marveling at how each elegant leaf carving fit together so perfectly. It took a certain thoughtfulness and planning to make the conch into a finished product. A single wrong stroke and weeks of work would be nothing more than seashell trash.

Candy slipped it on her wrist. Prospective mothers-in-law to her left and right haggled with jewelers over their own conch pieces. Just because they ached to wow wedding guests with brilliant gifts to their new daughter-in-law didn't mean they were going to be taken for a ride in the process.

"*Dhanyabada*," Candy said in a heavily accented Bengali, thanking the old jeweler while delicately handing back the piece. The price was about one dollar in 1969 prices. Another time, perhaps. She had a cocktail party with some Bengali friends that night but didn't want to overdo it. She made a mental note of a stunning pink pearl bracelet the jeweler also had; maybe she'd drop a hint to Jon, since their first anniversary was coming up soon.

Candy made her way back to the entrance without a single false step, stopping along the way to add a special spicy mustard-seed blend to her growing spice collection. The steaming, moldy monsoon air rushed against her face as she stepped over a mosquito-filled open sewer into the sticky street. She hailed a three-wheeled bicycle rickshaw to take her home.

While these man-powered taxis might not be as fast as the cabs back in Boston, Candy appreciated how every rickshaw was a brilliantly painted work of art. Palaces and man-faced tigers competed for space on the backs of some of these three-wheeled cycles, while others bore paintings of dragons and snow-topped mountains. Her sinewy driver slapped her seat free of flies with a rag while she took the time to admire the back of her ride, which featured a scene of a great Bengali king leading his army into battle. Then she settled herself onto the cracked red vinyl seat. The driver hopped back on the pedals for the twenty-minute journey, banging his rickshaw against the wheels of a few others in order to get out of the crammed parking lot.

Candy took in the view as they passed the open-air fish market. She spied a mélange of ice and blood draining off the white-brown fish boards and mixing into the gutter. The hilsa, perch, and porpoise here would soon fry in pans with secretive blends of oil, chili, lime, garlic, cardamom, and turmeric, and then make their way onto customers' banana leaves. Most Bengalis considered fish the lifeblood of their rich food culture, so even roadside cooks jealously guarded their recipes.

As she gazed out in awe at the kaleidoscope of colors that was so different from her last home, Candy thought back to six months earlier. She and Jon had been sitting at the kitchen table in their small apartment in Boston's Back Bay, flipping page by page through an old atlas and plotting their escape to a place where the authorities could never bother them. Next to the atlas lay a letter from the government, postmarked the day before. Jon was being drafted. Again.

Jon graduated top of his class at Harvard Medical School and was one of the brightest medical minds in the country. Yet as the Vietnam War dragged on, even the best were getting conscripted. Jon would have to report to the front lines as a triage surgeon, unless he and Candy could come up with a damn good reason for him not to. He'd already used his "heart condition" excuse last year, after his first draft letter. With the number of able bodies diminishing, those tall tales didn't fly anymore.

Jon was still wearing his blood-splattered scrubs from a thirty-six-hour shift at Boston City Hospital. There would be time for changing after they had explored every last latitude and longitude line on the atlas's ratty pages. They'd already agreed that fleeing for Canada wouldn't work—that would torpedo Jon's career right when it was supposed to take off. He flipped past Australia and Armenia, pausing briefly on the Bahamas to share a wistful smile with Candy.

Raised in the middle of an old Ohio apple orchard, Candy's parents dragged her aboard a mail boat bound for the Bahamas when she was four years old. They'd mapped a course through the then-deadly and mysterious Bermuda Triangle. As if being punished for their disregard, their boat chugged almost immediately into Hurricane Nine. (In the 1940s, nobody had yet bothered to come up with names for hurricanes.) The boat heaved for hours on the heavy seas, but the family survived the scare. Energized by the thrill of potential disaster, Candy begged her parents to repeat the harrowing ordeal, and they would return in the following summers to those Caribbean beaches.

Candy frowned as she and Jon turned the page. There was no

meaningful work for Jon in the Bahamas, either. They were already past Malaysia and Mexico, and nothing promising had come up so far. It was looking grim.

After being awake for two days, Jon could barely see straight. He flipped past the *P*'s absentmindedly.

"Wait, Jon, go back."

Jon flipped back a page.

"Didn't your friend Bucky work at a cholera lab in East Pakistan to fulfill his service?"

"That's right!" Jon said, tapping the page.

In an effort to win hearts and minds during the Cold War, America funded health clinics in developing countries in a ring all the way around the USSR's sphere of influence. Nestled between Soviet-leaning India and the Southeast Asian battlegrounds, East Pakistan was a priority target and in desperate need of Jon's services.

Candy didn't know much about the place, other than the occasional news clippings about assorted famines and floods that seemed to befall the poor people there every couple of years, but she thought it could be the perfect locale to escape the insanity of war. Besides, it looked lusciously green on the map sitting in front of them. She felt a thrill welling up in her, as that old adventurer's rush flowed through her veins.

The US Army approved Jon's exemption, and the pair packed their secondhand suitcases, bound for Dacca. But getting Jon out of the draft came with other sacrifices. Candy had just started teaching fifth graders at Newton Public Schools, the culmination of her master's in education. She loved the job. She'd even started designing a new curriculum and wrote essays to parents every semester about their children. But she would have to give it up. Candy hoped to develop something similar in Dacca, if given the chance.

In the months that followed, Candy slowly filled their cozy two-bedroom Dacca flat with carefully selected Bengali artworks and sculptures, while Jon did lifesaving medical research at the lab. Candy was less lucky finding her own calling in Dacca so far, but she was sure it was only a matter of time.

Candy's mind snapped back to the present as the rickshaw peddler slowed his vehicle to a stop. Traffic was at a standstill. Horns and drivers blared all around. Up ahead, two giant ox carts with wooden wheels blocked the narrow street. The oxen pulling the carts had stopped their labor to have a staring contest. Their owners pulled on the animals' horns and slapped their rumps, but the oxen remained implacable. Candy covered her face with her shawl as the old diesel minibus next to them belched its fumes their way.

The rickshaw driver paid no mind. He was used to it.

Then the rain started, offering a welcome reprieve from the stench of leaden exhaust. Candy pulled out her umbrella as she watched passersby scatter into sweetshops, whose glass displays were piled high with dozens of varieties of gooey, sticky, fried treats sure to be sold out well before sundown. The only food more quintessentially Bengali than fish was the sweets—most of which consisted of some combination of ghee (clarified butter), sugar, flour, cheese, milk, and a lot more sugar. Hindus, Muslims, and even the West Pakistanis living in Dacca devoured them.

The rain stopped just as quickly as it started, but at least the splash of water from the sky had motivated the two oxen to start moving again. The rickshaw sloshed through fresh knee-deep puddles, uphill to Candy's destination.

Once they crossed the river to Dacca's newest neighborhood, the streets grew wider. Trees lined the streets instead of trash. Yet the people carried the same determined look as they grided their way to survival through destitution as best they could. Children with protruding bellies played with bells that hung around their waists on black strings while their parents swept the boulevards.

Candy paid the driver the equivalent of ten cents as they rolled up to her house. The price included a healthy tip. She got down from the contraption and walked through her front gate. The flat was so new that one wall was still unbuilt, exposing their living room to the humid, water-logged garden. Their sparse home had little more on the shelves than Jon's brand-new top-of-the-line Nikon camera, for his favorite hobby. Though they'd been nearly broke back in America, moving to Dacca meant that the Rohdes could set themselves up in a mansion in the richest part of the city. But that wasn't their style, so they opted for a smaller space instead, one barely big enough for a small dinner party.

Candy loved the neighborhood. Cobras and jackals wandered across the streets from the jungle into the construction sites at night, a thrilling if potentially dangerous reminder that she indeed lived in the tropics. Brick by brick, sinewy, shirtless workers, ranging in age from preteen to postretirement, built the subdivision designed to attract Bengali writers, professors, businessmen, journalists, and even the occasional expat or two.

Candy was home.

4

Yahya Khan

LAHORE, WEST PAKISTAN

AUGUST 1969

Fifteen months before landfall

Yahya fidgeted on the red carpet as the wind whipped through his thick black hair. He was rarely nervous, but this was a rare moment. The leader of the free world was paying a visit to Lahore, and Yahya wanted to put on a good show for their first meeting as heads of state. He assembled a bagpipe orchestra on the airport tarmac, which launched into spirited military marches as Air Force One touched down. They played mostly in tune. Yahya had rows of gigantic, handwoven Kashmiri silk carpets put under the plane so that Nixon's leather wingtips wouldn't suffer the indignity of touching concrete.

The trip was Nixon's big overseas victory tour. Neil Armstrong and Buzz Aldrin had just returned from the moon, splashing down in the South Pacific. Nixon and his wife, Pat, congratulated the astronauts through thick panes of quarantine glass because nobody knew if the astronauts might be carrying killer moon germs that would wipe out the human race. Pakistan was the final stop of the trip, tacked on at the last minute because Nixon had an idea.

Nixon and Yahya shook hands. Then they hugged, smiling. The motorcade whisked them to the polo grounds, past a presentation of carefully choreographed sword dancers that Yahya was too impatient to watch. It was time to talk about those guns.

Nixon sized him up as they toured Lahore, wondering if this was a man he could trust with the biggest secret of his life. Apparently satisfied, after a couple of hours Nixon proposed a one-on-one meeting. He said he had a favor to ask, one that entailed the highest level of national security. The proposition intrigued Yahya. What task could he take on that was more important than ushering democracy into Pakistan? They excused themselves to catch up behind closed doors.

Nixon and Yahya sat together on Yahya's office couch, a two-seater covered by a cream-colored lace throw. Yahya waved out his security detail, and Nixon did the same. Nixon kicked off the meeting by giving Yahya a carefully wrapped box emblazoned with the presidential seal. Inside was something precious: a special gift that Yahya had asked Nixon to bring as a personal favor. Yahya cradled the package proudly. It was about the size of a small toaster and as light as a feather. He set it aside, unopened.

Nixon got down to business. Ever since he was a junior senator from California, he explained, China fascinated him. Mao Zedong's communists overthrew the Chinese government at around the same time as Partition. The Americans pretended that the ousted government holing up in Taiwan would come back any day, while Mao led the country in a radically new and, at times, horrific direction.

Twenty years had passed, and Nixon thought it was time to give up the charade. He saw China's potential to be a major world power and wanted to restore diplomatic and economic relations. It would be a radical break in American foreign policy and the most consequential change since World War II. There was just one problem: China was a complete black box for Nixon and his administration. They didn't have access to anyone in Mao's inner circle, and any attempts to reach out through formal channels would be an embarrassing display of weakness. It just so happened that America's four-year-old embargo had pushed Pakistan to make an alliance with China. Now Pakistan was a Cold War player in a prime position to help.

Nixon didn't grovel. But he needed a man whom Mao trusted to help set up a meeting. Even more difficult, Nixon needed a man whom he himself trusted in order to pull it all together. Yahya was the only man on the planet who ticked both boxes. In exchange, Nixon promised to deliver not only the guns that Yahya requested but also bombers, tanks, artillery, ships, anything that Yahya might need to squash any domestic or foreign threats, current or future.

Yahya recognized the opportunity of a lifetime. He said yes immediately. Although he needed the weaponry in the fight against India, the truth was that he would have done it for free. He liked Nixon, and he liked Mao. He promised Nixon that he would get along splendidly with Mao, in due course.

After an afternoon of deals and pageantry, everyone reunited over a regal state dinner. Crystal candelabras, giant bowls of apples, and hundreds of wineglasses filled the mahogany banquet table where the luminaries were seated. Nixon was all smiles. He regaled Fakhra, Yahya's wife of twenty years, with some sort of impressive tale or another, while Yahya and Pat giggled together.

After the extensive multicourse dinner and drinks, Yahya took the lectern for the first of the night's many toasts. He wore a black three-piece suit adorned with a red carnation. As usual, his suit's middle button pulled extra duty. Yahya grinned sloppily at the room. There was a lot to celebrate, and he and Nixon had started pouring hours ago. After some speechwriter-induced banalities, Yahya got rolling in a cadence that belied his level of inebriation.

"We in Pakistan are convinced that peace is mankind's most urgent need of the day," he slurred, almost to himself. "Nations need peace at home. And peace abroad! It is [an] essential prerequisite of progress. It is not . . ." Yahya paused, considering what he thought it might not be, before resuming on a different thought. "It is out of this conviction that we actively seek durable friendly relations with all countries. Especially our neighbors. It is for this reason that we have always been urging that the basic disputes between India and Pakistan be resolved. And got out of the way."

His speech meandered through the beauty of Americans landing on the moon and Nixon's plan to bring peace to the Middle East before he paused again, as if searching for something else to say. The inspiration vanished, so instead, he abruptly raised a glass to toast the American president.

With the night's VIP on deck, the band struggled through "The Star-Spangled Banner." Sharps became flats. Flats became spit dribbling down the reeds. It had been a long day for everyone.

Nixon began his own toast by lending a supportive hand to his friend: "I have the privilege to respond to those very eloquent words from the president."

Dressed in his usual drab gray suit and navy tie, Nixon tried small talk. He admired the "lovely ladies from Pakistan." He said his time with Yahya was every bit as special as the twenty-two hours that Neil and Buzz spent on the moon together. Nixon even said that maybe he and Yahya could work together to bring men to Mars.

Cigarette in hand, Pat Nixon sipped another martini at the table while not listening. She had her usual plate of cottage cheese. No slouch in the booze department himself, Nixon at least kept it together long enough to opine prophetically:

"In this region, we will soon see the greatest peace—or the greatest destruction—the world has ever known. What we do can affect the future of not just a billion and a half, not just three billion, but everyone on this planet. Let us raise our glasses to the president of Pakistan, and to the great and lasting friendship between the people of Pakistan and the people of the United States."

The band played him out, just in time for Yahya to order another round or three for everyone who could still keep their heads up. Fakhra took this opportunity to excuse herself. She'd seen how this night would end plenty of times before, but she'd never dream of chastising Yahya publicly for his boorishness.

The hours melted away as Yahya and Nixon bonded like long-lost brothers. After a farewell hug to Nixon, Yahya stumbled on a plane bound for Islamabad and President House, the official residence for the leader of Pakistan. Once there he carefully unwrapped Nixon's gift, his trembling hands trying their best not to rip the precious cargo inside.

He got the tape off and slid out the contents. Two packs of astronaut ice cream fell into his hands. It was a top-secret NASA project for the Apollo mission and wouldn't be available commercially for another six years.

Yahya slipped into a bedroom down the hall. He laid the packs next to his sleeping teenage son, Ali. Yahya smiled, anticipating Ali's reaction the next morning. Ali was Yahya's ultimate weak spot; he could never resist spoiling the boy with whatever baubles his position of power could muster. The day was a success, not only had he made some strategic progress for the nation, but he had also squeezed some dehydrated ice cream out of Nixon. And right now, it was the ice cream that really mattered. Yahya weaved back through the hallway, undressed, and collapsed into bed, trying not to wake his dutiful Fakhra.

The next morning, Nixon headed back to America, where he ordered the Department of Defense to break the arms embargo by selling Pakistan hundreds of armored personnel carriers and B-57 bombers. He wrote in his diary that Yahya was "a real leader, very intelligent and with great insight." Maybe the two of them launching rockets to Mars together wasn't such a crazy idea after all.

Hungover, Yahya meandered into his office. The yellow lilies were in full bloom outside his window. He felt honored to be asked by the most powerful man in the world to undertake such an important and dangerous mission. He made up his mind right then and there: Brokering a connection between the United States and China was going to be his life's greatest achievement. This was bigger than building Islamabad, maybe even bigger than democracy in Pakistan.

Yahya took out a blank manila folder and a black marker from a drawer. He wrote CHINESE CONNECTION on the cover. From that moment on, he would carry the folder with him everywhere. But time was tight. The country's economy was still careening toward a depression, and India was itching to fight again. Yahya had not only to get Mao to the table but also fast-track elections before the riots started up again, lest he be deposed like so many of his predecessors. Yahya figured he had a year, a year and a half at most.

5

Neil Frank

A few years ago, Neil Frank would have marveled at the images that the ESSA-8 sent to him from low-earth orbit. But at this particular moment he was just frustrated. The satellite circled the earth every 114.3 minutes and could snap and transmit a total of eight photos a day from a band across the Northern Hemisphere. Each image covered an area of two thousand square miles, and each pixel represented about two miles—a resolution only a weatherman could appreciate.

Frank unspooled a finger's length of transparent tape from a dispenser on the computer room's side table. He lined up the edges of the photos until they stretched out into a panorama representing a developing weather system in the Caribbean, while chain-smoking colleagues did similar patchwork tasks for other parts of the world. Frank's job at the National Hurricane Center (NHC) in Miami was to catch catastrophic storms in their initial stages and give an early warning to the places where they might hit. It was a laborious process, and the images landing on his desk often came days after the weather had resolved itself. But it was the best technology available at the time.

The clouds told the story of a tropical depression spinning counterclockwise and heading toward land, but he couldn't quite decipher if this was something noteworthy or just another fleeting moment in the skies. The resolution was too poor to know for sure, let alone calculate if the infant weather system might gain strength and grow into a megastorm with the capacity to kill thousands or even tens of thousands of people. At times like this, Frank felt like a destitute farmer looking at the skies to predict rain on his own fields. He needed better intel.

The NHC was a strange landing spot for Frank, given that all he ever wanted to be was a high-school basketball coach. Growing up in the heart of tornado alley in Wellington, Kansas, in the late 1940s, Frank cared infinitely more about spinning a ball on his finger than the twisters roaring past his window. But no school was going to hire a full-time coach back then. So the square-jawed midwesterner with a crew cut decided that the easiest way to live his dream was to become a science teacher and coach basketball on the side.

Frank excelled at chemistry in high school and college, but before he could get down to the business of teaching gangly teens how to dribble, he had to figure a way out of a new wrinkle. All the able-bodied men his age were getting shipped off to Korea. To avoid the grim and expendable life of an infantryman at war, Frank married his junior-high sweetheart and signed up to a posting at the US Air Force base in Okinawa instead. It was a detour—a quick one, he hoped.

The military was tired of being caught flat-footed every time a typhoon barreled through their fleet, so when his superiors realized that Frank had a knack for science, they assigned him to be a meteorologist. Three typhoons (what they call hurricanes or cyclones in Japan) hit Okinawa in Frank's first year, each worse than the last. Frank saw how deadly and damaging they could be, and how many lives could be saved with basic warnings. Even an alert just one hour before landfall could be enough for people to get to higher ground.

At the time, the only way to know about storms forming far out at sea was to make visual contact. So the air force sent reconnaissance aircraft out on daily cloud-scouting missions to give Frank and the other meteorologists in his unit the data they needed to predict whether or not a system might pose a threat. In the process, Frank also discovered the international code of military professionalism: How men in uniform—no matter the country—respected each other's sacrifice and were willing to cut to the chase.

Frank had found a new calling; basketball would have to wait. After finishing his tour of duty, he got a PhD in meteorology and moved to Miami to work at the NHC, the most technically sophisticated storm-tracking facility in the world.

Everyone in Miami knew the NHC because it had something curious on its roof that almost no other building in America had: a satellite dish. The agency had the latest, most expensive overhead projectors, top-of-the-line typewriters, and sophisticated ream-length spreadsheet printers that took up an entire room. The center's hub was an octagonal room, where half a dozen men put up hand-drawn charts, grainy radar images, and other breaking-weather events from around the world on backlit displays.

Broadly speaking, most tropical storms form over warm ocean waters between the tropic of cancer and the tropic of capricorn, with the equator smack in the middle. Here, sunlight causes the water surface to evaporate into huge masses of moist air. As the air rises, it creates a low-pressure area below, which then sucks in higher pressure air from the periphery. If the pressure differences are great enough, the convection starts to sustain itself like a massive ocean-fed engine. The system of clouds and wind spin around a center, moving faster and faster. According to the Saffir-Simpson Hurricane Wind Scale, if the storm sustains winds of more than 74 miles per hour, it is considered a Category 1 hurricane. For each increase of about 20 miles per hour, the storm's rating increases another notch, topping out at a Category 5—with sustained winds of 157 miles per hour or higher. Cyclones weaken when they hit land and lose connection to the warm water that fuels them. They dissipate and dump all of their water on whatever—and whoever—is unlucky enough to be in their path.

The deadliest hurricane to hit North America overran the levies in Galveston, Texas, in 1900 and killed somewhere between six and twelve thousand people—almost a third of the city. After the great hurricane hit, investors fled the climate-fragile boomtown and propped up Houston, a similarly sized but more inland town. Frank and everyone else at the NHC knew the Galveston story. It was the Big One, a devastating Category 4 that they always carried in the back of their minds.

Yet the South Asia situation was much more dire. In 1737 and again in 1864, Category 5 cyclones ripped through the Bay of Bengal, each time killing more than three hundred thousand people. Every hundred years or so, the low-lying delta region from Calcutta to Dacca was ground zero for a cataclysmic cyclone event. And by 1970, they were overdue.

History had proven that it wasn't just a city like Galveston that could be devastated; entire civilizations could rise and fall based on Mother Nature's wrath. The ancient cities of Harappa (in Pakistan) and Cahokia (in Illinois), once the largest population centers on their respective continents, disappeared from the face of the earth when the rivers that fed them changed course. The Vikings went extinct in Greenland with the coming of a medieval ice age. And the great Khmer civilization, best known for creating Angkor Wat, descended into chaos when they ran out of water. In these and hundreds of other cases, natural disasters did not only take human lives; they also wreaked havoc on entire political and social structures.

The NHC was theoretically a bulwark against that environmental destruction—offering predictions and warnings that could save lives and possibly even nations. Although the NHC's primary mission was to secure American interests, both Frank and his boss, Gordon Dunn, kept an eye on Asian events, too. Dunn believed that it was only a matter of time before East Pakistan was ground zero for another catastrophic storm and flew there to help develop an early-warning system. Once a warning came in from shipping reports or possibly even from the NHC's own sources, authorities could send an alert out to the most vulnerable areas.

So on Dunn's recommendation, the Pakistani government replaced their antiquated warning system. They installed speakers and told radio stations to alert people to get to higher ground. Dunn directed them to issue one loud alert for weaker cyclones all the way up to four alerts in a row for storms that promised cataclysmic disaster.

The US government wasn't pumping millions into storm research as an altruistic pursuit. The Department of Defense and the navy had just launched Project Stormfury, the government's first significant attempt to control the climate with technology. The idea was to spray hurricanes with silver iodine and other particles to try to weaken or otherwise change a storm's path or intensity. The potential military applications were so obvious that even Fidel Castro attacked the program, saying that the Americans were trying to weaponize hurricanes. The truth was probably a bit more benign, but given that a typical hurricane generated more destructive power than ten thousand nuclear bombs, Castro wasn't crazy to be afraid of the Americans directing a few his way.

Still, in 1970, most of the planet believed that megastorms were an unavoidable fact of life and that predicting them was as impossible as divining God's will. Frank was determined to prove them wrong. He worked fourteen-hour days developing better models to predict hurricane paths and intensities that could save countless lives.

The answer to at least some of Frank's frustrations was just about ready to be stuffed inside a rocket at Vandenberg Air Force Base in California. It was a new state-of-the-art satellite called ITOS 1, officially the world's most advanced weather tracker. A seven-hundred-pound octahedron that could transmit real-time weather imaging from its polar orbit, ITOS 1 was nothing less than a quantum leap in threat detection for the Department of Defense (DoD). After the Cuban missile crisis, the DoD fast-tracked funding for ITOS 1 as a key strategic asset in the Cold War fight against the Soviets. While weather events had brought civilizations to their knees in the past, a satellite like this might just be able to predict brewing conflicts by reading the clouds like tea leaves.

For all the reasons that a nation might look to safeguard their own shores first, the National Oceanographic and Atmospheric Association (NOAA)—the weather service charged with studying weather conditions across continents—was about to launch the ITOS 1 into geosynchronous orbit, which meant that it stayed in position. The ITOS generation satellites didn't have to circle the entire earth to take a picture like the ESSA-8 did. Instead, they hovered over the North Pole and beamed a steady stream of images back down to the weather center every thirty minutes.

Looking again at the taped-up monstrosity in front of him, Frank knew that ITOS 1 was about to change everything. Once the government started sending him satellite information, there wouldn't be any more cobbling photos together to make predictions based on events that happened five days ago. There would be real-time data that would help the NHC save lives anywhere in the Northern Hemisphere.

Finally, the agency would have enough technical know-how to make mass-casualty storms a thing of the past. The future was bright.

6

Yahya Khan and General Rani

Almost no one knew Akleem Akhtar by her real name. Instead, most people called her General Rani. And right now General Rani was scanning the room looking for a mark. It was an old habit. Yahya's parties at President House were a great place to do business. A drunk minister or corporate executive made an attractive and pliable candidate for her schemes.

Just like every other party she attended, Rani worked systematically. When she spotted an excellent prospect, perhaps a portly middle-aged interior minister trying and failing to charm a young socialite, her mind would cycle through the girls in her harem who would be more accommodating. She knew above all else that men in positions of power needed a vent, and the vent they required most was a bedmate provided through her reliable agency.

A muffled thudding floated over the din of rock-and-roll music blaring from the president's hi-fi. Rani heard a man yell "Yahya!" from across the room. She paid it no mind, gliding over to her mark. But halfway to her target, the Shah of Iran stopped her in her tracks.

The impeccably dressed Shah had been pounding his fist on the ornate door to Yahya's bedroom, over and over again, but it was no use. Iran's supreme ruler—and lavish Nixon campaign donor—had come to Islamabad on urgent business. He needed Yahya's military and strategic help against a rapidly growing Islamist insurgency. In turn, Yahya needed new trade partners as the 1965 sanctions were squeezing his country's economy like a vise and food riots raged in his cities. The Shah could help make those problems go away.

Rani and the Shah walked to Yahya's room together.

For ten years General Rani had sat in smoky, lecherous, sticky-carpeted army officers' clubs, watching respected men debase themselves in what they thought were friendly, no-questions-asked confines. She started a business in the early 1960s based on those years of careful study, offering prostitutes to officers and using the secrets they told in bed to extract favors later. Rani herself put it matter-of-factly: "I was determined to beat men at their own game. Dumb, pretty girls who come with no strings attached are a universal failing of men in power."

Rani was a natural madam. Charming and witty, she used each transaction as a stepping-stone to more powerful men who could offer yet more valuable information. Given the rampant corruption, gleeful backstabbing, and constant political turmoil that defined 1960s Pakistan, gossip was a currency more valuable than the rupee.

By 1965, Rani was working the Rawalpindi Club, the most elite officers' club in the country. When fishing for new clients, she liked to sit at the table closest to the toilets while sipping on a fresh lime soda. She surmised that the drunker an officer was, the more he had to pee. The more he had to pee, the more he'd pass by. The more he passed by, the more she could remind him of what was on her menu. It was a laughably effective strategy.

One night, Rani spotted the mark of a lifetime. A blind-drunk general with swaying medals clinking on his beefy chest stumbled by at least ten times on his way from the bar to the urinal and back. On the eleventh trip, Yahya Khan stopped to say hello.

The pair hit it off. Rani was smitten with Yahya's loose tongue and meteoric rise within the army ranks. Yahya liked women. They both adored discretion. Yahya bestowed on her the nickname of General

Rani (which translates to Queen General) to reflect that she, too, knew how to get things done. Calling Rani a madam didn't do justice to the empire she built. She wasn't just the country's premier distributor of carnal services; she was an essential data conduit to and for the elite.

Yahya and Rani floated in the same social circles, sharing a deep bond. Yahya loved the conversations at elegant dinner parties, the dripping high society of it all, and how even the air in the room could smell sophisticated. He loved seeing and being seen, and Rani helped him fill his Rolodex with the country's best singers, artists, and actors. Yahya started to import music and soon boasted the country's best and most up-to-date collection of 1960s swinging London vinyl sounds. Rani played matron, prying the whiskey bottle from Yahya's hand on the nights when he emptied it too fast.

As word spread of her deepening access into the country's political elite, Rani's client list grew. Yahya introduced her to then-president Ayub, who became a regular client. What Rani understood better than anyone was that connecting powerful men with women wasn't about the *money*. As she explained, "In this country everything works on mutual favors, and the profession I have chosen for myself entitles me to these favors." Rani signed movie stars and singers who feared their careers were waning, and showed them that a few uncomfortable hours in bed, when coupled with her skill at postcoital information management, led to *power*. Power to land a new recording deal, or secure financing for a lead role in a film. And sometimes, it meant the power to open the president's locked bedroom door.

The Shah's trip had started off well. Yahya showered him with pomp and circumstance on the tarmac. It felt like a good omen to the Iranian ruler. But then Yahya vanished while the Shah stewed in his suite, awaiting a invitation to talk privately.

After endless hours waiting for a man who gave no indication of when or if he was going to show up, the Shah ran out of patience. He stormed over to President House to locate the missing leader. Expecting a quiet, stately manor befitting a regal residence, he instead found a raucous bacchanal in full swing. It wasn't a one-off. A few months back, the local chief of police stopped calling the building President House. Instead, he offered up a new moniker: Pimp House. The Shah had his own decades-long reputation as a playboy, but, in his book, business always came before pleasure.

Sidestepping the revelers, the Shah discovered that Yahya wasn't busy glad-handing as president but was entombed in his bedroom. Though an all-powerful dictator at home, the Shah could only stare at the locked door like an impotent child. He scanned the room full of bureaucrats, diplomats, prostitutes, and military men, eventually finding just the madam he needed.

It hadn't always been like this for Yahya. After all, Islamabad was his city. Literally. When Ayub first hired Yahya in 1958, he tasked him with building Pakistan a shining new capital out of a patch of useless desert scrubland. Most everyone thought it impossible.

First, Yahya scoured the earth for architects who could create a modern urban administrative oasis, handpicking a world-class Greek team to lay out the new city. Like other planned capitals—such as Washington, DC, and Canberra, Australia—Yahya filled Islamabad with wide leafy boulevards and gleaming brick and stone buildings. There were no slums or signs of poverty as far as the eye could see. Yahya directed vast numbers of laborers at his disposal, ordering them to build this pristine bubble to epitomize a modern Pakistan. Excuses were to be left at the city limits. Just one year after breaking ground, Islamabad emerged.

But that wasn't the impossible bit. The true miracle was that Yahya built an entire city without a single complaint of corruption or embezzlement. Everywhere else in South Asia, even the smallest, most useless government-constructed ditch helped line someone's pocket. With up to 80 percent of Pakistan's budget spent on defense, it was standard for generals and officers to take a 10 percent cut of anything that passed through their hands. This doubled or even tripled the costs of just about every project.

Yahya scoffed at the bureaucratic naysayers and the advisers who begged him to pay off a local leader or clan head just to grease the wheels. Yahya's genius was in running a bureaucratic endeavor with military precision, and he was determined to see the vision through, leading by example and putting the glory of the nation over personal profits. The idea couldn't have been more removed from business as usual in Pakistan at the time. Yahya immersed himself in the task, overseeing the smallest details and keeping an iron grip on the accounting. Islamabad came together ahead of schedule and under budget.

When it was done, Ayub, Yahya, and the rest of Pakistan's senior officials moved in. Islamabad quickly filled with diplomats and businessmen, but it wasn't a place to raise a family. There wasn't much of anything to do. And venturing beyond the city limits was like stepping in a time machine; one stride took you from a paved road with modern villas to an ancient scrubland with nomadic hill tribes. Here, cloaked and bearded men lived in patchy tents and took long hookah drags at their campfires while they watched for jackals coming out of the wilderness.

Yahya found himself in a strange position. He had an army of loyal troops at his disposal, but they were bored and restless. He had already delegated all essential governance tasks, freeing himself from having any real daily activities despite his increasingly lofty positions of power. Surrounded by people celebrating his greatness, Yahya figured he could relax his rules a bit. One peg of whiskey a night—never during Ramadan—became two a night. Then three a night, but only one during Ramadan. Then a maximum of three before dinner. There was always someone to toast him and always another cadet honored to buy his next drink.

Yahya also started to get some serious disposable income, which he spent on disposable women. In Karachi, he was a regular at Le Gourmet, Pakistan's finest nightclub for belly dancing. It was a great place to escape the sandstorms that whipped through the still-treeless city he'd built. Yahya liked to tease the performers as they worked, borrowing their props to put on himself. The raucous *Mad Men* crowd of ambassadors and politicians loved every minute of it, and Yahya adored being the life of the party.

By the time Ayub gifted him the presidency, the madams and prostitutes were so entrenched in Yahya's orbit that he even promoted some of them to official positions. He made Rani the President House event planner, with a security detail matching that of the foreign minister, as a cover so she could continue her real job. He chucked protocol in the trash can whenever he had a more personal urge. After all, he was just an interim president. His legacy as Pakistan's Father of Democracy was secure. He'd delegated the election preparations too, and everything was running on schedule and exactly as planned.

Most everyone in Pakistan was sure that Yahya's successor would be Zulfikar Ali Bhutto, the head of the newly formed Pakistan People's Party, also known as the PPP. West Pakistanis loved Bhutto's promise to end the country's rampant corruption, throw the elites—whom Bhutto blamed for all the country's ills—in jail, and install a socialist democracy. Yahya liked how Bhutto treated politics like war, and they bonded over Bhutto's take-no-prisoners style when dealing with the career politicians they both hated. They became fast friends, slurping endless whiskey tumblers together late into the night in Islamabad's bars and officers' clubs.

Bhutto's main competition was a Bengali named Sheikh Mujibur Rahman—or, as everyone called him, Mujib. Mujib's party was the Awami League, one of several Bengali parties that most political pundits assumed would split the East Pakistan vote. Yahya and Bhutto, as well as every last adviser for the pair, were sure that Mujib had no chance of taking more than a minority of assembly seats. Bengalis, after all, weren't natural leaders like the erudite West Pakistanis. The Awami League was of no concern to Yahya, a nuisance that could be shooed away whenever he wished.

Problem was, visiting dignitaries continued to expect a modicum of competence, and they couldn't be waved away as easily as the butler with Yahya's breakfast cognac.

Rani and the Shah reached Yahya's bedroom door. Rani took out her private set of President House keys, already knowing what she'd find inside. Yahya's most recent object of desire was the actress Noor Jahan, to whom Rani had introduced him just a few hours earlier. In the 1950s Jahan was Pakistan's Marilyn Monroe, but changing popular tastes meant that her career had hit a rough patch. She needed a kick-start back to the top of the charts, and the president of Pakistan's support would do just the trick.

Rani slid into the room to find Jahan fellating Yahya. She pulled Jahan off Yahya's bulging midsection and helped him put his uniform on so that he would be fit for a diplomatic visit.

The Shah got his five minutes with Yahya. They struck a hasty deal in the bedroom's musty air, for a pittance of what the Shah was originally willing to give. They closed the deal quickly so the Shah could get the hell out of there with at least a modicum of his own dignity intact.

Yahya embraced his vices as his interest in governing diminished to nothingness. He outsourced responsibilities to his advisers, to Bhutto, and even to Rani. She, in turn, gave the most plum tasks to her best clients. By now, everyone knew that Yahya tended to parrot whatever policy position the last person whom he spoke with had said. So his more devious advisers guided his entire policy platform just by setting his schedule. Yahya never noticed the scheme. Sex and politics fused in his mind, the alcohol-damaged synapses crossing wires that otherwise would have stayed distinct.

The only thing that Yahya refused to delegate was his friendship with Richard Nixon and the CHINESE CONNECTION. Rubbing shoulders with the most powerful person in the world made Yahya stand a little bit taller. If he could find some way to advance Nixon's world agenda, and thus secure an alliance that would keep Pakistan ahead in the inevitable war against India, everyone would know and love the name Agha Muhammad Yahya Khan forever.

So Yahya drew up plans for a secret trip to China, where he could make his pitch to Mao in person and convince him that the United States could be a trusted friend. A trade summit would be the perfect cover.

7

Hafiz Uddin Ahmad

TEHRAN, IRAN

SEPTEMBER 1970

Two months before landfall

Hafiz lofted Pakistan's green-and-white crescent moon flag above his head at the opening ceremony of the games in Tehran. Twenty thousand Iranian football fans roared their approval. The Shah waved down from the Royal Gallery. The freshly snowcapped Alborz mountains made for a stunning backdrop. Hafiz's senses buzzed as the teams left the center circle for their respective sidelines.

Pakistan was about to square off against Iran, a World Cup contender, in a friendly round-robin tournament meant to support their regional economic alliance and spread goodwill among nations. Of the three teams competing, Pakistan was the weakest by a mile. Turkey was the best, and Iran wasn't far behind. Few on the Pakistan team dared even imagine that they could pull off a single upset, let alone win the whole tournament. Not only did the other teams have more skilled players but they were also physically bigger. Most of their players stood above six feet tall, while the bulk of the Pakistani lineup barely cleared five feet six inches. Hafiz was five eight, but he knew size and weight didn't matter once the ball went live. He was ready to shock the world, and this time no students were going to get in his way.

The transition from football star to soldier went much smoother than Hafiz could have ever anticipated. Most of Pakistan's soldiers hailed from West Pakistan, but he was happily entrenched in an all-Bengali unit at the military headquarters in Jessore. In basic training, he'd learned to shoot a rifle and handle the wide array of armaments in Pakistan's stockpile. Just as the major promised, the army made Hafiz a second lieutenant—high enough to command respectful salutes from the soldiers but not so high that the bureaucratic responsibilities would overwhelm his playing time.

Hafiz got the feeling that the army wanted to keep him on the pitch instead of in charge of live ammunition, which was fine by him. Everyone knew that his real job was to be the Army Team's ringer as it played against other semipro teams, like Pakistan Railways and Pakistan Airways, as well as in pride matches against the navy and air force. Once the toast of the nation, he now felt like a big fish in a much smaller pond. He'd gone from playing in front of crowds of thirty thousand to stadiums with a paltry three hundred—or less. But true to their word, the army still allowed him to play for the National Team when they had particularly important matches abroad, such as this one. Hafiz lived for these moments, though they were a lot rarer than he thought they'd be.

For Hafiz, this tournament was not only a chance to play on a bigger stage but also a window into a much more affluent nation. The Iranian hosts impressed Hafiz from the moment he landed, putting the team up at the Miami Hotel, right in the heart of Tehran. He walked around the city and marveled at the streets crowded with fancy new automobiles. It seemed that just about everyone here owned a car, compared to sleepy Dacca, where he often had the wide boulevards to himself as he wove his Vespa around town. In Tehran, women wore short skirts and makeup and the men donned flashy suits. He'd never been in a place so infused with Western fashion and values. Some of his teammates even shopped for sunglasses and records.

The first game was an embarrassing blowout for Hafiz and his teammates. The Iranians ran circles around them, scoring seven times, while Pakistan got shut out completely. Hafiz couldn't even manage a single shot on goal. Even worse, Captain Qadir Baksh, a midfielder with whom Hafiz had played ever since the Dacca days, mangled his knee when an Iranian striker came in for a slide tackle. Hafiz couldn't bear to look at the fluttering green-and-white flag as they trotted off the field.

The team sat in silence on the bus back to the Miami Hotel. They all dreaded playing another match against an even better team than the one that had just wiped them off the field—and without Baksh. Hafiz stared out the window at the slick suits and polished sedans, in disbelief that his football glories had tumbled all the way down from scoring game-winning goals to holding up flags.

Still exhausted from going all-out for ninety minutes, Hafiz wandered into the lobby in a daze, then did a double take when he spotted a face that any Bengali would recognize: the one and only Ravi Shankar. The classical sitar player traveled the world with the Beatles. He was arguably the most famous Bengali on the planet. And he happened to be playing a series of concerts in Iran.

The next morning, Hafiz saw Shankar again at the hotel restaurant. Starstruck, Hafiz walked up to the musician and introduced himself in Bengali. Though Shankar came from the Indian side of Bengal—and technically India and Pakistan were still bitter enemies—Hafiz hoped they could overlook that part while in a foreign country.

Shankar met the footballer with a wide grin at the sound of their mutual native tongue. When Hafiz mentioned that he'd grown up near Barisal, Shankar lit up. He'd visited the district, back before Partition, when they were part of the same homeland. He remembered a rustic scene of children playing cricket in lush fields and it made him homesick. When he learned Hafiz was in Tehran to play football, Shankar revealed that he barely knew anything at all about the sport.

"Do you play it barefoot?" he asked Hafiz, drawing upon old memories.

Hafiz smiled. "No, we wear shoes now."

"How do you play against players who are so much bigger than you?" Shankar asked innocently, for it truly did seem that the Pakistani players were up against giants.

"It's hard, sir, but luckily football is a game of skill. It's not boxing, after all," said Hafiz. He left out the part about how, based on the previous day's blowout, the teams they were up against were apparently also more skilled.

Still, the short chat perked Hafiz up and reinforced his sense that Bengalis, no matter where they lived, had a bond stronger than politics, careers, and language. Simply *being* Bengali meant something. It was a kinship that transcended borders.

After breakfast, the coach huddled the team on the bus, as the diesel contraption chugged to the stadium. Baksh sat with them, his leg in a cast. The coach asked Hafiz if he could step in as captain. He paused on the question. Who in their right mind would take on a suicide mission like that, given what had happened at their last game? Hafiz had captained Bengali teams in Dacca before, but this was different. Most every other player on the team was Punjabi. Would they even follow him?

Then again, wasn't it just a game, after all? What did he have to lose by trying? He had a few ideas on how the team might improve their offensive strategies, and he knew what motivated his teammates much better than the coach did.

"Yes, I'll do it."

The coach appreciated Hafiz's willingness to be the sacrificial lamb. Everyone in Tehran—even the Bengali musician who knew next to nothing about football—knew that Pakistan was about to get obliterated.

As usual, Hafiz led with his foot, scoring the team's only goal. But as captain, he also led with his heart and voice. As their leader, he surprised himself with his decisiveness and marveled at how the other players soaked up his guidance. Following Hafiz's example, they came together as a team. Without hope of winning, the Pakistan squad attacked Turkey's defenses relentlessly, keeping the much better team on the backfoot for the entire ninety minutes. Under Hafiz's command, the less-talented, undersized Pakistanis flew around the field like gnats, disrupting Turkey's game plan just enough to make it a real battle.

There was no fairy-tale ending—Pakistan still lost—but Hafiz and his teammates held their heads high as they shook hands with the Turkish players after the match. The final score was 1–3, but the outcome of the match was in doubt right up until the last ten minutes or so.

Walking off the field at Amjadiyeh Stadium, arm in arm with his Punjabi teammates, Hafiz couldn't help but be proud of himself and what he had inspired in his teammates. *Maybe I am a bit of a leader*, he thought. For the first time, he was excited to get back to his men at the barracks.

8

Mohammad Hai

Mohammad Abdul Hai's uncle gripped the tiller of the pontoon boat with one hand and the rope controlling the sail with the other. Hai couldn't see his face but knew that his uncle was smiling. He always did when the family headed out into the Bay of Bengal to catch dinner. About ten feet away, two other uncles matched their course and speed in a nearly identical boat. Between the two crafts, eighteen-year-old Hai and his cousin each held one end of a simple mesh that looked something like a volleyball net.

Usually they managed a few carp or eel on their excursions. But as they trolled through the shallow latte-colored waters, both net men felt a sharp pull. It was so strong that it almost crashed the two boats together.

Hai couldn't believe their luck. The beast splashed its tail above the surface and writhed around desperately as it sought a hole in the unexpected trap. It was a helicopter catfish, also known as the piranha of the Ganges. Unlike the five-inch predator version in the Amazon, helicopters could grow to be more than six feet long and had a nasty tendency to bite off the hands of fishermen when cornered—or caught in a net.

Technically a member of the catfish family, the helicopters were more like prehistoric horror shows with ball-like eyes and bulging lips. They also sported two large tentacles that extended from either side of their nose, looking more like spikes than whiskers, which they used to search the mud for prey. But the real danger lay in their three rows of razor-sharp teeth, each hooked on the end to make it impossible for anything to escape once the beast closed its jaws. Fishermen told stories of finding dogs and even small children in their stomachs.

Then again, the helicopters rarely came this far south. They were a freshwater fish, and this one clearly took a wrong turn somewhere. Not that any of this would make it any less delicious. Together, Hai and his uncles wrapped the net around the chomping helicopter and heaved it onto the pontoon boat's floor. Hai kneeled on it until it slowly drowned in the damp seventy-five-degree air.

They'd snagged the forty-pound behemoth in the brackish water right off the coast of Manpura—just one of hundreds of islands clinging to the southern third of East Pakistan. The very last spit of land before the open water of the Bay of Bengal, Manpura was a pencil-shaped splotch of snake-filled mangrove swamps that maxed out at four miles wide and five feet above sea level. Hai was born and raised here, alongside all twenty-five of his family members and about fifty thousand other people who called it home.

Manpura was about as disconnected from global intrigue and high society as one could get. It was one of those places that retirees might call tranquil and younger generations would just call boring. Ferries were the only way in or out. Newspapers would arrive weeks late, if at all. Shortwave radios were the sole source of immediate information, although batteries were always in short supply. This meant that islanders had to rely on the news and rumors that passengers on commuter ferries brought with them from the other islands and sometimes, when they were lucky, the capital of Dacca. Residents spread this gossip through the rest of the island with the enthusiasm of fishermen coming to shore with a big catch.

Yet the pancake-flat parcel of land was still a geographic hotspot.

It formed a choke point for East Pakistan's main sea conduit to Dacca, meaning that anyone who wanted to get something in or out of the capital by water would need to pass by. It was a perfect place for pirates to steal spices in 1570—or for an eighteen-year-old aching for more out of life to daydream about as he watched the world go by in 1970.

But Manpura had dangers too. The island was ground zero for several of history's worst cyclones, and almost every year residents either endured a direct hit or at least the threat of one. This could sometimes be a boon. Hai never forgot the day that thousands of multicolored barrels of heating oil washed ashore after a cyclone just missed them but sank a container ship thirty miles out. The detritus littered the beaches for weeks and sparked a cottage industry of oil resellers.

That's not to say that life on the island was all barrenness and destitution. Manpura's silt-rich earth made for exceptional rice farming, fishing, and birding. Every fall, the sky would fill with thousands of migratory birds that used Manpura as a rest stop on the way to Siberia, Nepal, or China. Hai's favorite childhood memory was of hearing the varied sounds of the flocks slowly build and then unite into an orchestra of birdsong.

Still, like most teenagers growing up on the periphery, Hai ached for a taste of the center. At Manpura High School, Hai and his best friend Malik Mahmud were the island's homegrown version of political rabble-rousers. Malik was a rich kid by Manpura standards. It meant he could just afford the fare for him and his friends to take the ferry to Dacca. A couple of months back, he finally convinced a few student leaders at the Awami League that he and Hai weren't just some bayou bumpkins but committed community organizers who could help spread the gospel back home. That was Hai's first trip out of the delta.

Malik's silky words cracked open the door into the world of underground organizing, but his golden foot kicked it down. Even the Awami League students had heard the rumor that Dacca's famous

Mohammedan Sporting Club was grooming Malik for a roster spot. A politically active player was just what the league needed. And Malik felt anything was possible. Every kid on Manpura knew that just a few years earlier the Mohammedans signed local hero Hafiz Uddin Ahmad from the neighboring island of Bhola and turned him into a superstar.

Though Hai was happy to ride Malik's coattails, his own life seemed boring in comparison. Hai lived next to the high school, where his dad taught and his mom led the local school board. Hai and Malik played endless pickup football games on the salt-crusted school grounds, using their shirts as goal markers. The final whistle was inevitably Hai's mom calling him in to hit the books. She pushed Hai hard, throwing huge parties each time he got top marks and giving punishing night lessons to prepare him for Pakistan's civil service exam. Passing it, she told Hai, would guarantee him a good job for life. Only a few dozen spots were available each year; maybe only one in ten thousand graduates landed one.

"Use your brain. It's the only way out of here." She said it so much that he usually repeated the line with her, while rolling his eyes.

The truth was that Hai craved bigger adventures. That's why Hai and Malik took that twenty-two-hour ride to Dacca on a leaky wooden steamer ship and joined impromptu student protests with their idealistic counterparts from all over East Pakistan. They chanted slogans of Bengali autonomy in groups of a few hundred. They zigzagged around Dacca, yelling loud enough for even the rich foreigners staying at the InterContinental Hotel to hear. Wearing all white as a symbol of solidarity, their marches usually ended under the old banyan tree at Dacca University.

At night, they'd talk about what they knew of world politics. Everyone agreed that with Mujib leading their movement, they had a real chance to make a difference. The college kids explained how British colonial legacies and the Cold War stifled their chances for freedom. Hai held his own with the fiery students. He gave supporting data to their inequality arguments and refuted the occasional nonsense conspiracy theories. They were impressed.

Hai fell in love with every last bit of it. He fantasized about one day studying at Dacca University—East Pakistan's intellectual epicenter—and taking part in the great debates under the banyan tree. After all, Dacca University wasn't just East Pakistan's Oxford; it was also the launching pad for almost every major Bengali political movement since Partition. That included the 1952 protests that prevented West Pakistan from forcing Bengalis to write in Urdu and the 1969 protests that freed East Pakistan politicians who were jailed for demanding equal rights for Bengalis.

Hai dreamed that, one day, he might even be able to see one of Mujib's speeches in person. Lately, the Awami League leader was shaking his fist over taxes, saying that the politicians in Islamabad treated East Pakistan like their own personal cash machine. The Bengalis got crumbs while the Punjabi-speaking elites treated them like indentured servants.

Mujib barnstormed from village to village, giving incendiary speeches on football fields and in town squares, arguing that West Pakistan thought of East Pakistan as little more than a colony. Still, most Bengalis had a hard time seeing how his lofty talk would mean real change. Yahya's big election was less than a month away, and it was the first-ever chance for Bengalis to take part in democracy. If the election was going to mean anything, Mujib needed a catalyst to show Bengalis how little West Pakistan cared.

Hai snapped back from his revolutionary thoughts and turned his head toward the shore. With their now lifeless catch secured and stowed, Hai and his uncles turned homeward. The wind picked up, and rows of dark hammerhead clouds rolled over their heads. It was early afternoon, but the sky had turned the same shade of greenish black as the sea that stretched to the horizon.

This looked like a big one.

Hai paddled quickly while his uncle adjusted the sail. They hoped to make it back before they got drenched. Rowing and pulling in unison, they angled toward the dock as other boats bobbed and heaved on the choppy waters.

Hai ran the boats aground and jumped out to pull the tow ropes from the mud and tie them to a date palm. The mud felt like home. He loved digging his hands into the dirt and seeing things grow out of it, which was easy here, where rice stalks could grow almost an inch per day.

They walked past the houses and huts that dotted the landscape, none constructed more than a few feet above sea level. Stands of coconut palms, planted hundreds of years ago, provided shade to clusters of houses built under their branches. There were no fences; everyone just knew what was what and whose was whose. Hai's uncles shouted greetings to the cigarette and vegetable sellers operating out of bicycle carts.

With sinister-looking green-orange colors on the horizon, Hai and his uncles, lucky again, made it home before the clouds spat out anything more than a drizzle. They dumped their massive catch on the kitchen floor. Contagious smiles spread all around the house at the sight of the helicopter catfish; breaking the Ramadan fast tonight was going to be a real celebration. Hai flipped on the shortwave to catch the Pakistan Radio news hour. There had been a few warnings over the last couple of days about a coming storm, but they didn't seem any different from the five or six other times this year that the serious-sounding warnings interrupted bulletins about events in far-flung parts of the world.

The reporter droned on about President Yahya Khan's upcoming visit to Peking for a trade summit, then about a United Nations summit in New York. Hai imagined New York City to be a fantastical land of luxury. Having never seen a picture of it, he envisioned important people rushing about, deciding the direction of the world. Never mind traveling to New York or even the mysterious Peking; it would be enough just to get off Manpura, where he was as much a slave to the weather as to his own lack of social mobility.

Still, it was better to be safe than sorry. With his father away to collect his paycheck at the district headquarters on Bhola, Hai followed the same procedures that his dad always did when the wind picked up. First, he welcomed his extended family members who lived in palm-frond huts into his parents' new brick house where they could ride out the storm. Then, he told his mom to prepare a good meal for everyone while he secured the home. He gathered his grandmother and cousins, who played with his seven-year-old brother, Emdadul, while Hai rustled chickens and goats into the tin pen attached to the side of the house.

He noticed the yard's marsh ground turning spongy. The water table was rising.

Over dinner, they talked about dogs. While wolfing down bowls of fish curry and piles of vegetables after not eating all day, everyone agreed that it was strange that the animals would just not shut up today. It seemed like every stray on Manpura was either yelping and whimpering alone, or roaming around in annoying packs. Hai's uncle said that Allah was sending them a message, and the older generation took turns speculating what that might be.

Hai had lived through cyclones before, of course. One came nearly every year of his life. Usually they made a mess of things, but it wasn't anything a hard day's work couldn't fix.

On the radio, a new storm alert came through. The announcer repeated the signal "Red 4, Red 4" over and over again.

Nobody knew what that meant. The announcer offered no explanation or guidance about what to do next. A second warning just said "big danger coming" with no further instructions—as if that wasn't obvious by simply looking outside at the unnatural sky. Hai's family, like most everyone on the island, reacted by deciding to ride it out in their homes and huts.

What Manpura's residents weren't told was that Red 4 was from the warning system designed by Gordon Dunn of the National Hurricane Center, which rated storms on a scale of 1 to 4. Dunn defined Red 4 as:

"**Red Alert. Catastrophic destruction imminent. Seek high ground immediately.**" But most islands still used the older warning system's 10-point scale. This hodgepodge of systems and ratings was so confusing that even a World Bank coastal mission near Manpura at the time had to call headquarters to figure out what was about to happen.

Everyone in Hai's home shrugged; 4 was certainly better than 10. And they were already cozy inside one of the island's sturdiest houses. They finished the last of the rice and vegetables. The meat was long since stripped clean off the helicopter's spine.

Hai looked out the window as darkness set and thought of his dad. He was likely sitting on one of the diesel-leaking, smoke-belching deathtraps that passed for commuter boats. They were barely seaworthy under clear skies. Hai could just make out sheets of rain falling off the coast. He hoped that his dad would have the good sense to stay on land.

Stuffed but uneasy, Hai sent his exhausted mother to bed after she finished washing all the bowls and pots. Nineteen people were now crammed into the three-bedroom, two-story house. Another twenty relatives and neighbors were at his uncle's place next door. Hai was thankful that his father had installed imported Australian tin for their roof. It was a luxury few could afford on Manpura—and had almost bankrupted them. But on rainy nights, like this one promised to be, the lack of leaks and cracks was worth every rupee.

Raindrops pinged on the roof. Most of the men in Hai's house were downstairs. Their thin blankets offered little comfort from the damp floor and oddly cold draft coming from under the front door. The kids and grandparents got the beds upstairs. Hai herded them up as the tin roof began to rattle on the brick walls.

Hai laid down on his skinny twin mattress with Emdadul. A sharp rain started pelting the windows. He closed his eyes and tried to ignore the howls of wind and the groaning whines of the family's animals.

9

Candy Rohde

Candy hurried to the bedroom to put on one of her good saris. Jon would be here any minute to pick her up for the party. But wrapping six meters of fabric around her thin body was no easy feat. Even after living in Dacca for two years, she still struggled to get the folds in the front just right.

She heard the front-door lock click open and Jon's voice. "I'm home!"

Candy frowned at her handiwork in the mirror. It would have to do.

Jon gave her a quick kiss, then swapped out his scrubs for a Bengali kurta with woven gold threads. Five minutes later, they hopped into their VW Beetle and pulled out onto the street.

They passed their boat, docked just a little way from their house in exclusive New Dacca. Candy and Jon bought a small sailboat to laze about on weekends on the river that ran though their neighborhood. They'd weave past the porpoises, fishermen, and colorful paddle-wheel riverboats with people packed on every deck.

Jon filled Candy in on his day as they drove. The Cholera Research Lab was one of the world's premier centers of study on the devastating disease. Primarily because of how terrible cholera epidemics were in East Pakistan, there was never a shortage of cases or willing trial participants. Before Jon began his work in Dacca, the US government sent him to Oak Ridge, Tennessee, for training, where he learned to use radio isotopes to track how electrolytes moved across intestinal membranes. Cholera causes catastrophic diarrhea, and most patients die from dehydration. Jon researched ways that certain electrolyte solutions might keep a person hydrated through the most acute phase of the illness. If they could just keep hydrated, most people survived. It was all about giving the body enough time to heal itself.

Jon eagerly told her about a new technique he was testing that looked promising. Candy smiled and looked back out the window at the darkening city they now called home. If Jon's work could save thousands of lives, it was probably worth leaving her budding career behind in Boston.

The Beetle sputtered happily through New Dacca. This side of town was a world away from the city's twisting old bazaars. "London Lipstick" boutiques, billboards for ladies' cigarettes, and big English signs wedged between the more typical sari shops and tea stalls advertising their wares in the Bengali script that peppered the roads. There was even a discotheque that played Beatles records every Friday.

Although much of the late 1960s sex and music liberation scene hadn't made it all the way to Dacca, the modernist construction style sure did. In an attempt to strong-arm the jungle out of the city, New Dacca had wide, gleaming concrete boulevards. Pedestrians and bicycles outnumbered vehicles by a hundred to one, so the roads were calm enough for groups of men to sit in the middle of them and drink tea while rickshaws ambled by. Jon hung a left at the new InterContinental Hotel, the closest thing that Dacca had to true luxury.

Candy wished they were going to that all-white marble-and-sandstone landmark hotel tonight for their weekly tea at the hotel's Saqi Bar instead of a party at the US consulate. At the Saqi Bar, they talked poetry and Shakespeare over cups of steaming Darjeeling with a mix of journalists, generals, and politicians and daydreamed about their bright future back in America. Pretty much everyone was on a first-name basis. Expats gave their kids swimming lessons at the pool out back under the watchful eye of ravenous cawing black crows. The Beetle puttered past the hotel.

They arrived at the consul's residence right on time. Bengalis weren't exactly known for being punctual, but Candy was a stickler. On nights like this, she wondered why she bothered.

When the US consulate threw a cocktail party, it was the hottest ticket in town and *the* place for up-and-coming elites to schmooze. The Rohdes were always on the guest list. From Candy's perspective, the evenings were too full of bureaucrats bragging and posturing about their own importance or, worse, foreigners complaining about whatever minor nuisance befell them that day.

The US deputy chief of mission greeted them warmly as they arrived. Then he motioned to the cluster of Bengali chauffeurs outside and said, "At least the natives aren't restless tonight." Candy's smile morphed into pursed lips.

Candy and Jon joined the other guests on the veranda, where a tuxedoed butler served them fresh lime sodas. Looking around, it was a bit of a role reversal; all of the Pakistani guests wore suits and dresses, while many of the foreigners, like Candy and Jon, showed up in formal Bengali attire.

Most attendees congregated around the open bar. The Pakistanis preferred their whiskey, the British their gin, while the Americans gravitated toward imported light beer. Any good host in Dacca always had all three at the ready. They even had tonic water. The British were jealous in a stiff-upper-lip kind of way. Their own consulate's shipment had been delayed for months, and that crisis was on everyone's lips.

Candy hated every minute of it. It wasn't the guest list or superficial conversations that grated the most. It was the fact that she was expected to stand politely in the corner, thin cigarette in hand, and talk recipes with the other wives. She felt insulted: filled with curiosity and ambition but stuck in a country where women didn't work outside the house. Candy half listened to talk of children's milestones and warnings about thieving servants.

But she perked up at bits of a conversation ten feet away that seemed much more interesting. A smattering of foreign and Pakistani officials were deep in discussion about the upcoming election, now just three weeks away. They all agreed that Mujib's tactics, while effective in rallying votes, risked upending the careful, orderly society they'd all helped build.

Candy inched close enough to hear a local official wonder out loud why Bengalis had to make it so hard on themselves. Strikes simply hurt the economy, after all. And since they threatened violence, the army was justified in breaking them up by force.

The consul gave a polite nod as others joined the circle. One newcomer, an American, complained that someone threw a brick at his chauffeured car and made him late for tennis that morning. Others shared their own stories of strike-induced inconvenience.

Candy fantasized about giving them a piece of her mind. Maybe everyone here should be talking about the reasons that people went on strike instead of how irritating it was for the elite. If they just cared enough and wanted to, the people in this room could actually do something helpful.

No, thought Candy. She knew how that scene would play out. They'd give her a figurative—or worse, a literal—pat on the head for her "heartfelt" contribution, have a chuckle and a refill, and then move on to another topic. They'd see Jon as the man with a rabble-rousing wife. Then the social invites would dry up. Shortly thereafter, funding for the Cholera Research Lab could dry up too. So instead, Candy made the calculated choice to stew.

She went back to not listening to recipes and gave Jon a look from across the room, raising her eyebrows and motioning her eyes toward the door. He smiled, relieved. Jon gave a quick excuse about getting back to work. They went out of the consul's residence and back into the real world.

The next morning, Candy was still bothered by the event and the vapid role that she was forced to play. She loved Dacca but missed being taken seriously. Most of all, she missed teaching and the sense of purpose it gave. Her repeated efforts to find that one thing that would give her life meaning here hadn't quite panned out. In the last year she'd learned an Indian dance style called *Bharatanatyam* and took up yoga with an old sage who told his disciples endless stories of how he could walk on water—but only if you promised never to ask him for a demonstration. Entertaining to be sure, but it wasn't enough.

What really excited her were conversations with the Bengali intelligencia. She gravitated toward Bengali writers, journalists, artists, poets, and professors. These people welcomed the few foreigners who showed an interest in embracing their culture. Candy and Jon earned a reputation as a driven, loving couple who actually cared about the country they lived in.

Candy loved flying kites with her Bengali friends' children whenever a festival rolled around—which luckily seemed to be every other week. She formed deep friendships by talking politics and prose. Even mundane topics like the weather took on new meaning as her Bengali friends taught her about the psychological and cultural importance of the monsoon, the rivers, and the storms that spun up out of the Bay of Bengal.

Yet Candy itched for more. Chatting with people wasn't a job; it didn't give back like teaching did. When she looked outside her kitchen window, emaciated children monotonously pounded bricks into rocks for road filler and the sight taunted her to do better.

Candy picked up the paper and scanned the headlines. The front page concerned Mujib's strikes, which came nearly every day now. The article reported police beating students to death with sticks but was vague about who started what. Only the riots and lockdowns afterward were predictably grim.

Candy and Jon usually stockpiled beer in anticipation of police lockdowns so they could throw neighborhood parties. They played endless games of horseshoes, poker, and dominoes until dawn. But they also knew that for nearly everyone else in Dacca, the curfews and strikes meant a much more dangerous evening. For Mujib's Awami League supporters in particular, alleged "agitators" got arbitrary beatings and imprisonment.

Candy's eyes scanned down the page to a weather report that predicted unseasonal rain and possibly a big storm. Details were sparse. Just in case, she'd better put the tarp up to shield their unfinished balcony. She took one last deep breath of the jasmine air wafting in from outside, then she started shutting the windows.

10

Mohammad Hai

Hai jumped out of bed with a start. A tin sheet ripped off the roof, crashing down on the animal pen. He tuned his ears to the bleating outside, which sounded more scared than hurt. It was ten p.m. His bed hadn't even had a chance to get warm yet, but if one tin sheet could blow off, more might follow. Hai threw on a shirt and ventured out into the darkness.

The kitchen candles gave no help as he rushed to nail up wooden planks and patch tarps over the windows. The windy drizzle of an hour ago had mutated into a near-horizontal downpour. The cows whipped their heads back and forth in a vain attempt to break the ropes around their necks. They moved as though possessed by evil spirits. Hai had a sinking feeling that there would be no sleep tonight.

While he fumbled around, his family gathered in the living room. They squeezed themselves into a semicircle, with Hai's mom in the center. She cracked open the family Qur'an and began reading aloud. The words comforted the uncles, and the sound of her voice calmed the children.

With his dad gone, Hai was the man of the house. With a few boards over the windows, the house was about as secure as he could make it. He turned his attention to the animals. Livestock was the lifeblood for any farming family. If they lost too many cows or goats, it would take Hai's family years or even decades to recover. He needed to get them out of the rain and into the safety of the barn.

He sang a gentle song as he ran his hand over the family's ox, but getting a terrified, thousand-pound beast to calmly follow orders while needles of rain stung her rump would take a true cow whisperer. Hai wasn't that shepherd; he could barely get them to the trough. For half an hour, he slammed his shoulders into the cows' butts in vain, trying to push them into the barn. He slipped over and over again on the muddy water that pooled under their immovable hooves. Whenever he stopped pushing and tried to catch his breath, the wind was so strong that he realized he needed to use more energy just to stand still. At least the chickens and goats had the good sense to huddle in the corner.

By eleven, Hai gave up. With the cows shrieking in unholy wails and debris flying past like missiles, he clawed his way to the front door, sloshing through the yard in his flip-flops. The animals would have to take their chances. Hai opened the door, too ashamed to look his mother in the eye. She gave Hai an appreciative smile and motioned for him to sit next to her while she read. God would provide. Her kind words did little to assuage Hai's guilt. He tried not to think about having to explain this failure to his father tomorrow.

Just before midnight, the Qur'an started losing its usefulness as a source of comfort. All the cyclones they'd lived through before had peaked in intensity before now. But this one kept growing. Its roar was too loud to ignore over the holy verses. The clattering roof sounded like it was about to disintegrate. The winds started to rip the fronds off the palm trees in the front yard. Hai's mom kept reading, but she lost her focus, repeating lines.

Hai scanned his family's faces in the flickering candlelight. He could sense their rising panic. They hadn't experienced this before. Not knowing what would come next terrified them, but they were all trying to keep it together for the kids' sake.

Hai went over to the radio on the shelf. He turned the dial, cycling slowly across the frequencies. He inched the knob back and forth, where he knew stations should be, hoping that the right tiny tweak would lock in a signal. Hai leaned closer to the speaker, squinting at the row of numbers as if that would help him hear a faint broadcast. He found only static.

Suddenly, they heard a wet slap against the side of the house—but this wasn't the clap of a wooden plank or metal sheet. It was a sound totally out of place, like hard surf slamming on rocks. Hai stopped his fiddling and looked up, puzzled.

That can't be right, Hai thought. Their house was more than half a mile from the shore. *My ears must be playing tricks on me.* Hai switched off the radio and focused.

Ten seconds later, they heard another splash. Then another, a few seconds later. The family looked at one another, their faces full of confusion. What *was* this? Hai rushed to a boarded-up window and peeked through a slit. His eyes grew wide with horror.

The sea lapped at their doorstep. Hai braced himself as a wave rushed in, hitting the house and spraying him with a salty mist through the gaps in the window boards. Mesmerized by the sound and paralyzed by the impossibility of it all, he stared out at the water as it enveloped the property. He tried to process what this meant.

Up! Hai thought.

Then to everyone: "We have to go up!"

He guided his aunt up the worn wood steps and silently thanked God that they had a second floor to go to. Most Manpura residents lived in palm-frond huts or mud lean-tos.

The surf grew louder with each collision against the foundation. Water flooded in underneath the front door, soaking the carpets, as Hai sprinted back down two steps at a time. He cradled his grandmother and carried her up the stairs, gently setting her down on the floor next to his mom.

The house creaked from the weight of the water. Moving with a speed he could barely recognize in himself, Hai managed to get everyone upstairs just before seawater started pouring in through the downstairs windows. Somebody screamed. Hai couldn't tell who. Only a single wick in an old lamp provided light to the twenty people packed together in a space meant for three. Black shadows flitted across walls and ceiling. Hai's mom prayed through panicked sobs.

Outside, the ropes around the cow's necks became nooses. The wind blew so strong that it dragged the cows sideways until they strangled to death. The waves then pushed the silent floating beasts against the house with sickening thuds.

Hai went back downstairs, feeling his way in the darkness. Halfway down, he stepped into the sea. He swam through his living room, feeling around furniture, hoping to salvage any valuables before they got too soaked.

More waves crashed against the house, shoving hundreds of gallons of seawater inside with each pulse. Hai spied a few candles bobbing on the surface and grabbed them, then swam back to the stairs.

Hai's younger brother and cousins wailed as the cold, salty water crept up the stairs. The aunts and uncles tried to calm the kids, but their words were nothing more than feeble attempts to comfort themselves. They began to whisper prayers for salvation.

Hai stood watch at the top of the stairs. "Stop . . . Stop!" he yelled, ordering the water to recede. Every half minute, the ocean rose farther up the staircase. Only three steps remained. Outside, sea-foam licked at the second story.

Soon there were only two dry steps. A wave shattered an upstairs window.

As the water claimed the final step, the wind screamed through the broken windowpane and blew out the lamp.

Salt water poured over Hai's feet. He backed up against the wall. The ceiling here was lower than the main floor; if the water kept rising, there would be nowhere left to go. It was pitch black, but they could hear the water rushing in through the second-story window, blown in by the gales. They had to yell to hear one another over the cyclonic roar.

Even the men sobbed and screamed, begging God for the knee-high water to go back down. Emdadul cried out, "Brother! Please, save our lives!" But what could Hai do? It had been only eight minutes since the first waves tested the walls of his house.

Hai needed to try something desperate if he was going to save his family. He told an uncle to steady a chair, grabbed Emdadul, and ripped off an access panel to the roof. He climbed up, carrying Emdadul in one arm while lifting himself up with the other. They stuck their heads out and impossibly powerful winds answered their faces. The raindrops punched their skin like BBs.

Every nerve in his body told Hai to turn back, but he resisted. Shielding Emdadul from the rain with his torso, Hai felt around in the darkness with his fingers for something solid to grasp. The brothers crawled up and out of the hole and were almost blown off the slick roof into the sea. Hai's idea was that everyone could huddle here together, giving them a few more precious feet to escape the flood. But as Hai and Emdadul lay down to minimize exposure to the wind, the tin roof bent under their weight close to the breaking point.

Hai's heart sank. The wind had already damaged the roof so much that it couldn't support two people, let alone twenty. Hai took Emdadul back down to shelter while his mind raced, searching for new plans.

The water now reached waist-high on the second floor. Hai's uncles held the children up on their shoulders to keep their heads above the surface. The ceiling and the water were three feet apart. The space continued to shrink. Everyone swayed as if they were bobbing on a canoe when each new wave hit the structure.

Grasping at whatever ideas his mind could conjure, Hai had a eureka moment. The tallest thing around was their old coconut palm tree, a fifty-foot giant that had weathered dozens of cyclones. It was tall and sturdy enough to save everyone, if they could get to it.

Hai yelled his frenzied strategy to the room: He'd climb back up to the roof and jump onto the tree, which was just a couple of feet from the house. It was an easy feat under clear skies. From there, he could help the rest of his family follow.

Hai knew that if he missed the jump he'd land in the fast-moving current and be swept out to the Bay of Bengal. Missing the jump assured his death. But he kept quiet about that part.

It was their last, best chance.

Hai climbed back up through the hole, this time better prepared to brace himself when the wind hit him so hard it carved ripples across his skin. It was impossible to stand up so Hai dug his hands along the gaps in the wet tin as he worked his way across the rattling roof. In the darkness, he would not only have to calculate the wind's effect on his jump but also guess, from memory, the tree's exact location. Muffled screaming from the room below managed to pierce the wind's incessant howls.

Hai crawled to the roof's edge. Waves rocked at his feet, peeling back the tin. He took deep, confidence-building breaths as rain bullets pelted his back and neck. Hai crouched, trying to angle himself so that the crosswind wouldn't trip him up. He opened and then closed his eyes. It made no difference. He thought he could hear fronds creaking against the wind. The sound helped him fix the trunk's location—or, at least, his best guess at it.

This would be a leap of faith. Hai curled his flip-flops over the edge of the roof, trying to maintain his balance. He jumped like a frog, putting all his energy in his quads and glutes. He stretched out his arms and smashed face-first against the tree trunk. A direct hit.

Hai wrapped his arms around the rough cylinder, exhaling in relief. He shimmied up the tree to make room for the next person to come. Slipping would mean letting the depths swallow him. He wedged his fingers in between cracks in the scaly bark. He kicked his flip-flops off for better traction with his bare feet. Adrenaline pulsed through his body.

"I made it! I made it!" Hai screamed out. He heard a wave crash against the roof a few feet away.

Hai strained his ears and tried to hear voices through the roaring storm.

"I made it!" Hai yelled into the void. Surely the others would be coming any second. Even his mother could do it.

"I made it!"

The waves punished the roof with their damning, unrelenting frequency. The water continued to rise.

Hai screamed for minute after agonizing minute, clinging as the winds flattened him against the palm. His cries turned from triumphant to desperate. He called out to his mom. He called out to God.

For the next hour, Hai held on to the violently swaying palm, grinding his forearm flesh into the bark. He held on while the winds tattered and then ripped the clothes off his body. He held on, bleeding from his arms and legs, though his exhausted muscles begged to give up. He held on through the howling darkness.

Hai held on alone.

He knew he could not hold on forever. Hai prepared to give in and join his family below. If his family was dead, he should be too. Then, suddenly, everything stopped. In the span of just a few seconds, the wind went from the hardest of gales in a generation to a pleasant breeze. The rain stopped too. His overstimulated ears ached in the quiet.

Hai wondered: *Am I dead?*

Then screams shook Hai out of his stupor. They were close, coming from his uncle's house next door. A full moon emerged and illuminated a scene more horrifying than anything he'd imagined in the darkness. Hai saw that the water submerged most of his house—and all of Manpura. Debris and dead bodies floated past. The ocean stretched as far as he could see. The only real structure he could make out was the top ten feet or so of the three-story Manpura High School.

If only someone had warned us, Hai thought.

Hai turned his attention back toward the screams. His trapped uncle called for help. By sheer coincidence, the foundation of his uncle's house lay about one foot higher than Hai's. That foot meant the difference between drowning and survival. Hai heard similar cries from two other mostly submerged roofs a few hundred yards away.

His own house was silent.

Hai peeled his bloody arms and legs off the palm, landing with a splash. He dog-paddled the fifty feet to his uncle's roof as fast as his torn-up limbs would allow. His wounds did not appreciate the salty bath.

"I'm here, Uncle!" he yelled through the tin. Hai pulled away a few panels while his uncle clawed at the roof from within. It took time—their roof was better built than Hai's. Finally, Hai tore open a small hole. He grabbed his uncle's hand and pulled him and his aunt up to safety. "What about everyone else?"

"They're gone, Nephew. They're all gone."

Hai swam back home. Dread rushed up inside his chest, and he had to force himself to peer into the hole. Silent wet blackness met him inside. Too devastated to cry, Hai sat quietly under the full moon, unable to form a coherent thought.

Then he heard it. Somewhere far over the ocean at first: an angry growl from the sky, like a convoy of diesel trucks all starting up at the same time. The wind whipped up. Thick clouds covered the moon, plunging Manpura back into darkness.

Satan's storm was coming back.

"Go to a tree, Uncle! Go to a tree, Auntie!" Hai yelled from his roof. He paddled back to his own palm just before the cyclone's southern eyewall smashed back into Manpura. Within seconds, the wind hit 125 miles per hour; gusts topped 150. Holding on to anything at those speeds was all but impossible. Humans and cobras jumped onto palms together, sharing the only safe place above the surface that either could find.

Screams traveled on the wind as the storm's eye finished passing over the village. Hai could only make out broken phrases as the screams swept past.

"We are going to die!"

"We can't survive. Please God, help us!"

Hai dug his bloody arms and legs back into the palm bark. His aunt and uncle hugged along with him at his feet. At least someone other than him survived. He decided that no matter what, he was not going to let this cyclone beat him. He held on through rain that welted his naked skin and gusts that tried to pry him off. Like a mountain climber without a rope, Hai's only thoughts were on his grip. Whenever the muscle pain became too much, he would relax one limb at a time, shifting his body around the trunk so that the wind would push him up against the tree instead of off it.

Hai kept his face pressed against the palm until the wind began to drop. From here, he could make out the faintest outline of his house. At four in the morning, Hai collapsed back onto the roof after it poked securely above the waves. He lay motionless as the cyclone's outer bands passed over him. The bodies of almost everyone he loved floated fifteen inches below.

He was exhausted. Broken. And all he wanted to do was die.

11

Candy Rohde

Candy stretched, yawning, as she slowly extracted herself from the big, warm, teak bed. She'd slept later than she'd planned—Jon was already at work—but the sound of rain pinging against the roof always lulled her into a deep and restful sleep.

She peeked outside. Still a bit windy, but a bright sun was quickly making work of the muddy puddles. A newly planted tree across the street was half uprooted, but nothing else seemed out of place. The few Bengalis who were out bundled up in polyester sweaters to brave the chilly seventy-degree winter morning.

Candy put on the tea and prepared for her friends Runi Khan and Marty Chen to come by for brunch. Runi and Marty were begrudging housewives, just like her—brilliant minds stuck with domestic duties. Marty, tall and striking, grew up in British India but attended college in Connecticut. Runi was a Dacca-born socialite who took great pride in introducing Candy to all things Bengali, starting with the correct way to wrap a sari. The three invariably launched into societal debates great and small. Runi reeled in Candy and Marty whenever they got a little too unintentionally colonialist in their prescriptions; Candy preached the importance of pinpoint accuracy and thorough- ness to Runi whenever she suggested a rash political upheaval.

Runi arrived first, carrying a copy of the *Pakistan Observer* under her arm. Marty was right behind. They wasted no time with pleasantries. The debates started before they even made it into the living room.

Runi clicked her tongue with a mix of annoyance and delight at Mujib's latest mischief-making. "They say Mujib wants a *Bangla Desh!*" she said. *Desh* was Bengali for "nation," and it carried the whiff of revolution about it. Mujib's Awami League was rocketing up in the polls, and Runi hoped that it would be the biggest party in East Pakistan after the election in December.

Candy popped a handful of spicy dry kitchari into her mouth and raised an eyebrow. A new anti-Pakistan, pro-socialist state might also shift the Asian balance of power against the United States.

The trio munched on crispy dal puris and sipped cardamom tea. Marty casually flipped over the paper, looking for more fuel for their debate. Instead, she found an unusual weather-related headline. She read it out loud: "50 Feared Lost in Coastal Cyclone."

"Oh no," Candy said. News figures right after disasters always had a way of underreporting the destruction at first, especially in these parts. The real number might be ten—or even a hundred—times higher. Plus, they all knew that everyone was dirt poor in the delta, most of the population working as subsistence fishers. "Somebody should do something to help those poor people."

Marty and Runi nodded. They searched the paper in vain for any mention of a relief effort, but all they found was confirmation that the governor's all-day reception with the Asian Highway Motor Rally would go on as scheduled.

"Something's got to happen," Candy said.

"Clearly the governor has other priorities," Runi replied.

If no one else is doing anything, Candy thought, *maybe I can make a small difference.*

"Well, then, we have to do something!" Candy said. It wasn't the most articulate idea in the moment, but her insistence won them over.

They brainstormed all day, asking themselves two main questions: What needs to be done, and what can we do about it? The problem was that they didn't really know the answer to either. So they called up their mutual friend Fazle Hasan Abed, a local Shell Oil executive, hoping to get a sense of what kind of logistics such an effort entailed. He said it wouldn't be impossible to put something together, but it wouldn't be easy either. Not without an army of volunteers, a bunch of cash, and a lot of luck.

Then Candy and Marty called their husbands, who both were frustratingly unconcerned. Jon told Candy to go ahead and try, but he warned her that it was unlikely that her efforts would come to anything. After all, they'd never even been to those islands before. Jon couldn't take time away from his own work to aid in the relief, and anyway, there was sure to be a government response soon.

While Jon preferred to call it realism, Candy was skeptical of what she saw as his pessimism. She knew instinctively that the first few days and weeks after a disaster were the most important. Waiting for a government response wasn't good enough. If anything was going to happen, they'd have to do it themselves.

The first order of business was coming up with a name for their mission. According to the papers, the cyclone hit an island called Hatiya hardest, so Candy, Marty, and Runi called their new organization the Hatiya Emergency Lifesaving Project—or HELP. There was a near-total vacuum of information, but they imagined that there might be thousands of people needing immediate assistance and figured that they could do something akin to a food or charity drive. It would be something that could aid the victims alongside other, more organized efforts. Every little bit would help, surely.

Next, the trio solicited Dacca's high society for donations. Candy popped by the houses of everyone she knew from those awful cocktail parties. Most offered a pittance, perhaps out of guilt, but none of them gave more than twenty dollars or so. Candy wished she'd faked more interest when listening to their self-absorbed stories.

Runi's Bengali intelligencia friends were a different story. They immediately opened their wallets and shared their resources. Abed offered his Shell warehouses and petty cash for the cause, so they made him a partner in HELP on the spot. Within twenty-four hours, HELP had scraped together their first thousand dollars.

Candy rushed to Shankar Bazaar in old Dacca with the wad of disorganized bills, ready to buy anything that might help survivors. She cleaned out the first few rice and cooking-oil sellers, rushing back and forth between their shops and her wooden oxen carts at the bazaar's entrance. She pushed a wheelbarrow through the alleys and scavenged up an outboard motor and petrol cans. Then she bought all the matches and stoves she could find, before spending the last of her money on milk, saris, and lungis.

Only then did the real problem became clear: How would they get everything to the delta? There weren't any roads or even maps of the islands. In the time it took to organize her supplies, it was starting to be clear that the damage was worse than anyone had thought. The cyclone rendered the waterways largely inoperable and destroyed almost every boat. The few undamaged vessels were already allocated to rescue operations.

One option remained: They'd need to go by air.

12

Mohammad Hai

By daybreak, the water retreated into the sea like someone had pulled a plug out of a giant bathtub. Hai scanned the horizon. It looked like the aftermath of a bomb blast. Bodies of animals and people lay everywhere, caked in mud. Almost everyone was dead.

Hai took a deep breath and climbed through the hole in his roof. The dawn filtered through the broken windows. It illuminated the corpses of his mother, brother, and the rest of his family. Of twenty family members in his house, Hai was the only survivor. The bloated bodies twisted and piled together in a corner. Hai begged God to forgive whatever sin they must have committed to deserve this fate.

Hai didn't understand why none of them made it out to join him on the tree, but he did know that he needed to dig their graves. According to Muslim tradition, a body must be buried as soon as possible after death. He may have failed to save his family, but he could at least respect their journey to the afterlife.

Hai walked outside, weaving around their dead animals to look for a shovel. Manpura was eerily silent. No birds sang, no dogs barked. The wind and rain were gone. The screams had stopped. And all their tools had washed away. So Hai dug into the sodden earth with his hands.

After about half an hour, he looked at his pathetic progress and realized that he couldn't do it alone. He went looking for survivors to help him.

Naked, Hai stumbled around the island's remains. Horrific sights greeted him. A dead woman hung from a tree by her tangled hair, still holding her baby. He walked to what used to be the town square, where he found Manpura's chairman—a mayor figure—alive. The chairman was a corrupt landowner who ran the island like his own little fiefdom. There was someone in his position in most of East Pakistan's villages. The forty-five-year-old chairman lay in a stupor. Like Hai, most of his family was dead, too.

The man stared vacantly at his family's bodies, acting nearly as lifeless as the corpses. Hai tried to get a word out of him, but the chairman was too shell-shocked to speak. A few other scattered survivors made their way over. There were no women or children. Nobody knew what to do.

For some reason, Hai felt that he did. Or, at least, he knew that they had to start somewhere. Even though most of them were naked and bleeding from their tree-scraped torsos, just like him, Hai reminded them that God hated excuses and that they had a job to do. He picked the most able-bodied and looked around for tools. The chairman's brick storehouse was intact, so Hai took half a dozen shovels. The first order of business was to go house to house and bury as many of the dead as they could.

Hai brought them to his home. They dug out a large pit, ten feet long and eight feet wide. Those who didn't have shovels pulled through the mud with their hands. They got only a couple of feet deep, but that would be enough. While they excavated, Hai pulled his little brother, aunts, uncles, and cousins down the stairs and out of the house, one at a time. He never found his grandmother's body. She had apparently floated through the window and out to sea. Hai said a quick prayer each time he rolled a body into the pit.

Last, Hai carried his mother out and laid her next to his little brother. He closed their eyes, one by one, and placed handfuls of mud on their faces.

Hai and his men collected more bodies around the neighborhood, repurposing overturned vegetable carts to transport bodies like open-air hearses. He made sure to say prayers for each one as they dumped them in the shallow pit. Hai deposited friends, teachers, and neighbors. He buried Muslims and Hindus alike. Since Hindus were supposed to be cremated, he hoped that they would still find their way to a happy afterlife when he put them into the ground out of necessity.

The sun came out in full force as they filled the rest of the pit with dogs, chickens, and goats to help avoid the spread of disease. Last, they shoveled about nine inches of mud on top. The cows, strewn about the yard with rigor mortis, their legs stiff in the air, would have to wait.

Hai worked all morning, rubbing away tears as he dug in the mud and dragged bodies. He seeded his family's land, one of the most fertile places on the island, with bodies. There were so many that he should have lost count, but his mind would never let go of that dreaded number. Before noon, Hai buried a hundred and eighty people in his front yard.

Hai was numb. What they would all soon call the Great Bhola Cyclone had obliterated every one of his senses. The next forty-eight hours were a blur, as two urgent tasks consumed him. First, they needed to bury both people and animals as quickly as possible. By his calculation, more than forty thousand of Manpura's fifty thousand residents were dead. Hai dug from dawn until dusk, wrapping a scrap of white T-shirt around his face in a feeble attempt to mask the stench.

Second, they had to figure out what the living would eat. Most of Manpura's food had washed away, and seawater inundated the wells. Within days the survivors became scavengers, gnawing on anything that looked like it might be food. They ate tree roots and raw snake, coconut rinds and bark. They had no word from off the island, no idea if help was coming. Hunger and grief were everywhere. People paced around with a wild, irrational look in their eyes. Some raved with madness. Manpura teetered on the verge of animalistic anarchy.

Even though they were weather-bombed to near oblivion, Hai remembered how Awami League organizers would look out for their fellow men and how they went to great lengths to ensure that if there was a share to give, every man got one. Hai had no idea if Malik had survived—or Mujib for that matter—but hoped that he could honor the league's spirit. So he set up a simple wooden stand, just beyond his mother's grave, where people could bring supplies to share and exchange, as well as to trade tips about food and water sources. During his breaks from burying, he'd man the stand and try to help his people.

With the chairman still catatonic, desperate survivors leapt at this plan. Just about everyone on the island came to Hai to contribute. He made sure that their meager rations were shared equally, regardless of religion or social status. A couple of people brought gold to try to get more than their share, offering prices a hundred or even a thousand times higher than what the supplies would have been worth before the storm. Hai refused them at every turn. His efforts to distribute what little they had fairly and prevent hoarding by the rich probably saved hundreds of lives.

Two days after Bhola, the first boat since the storm docked at Manpura's concrete jetty. Hai sprinted there as fast as his broken body would allow. His father was not on board. Hai asked the captain if anyone had heard about his dad. The captain shrugged, shaking his head. He told Hai that dozens of other islands were hit just as badly.

Soon helicopters flew overhead in a military formation. Small boats started to land every few hours, each one with a dozen or so people who survived elsewhere. Each time, Hai greeted them, first looking in vain for his father and then offering his relief services.

On the third day, Hai experienced a miracle. His father walked off the same commuter boat that he had left on, looking little worse for wear. They embraced, Hai nearly hyperventilating as he did so. Hai wanted to hug him and never let go. He didn't pay any attention to the pain of his scabbed-over arm wounds. Hai's dad said that when the cyclone hit, he had the good luck to be collecting his paycheck in the municipal office, a concrete building that was three stories tall. Crammed in with a few hundred others, he rode out Bhola with relative ease.

"Come, my son, take me to the others. I've missed their faces so much."

Hai couldn't look at his father. They began the short trek home.

Hai walked in silence while his dad peppered him with questions: "How is the house? How are the animals? What happened to your arms? Have you eaten? Was anyone badly hurt?"

And finally: "Why aren't you talking, son?"

What could Hai possibly say? He could only show. They arrived at the house. Hai's dad saw the mounded mass grave. The cow corpses. He saw the torn roof, with a stained saltwater line inches from its apex.

Like the chairman, Hai's father collapsed, dumbfounded. He sat in silence as Hai finally found the words to relive the night. Everything that his father worked for, that he and Hai's grandfather had built, his daughter, his wife, his sister and brothers. His mother. Gone.

Hai sat down next to his father on the dried, cracked mud. They cried together under the sun.

13

Hafiz Uddin Ahmad

JESSORE CANTONMENT, EAST PAKISTAN

NOVEMBER 14, 1970
Two days after landfall

Hafiz leafed through the stack of day-old newspapers in the officer's mess, scanning headlines in Bengali, English, and Urdu. He scrounged for details in articles that had precious few to give. Some papers said fifty dead. Others reported that a thousand people along the coast had perished. Hafiz guessed it was probably a lot more than that.

The night of the cyclone, Hafiz slept under a clear sky at Jessore Cantonment. The base was a hundred and fifty miles northwest of the Bay of Bengal and didn't see a single storm cloud that evening. His family, on the other hand, lived right in the cyclone's path, on Bhola, the next island over from Manpura. Worse, his father was in the middle of a busy reelection campaign—he was pushing Mujib's Awami League platform of Bengali self-determination and autonomy throughout his coastal district—and was likely to be away from home. Exposed.

Hafiz hoped his family was safe, but there was nothing he could do but wait for news. He reread the papers, hoping—and fearing—that he'd missed something. No luck. He finally gave up and went outside, where he watched the clouds grow thick, then gradually clear away in a perfect November breeze. The soldiers in front of him drilled lackadaisically. Hafiz was too distracted to reprimand them.

After a day of waiting and praying, a telegram arrived for him on yellow paper. It was from his mother. She never sent telegrams. Hafiz took a deep breath to calm himself before reading it.

HAFIZ. PLEASE COME HOME. MANY PEOPLE DEAD. INCLUDING FAMILY.

Hafiz exhaled in relief. If his sister or brother or father had died, surely his mother would have mentioned it. At least he hoped so, but there just wasn't enough information to be sure. "Including family" was ominous. His mind raced through images of favorite cousins, uncles, and aunties. His battalion commander, Lieutenant Colonel Jalil, sympathized with his plight and granted him leave to go home.

Hafiz rushed out of the cantonment, hiring a rickshaw to take him to the nearest river launch. From there, he caught a coal steamer to the port at Barisal. Shortly after they pulled out onto the river delta, the landscape started to change. Hafiz saw more and more bare palm trees with their fronds spilled across the ground and the battered thatched roofs of hundreds of shacks. But he still wasn't anywhere near the coast where the papers said that the storm's most violent winds thrashed the land. At Barisal, he caught a small ferry, which was currently the only vehicle able to navigate the narrow passages to Bhola. It was a four-hour journey.

He saw the first dead body about two hours after launch. It was a man's corpse, completely naked with fingers clenched toward the sky in some sort of grim repose. Hafiz motioned to the boatman, who simply nodded grimly.

The boat motored on. The engine's hum drowned out the sound of water lapping along the bow. Hafiz saw the next corpse just a few minutes later, followed by a trio of bodies—perhaps a family—caught in an eddy along the riverbank. It seemed that more people had died than the papers reported. A lot more. They'd gone only half of the way, and the number of corpses in the river seemed to grow exponentially.

Dread didn't truly take hold of Hafiz until the wind shifted and he started to smell the devastation. It was faint at first—almost sweet—but that didn't last. Notes of decay filtered in. The farther they traveled downriver, the more pungent and fetid the odor. This wasn't the smell of an odd corpse rotting on its own in forgotten wallow. It had a darker character. It was the smell of mass death. When the boat approached a river bend, Hafiz made out another twenty bodies clustered in a cove, mixed in with rotting buffalo and goat corpses. He'd already seen as many bodies on this one short stretch of river as the papers reported dead in the whole country. And they were multiplying.

The boat puttered along slowly, giving Hafiz an uncomfortably long time to take in each contorted, lifeless body. Each time he dared to look at a face, he steeled himself for the possibility that it would be an auntie or a cousin staring back.

The clusters of bodies gave way to massive rafts of decay. The corpses of men, women, children, and animals, along with the flotsam of a thousand houses, clogged the waterway. At times, especially in the smaller channels, it was impossible to navigate through the water without corpses thunking against the aluminum frame. The boatman was careful to slow down when he got near women's bodies, lest their long, tangled hair get stuck in the propeller.

Hafiz wanted to vomit, but he fought to keep it in. How many of these deformed souls had he known in life? How many people were still alive on his island? There was no way to know. Hafiz closed his eyes, but it brought no reprieve. He pictured empty villages with the entire population swept into the rivers. There, the fish that Bengalis traditionally ate would instead nibble on the Bengalis.

Though it took only four hours, Hafiz felt he'd aged a year when he finally arrived at Bhola jetty. He desperately scanned the motley group of survivors for familiar faces, then when he saw his father, a man in his fifties with a regal demeanor, waiting in a hastily assembled shed by the boat launch, Hafiz's face cracked into an impossible smile.

His father smiled back, with perhaps a hint of pride creeping into the corners of his mouth, at the sight of his son in a crisp officer's uniform.

"How did you survive?" Hafiz asked.

"I was on the roof of the Arzu Hotel," his father replied. The Arzu was a dilapidated tin-roofed hotel-restaurant, which just happened to be the tallest building on this part of the island. "I was there all night. I was safe, but there was nothing I could do to help our people. My sisters died. Our village is . . . gone."

His father then explained that Hafiz's uncles, cousins, sisters, and brothers—at least twenty of his family members—had vanished without a trace. His grandmother had survived only because her servants tied her to a tree. Over the course of the storm, she watched them all drown, one by one. Both men wanted to cry. Both held it in. His father, ever the politician, wouldn't dare blubber in front of constituents. Hafiz would betray his duty to the uniform if he shed a tear in public. Men did not do such things.

Hafiz looked out at the sea of floating bodies. He'd seen enough to know that corpses littered more than just their small nook of the delta; they were scattered along its entire length—across dozens of islands and clogged channels. It would take more than a few families coming together to rebuild. Simply burying the dead would require the organizational capabilities of the entire nation. Hafiz stiffened his spine to the task ahead.

There was no telling how any of this might affect his father's election, which was just a few weeks away. There was no time to think about those things right now.

Hafiz felt his father's hand rest on his shoulder. He watched his dad studying his uniform in admiration. Hafiz felt it was the first time his father saw a man as he stared out at the wreckage, not a footballer.

Yahya Khan

HALF A MILE ABOVE MANPURA ISLAND, EAST PAKISTAN

NOVEMBER 16, 1970

Four days after landfall

"It doesn't look so bad."

Gripping an ice-cold beer, Yahya directed his casual assessment both to the pilot and to himself as they hummed around in a Fokker Friendship propeller plane three thousand feet above what was left of Manpura. Yahya took a swig and peered out the window again. Only the occasional palm tree jutting above the water pierced the rice paddies.

Yahya chucked the empty out the window then reached for another. He drew the aluminum hoop back with a pudgy finger adorned with a dictator-size ring.

Yahya thought the whole flyby was a waste of time. He'd arrived in Dacca the night before from Peking, where he'd single-handedly negotiated what was possibly the biggest diplomatic coup in Pakistan's history. That deserved a celebration. After landing, a boozy Yahya shooed away the governor and made a beeline for the house of a Bengali businesswoman who was throwing a party in his honor.

The next morning, Yahya's advisers reminded their hungover boss that the situation in the delta was quite serious. It would be good to show a display of concern. So he boarded the plane, a gold-tipped cane in one hand and plastic cooler of imported pilsner in the other.

Now he was staring at watery trash. He was ready to get back to Islamabad.

In truth, Yahya's visit to Peking had been a roller coaster. Formally, the visit was called a trade mission, though Nixon had asked Yahya to act as an informal US emissary. The plan was that Yahya would dangle a few enticing ideas, then lay the groundwork for an official visit by Nixon's right-hand man, Henry Kissinger, next year. Yahya expected that the trip would be a raging success: China would welcome Nixon with open arms and sign some impressive trade agreements that would make Yahya look like a major dealmaker who pulled his country's economy out of the doldrums.

Mao knew that Yahya was the impressionable sort and that every minute of his experience would be relayed back to Nixon, so he pulled out all the stops. He threw an impossibly lavish welcome party. Color guards and bands filled the tarmac as Yahya's plane opened its fuselage door. More than a hundred thousand cheering fans heralded his motorcade along the roads to the Imperial Palace.

In a bid to sweeten whatever diplomatic offering might come of their relationship, Chinese emissaries plied Yahya with liberal helpings of liquor, women, and compliments. Yahya didn't realize until too late that he'd walked into an ambush. The regal welcome quickly gave way to a daylong scolding by Premier Zhou Enlai, who made it clear to Yahya that any meeting with the Americans was going to happen on China's terms or not at all. Yahya hadn't told a soul in his delegation about the secret agenda of his visit, so he was alone with his wits while Zhou had an army of advisers at his disposal.

The talks dragged into a second, then a third day, but they felt like they were going backward. With the pressure high, Yahya cracked, stumbling over words at crucial moments. Zhou remained unimpressed. The Chinese were wary of Kissinger; they agreed to see the American secretary of state only if Yahya could smuggle him in without anyone knowing. Yahya knew that Nixon wouldn't be happy with this.

Even the trade talks, which were the simplest part of his visit—and really more of a formality for the newspapers—were falling apart. Yahya feared what he would come home to if he failed to close the deals he'd promised to everyone. He didn't care about losing the support of the Pakistani bureaucrats, but the military was a different matter. He knew all too well that leaders rarely caught wind of a coup until it was too late.

Above all, Yahya's biggest concern was losing the people. He needed to raise the specter of something more terrifying than his own failings in order to distract the press. They were always suckers for India fearmongering, so he'd rattled some sabers in that direction before he'd left for China, blaming Prime Minister Indira Gandhi for all of Pakistan's ills. After all, everyone in Pakistan hated her. But even that favorite song was getting played out.

Pakistan was ailing after five years of crippling economic sanctions, and now Yahya's former Punjabi supporters in West Pakistan were up in arms. Unemployed students and underpaid workers rioted against factory owners and the police. One fanatic even tried to scuttle a trade deal with Poland in the most spectacular manner possible. When the Polish delegation landed at Karachi airport, the fanatic stole a green-and-white Pakistan International Airways baggage cart. As the delegation deplaned, he floored the cart in their direction, aiming for the Polish president Marian Spychalski. He missed, slamming into a reporter and the Polish deputy foreign minister instead, killing the deputy upon impact. The assassination on Pakistani soil made Yahya look impotent.

Yahya started to panic. The democratic election that was meant to cement his legacy was taking place in just three weeks, but what if that wasn't enough to save his rapidly eroding popularity? Everything was spiraling out of control, and everyone pointed at one man to blame: General Yahya Khan. Yahya needed some way to show the people that he was the man they needed most—the only man who could save them.

Yahya needed a miracle.

As day three of Yahya's talks with Zhao neared its end, a staffer wearing a squarish, ill-fitting suit that epitomized Pakistan's sluggish bureaucracy, interrupted the president's ramblings. He waved a telegram in Yahya's face. The exact text is lost to time, but it likely would have had something typed out about a once-in-a-lifetime storm hitting East Pakistan.

Yahya couldn't believe his luck. The cyclone news added the very sense of urgency to the China talks that he'd been trying—and failing—to achieve. He immediately told Zhao, who shared the news with Mao. Both men were concerned about the storm's impact, so they relented on their posturing and offered to get at least the economic trade package squared away. After that, Mao relented on the military deal, which, to be honest, was in both of their interests anyway.

His confidence suddenly bolstered, Yahya turned on the charm for his coup de grâce, and even Mao succumbed to Yahya's silver tongue and infectious smile. He convinced Mao to start secret communications with Nixon, under two conditions: First, the only communication would come through secret couriered letters; and second, those could only go through Yahya himself. The cyclone telegraph had turned everything around.

While the cyclone might have saved Yahya's hide, that didn't necessarily mean he thought it worth touring its aftermath a few days later. The whir of the propellers just a few feet away gave him a headache that beer wasn't powerful enough to numb. He tried anyway, downing the entire six-pack in the hour they circled over Manpura. This whole cyclone business seemed blown out of proportion. Hell, one hit the coast two months earlier and killed only a few people. The delta always recovered.

He glared down at the black flecks of corpses bobbing on the surface of the water. The pilot suggested landing for a closer look at the damage. Yahya recoiled. He had no interest in stumbling over debris in front of some destitute peasants who would just claw at his suit. The press knew that he'd seen some of the devastation himself, maybe that would be enough.

They flew back to Dacca.

Yahya boarded his personal plane for Islamabad without leaving the airport—or meeting the officials tasked with the Bhola response. He refused to declare East Pakistan a disaster area or worthy of a national emergency, two actions that would have allowed the local government to reallocate their meager resources to relief.

Yahya had more important things to worry about: spectacular news that he wanted to telegram to President Nixon as soon as possible. Abandoned by Yahya, the first responders held a press conference later that day, asking the journalists in the audience what they should do. The presser ended with journalists and bureaucrats walking out of the room together in a confused, dreadful silence.

15

Candy Rohde

Candy and Marty stood on the Dacca airport tarmac alongside two ox carts full of rice and two others full of clothes and cooking oil, with no way to get it where it needed to go.

"I'm sorry, madam, but this helicopter is reserved for VVIPs only. Very very important persons." The army colonel wouldn't budge.

"But it's the only one in East Pakistan! We need to get this rice to the islands!" Candy pleaded, incredulous at his apathy.

HELP now employed a dozen people. Candy had secured money and supplies from a global hodgepodge of governments and aid organizations. But there still wasn't a way to get it to the delta.

Never mind that Yahya had long since gone back to Islamabad. This chopper was staying put, and trying to finagle any other official aircraft for relief purposes was out of the question. Too expensive. Too much of a hassle.

None of Candy's pleading could crack the colonel. Getting fired and court-martialed would be the least of his worries if Yahya came for a surprise visit and his helicopter was off running errands for Bengalis and foreigners. He assured Candy that now that Yahya had seen the destruction with his own eyes, a massive government aid effort would undoubtedly be underway.

Candy refused to risk lives on that charitable reading.

Marty flipped through a copy of the *Observer* for ideas. The headline said that the confirmed deaths had gone up a hundredfold—to five thousand.

They brainstormed together on the tarmac, next to Yahya's gassed-up chopper. Maybe they could buy all the seats on a passenger plane and fill it with sacks of rice—no, too expensive—or maybe they could just commandeer something. Did helicopters have keys?

Candy had another idea.

She led Marty to the airport bar. It was a seedy building on the edge of the terminal where pilots from all over the world, most of them on their way to or back from Vietnam, told tall tales of close shaves in war zones. The duo ordered drinks and struck up a conversation with a couple of men in jumpsuits.

An hour or so later, the flight crews were more amenable than the colonel on the tarmac had been. West German pilots seemed to be the kindest and most respectful of the bunch. The ladies wooed them with beer, eventually convincing them to look at their Dacca stopover from a more altruistic perspective.

It was agreed. The West Germans would help them deliver goods later that week, off the books. Candy had just figured out a way to get past the military blockade, but with relief provisions piling up, they would need more than just the West Germans' planes. So they headed over to the bar at the InterContinental Hotel to pitch every pilot on the premises.

Bouncing between the airport, the InterContinental, and their logistics offices across the street from Dacca Stadium, Candy and Marty found a rhythm as they cajoled pilots into abandoning their formal duties to deliver lifesaving aid supplies instead. They didn't need to flirt, not exactly. Camaraderie with any woman was a rare enough reward for military men, and Candy presented the cause with such passion that they couldn't help but be swept along for the ride.

HELP wasn't the only group searching for available planes. A couple of enterprising Punjabi merchants offered a 500 percent bonus to any pilot who would fly their food down to the delta to sell at insane markups. With this competition in mind, Candy and Marty worked over the pilots for hours, alternating between pulling at their heartstrings as good Samaritans and browbeating them for having the nerve to even think about profiting from the disaster. Nobody signed on with the Punjabis.

Eventually, all the aviators asked the same thing: "What do you need?"

In addition to their new West German friends, they also convinced American and French pilots stopping over from Vietnam to load up their helicopters and rusty prop planes with supplies—at least five hundred bags of rice plus anything else they could secure—and deliver the relief aid as fast as HELP could get it together. Candy agreed to go with the West German team to help with distribution.

Candy and Marty were making progress, but they still needed Pakistani support if they were going to help the entire affected area. One helicopter-load of rice would barely be enough for one island for a week. More than thirty-five islands needed immediate help.

On November 21, Candy arranged a meeting with two senior officials from the Pakistan Army—men who could give serious infrastructure to HELP's efforts. The officials set up an evening meeting back at their InterContinental suite. Candy and Marty walked in, ready to do business. The men had drinks in hand, looking to party with foreign girls. Candy tried to talk logistics. One officer told her to relax. Marty tried to talk supplies. The other officer closed the door.

This was turning sideways, but these men were the gatekeepers to fleets of planes and helicopters. They could save tens of thousands of lives with a phone call. Candy and Marty tried to steer the conversation back to HELP, but when the officers put on some music and started dancing instead, the women realized that these men—the most senior officials for Pakistan's aid effort—were never going to make that call. Candy and Marty got the hell out of there.

The next morning, Candy read the latest *Observer* headline. The number of confirmed deaths had gone up tenfold again, to fifty thousand, and horrific field reports trickled in from the islands. Outside of Pakistan, a meager aid campaign began to coalesce. Iran and China sent planes, helicopters, and grain. The US military sent a fleet, as did the British. The Soviets sent helicopters and ships. But supplies piled up at Dacca airport as the Pakistan Army argued with aid agencies over who got to deliver the goods. The army annexed whole warehouses, saying they knew best who needed it the most. The grass beside the runway turned into an air show. The Red Cross told donors to stop sending food because they had no way to get it to the delta.

Seeing the warehouses filling up, Candy had an idea: What if she expanded her operations to cut through the red tape that stymied every other aid agency in East Pakistan? If she could pay her new network of pilots, they could take more trips and get this food to the delta faster than the Red Cross—and certainly faster than the Pakistan Army troops who just sat in the barracks. Combined with Runi's impressive work in getting the Bengali elites to fund food and supplies, they just might have a way to save thousands of lives.

Two days later, Candy and Marty got their pitch together and met with the United States Agency for International Development (USAID). Yellow legal notepads in hand, they went to the administrator's office and gave a short presentation, complete with hand-drawn flow charts and lists that detailed what was needed, what they'd already done, and what they could do, step by step. The administrator listened patiently, asking no questions.

"That sure is a fine idea you ladies have. Why don't you have your husbands give me a call so I can go over the details with them?"

Candy could feel the condescending pat on her head. Marty wanted to rip her legal pad in two. They politely thanked the administrator for his time and said that their husbands would be in touch.

The problem persisted. Each time they approached the head of an international agency, showing the logistics networks that they'd already set up, the donors asked to meet with their husbands instead. They were treated like receptionists at best, vacuous housewives at worst.

Candy anguished over the latest *Observer* casualty numbers and fretted about the hundreds of thousands more left without food or clothing. The figure was unimaginable. There was no more time to lose. She rushed to the airport, woke up the West Germans, and together they set off for Hatiya, the closest airstrip to the worst-hit areas. The place was going to be a zoo, but she hoped she could at least land, make contact with the experts there, and hand off all her goods, before rushing back to Dacca for the next load. She was sure it would all work out.

16

Neil Frank

NATIONAL HURRICANE CENTER, MIAMI

NOVEMBER 19, 1970

Seven days after landfall

Eighteen days until the election

Seven days after the cyclone a mail clerk dropped off a letter and a grainy black-and-white photograph on Neil Frank's desk. Frank took one look at the picture and sat upright in his chair. The snapshot showed the spinning vortex of an immeasurably powerful cyclone as it barreled northeast through the Bay of Bengal, directly into the most densely populated region on earth. Even a first-year meteorology student could extrapolate the death and destruction that the massive solid white bands were about to unleash. The storm of the decade, maybe worse.

Frank kept his eyes on the photograph. This looked like a worst-case scenario—exactly the reason why his former boss had flown to East Pakistan three years ago to create a state-of-the-art warning system. It was the sort of image that would make a weatherman ring every alarm bell that he could get his hands on.

Then Frank looked at the picture's date. It was one week old. He exhaled and banged his fist on the desk. There was nothing to do now except read the news over the coming days for details of the devastation.

Instead of receiving the data from ITOS 1 in advance, Frank

learned about the Great Bhola Cyclone from news reports just like everyone else. A day earlier the *New York Times* reported "The Survivors on Devastated Island Wait for Food, Water and Medicine" on page A16. Frank shook his head while he read about how three-quarters of the residents of a coastal island called Manpura had drowned. Frank knew that Manpura was just one of dozens of similar islands in the cyclone's path. Worse, some calculations put the storm's surge at an unimaginable thirty-three feet high in places, confirming his fears about its potential for devastation.

ITOS 1 captured the image from orbit just before Bhola's landfall and transmitted it back to earth to anyone who was watching in almost real time. Yet this was the first time anyone at the National Hurricane Center had seen it, because their mission wasn't to report on dangerous weather developments around the planet—only those in Hawaii and in the Atlantic and Caribbean basins, where they might hit the United States. The slow-turning wheels of the government bureaucracy hadn't yet synced with the possibilities of the modern, intimately connected world. Given the right lead time, Frank would have instantly known the danger the storm presented. He could have amplified any warning that came out of the center. But given that no urgent bulletins reached him, clearly nobody knew what the ITOS 1 transmission meant when they saw it.

Frank surmised from the image that Bhola was huge, but not the most powerful storm they'd ever recorded. It was technically only a Category 4 cyclone. It certainly had enough power to cause mass devastation in a country where most people still lived in thatched palm-frond houses. Still not knowing the scope of the damage, Frank made some quick calculations, worried about a confluence of factors. Bhola made landfall at high tide, during a full moon—two events that dragged water upward and inward to land. This amplified the storm surge. Frank wrinkled his brow and imagined the devastation when a storm like this hit a county where one-third of the land lay less than ten feet above sea level.

Officials later estimated that between 350,000 and 500,000 people died, making it the largest loss of life in a single weather event in all of human history. The Indian freighter *Mahajagmitra* and its entire crew were the first official victims. Economists estimated that the storm caused only $84.6 million worth of damage—mostly in terms of crop damage. Back-of-the-envelope math suggested that each Bengali life was worth just seventy-three dollars.

Frank couldn't understand why Pakistan's or India's weather services hadn't warned the entire country to reach higher ground. Surely they must have seen the satellite image in real time. While the ITOS 1 was US hardware, its signal blanketed the entire Northern Hemisphere. Anyone with a receiver could have tuned in to its transmissions, and there were receivers all across South Asia. Yet as far as he could tell, no urgent warnings had ever gone out.

In what must pass for irony—or maybe the satellite's own metaphysical admission of failure—on November 16, just four days after landfall, the ITOS 1's tape recorder malfunctioned, putting half of its sensory systems permanently out of commission. The Great Bhola Cyclone was ITOS 1's first and last chance to save lives.

As it turned out, Frank wasn't the only one asking himself what went wrong. The return address on the as-yet-unopened letter to Frank read: "World Bank, Washington, DC." It wasn't often that the most powerful economic institution on the planet wrote to a meteorologist. He was apprehensive about opening it, but unsure why.

He inserted a letter opener into the fold and cut the seam. As he scanned the document, his eyes morphed from puzzlement to determination. Over the last few decades, the World Bank had invested millions into economic development in Pakistan. Now they were concerned that the devastation would create fundamental instability. They'd learned that the NHC helped develop a cyclone warning system and that, for some reason, the system failed. Since Gordon Dunn—the system's inventor and Frank's former boss—had retired in 1967, they wanted Frank to head to Dacca to write a report.

Here was his opportunity to figure out what the hell had happened over there. People at the NHC didn't get chances like this to study the big picture—the societal consequences of storms. Ever. More important, maybe he could decipher what sort of technical error occurred, and stop the same thing from happening in the United States or elsewhere in the world.

By the time he came to the end of the letter, Frank was already trying to figure out how to tell his wife and young daughter that he would be taking the next flight to East Pakistan.

17

Mohammad Hai

Malik raced down the dirt path, waving his hands and yelling from two fields over.

"Come, come quickly! He's here! He's here!"

Hai looked up from the table where he was testing donated D-cell batteries. The cloth scrap over his face itched incessantly. With twenty thousand more people left to bury, they were losing the race against decomposition, and the smell was unbearable. Malik had returned the day before; he happened to be taking an exam up north and missed the worst of Bhola. Hai appreciated the chance to see his friend's goofy, excited gait again. He smiled for the first time since the storm.

"Who, Malik?"

"Mujib! He's really here!"

Hai sprang out of his chair. They sprinted side by side to the jetty where a decent-size tugboat prepared to dock. On the bow stood a man wearing all white. His thick, black mustache complemented his thick, black-rimmed glasses. He was a foot taller than most Bengalis and enjoyed maximizing the effect of his regal posture. He ordered two junior staff members to grab boxes from below deck while two others tied up the boat.

Sheikh Mujibur Rahman, the head of the Awami League and an inspiration to Bengalis across East Pakistan, had arrived to Manpura. He was campaigning near Dacca, building support for his six-point plan for equal Bengali political representation, when Bhola hit. As the scope of the devastation became clear, Mujib wanted to show through actions—not just a politician's words—that only Bengalis could be trusted to look after fellow Bengalis.

It wouldn't be that hard. After all, when the *Dacca Morning News* uncovered the disaster's magnitude, two days after the cyclone, with a headline that read "Tens of Thousands Killed," the Punjabi officials running East Pakistan spent hours feasting in Dacca with a group of Asian Highway Motor Rally drivers instead of launching a relief effort. That same day, Mujib filled an Awami League boat with rice sacks, fuel cans, and clothes and set out south to the delta. Officially, he'd postponed his election campaign. But Mujib calculated that the trip might be ten times more effective for earning votes than yet another stump speech.

Hai couldn't believe it. Even in his daydreams, he never got closer to Mujib than standing in the background at a student rally—or maybe, just maybe, a quick hello in passing. Yet now, he stood just a few feet away. Hai was starstruck. The fog of his mother and little brother's deaths was momentarily suppressed as he allowed himself a glimmer of excitement.

Mujib was long accustomed to visiting scenes of suffering and despair, but even he was shocked at Manpura's utter destitution. Scanning the horizon, he said, to no one in particular: "God, why have you destroyed everything?"

Mujib was the first person to bring any sort of aid since the cyclone hit. Hundreds of people surrounded the dock, begging for their first scrap of real food in almost a week. Mujib steeled himself and spoke with determination.

"I am Sheikh Mujibur Rahman, from the Awami League. I am here to help our Bengali brothers in their time of need. Who is leading the relief effort here?"

Hai tentatively stepped forward. Malik and others gave him a friendly push to get him to the front of the throng.

"I am, Sheikh sir. My name is Muhammad Abdul Hai, and I am helping the chairman while he is incapacitated." Hai felt embarrassed to be seen in just a tattered, mud-stained waistcloth. It was the only clothing he could find.

"Please take this help for Manpura's people. I'm sorry I do not have more. I must bring something to each of the islands, but I will send more soon. See that this is shared fairly, Abdul Hai."

Mujib's helpers unloaded the goods. It was nothing much—some used clothes and maybe two days' worth of rice. Hai stood next to the burlap sacks, beaming. This famous politician, the one he'd heard countless times on the radio, actually cared about little Manpura, even if he had only a little to give.

Mujib grabbed his tailored knee-length coat off the railing and handed it to Malik to pass on to any elder who needed extra winter warmth. He placed his right hand on Hai's head, then on Malik's.

"My sons, you have the honor but also the responsibility to take care of Manpura's survivors. The Awami League puts our trust in you."

Mujib's men untied the ropes from the jetty. The visit lasted less than five minutes.

As he watched the steamer chug away, Hai promised himself that he would never let Mujib down. Anything Mujib asked of him, anything at all, he would give.

Over the next few days, Hai's concern grew as Mujib's stockpile shrank. He looked skyward for planes that might carry supplies. Maybe they would drop something, even if they couldn't land. But all he saw were military jets.

A couple shopkeepers got a radio working, so Hai and others would gather around it, two hundred at a time, to get tinny BBC updates on their situation. Most of the bulletins dealt with Mujib and President Yahya arguing about whether the elections should be postponed because of the cyclone. A few listeners murmured—using the disaster as a pretense to deny democracy was just the sort of dirty trick that the West Pakistanis had been using for a generation.

Other survivors paced around the island endlessly looking for loved ones. One father peered into the faces of more than a thousand dead children in a fruitless search for his son. Hai wondered why the government hadn't come yet. Surely if Mujib could make it, the bureaucrats, or even the army, could too.

Nine days after Bhola, Hai and Malik heard the chopping whir of a military helicopter approaching Manpura. They and hundreds of others ran toward it. People were so desperate for food that they rushed underneath the helicopter's shadow as it flit from field to field. The crowd was so thick it was impossible to land. The crew yelled at the crowd to move back, but hunger breeds irrational actions.

So the pilot increased his altitude for the drop, flying so high the crowd could barely see it. Malik thought it looked like a matchstick. The crew pushed out three tiny specks and zipped away. Everyone tried to figure out which speck they could be closest to when it landed. The crowd dispersed into three groups and the specks got bigger. Slowly, then quickly. The fifty-pound rice bags slammed into the earth at terminal velocity, 120 miles per hour—two landed on hungry men, killing both instantly. The helicopter was long gone. The police rushed in. Ignoring the bodies, they commandeered the bag that didn't kill anyone, saying it was official government property.

Other officials tried similar charity drops. On another island, the US ambassador Joseph Farland rode in on a helicopter to hand out sacks of rice, molasses, and salt. Starving people rushed the ambassador in his presumed moment of triumph. Scared of the mob, he kicked the bags out and ordered a retreat. The pilot whisked him up to safety, slicing three people with the tail rotor as he swung the helicopter skyward.

Hai took the two bloodied bags back to his stand. He allocated a puny portion of rice to each of the five hundred people who lined up. They were on the brink of starving to death, and a few grains weren't going to cut it.

Hafiz Uddin Ahmad and Yahya Khan

BHOLA ISLAND, EAST PAKISTAN

NOVEMBER 21, 1970
Nine days after landfall
Sixteen days until the election

Hafiz stood on a large berm near the banks of the mighty Tetulia River. He could barely make out the outline of another island from across the mile-wide stretch of fetid water. He'd spent a week burying bodies at his ancestral village. Most of the corpses weren't even from the area but had floated downriver during the tidal surge. In this way, every village buried its upstream neighbors. The work was far from over. Every time they pulled a dead body from the river, two more washed up.

After more than three days of work, his achievements seemed minor, but at least now most of the corpses were pulled down from the trees. The army had given him only a few days leave to check on his family, but right before he boarded a boat back to his barracks, he received a message from his commanding officer, Lieutenant Colonel Jalil. Bravo Company was assigned to humanitarian duty, and his unit would meet him in the delta.

The next day, Hafiz was organizing mass graves. He directed teams of shovel-wielding men to excavate a massive trench so that his unit could fill it with bodies. It was slow work. What they really needed was a fleet of bulldozers.

The cyclone stripped away any sense of identity from the corpses around him. Two weeks before, every one of these bodies was a person with feelings, a family, some scrap of education, and hopes for the future. Now they were rotting meat that had to be dumped underground at double-time to stop cholera and other diseases from poisoning the survivors. After a few days of working knee-deep in the dead, Hafiz got used to the smell enough that he could focus and not spend hours fighting back the urge to vomit. He wasn't sure if this was luck, exactly, but at least he could finish the job.

When the first mass grave was full, Hafiz ordered another. He was debating with himself about whether the next trench, spaced between two sets of palm trees, would be big enough, when a courier ran out to him from the makeshift army headquarters. In truth, the command center was little more than a room with a working—and, therefore, precious—telephone. The breathless messenger said there was an urgent call for him from Dacca. Hafiz held the black receiver in his hand and made out the familiar military staccato of a Punjabi noncommissioned officer. They spoke in English.

"Hello, Hafiz. I hope everything is going well. We have an important question for you. Is there black dog on your island? What do you think?"

Hafiz was sure he misheard something. His mind raced to the carnage outside. He'd seen dogs of all kinds, black and otherwise, gnawing on the corpses and making nuisances of themselves.

"Of course, they're everywhere. What do you need them for?"

The echo of the man's chortle flew across the phone lines and into his ear. "Even with all of your world travel, you really don't know anything but football, do you? I said 'Black Dog.' As in the whiskey. It's our dear president's favorite drink. He's coming to your island the day after tomorrow to survey the relief work with his own eyes. He'll have lunch with us there. So if we want to keep our jobs safe, we need Black Dog whiskey for him."

Hafiz was surprised. Since the storm had hit, the president had done nothing more than fly over the destruction. Hafiz knew that he had gone to Dacca, but there was no indication he was planning on a return trip.

The officer on the phone informed Hafiz that the president would not only need to be good and drunk if he was going to witness the horrors on the island, but he also wasn't in the most spectacular physical shape, so walking was out of the question.

"Why don't you gather up a few dozen dead bodies and drag them over to the landing zone? That would be easiest for everyone, wouldn't it?" he asked.

Hafiz blinked, speechless. Never mind that his faith forbid alcohol, was *this* the time for a drink? And wait a minute, was he really being ordered to construct a grotesque diorama so that Yahya wouldn't have to walk a few dozen feet to the river? Twenty of Hafiz's relatives had vanished in the storm; their corpses were still missing. There was always a chance that he was related to any bodies he dragged from the river. Would he want his cousin's corpse to be a prop?

"Don't worry, the president won't have any trouble seeing dead bodies," Hafiz said, after considering the field of decay he'd been toiling in all morning. "But you can tell the president that he can stick that Black Dog up his own ass. I'm not going to waste my time with that."

Hafiz hung up the phone without waiting for the man's protests, orders, or, maybe, pleadings. He had work to do, and as far as he was concerned, Yahya Khan would just get in the way.

Back in Islamabad, Yahya's mind was far from the plight. He spent most of his time holed up in his office at President House. His advisers had no idea what he was doing behind the locked doors. They couldn't know that Yahya was deep in thought, ruminating over a letter that he had brought back from Peking, which confirmed China's interest in exploring a normalization of relations with Nixon.

In accordance with the agreement he'd struck with them, the letter couldn't look like it came from a Chinese hand or be on Chinese paper, so Yahya carefully rewrote it himself and sent it on to Washington via encrypted cipher. Even the carbon copies of his letter were dutifully burned. He ordered his ambassador in Washington, DC, to read his letter to Kissinger aloud, then destroy it before he left the White House.

While Yahya daydreamed about filling the CHINESE CONNECTION folder with copies of every letter and message that he would shuttle back and forth between Mao and Nixon, politicians and power brokers piled up outside his door with urgent messages. To shut them up, Yahya decided that it was time for a display of magnanimity. He had his public relations guru set up a private flight to Bhola for the perfect photo op with a football-star-turned-army-captain who was leading a relief effort.

Two days later, the rhythmic thumping of Yahya's helicopter cut through the air above Bhola, while Hafiz and his superior officer, Lieutenant Colonel Jalil, stood at attention along the perimeter of a hastily cleared landing pad. A teeming mass of villagers and cyclone survivors gathered behind the soldiers. Stripped naked by the cyclone, most survivors wore only the few scraps of cloth they had been able to salvage.

In the past few days, aid had trickled in at a painfully slow pace—and, Hafiz noticed, it wasn't coming from Pakistanis. A British Royal Marine Commando Team ferried a few supplies from Singapore to the delta's worst-hit areas on helicopters. Survivors understood that helicopters meant food, water, and fresh clothing, but only the first people on the scene had any chance of getting something. Hafiz knew that most of the people here weren't waiting to catch a glimpse of the president. Rather, they hoped for anything that might help them make it through another night.

The wash from the rotors beat back the low bushes and loosened fronds from the surviving palm trees—a miniature reenactment of the cyclone that had devastated the region. When the helicopter finally touched down, Hafiz immediately recognized the hawklike eyebrows and expansive gut of the past-his-prime soldier. President Yahya climbed down from the dark green military helicopter in a tan raincoat and civilian's fedora to keep the sun off his brow. A junior officer behind the president abruptly stopped in horror on the aircraft's stair when he caught sight of the number of corpses rotting in the hot sun a few feet away.

Yahya walked briefly among the dead, posing just long enough with the corpses for the state press photographer and foreign TV media to capture the moment. He stuck his hand in a bucket of rice, pretending to inspect it, for another photo op.

Hafiz then ordered two subordinates to bring up the closest body. They carried it over to Yahya on a wooden plank. The corpse had already started to decompose, the legs blackened from decay, exposing bits of femur. One arm slid off the plank as they carried it, and the rotting stick swayed gently through the rice stalks as the subordinates brought it to Yahya like a gift. He contorted his face into a simulacrum of concern and nodded solemnly, doing his best to hide the fact that half a bottle of spirits had dulled his senses.

The junior official gave a small, satisfied smile and nodded at the officers for a job well done in arranging the bodies. He didn't realize that Hafiz hadn't made any special efforts. Bodies were the only thing in high supply.

But Yahya came to deliver a show. He began an impromptu speech in front of the ragged refugees, whom Hafiz would never forget. Yahya spoke of the importance of people pulling themselves up by their bootstraps and of the indomitable spirit of the people of Pakistan. He praised the aid efforts and predicted Bhutto's victory in the polls.

The crowd looked on, dumbfounded, while Associated Press cameras rolled. Who was this fat man speaking to them in English? Where were the bags of rice and cloth?

The president asked nearby officers who was in charge of the local operation. Lieutenant Colonel Jalil puffed out his chest and pointed to Hafiz. "Hafiz is a real hero here. He lost twenty-five family members in the floods and has been on the ground, helping with relief, almost since day one."

Hafiz sweated inside his uniform as the sun beat down.

The president smiled and extended his hand. Hafiz took it reluctantly, burning inside as they locked eyes. He wanted to scream at Yahya, *How can you arrive so late and do so little, you old drunk?* But he bit his tongue. Protocol, above all.

Interrupting this manufactured media moment, an old man with deeply fissured skin, forged from years toiling in the sun, stomped up to Yahya and Hafiz and asked in Bengali, "Where is the rice? Please sir, we are starving! We need clothes!"

The angry Bengali's words washed over Yahya like a baby's babbling. His expression soured. He'd flown in to get some snaps with dead bodies, not to deal with the destitute. Mindful of the nearby camera, he asked Hafiz to translate.

"He says that he lost twenty people in his family, and those who are left have no food or clothing," Hafiz began, translating for Yahya into English.

The old man cried as he told more of his story.

Yahya raised his hand to stop him. "Tell this old man how many relatives you lost, Hafiz."

Caught between Pakistan's most powerful man and a starving survivor, Hafiz said the only words he could, "Don't be sad, Uncle. Like you, I have also lost people close to me. May God bless us both with patience."

Pleased at how Hafiz dispensed with the beggar, Yahya looked out over the crowd and resumed his rousing pep talk. "Look, there's no profit in crying. Keep working with a cheerful mind. Eat roti instead of rice, and you will be stronger and more able to tackle the challenges in this difficult time. It will all get better soon," he advised in stately Urdu, another language that almost nobody on the island understood.

Satisfied that his media contingent captured the message, Yahya tipped his hat toward Hafiz and went to lunch. Yahya and a few other VIPs had a closed-door biryani feast a few hundred yards from the relief site. Yahya smiled when he saw the table's centerpiece: a gleaming, sealed bottle of Black Dog. The officer on the phone had commandeered a relief speedboat the day before and gunned it all the way to Dacca and back in order to have it there in time, using relief-aid funds to pay for the gas and booze.

Watching Yahya and his entourage walk into the mess hall, the frustrated old man turned to a college-aged student in the crowd. He asked, "Who were those assholes?"

Hafiz let out a somber chuckle. The black times rewarded black humor. The farmer never once realized that he was speaking to the president of Pakistan. All he wanted was rice.

An hour or so later, Yahya returned to a Dacca tarmac packed high with relief supplies. Most of it had been sitting there for a week. Yahya zipped past it without a second thought.

That evening, at a banquet at the InterContinental Hotel, Yahya recounted his day to reporters. He said that he had his best and brightest on the case. In particular, he said, "Lieutenant Hafiz continues to work in the unit despite the loss of several close relatives in the tide."

After seeing his story on TV, army officers and officials from around the country sent telegrams to Hafiz, expressing their condolences. One of them even promised that they'd put his name in for a prestigious award.

Hafiz had priorities other than awards, like selecting which mountain of dirt was going to cover the next mass of dead bodies. They'd made some progress in this small village, but there was more work to do.

19

Candy Rohde

HATIYA ISLAND, EAST PAKISTAN

NOVEMBER 21, 1970
Nine days after landfall
Sixteen days until the election

"Hello?"

Candy wandered around the vacant Hatiya airport about an hour after sunrise.

"Hello?" It was a ghost town. Her plane, with its hundred bags of rice, was the only vehicle around. Finally, she found a security guard half asleep by an empty hangar.

"Where is everyone? Did the other agencies already go to the countryside? Where is the army?"

The guard gave her a funny look through bleary eyes. "Army? No army here. No one has come since the storm."

"What about doctors, hospitals?"

The guard frowned and shook his head.

Candy stood there, speechless. It wasn't possible. How could she be the only one here after the biggest natural disaster in Pakistan's history?

And yet the guard was right. The airport was deserted. No deliveries, no cargo transports, no army or police milling about, no government personnel, no triage tents, and not a single relief worker in sight. The security guard went back to watching over the empty airstrip.

Candy's stomach churned. Marty, Runi, and she were just winging it, after all. They weren't aid experts. Maybe there was an entire operation going on somewhere else, and they'd just missed it. Where did the army go with all of that food?

Where was everyone?

A horrible thought crept in, a little gnat burrowing into Candy's consciousness: What if the army didn't want to help? It was almost too terrible to work through. No government could be that callous, that evil.

Candy swatted out the thought. But her mind kept coming back to the cocktail-party conversations and the officers in the suite. The army had warehouses full of grain in Dacca at that very moment. She'd seen them. They had planes and boats. It wasn't a logistics problem.

Yahya was going to let hundreds of thousands of people starve to death. She needed to make HELP much bigger, as quickly as possible.

Candy ran back to the plane. "Hurry! We have to get back to Dacca! Right away."

She and the pilot unloaded the bags of rice and set them against the hangar wall. Then they jumped in the plane. The propellers churned into action. As they took off, Candy saw dark shapes bobbing on the surface of the water, which could only be one thing.

Forty-five minutes later, she gripped the handle of a pay phone at the Dacca airport while an attendant looked on, dutifully monitoring the seconds as they clicked by to calculate the correct price to charge her. Candy tried to keep her composure as she begged her husband. She was making the biggest ask of their relationship: She needed Jon to drop everything he came here for and adopt her mission.

"You know I can't leave my work at the hospital. They need me here. Why are you asking me?" Jon's tinny voice came through the receiver.

"Tens of thousands more people need your help here," she replied.

"Candy, I'm too involved in experiments, and the hospital is full of cholera patients. Besides, I can't leave," he said. The unspoken threat of Vietnam dangled between them.

"Jon, this is the work we're meant to be doing. I'm sure of it."

On the other end of the line, Jon looked around at the research facility that might one day develop a treatment for cholera that could save countless lives. Leaving now felt like abandoning his team and the last two years of work.

But deep down, he knew Candy was right: They needed to save lives *now*. Without any triage doctors, hundreds of cyclone survivors would perish from infected wounds and communicable diseases long before Candy's aid could take effect. Even if he got shipped to Saigon immediately after, it would be worth it. The cholera research would have to wait.

Candy made hundreds of pay-phone calls that week, telling everyone with any clout in Dacca what she'd seen in Hatiya and how they were the only people who could stop a Yahya-induced famine. In just nine days, Candy and HELP organized one of the most massive relief movements in human history. Their telegrams, letters, and phone calls miraculously transformed into a torrent of supplies and cash. They scored the use of everything from military landing craft akin to the boats that delivered troops to the beaches of Normandy in World War II, to the last working paddle boat in Dacca, which sported giant wheels on both sides to power through the delta's shallow channels.

The Shell Oil warehouses and garages, just off the airport's tarmac, served as their supply depot. Candy loaded supplies by hand on every last aircraft she could find. Soviet helicopter pilots—technically, the United States' enemy—gave her medical supplies. She even managed to convince Ambassador Farland to lend them his private plane.

The organization grew so fast that it was difficult to get name tags for all the workers. Instead, they wrote "HELP" on pieces of paper and pinned them to their shirts.

Candy embraced the role, coordinating ever-larger shipments of supplies dumped at her feet by desperate donors. Each burlap package was a ticking clock that represented maybe a hundred lives. Either Candy got the supplies where they needed to go or they rotted and their intended recipients wasted away. Candy built the supply chain through sheer determination, while the Red Cross and others were still stuck on the tarmac dealing with bureaucrats.

Meanwhile, the *New York Times* and *Washington Post* eviscerated the nonexistent government-aid effort and the US government's thumb-twiddling. Nixon responded by complaining that the media was being too negative about Yahya, a close friend and important US ally who was doing his very best. He ordered Dacca's consul to spend his days not on aid but on public relations, to counter every negative article with a corresponding press release that showed the positive side of things.

Armed with a small fleet of planes and helicopters, as well as a boat stuffed with supplies, Candy was ready. Eleven days after the storm, she went back to the delta—this time with Jon and thousands of pounds of relief supplies in tow. They got a few other friends from Dacca to come with them and quickly went to work: Candy distributed goods, Jon did triage.

In Hatiya, they began distributing supplies. A quarter of Hatiya's inhabitants were dead, but rumors came up from the jetties. Ignoring their own starvation, the Hatiya survivors told Candy and Jon that, somehow, things were even worse on the next island over, Manpura. They said that Manpura was little more than a long bar of silt and totally exposed, and things would surely be much worse there. It wasn't even on the map Candy had. Jon offered to check it out.

Candy listened to the islander's directions and drew her own maps for Jon. Jon weighed a little boat down to the water line with food, then scrounged up two derelict sailboats and did the same with those, connecting the vessels with a tow line. She figured Manpura was about twenty miles away, so Jon loaded what he estimated was enough gasoline to make it there and back. It was a careful calculation. Bringing too much gasoline meant a half dozen people might starve. Bringing too little meant he'd be stranded.

Jon pulled the motor's starter rope. It whined and gave a couple of half-hearted chugs, then silence. Candy gave Jon a look.

"I'll be fine!" Jon promised Candy. He didn't even have a compass.

She glanced at the local HELP staff, all of whom had refused, point-blank, to take such a dumb risk. Candy and Jon both knew that if he got off course—or if Candy's maps were wrong—he'd float out to sea with no way to paddle back. There'd be no way to communicate with anyone, and no hope of rescue if things went sideways. Jon cajoled two doctor buddies he brought from Dacca to join him.

"It's a good boat," Jon said as he slapped the side of the hull, half trying to reassure Candy and half trying to reassure himself. He primed the motor and pulled the starter rope again. It lurched to life ever so reluctantly.

"I love you, Jon," she said. "Be careful."

Jon pushed the boats off the bank and turned west. Candy watched Jon's silhouette as he gripped the tiller and slowly disappeared into the Bay of Bengal.

Candy raced back to Hatiya airport to make some calls. She coordinated the incoming shipments and her growing mass of volunteers, both foreign and Bengali, all from a public phone, like a fast-speaking general positioning distant troops onto various locations on the front. By now, HELP had swelled to more than one hundred volunteers and could feed more than fifty thousand survivors a week. Candy kept track of everything on a clipboard that was always within arm's reach.

Perhaps shamed by the negative press from around the world the government finally, almost two weeks after the cyclone hit, deployed the army to the delta in what was supposed to look like a real relief effort. But the mighty Pakistan Army, with all its resources and logistical capabilities, was flat-footed compared to Candy's gang. The army had commandeered a warehouse in Hatiya and filled it to the two-story roof with rice and kerosene, saying that they needed more orders before distributing a single grain. Candy offered to work together, or even distribute their goods for them, for free. They refused.

Anyone sending aid from outside Pakistan had a choice: They could give it to a government that let it rot or they could give to Candy and hope that a scrappy group of expats and Bengalis could do the job better. As word spread of Candy's success at breaking through the logjam, more agencies gave Candy their supplies. Yet as big as HELP was getting, it still left millions to fend for themselves.

Somewhere out on the delta, Jon opened the gas cap and peered down. Almost half of the tank was gone, and there was still no sign of Manpura. The only thing that he and the other two doctors had seen in the last three hours were a couple of lonely sandbars. One had a buffalo carcass resting atop it. On the other, a dead child's arm and leg stuck out of the mud: a macabre warning. Jon puttered on, squinting for land as the noon sun reflected like a glistening prism across the choppy water.

An hour later, Jon looked down again—this time, putting his eye nearly onto the gas-cap ring. Fumes wafted across his cornea. There was maybe a third of a tank left and still no Manpura in sight. Chugging along at a walking pace, it felt like every breeze pushed them backward. Jon steeled himself for the possibility that the storm could have washed the entire island away.

This was the point of no return. If he had any chance of making it back to Candy with the fuel he had left, Jon would need to turn around immediately.

Instead, he plowed ahead. His hand ached from gripping the diminutive motor's vibrating tiller for hours. The wind suddenly shifted to a light headwind, and with it, the men all sat up, suppressing their gag reflexes. The gases of decay wafted over the boat.

Suppressing his natural impulse to flee, Jon crawled onward, through the cloud of departed souls. It must be close now.

20

Mohammad Hai

MANPURA, EAST PAKISTAN

NOVEMBER 25, 1970
Thirteen days after landfall
Twelve days until the election

Hai walked past the piles of mud and debris that lingered around the Manpura jetty, scanning them half-heartedly for anything salvageable or memorable while he waited. Every day at around noon, he came by, hoping against hope that Mujib, another Awami League leader, or even the army would bring a supply boat. The starving survivors were growing more desperate for food, eating tree bark, dog corpses, or anything else that could keep them alive for another day.

Hai looked up at the horizon, then slunk his shoulders when he saw a small passenger ferry and nothing else. The ferries started up a few days ago to get people like Hai's dad back to their home islands. Hai knew that the ferries carried only two things: more hungry mouths and grotesque, impossible to believe, rumors.

The boat docked. New arrivals told Hai that army officials around the delta had started to show up at a few islands, but they were far from saviors. On Bhola island, they played badminton in starched whites while bodies rotted in nearby fields and starving locals wailed for food. Rumors circulated that soldiers traded food for sex with desperate mothers or stole ration boxes to resell. When reporters asked Yahya to explain his soldier's actions, the president replied "My government is not made up of angels."

Hai couldn't imagine how anyone could be so cruel. Who could possibly see a starving mother begging for baby food and think it was a great chance to get off? Maybe the West Pakistanis really didn't see them as human.

Hai left for the town square about a mile away. When he arrived, a shopkeeper turned on one of the island's last working radios. Mujib's daily speech was about to begin. It was the one break Hai allowed himself, while eating his daily handful of rice. Mujib's voice crackled with energy, mixed in with the roar of a Dacca audience that punctuated his pauses with cheers. Mujib lacerated Yahya for his anemic aid response, sharing the horrors he'd seen when he visited Manpura and other islands just a week earlier. Mujib said that there were mountains of food rotting at the airport in Dacca while the army argued about who would get to deliver it. Food that could be in the stomachs of starving people in less than an hour if they'd cared at all. Hai envisioned the scene, wishing that his uncle's boat hadn't vanished after the cyclone. He would have jumped in it and gone there himself.

But this wasn't incompetence, Mujib warned. He promised to arrest every last official who refused to allow aid deliveries to the islands after the cyclone. These officials, he said, were responsible for the "cold-blooded murder" of up to one million people. Mujib's message was so decisive, and so heartfelt, that even leaders of competing Bengali parties joined the Awami League. Mujib had always been a great agitator; now, for the first time, Bengalis saw him as a true leader. He said that there would never be a better time for Bengalis to lead themselves than by voting in the upcoming election. Their very lives depended on it.

Then Mujib recited his six-point plan for building a better government. Hai knew it by heart but listened anyway, nodding as Mujib zoomed through the points, which he introduced four years ago and had been fine-tuning ever since. Designed to be simple enough for everyday people to grasp, the points were: (1) create universal suffrage and a national, democratically elected parliament; (2) reduce the federal government's activities to only defense and foreign affairs and let local governments in East and West Pakistan run the rest; (3) allow local governments to tax and spend their own revenue; (4) ban corporate wealth transfers from East to West Pakistan; (5) allow East Pakistan to conduct foreign trade without going through West Pakistan; and (6) give each wing its own independent military force.

But Mujib wasn't done. He was about to drop the most incendiary sentence he had ever uttered: "East Pakistan must achieve self-rule by ballot if possible, and by bullet, if necessary."

Would the Awami League really take up weapons? Hai wondered. It seemed impossible. Then he wondered if there was any other choice. Rumors off the ferries warned that the government planned to rig the election with thousands of fake ballots. How could they trust Yahya to give them a vote, when he wouldn't even give them rice?

Hai shivered. Mujib had never spoken like this before. Hai thought of his mother—a woman who resisted British rule—about how proud she would be to hear the ideas that so few dared to speak even a month ago. But how scared she would be too. And here Mujib was forging a new future with his words and daring Yahya to shut him up. So far, Yahya hadn't done much other than yell at the foreign reporters who reported rumors about aid mismanagement. He said the relief efforts were, in fact, going splendidly, and any news otherwise was fake.

Like millions of other Bengalis around the country, Hai cheered Mujib with a righteous anger. If the rumors were fake, where was the army? Where was the food? Soon the broadcasts began to feel more like football matches. Mujib's audience whooped so much they missed half of the speeches, but it didn't matter because there would be another one tomorrow and the day after that.

Mujib's Dacca crowds were even bigger and more rambunctious. His deputy said that the Great Bhola Cyclone was God's sign for a Bengali uprising. The growing crowds fueled the flames of Mujib's fiery rhetoric, which in turn fueled even bigger crowds. The election, now just two weeks away, couldn't come fast enough. Assuming Yahya let the election happen as planned, some Bengalis began to imagine an outcome in which they won an outright majority. After all, East Pakistan out-populated West Pakistan. Mujib and the Awami League knew it was the longest of long shots, but they realized that the despicably bad aid response could play directly into their hands and galvanize every last Bengali to vote for their cause.

When the speech was over, the shopkeeper flicked off the radio to conserve the battery for the next day. Hai and the others looked at one another, then dispersed. The afterglow of even the most inspirational leader's words faded fast in a starving person. Hai made his usual daily trip down to the jetty, praying that Mujib had sent a new supply ship to back up his words.

Far off in the distance, Hai could just make out a glaring speck. It wasn't coming from Dacca to the north but from Hatiya to the east. And it wasn't a passenger ferry. *What could it be?* he thought, trying to temper expectations. *Maybe Mujib's back!*

The speck grew, ever so slowly. Minutes passed.

Eventually, Hai realized that it wasn't Mujib at all. It was a ratty supply boat, towing a couple of overloaded sailboats behind it. Inside the main aluminum dinghy, a flailing white man was trying to find a place to land. He was having a hard time of it against the current.

Hai tilted his head and squinted. He'd never seen a white person before. *What in the world was he doing here?*

More important: What was in those boats?

21

Jon Rohde, Mohammad Hai, and Candy Rohde

Jon spied some bare sticks along the horizon. Palm trees, stripped by the storm. Candy's hand-drawn map was accurate to within a quarter mile. He gripped the tiller harder, trying to will one bit of horsepower more out of the engine so the three boats could get to their destination before the gas gave out.

As the water got shallower, Jon realized he'd have to weave around rotting bodies before he made land. He floated nearly a mile along the shore before he found a corpse-free stretch of beach. Ten feet away, the body of a cow lay bloated to the point of exploding under the Bengali sun. In the other direction, a dog chewed on a man's lifeless torso.

In his worst nightmares, Jon hadn't imagined such devastation. It was eerily calm. There was no breeze, no waves. Just endless bodies and animal carcasses bobbing gently all around him, up and down. A few curious starving souls wandered to the shore to watch him.

Jon called out in a mishmash of English and broken Bengali for help securing the boats. One skinny teen stepped forward, with scars on his arms and wearing only a scrap of dirty cloth. Jon introduced himself, saying his name as he put his hand to his chest.

Mohammad Abdul Hai returned the gesture.

Jon said that he and his wife, Candy, were Americans bringing help to cyclone victims. His Bengali was a weird Dacca dialect, but Hai got the gist. The real message came with the cargo. The boats were filled with rice, milk, shirts, kerosene, lentils, and matches. It was everything the island needed most.

While the other two doctors set up a makeshift triage tent, Jon unloaded the first box by himself, balancing a bulky fifty-pound crate on his head. He made it about a hundred yards through the sand and mud before collapsing. Hai rushed to bring a box to shore himself, straining just as much, and yelling at others to stop sifting through debris and instead join the effort.

A few children gathered, watching the procession greedily with all the desire of someone who hadn't eaten in more than a week. Hai opened a box and found cans featuring a cartoonish face of a child. He passed one to a girl who was too weak to hold it for herself. Neither Hai nor the child knew what was inside.

News of the trio's landing spread so quickly that it might as well have been broadcast on the radio. So many were so close to starvation that Jon knew hundreds here would be dead tomorrow, if not later today, if they didn't ingest something. He tried to explain the contents of the mystery cans.

"Milk! Milk!" Jon said in English, pointing at the cans. Then he tried "*Dudha!*" in Bengali. People who had only known dairy from the udder of a buffalo couldn't understand what cans had to do with milk.

Equally confounded, Jon eventually opened a can, took a drink himself, then put it against a child's lips. Her eyes widened when the liquid hit her tongue. She gripped the can with emaciated fingers and gulped ravenously. In minutes, everyone in the crowd had their own cans, traces of white liquid dripping down their chins.

Jon, Hai, and a few other volunteers distributed what was on the

first boat. After an hour ashore, the stench coming through Jon's nos-
trils was still every bit as strong as his first inhalation. He covered his
face with a rag to muffle the smell.

Hai helped Jon unload the second boat onto the jetty. As he
strained against the boxes, Jon noticed pus leaking out of abrasions
across Hai's forearms, biceps, and inner thighs. He offered to clean
them, but Hai motioned at the boxes. Others had more severe wounds,
and Hai wouldn't accept any tending to as long as there was still food
to bring to his starving brothers.

The other distributors weren't going to get much rest, either. People
from across the island trekked to the jetty on the mere whisper of the
foreigner's boat; hundreds were now pushing for a glimpse. A scuffle
broke out as panicked survivors in the back of the throng feared that
there wouldn't be enough food to last and shoved their way forward.
Others shoved back. Hunger and fear spread through the crowd like
a virus.

"Stop! Everyone will get a fair share," Hai said, surprised at his
own directness with people who were very much his senior. He remembered how Mujib acted in similar situations, and told the crowd
sternly that if they just stayed orderly and a bit patient, he'd make sure
they all got their equal share. Jon nodded at the words. He couldn't
quite understand them, but he got the idea.

Hai kept his word. In the next few hours, he made sure that his
comrades all got something, regardless of whether they were Hindus,
Muslims, Punjabis, or Bengalis. In one day, five hundred people ate
their first real meal in two weeks.

Meanwhile, Jon tended to a long line of his own, cleaning the
wounds of dozens of men who'd survived by holding on to tree trunks
for an entire night. He called their injuries "palm tree syndrome."
When he ran out of gauze and disinfectant, he went back to talk with
Hai, who he also treated. Jon felt lucky to find someone on Manpura
who emphasized fairness and order; it was all too easy to let chaos
envelop these sorts of missions.

So Jon signed Hai on as HELP's coordinator for the island, one of the organization's first paid positions. Hai agreed, and they made a badge out of paper that read "HELP Manpura." It was all the authority Hai would need.

Jon and Hai worked past dusk and into the night. With only a sliver of moon interrupting a cloudless sky, Hai fell fast asleep under a tarp on the dirt, while Jon did the same but without a tarp, staring at Orion before passing out from exhaustion.

The next morning, Jon promised more rations once they figured out how to distribute the bounties from foreign countries. In truth, Jon had no idea if there was going to be anything left by the time he got back to the Hatiya airstrip. After all, Manpura was only one island out of dozens that needed aid. Jon hoped that Candy could conjure a miracle that would let him honor his rash promise.

Hai gave Jon some of Manpura's last reserves of gasoline to refill his tank, then watched Jon's boat vanish on the horizon as mysteriously as it had appeared. It could well be another week until the survivors' next meal.

Two excruciating days passed before Hai saw Jon's little boat dawdling back to Manpura. At first, the sight filled him with joy, but as the boat drew nearer, his heart sank. Jon was alone, his boat empty.

Jon came ashore and brushed off Hai's questions about supplies. Instead, he arranged empty kerosene cans on the ground into a large X, then made another X a few yards away. Then he took out a beat-up pair of army binoculars to scan the sky.

"There! There she is!" Jon ran up the mud embankment above the flat rice paddies. He waved his arms furiously at the two X's. A propeller plane came buzzing in, low and slow. It was an old two-seat crop duster flying just fifteen feet off the ground with its cargo door wide open.

The pilot held steady on his course until just about a hundred yards before crossing over the X's. Then he pulled back on the stick. Ten heavy bags tumbled earthward. With memories fresh of the last airdrop gone wrong, this time the residents kept their distance. Hai could just make out a woman, grinning from ear to ear, next to the pilot. She threw a small cylinder out of the cockpit window and waved at Jon. It twirled end over end, landing in a thick patch of rice paddy. Jon ran over to it, cracked it open, and waved back as the plane banked right and flew out of sight.

Hai surmised that the mystery woman must be Jon's wife. Without a phone, telegraph, or even a two-way radio, this was the only way that Candy could reliably get instructions to the island: one tube at a time. Malik joked that it was a love letter. Hai didn't find that particularly funny. Meanwhile, Jon eagerly ripped open the tube:

> *How's the smell today? Hope you are using nose masks. I've been operating on two hours of sleep per night and no food today until 5:30 PM. I'm afraid what I have to say is not going to be too coherent. I'm working on these things for you now: people, tents, kerosene, blankets, shovels, food and medicines. All organizations in Dacca are trying to funnel through us now. It is really snowballing. Right now we're concentrating on helping you first and foremost. We are going to drop water this afternoon in plastic cans, hoping they won't break. It is not boiled because we're hurrying to get it to you. Happiness is knowing where you are. I love and adore you.*

It wasn't long until Candy started coordinating airdrops on Manpura from other countries too, while Jon stayed on Manpura to lead the relief effort. The Germans and Soviets dropped rice and medicine; the Italians gave blankets. Hai heard over the shopkeeper's radio that the pope (whoever that was) flew into Dacca and that the US president was sending helicopters from North Carolina (wherever that was).

The Americans dumped bacon and eggs from their Vietnam military rations. Hai and the rest of the island grimaced at the canned bacon. The Qur'an forbids eating pig flesh, and they recoiled from the thought of having to sin in order to survive. On the other hand, the Qur'an allowed for exceptions in emergencies, so some survivors choked down the pork.

There was still no sign of the Pakistani authorities.

Five days later, Jon spent a chilly Thanksgiving night alone under the stars, with his horn-rimmed glasses on, reading and rereading Candy's air-dropped daily letters by candlelight over a stale batch of reconstituted US Army eggs. He'd worn the same unwashed beige cotton kurta and khaki shorts for a week. Hai collapsed alone in exhaustion about a mile away, lying inside a donated tent, shivering under a donated blanket, wearing a donated shirt, eating the same donated eggs.

As he looked up at the clear night sky, Jon couldn't stop thinking about the little girl and the milk. It was probably the first thing she'd ingested since the storm, and there must be tens of thousands of children in the same circumstances all around the country. What if there could be some sort of high-caloric packet that aid agencies could throw out of planes in disaster zones before more substantial relief arrived? If people could just make it through the first days after a crisis, their chances of surviving increased exponentially.

The next morning, two weeks after the cyclone, the Pakistan Army finally came to Manpura. The cavalry consisted of a single helicopter. A dozen Punjabi soldiers bearing only ten bags of rice to distribute to ten thousand people. At any other time, Hai would have laughed in the face of this pathetic display. But that rice would save hundreds of lives. He bit his tongue and showed them HELP's allocation strategy.

Jon buttered up the colonel to make sure that the army wouldn't kick HELP off Manpura. Candy wrote that the Pakistan Army was giving her problems on the neighboring island and had banned foreign aid agencies from using the Dacca airport. Hai was wary of the military officer but played along. Jon and Hai continued their fourteen-hour days, while the soldiers lazed about. Some evenings, Jon dined with the colonel leading the local army contingent, humoring his monologues about all of the wonderful things that Pakistan was doing to care for the poor, weak Bengalis. The international media came too. Jon showed the HELP operation to a BBC journalist, who had stopped by the army camp before flying out. Jon thought nothing of it at the time.

But some people on Manpura benefited more than others from the new arrivals. The chairman's son, jealous at Hai's new status, told Jon that if he weren't put in charge of HELP, he would make sure that the army banned them from the island. The chairman and the army had a certain understanding about things.

Jon felt stuck. He was desperate for HELP to continue, but he didn't trust the son, who hadn't done anything to help out so far. Sticking around for a trial period wasn't possible. Candy needed him back in Dacca. So Jon reluctantly gave in to the son. With no idea when he could come back, he couldn't risk a big blowup. If HELP lost their access, all of Candy's work here would be for nothing.

On his way off Manpura, Jon told Hai and the others of the change, thinking it wouldn't be that big a deal.

The language barrier, and the respect he gave Jon as a benefactor, meant that Hai didn't utter a word of protest. Not a word about how these corrupt landowners—the same ones who cared more about making a few rupees than helping their fellow Bengalis in their deepest times of need—were in charge all over again. Hai conceded silently, but inside, he screamed. He knew it meant that all the old favoritism would get mixed in with the rice going forward. Not even the worst cyclone in history could wash that out of the system.

And now, just like that, Hai reported to the chairman's son.

Hai sat on the muddy, grassy bank, staring in disbelief at Jon's slowly vanishing silhouette. Despite all he'd done, despite how well he'd done it, Hai was back to being a nobody. The chairman's son smiled and waved until Jon was out of sight. With the send-off complete, he ordered Hai and the others to take the rest of the supplies to the chairman's house.

———

Back in Dacca, Candy fidgeted, turning her cup of Darjeeling around and around on the InterContinental café's table. Candy never fidgeted. But Germans were known for their punctuality, and it was five past the hour now. Maybe picking her and Jon's favorite table wasn't so lucky after all.

Next to the cup lay a legal pad with a hastily drafted budget in longhand. Candy had arranged a meeting with the German organization Brot für die Welt (Bread for the World). Word was they had some money to spend on relief, but like everyone else they were blocked by the Pakistan Army from doing anything. So Candy invited them for tea. She studied the figures on the sheet one last time. She was about to ask for more than a quarter of a million dollars for her four-week-old organization.

Finally, the Germans arrived. Candy waved them over. They were delayed by a Mujib rally that blocked the roads for miles. Candy launched into an impassioned speech, filled with details about what HELP had done so far and the scope of the problem.

The two men listened patiently, without asking questions. A pat on the head this time would be devastating.

Candy closed her pitch with a figure that she said would feed and shelter everyone left on Manpura for the next six months: $383,000.

The German director frowned. His brow wrinkled.

Candy remained stone-faced. The odds of the Germans asking to speak with her husband seemed to double with each passing second.

Finally, he spoke. "Ah. That is too bad, because I want to give you half a million, and my friend here wants to give you a million and a half."

Candy was shocked, but her poker face held firm. Together, they worked through how the additional funds could be allocated—and where. By the end of the meeting, Candy had secured more than one million dollars for relief work in Manpura, Bhola, and Hatiya. At some point down the line the Germans promised another million to see the job through to the end.

This was no time to celebrate, though. After leaving the hotel, Candy rushed to the pier, where she'd heard that a Soviet freighter had come in with medical supplies. She hoped to use some of the new funds to buy scarce, lifesaving implements. It wouldn't be easy. America and the Soviets were still mortal enemies.

Candy approached the captain. He gave her a warm welcome; he'd already heard great things about her. Before Candy even asked, he told her about the nine tons of supplies on his ship. Since the Russians were friendly with India, the Pakistan Army wanted nothing to do with their aid. Maybe Candy could help? The captain gave her run of everything on the ship, for however she felt it could be put to the best use. For free.

22

Neil Frank

Neil Frank emerged from the InterContinental Hotel's stately lobby into the pleasant seventy-degree morning sunshine. The concierge saluted the meteorologist and called over a white Vauxhall Victor thrumming at the curb. The driver rushed to open the back door so that Frank wouldn't need to spend more than a split second at the taxi stand.

The World Bank had given Frank a task he thought would be simple: Find out how and why the cyclone warning system had failed so badly. But one week into his mission, Frank was getting frustrated at his lack of progress. So far, bumping around through assorted conference rooms and weather offices led to little more than sob stories from heartbroken counterparts. He hoped he'd have better luck today.

As he drove to a meeting, one particular visit weighed on Frank's mind. He'd met with the person in charge of East Pakistan's meteorology department. Everyone in the country, from rickshaw drivers all the way up to Yahya Khan himself, blamed this man for botching the warning. They blamed him for the deaths. Many called for his execution. In the middle of a typical bureaucratic spiel about protocol, the man stopped and looked over his desk at Frank. His calm cadence gave way to a crushing dread. "I did everything I was supposed to," the man said.

The man's tone wasn't defiant or excuse-making. It carried the weight of a decisive person who knew all too well that, if he'd only had the right information—the right guidance—he could have saved tens of thousands of lives. Maybe hundreds of thousands.

"I did everything I was supposed to." He repeated it over and over, looking deep into Frank's eyes as if Frank could absolve him.

The bureaucrat told Frank that as soon as he received the first signs of the brewing storm, he passed the message down the line to channels that issued warnings to coastal communities in the storm's path. But West Pakistan sent the message too late and too garbled to make people realize that they needed to take immediate action.

Frank's heart went out to the guy. He had a similar feeling anytime a hurricane killed just a few dozen in the States when better warnings could have reduced the toll. It was an inconceivable burden to bear. Frank tried his best to console the department head, to remind him that meteorology is not the exact science either of them would like it to be.

Problem was, all the scientific camaraderie in the world wasn't getting Frank any closer to understanding where exactly the system broke down. If he was going to fix the storm-warning operation, he needed to know where the weaknesses were. So today he was going to try something a bit different.

An hour earlier, Frank read a couple of local newspapers over breakfast. The death toll seemed to have settled at a number equivalent to the entirety of Miami and Orlando perishing in an afternoon. The papers blamed foreigners, claiming that the American and Indian weather services hadn't shared information fast enough.

Frank knew that wasn't the problem. Pakistani authorities could pick up the ITOS 1's signals from their own satellite receivers in West Pakistan just as easily as the American's could back at home. He started to fear that the real problem was that his boss, Gordon Dunn, had messed things up. Not only because his changes to the hurricane warning system never reached the public but because the system he had set up required leaders in East Pakistan to get permission from West Pakistan before they could issue an alert. The bureaucrats in Islamabad gave no such approval.

That damned bureaucracy, Frank thought. *Confusion and delays caused this catastrophe.* Preliminary estimates showed that 90 percent of people on the coast knew that some sort of storm was on the way, but less than 1 percent sought out higher ground or stronger buildings because of a delayed, incomplete alert.

The car inched through the traffic past walls full of political slogans splashed in red paint in the Bengali script. Frank had no idea what they said, but they were at least a colorful distraction. Eventually, the car arrived at a military compound, and attendants ushered him to an army general's office.

The man wore a khaki uniform with stars shining on his epaulets. The two men eyed each other as Frank fished out a notebook to record the details. The general led with a rhetorical question: How can Pakistan ensure it was never caught unaware again?

Frank zipped through a few obvious options: better satellite uplinks, coastal radio transponders, and a new organizational structure. One by one, the general shook his head at Frank's replies, as if he hadn't hit on the right solution just yet.

Stumped, Frank thought back to when he'd worked as a weatherman in Okinawa, when the military sent planes out to spot typhoons.

"Surveillance aircraft?" Frank asked.

The general's eyes lit up. "Exactly!"

Frank mentioned his time in the service, and the general was thrilled to hear that Frank was a fellow solider. Now they could get down to business.

"You work for the World Bank," the general said. "We need you to send us a C-130 to monitor the Bay of Bengal. Think of how many lives a single plane could save."

Frank jotted down C-130 in his notepad, along with several question marks. The Lockheed C-130 Hercules could certainly fly in a circle, but it was a massive combat transport plane meant to move troops and military cargo. It was also a solution from a bygone era. Satellites could do the job much better, and he told the general so.

"Besides, I don't know if the World Bank is going to authorize a plane that doubles as a troop transport," Frank said.

"Of course they will. They have to!" said the general. "It's the only way." Frank was perplexed. Only way for what?

He then waved his hand cautiously at Frank's notebook. Once Frank put down his pencil, the general leaned over the desk and spoke quietly. "You see, Neil, this cyclone solved about half a million of our problems."

Frank grasped for words while a squeaky ceiling fan whirred above. He came up empty.

Being military men, the general said, they could drop all the bullshit and be candid. In just a few weeks, the entire country was going to stand for an election, and Bengali voters didn't have the interests of the country at heart. The more Bengalis that perished, the better Pakistan would be for it in the long run. And that C-130 could watch the skies during the days and get his boys embedded across East Pakistan to sniff out insurgents in the nights, a perfect match.

Then the general abruptly sat back in his chair and returned the conversation to all the great things that the World Bank could do to help Pakistan. Frank picked up his pencil and jotted, only half listening. His mind cemented itself on the comment.

Had the general all but admitted this was a man-made disaster?

Perhaps reading Frank's lack of focus, the general tried to soften the edges: "But that doesn't mean that we want it to happen again, of course."

Frank packed off to the InterContinental. He stared at the back of the driver's seat the entire ride. The system failure wasn't technical. It was political. West Pakistan didn't care if Bengalis died.

The general sent him a message over breakfast every morning, reminding him that they really did need that plane. And every morning, Frank left the note on the table under his coffee cup.

The last night of his stay, Frank heard what he thought were gunshots in the distance. As he looked out the windows of his big, beautiful suite, he saw the city clearly for the first time: the graffiti, the demonstrations, the troop movements. The whole place was a powder keg. Whatever was happening with the government, the military, and the weather service, it wasn't anything a better warning system could fix on its own.

On the series of planes back to Miami, Frank sat in a stupor, shell-shocked and overwhelmed as he looked at his notes while passengers drank and chain-smoked around him. He longed to hug his baby girl, then get back to the National Hurricane Center's Atlantic desk, a place where he knew his alerts would be taken seriously. He started to pen the technical report that the World Bank had asked for.

One thing was for certain, though. Frank would be damned if that Pakistani general was going to get his greedy hands anywhere near a C-130.

23

Yahya Khan and Zulfikar Ali Bhutto

ISLAMABAD, WEST PAKISTAN

NOVEMBER 30, 1970

Eighteen days after landfall

Seven days until the election

"After these elections, is it your intention to remain as president?"

Surrounded by squat, potted palm trees and brilliant marble slabs, Yahya took a long drag off his Chesterfield in the President House courtyard and contemplated the question. He put the cigarette down and exhaled, giving a little grin, as the folds of his neck jiggled over the too-tight collar of his starched white shirt.

"In our process of democracy, the people will elect their president. Unless I offer myself in the election, I cannot remain the president. And I am not offering myself in these elections."

"You will not?" The off-camera Associated Press interviewer was skeptical that Yahya, or any leader in Pakistan for that matter, would ever relinquish power so freely.

"No. My temperament is not to be president. My makeup is not that way. I joined the army to be a professional solider, and my aim is to go back to my army. I have three years of service left, then I can retire. My only satisfaction is in restoring democracy to the nation—as a soldier. Does that answer your question?"

Indeed, it did. They wrapped the interview, both satisfied. Yahya was sharp today, sober, and it was time to put his foot down. Some of his generals suggested that he postpone the election or cancel it entirely. Nobody would be that surprised. There was always some excuse or another that they could use. National security, or the Indians maybe. But Yahya wouldn't of hear it. He'd spent six months installing an unimpeachable electoral commission, and he'd funded it lavishly with one sole aim: to deliver a legitimate, fair, and free election. What use would it be to throw all that hard work away now?

Even Bhutto nagged Yahya about it. He suggested they stuff a few hundred ballot boxes—or at least close a few hundred polling places in East Pakistan to give them a little edge. Nobody would notice. Or better yet, he could just cancel the elections, then "kill 20,000 Bengalis and all will be well."

Yahya scoffed. Gumming up the works now, so close to the finish line, would be like failing to build roofs on the buildings of Islamabad. It was preposterous.

Yahya would see this to the finish. He would deliver real democracy through real elections, not a fake democracy through fake elections.

Things weren't always this tense between the pair. In fact, they drained a bottle of whiskey together almost every night. Tumbler in hand, Bhutto bitched to Yahya incessantly about the softness of former Pakistani leaders. Why couldn't they be more like Stalin, a man who had just the right gut instincts? For Bhutto, the more grandiose the plan, the better. He thought that a thousand-year war with India would be Pakistan's ideal policy.

A few years earlier, Bhutto invited Yahya to share a meal at his Karachi mansion. Yahya stood in Bhutto's opulent reading room, looking up at the shelves. His eye caught a beautifully embossed silver book displayed smack in the center. Puzzled, Yahya read the title: *Mein Kampf*.

"Aha! I see you are admiring my collection. That one is my absolute favorite, aside from the Mussolinis to the right, just over there," Bhutto said. He thought that reading and rereading such works made him sophisticated, showed that he was learning from Europe's great men.

Bhutto got his first taste for politics as a student at the University of California at Los Angeles and then the University of California at Berkeley in the early 1950s. He organized against Richard Nixon's senatorial effort—the one where he earned the moniker "Tricky Dick" for slandering his opponent as a communist. When Bhutto returned home to Islamabad, his dad bought him a position as the country's finance minister as a thirtieth birthday present. Bhutto loved the power that the position gave him, the control over other people' lives. He married his first cousin, and when she couldn't give him kids, he bought her a cottage a thousand miles away and then took a student as his second wife. As an Italian journalist described him, he was "born to charm [and] . . . he looked like a banker who wants to get you to open an account in his bank."

Yahya knew in his heart that Bhutto was a true friend.

But now, just seven days before the election, Yahya couldn't understand why Bhutto insisted on putting his thin banker's thumb on the scale.

Bhutto made his case late into the night, trying to lean on Yahya's army sensibilities: The conventional wisdom was that any Punjabi who would let a Bengali rule him would be a laughingstock; any leader who let it happen would be the ultimate disgrace to his clan and country.

But no matter how much he schemed, Bhutto never understood that Yahya's mission from Ayub was to hold a free and fair election. Yahya refused to cheat, laboring under the same belief system that built Islamabad without a single kickback. He'd complete the mission to the letter.

Bhutto had a legitimate reason to worry. There were three hundred seats up for grabs in Pakistan's National Assembly, a parliamentary body roughly similar to the US House of Representatives. The main difference from the American system (besides not having anything like a Senate) was that whatever party took a majority got to pick Pakistan's next prime minister. If population were all that mattered, then the Bengali-speaking East Pakistan had an advantage with 162 seats against 138 in West Pakistan.

Although polling was nearly nonexistent, most pundits agreed that Mujib's Awami League might secure about eighty seats at best, with the other eighty-two eastern seats split between Bhutto's Pakistan People's Party and an assortment of local parties. It would be a solid showing; Bhutto would be in charge, but Mujib would have enough power to influence policy.

Not to be stymied by Yahya's unexpected backbone, Bhutto opened a new strategic front. He ordered his campaign manager to strike a deal with the opposition's team. Three weeks before the election, at the InterContinental Hotel bar in Dacca, Mujib's and Bhutto's campaign managers hammered out a power-sharing agreement. Regardless of the exact number of seats either won, the deal ensured that Bhutto would be prime minister, and Mujib would get a bit more autonomy for Bengalis.

Bhutto loved dealing with Mujib. He was always so willing to believe in the words of men.

24

Mohammad Hai and Yahya Khan

MANPURA, EAST PAKISTAN, AND ISLAMABAD, WEST PAKISTAN

DECEMBER 7, 1970

Twenty-five days after landfall

Election Day

A golden dawn broke over Manpura on December 7, 1970. Election day. Hai ambled toward the town square. Debris was everywhere, but at least most of the bodies were buried now. A grizzled shopkeeper fired up a burner to make a pile of oily snacks for the long day ahead. He flipped on his radio and tuned it to a staticy Radio Pakistan broadcast.

A few dozen other early risers joined Hai around the shop. The shopkeeper turned up the volume as loud as it could go so that people in the back could hear the distorted sound. Hai said a quick prayer for a miracle—a free and fair election. They had no recourse if Yahya rigged it, and in Pakistan, elections were always rigged.

But no one knew for sure what would happen. Hai chose to stay unrealistically optimistic, a feeling familiar to any fan of a team that's a massive underdog right before playing the champs. He couldn't help dreaming, *What if every Bengali voted for one man?*

The radio broke in with a bulletin about long lines at polling stations in Dacca and Chittagong and irregularities with unsecured voting boxes. It was concerning but nothing cataclysmic when fifty million people were voting for the first time in their lives. Hai could only listen as a spectator. The government told Hai and the rest of Monpura's erstwhile voters that they'd have to wait a month or two to cast their votes, because it would be impossible to get poll workers to the island.

Hai tried to cheer up Malik while stoic broadcasters went over various scenarios. Malik wasn't upset about the election prognostications but, rather, about the fact that he was spending his nineteenth birthday on a makeshift cot. Earlier in the week, he'd jumped on the back of a horse for the first time since the storm. Most of the animals were still too spooked to ride, but a wealthy relative let Malik borrow her, just to get her some exercise. Malik took off in a blaze. All he wanted to do was run at top speed and forget his surroundings for an hour or so, but when he willed her over a too-high jump, she landed hard on unseen storm debris.

The horse bucked Malik, and he landed on his shin. The sound of the shattering bone replayed in his head again and again. When he looked down, jagged white ridges protruded out of his lower leg. A doctor told him that while the bone would heal and the pain would go away in time, his dream of playing in Dacca Stadium was over. Worse, with it, maybe their dreams of being big shots in the Awami League were gone too.

Hai manned his post by the radio all day. Finally, at dusk, the announcer said that the polls had closed. Election officials—mostly Punjabi—collected unlocked boxes of ballots from around the country and delivered them to a select few counting centers, also mostly Punjabi-run. They tallied the fingerprint-smeared paper ballots through the night, refusing attempts by journalists to get a sneak preview of results or monitor their actions behind closed doors.

The next morning at President House, fifteen hundred miles west of Manpura, Yahya's boxy black-and-white televisions were all tuned to the government channel: Pakistan Television, otherwise known as PTV. At midnight, PTV started airing what it promised would be twenty-four nonstop hours of election coverage. This was an innovation in election entertainment. By contrast, NBC's 1968 presidential election coverage in the United States lasted less than three hours. Dressed in black slacks, white starched shirts, and skinny black ties, half a dozen dashing PTV anchors posed in front of a huge display that looked like the Fenway Park scoreboard. Below it, piles of green-and-white wooden number squares were ready to slate into place as results rolled in.

Yahya's advisers claimed victory for Bhutto before a single vote tally was announced.

"Pakistan is saved!" Yahya intoned with triumphant bravado on Election Day. He told advisers, journalists, and anyone else within earshot that democracy would be the only thing that could make Pakistan truly great, that he was right all along in pushing so hard for it, and that, in the coming hours, he would fulfill his audacious promise to deliver Pakistan its first-ever free and fair election.

And by God, he delivered. Yahya ordered the votes to be counted transparently and the results reported in real time. His own thumb still stained with black ink from when he voted yesterday, Yahya pulled off what no other Pakistani leader could in its quarter century of existence, shutting up the naysayers. Yahya was sure he would be remembered as a hero and a patriot—Pakistan's father of democracy. He probably pictured his face on the hundred-rupee note. He poured himself a double Black Dog and leaned back in his executive chair to soak in the glory of his creation.

Just after breakfast, Pakistan Radio announced the first results. The Pakistan People's Party got three of three seats in West Pakistan, and the first five East Pakistan seats went to the Awami League. The five seats didn't mean anything in the grand scheme of power, but they were thrilling nonetheless: They meant that rumors about ballot stuffing and outright fraud probably weren't true. The election would be legitimate, not some dictator's majority of 99 percent.

An hour later, the first big numbers hit the wires. Yahya watched as the PTV anchors placed a bunch of 1s and 2s to Bhutto's side of the big board. Bhutto was coming in much stronger than expected, with a flurry of seats. While Hai grimaced in Manpura, Yahya called Bhutto to invite him over for a celebratory dinner.

The PTV anchors continued to stack the numbers up on Bhutto's side of the board without much commentary, their starched shirts now rumpled after eight hours of nonstop pontificating. The coverage was getting stale. The presenters ran out of real material hours earlier, and the numbers weren't that hard for viewers to grasp. With twelve hours of airtime left to fill and election updates coming only once an hour or so, one anchor grabbed a book of elephant jokes from his bag. He read through it twice, asking celebrities who passed through the studio to comment on the quality of his jokes. One producer had the bright idea to add some dramatic music during the dead time whenever they switched anchor teams, a tactic later copied in TV newsrooms all over the world.

Results in East Pakistan took longer than in West Pakistan. Hai paced outside the shop, trying to keep perspective. No matter who won, they'd all still be hungry tomorrow. More people arrived to the square every few minutes, including Malik on a pair of crutches. He and Hai shared a little bowl of rice and lentils. By noon, Bhutto's PPP scored seventy seats in West Pakistan, with dozens more likely to come. If they got anywhere near their expected fifty seats in East Pakistan, Bhutto would become the prime minister and could shut Mujib out of power entirely. Hai braced himself for the worst.

But then Dacca delivered a shock wave. The Awami League swept almost every seat in the city—fifty-six out of fifty-eight districts. The Manpura crowd let out a surprised cheer. Hai yelped along, then tried to calm himself, calculating the remainder of the votes. Of course the intellectuals of Dacca all voted for Mujib. It was the countryside voters that would make the difference. People like him. Could Mujib deliver rural votes?

Radio Pakistan broke in with another big update. Bhutto's PPP now had eighty seats in West Pakistan alone, an avalanche. The Manpura crowd fell silent, then a wave of murmurs set in.

Hai and Malik shared a worried glance as the last wisps of sunlight vanished in the dusk. A big PPP win might mean a crackdown on Dacca's student protests. Hai's and Malik's thumbprints were literally all over those Dacca student protest petitions. Hai shuddered at how easy it would have been to simply leave his name blank. Depending on the mood of the moment, they could be arrested by the end of the week. Hai could hear his mom's voice saying "I told you so" about the dangerous world of politics.

The anguish didn't last long. A young newscaster interrupted with a breaking bulletin. The announcer warned the millions of people hanging on his every word that the news would be a shock. Everyone at the shopkeeper's stand held their breath.

The Awami League had secured a hundred and three of East Pakistan's first hundred and six seats.

The crowd roared as if Hafiz had knocked a game winner into the back of the net. Hai crunched the numbers himself with a pencil and paper, in partial disbelief at the figures. A hundred and three meant, at the very least, a strong minority government for Mujib.

Bengalis were mystified, incredulous. Yahya had kept his promise: free and fair elections. The people were speaking. Foreign reporters rushed to the PTV studios, craning their necks around the cameras to the big board onstage. They wanted to witness history, too.

The hits kept coming: a hundred and fifteen of a hundred and seventeen for Mujib in East Pakistan, then a hundred and thirty-three of a hundred and thirty-five. Malik got up to dance around the little radio until the pain in his leg forced him onto a chair. The shopkeeper used the last of his generator's fuel to power a single lightbulb for the crowd. Hai circled and recircled the magic number: a hundred and fifty-one. What if Mujib got enough votes to lead all of Pakistan? Was Yahya going to be their unintended savior after all?

As the sun set on Manpura, Radio Pakistan made it official: The Awami League won a hundred and fifty-one of East Pakistan's first hundred and fifty-three seats, guaranteeing that Mujib would be Pakistan's first democratically elected prime minister.

Hai couldn't find words to fit his emotions. For the first time, Bengalis had equality. They had power. Hai thanked God and hoped that his mom was smiling at the results as she looked down from heaven.

Hai hugged Malik. This was a time for a new beginning. In the afterglow, they talked about the future—about how they could be leaders of Manpura and help build a more equal society. They found a space for hope for the first time in their lives. Malik thought it was the best birthday present he could have possibly gotten.

At President House, Yahya squinted at the TV screen. The numbers were right there in black-and-white. The anchors spoke matter-of-factly about the results, impressed by how smoothly everything had gone off. They complimented Yahya on his stewardship. The nice words cooled Yahya's temper, but he couldn't shake the feeling that something was very wrong in his country. When the entire vote tally finally came together a few months later, the Awami League beat the PPP a hundred and sixty seats to eighty-one, with sixty-two seats going to other political parties. It was a blowout.

To get his mind off of things, Yahya opened the CHINESE CONNECTION folder, gathered his thoughts from the China trip last month, and wrote an overdue telegram to Nixon about the progress. Only then did he bring in his election advisers to make sense of the situation.

"What in the devil's name is happening here? Where on earth has your assessment gone?" he demanded. The day before, his advisers had assured him that Bhutto would win. Bhutto himself guaranteed it. Now they assured him that the whole country was beaming with pride that Yahya brought Pakistan real democracy; only Yahya could have done it so well.

Still uneasy, Yahya comforted himself in the fact that at least the nation would remember him as a hero.

With General Rani at his side, Yahya called Bhutto to congratulate him on his strong showing in West Pakistan. They had that at least. Maybe Bhutto would have some insight on how this result could even be good for them—and perhaps help them win the next election.

"You idiot, Yahya!" yelled an apoplectic Bhutto in place of a hello. "Now the bastards will think they deserve to rule this country!"

Surprised by the outburst, Yahya tried to conceive of some political ploy that could salvage the situation and make everyone happy. Rani came up with a bright idea: What if Bhutto and Mujib could be co–prime ministers? Yahya asked Bhutto if that might work.

Bhutto screamed some more at Yahya's absolute thickness.

"I don't see what all the fuss is about, Bhutto. You've won the minority party convincingly. You can sit in the minority and still be a very powerful man."

Bhutto laughed in the president's face at his naivety. It was time to poke the soft spots. He blamed Yahya for Pakistan's inevitable downfall at the hands of the Bengalis. "You're nothing but a Queen Elizabeth," Bhutto said, "a useless figurehead. A *woman*."

"Don't think I'm a soft chap, Bhutto! Never!" Yahya's manhood was under attack. That would not do. "You are simply a clever and venomous toad."

Yahya's horrified advisers huddled in whatever dark corners they could find. This was the sort of strategic disaster that gets scapegoats thrown in prison. And no one could quite tell yet where Yahya's mood would end up.

Despite all the promises to destroy each other's reputation—all the rapid-fire claims and counterclaims of incompetency and mother fucking—the two men had one thing in common: They'd be damned if they'd ever let "those black bastards," "those pretend Muslims," "those secret Hindus from Bengal" rule their nation. Not after they'd both sacrificed so much to get to this point. Even Yahya's advisers did a one-eighty after hearing the conversation; now they said that history would never forgive Yahya if he gave that traitor Mujib power. Surrounded by men telling him that his beloved country was on the precipice of disaster, Yahya came up with a new mission: He would save Pakistan from itself.

At midnight, Yahya hung up and poured himself another double Black Dog. He kicked his advisers out. The whiskey cooled his temper as the ice cubes bounced against his lips. Bhutto had his chance and failed, that much was sure.

What Yahya needed now was not some politician with promises but a man of action, someone like him. Yahya switched off the blabbering TV and had a deep think. Step by step, he sketched out a scheme of how the coming months could play out. His dreams of being Pakistan's father of democracy might have to wait, but law and order had to come first.

Yahya picked up the handset of his black rotary phone and asked the operator to patch him through to an old friend, a man whom he'd fought Nazis with. A man who'd saved his life. A man who had the fortitude to do what needed to be done.

The man they called the Butcher of Balochistan picked up on the first ring.

Yahya Khan and Tikka Khan

A fit and trim Lieutenant Yahya Khan stood tall in the darkness, or at least as tall as one could while entombed in an American M3 Stuart tank that barely cracked seven feet itself. A few subordinates gazed in awe at their leader, awaiting his genius orders.

It was ninety degrees outside but must have been over a hundred and ten inside the rolling hotbox. Punishing summer sunlight flittered in through the steel plating's few open slats. Yahya's khaki uniform and brightly polished boots flickered in and out of view whenever someone stuck their face against a slat to peer outside.

The Nazis were half a mile away, give or take. It was hard to tell for sure, since the entire horizon was flat and shimmered with endless blowing sand. Yahya's tank—and the two hundred men under his command behind him under the Third Indian Motor Brigade—lay right outside the nondescript town of Tobruk, Libya. The British Indian Army had just launched a new offensive against the German general Edwin Rommel. Yahya's team was one of a dozen Indian companies fighting for the Allies in the North African desert.

Fifteen years of nonstop training all came down to this moment. Yahya was the son of a lawman, raised behind gated enclosures of one kind or another throughout his childhood. Guided by his strict father, he made first in his class in British India's most prestigious military academy. There were better shooters in his class, better athletes too, but nobody was going to out-patriot Yahya—or outwork him. Yahya studied late every night while his classmates knocked off to get drunk and chase women. He completed every assignment, every mundane task, to the letter. He even adopted a thick British accent, in what he thought was a posh dialect, to impress his superiors.

His efforts paid off. Yahya already stood out to his British Indian Army superiors as a rising star when World War II began. They loved the way that others gravitated toward him in the mess and barracks. He was a natural leader, serious yet jovial at the right moments. Yahya made lieutenant at twenty-two, earning him the privilege of leading men into battle.

Yahya gave his company the order: Full speed ahead, knock out those Nazi chaps with everything they had. If he could prove his bravery and honor here, he'd be on the fast track to moving up the ranks.

Or at least that was the idea. On his first day of North African combat, Yahya directed his entire company right into an ambush. Whether it was because of an exceptionally bad series of coincidences or due to his exceptionally bad tactical maneuvers is lost to time. Either way, they were surrounded. They didn't even have the chance to fight their way out. The entire company surrendered.

The Nazis imprisoned Yahya and his men and made plans to ship them to a prisoner of war camp in Italy. While awaiting their fate, the men shared stories they'd heard of how the Nazis treated prisoners, none of them good. Yahya did his best to keep morale up, but his jokes fell flat. The men were too busy thinking about hard labor and starvation to be in a laughing mood.

The Nazis packed Yahya and his men in the cargo hold of an old transport boat for the trip. Every now and then, their Italian captors let a few prisoners come up for a few precious breaths of fresh air. Those lucky prisoners had a mysterious habit of accidently falling overboard into the azure waters.

The imprisoned unit trudged ten kilometers in chains from the Naples pier to camp PG 63. Yahya expected the worst. He and his men shared space with a few hundred other British Indian POWs that the Nazis had captured around North Africa. The advance hadn't gone that well for anyone, apparently. Together, they stumbled their conjoined feet across the camp threshold into a truly shocking scene.

The place looked like a hotel.

As it turned out, the Nazis courted anyone who could be considered an honorary part of the Aryan race—and if they could dismantle the backbone of the British Empire in the process, all the better. Decades earlier, German scholars parsed linguistic evidence that pointed to ancient migrations and technically made Indians the original Aryans. Indeed, that's why the Nazis adapted the ancient Hindu symbol of the swastika to their own purposes.

For Yahya and his compatriots, this meant the Germans treated Indian POWs with country club–level kid gloves. The Nazis fast-tracked cigarettes, ice cream, and wine for the prisoners. The pope visited and donated a violin for the prisoner orchestra. Their library carried Aristotle and Plato in multiple languages. The POWs had so much extra chocolate that they handed it out to destitute Italian children who came by to watch their twice-monthly concerts of Indian song and dance.

Now this was a place a funny man could get some jokes in. Yahya had a ball.

Yahya met a fellow prisoner from his homeland by the name of Tikka Khan. Given their officer status, Yahya became second in command, behind the camp's senior officer, P. P. Kumaramangalam, with Tikka third in rank. Like everyone else, Tikka loved commiserating with Yahya. He quickly became Yahya's right-hand man.

Yet Tikka was cut from a different cloth. Born Mohammed Khan, he took up his middle name, Tikka (meaning: red hot), as a symbol of pride. Tikka was fiery and ruthless, a vicious boxer who loved the dopamine rush of meting out punishment. He especially loved pulping anyone who dared tease him about his bent nose. While Yahya grew up wanting love and adoration, Tikka wanted people to fear him. Tikka loved the British Army through and through, but he also admired the Nazis' way of total warfare—how they saw even their own civilians as not only an expendable nuisance but also a tactical soft target.

Where Yahya was a straight-laced soldier, Tikka was a straight-up killer.

And Italy bored Tikka out of his mind. He didn't join the army to sing. So Tikka hatched an escape plan for the pair. He convinced Yahya that all the chocolate and violins in the world wouldn't mask their stink of being lazy prisoners after the war while their brothers bled on the battlefield. They made their move. It failed. Tikka tried again. That failed too. The camp commandant told Yahya and Tikka that if he caught them again, original Aryans or not, he'd order their execution.

Then Tikka had one last idea. It was brazen, yet simple. On a crisp October night, Tikka, Yahya, and a few others tunneled out from their quarters, using the shovels and pickaxes that the Nazis gave them to keep in shape.

Once free from the camp, they were still stuck deep in enemy territory. The Allied lines lay two hundred miles away. They dashed east to avoid Naples, through endless rows of Aglianico wine grapes, traveling only at night. They weaved southward, around Nazi battalions that littered the rolling Italian countryside, figuring that the Germans were too busy raiding Renaissance-era farmhouse cellars to notice them. They hid under the floorboards of peasant shanties during the day, grateful to eat any table scraps that the impoverished farmers could spare. They circled back south of Naples, in the shadow of Mount Vesuvius. Somewhere along the way, Yahya lost a shoe and pushed on with one bare foot.

All the while, Tikka looked out for Yahya, and Yahya looked out for Tikka. They bonded in that struggle to survive.

Eventually, Yahya and Tikka made it to the Allied front lines—as luck would have it, right near a British Indian Army battalion. Wracked with hunger, they hugged comrades and lapped up the sunshine and awaited new orders.

A month later, Yahya and Tikka bid adieu as brothers in war. For Yahya, it was time to go home; his rise up the ranks had already begun. Despite his failure in North Africa, he became a major and then the youngest colonel in the British Indian Army. He started teaching military strategy at Quetta Staff College alongside two other war heroes: a brash loudmouth named A. K. K. Niazi and the thinker of the bunch, a Bengali named M. A. G. Osmani.

Tikka didn't want an academic life. He wanted action. So he raced to the Burmese front lines for another dose of slaughter against the Japanese. Even after the war, Tikka continued his career with the single-minded goal of remaining as close to combat as possible. He made colonel in 1954, when he headed up an artillery division in central Pakistan, then he found a chance to advance again in 1958 when an insurrectionist movement in Balochistan tried to claim independence from Pakistan. Tikka modeled his counterstrike on the Nazis' scorched-earth tactics. He shelled towns and villages with indiscriminate artillery for a decade. With eighty thousand troops under his command, his vicious reprisals eventually exterminated the thousand or so rebels, along with a large swath of the civilian population. The heavy-handed tactics crushed the rebellion, and his actions earned him the moniker the Butcher of Balochistan.

Publicly, he eschewed the nickname.

Privately, he loved it.

ACT II

OPERATION SEARCHLIGHT

25

Yahya Khan

Pakistan's prime minister–elect, Sheikh Mujibur Rahman, couldn't get Yahya on the phone. Almost two months after the election—and only a matter of weeks before the official transfer of power was supposed to take place in the National Assembly—Yahya still wouldn't take a single call from Mujib. They wrote letters back and forth. Yahya's were filled with platitudes and contained absolutely no clarity about what a transition of power would look like. Exasperated, Mujib invited Yahya to Dacca for a summit. Surely it was all just a misunderstanding.

Yahya gave a noncommittal reply, reminding Mujib that the country wasn't yet his. He told Mujib, "You have the votes, but I have the power."

If Mujib didn't know any better, he would have thought that Yahya, the self-styled steward of democracy, wasn't going to honor the election after all. It was an ominous thought, so Mujib tried to woo Yahya by backtracking on parts of his signature six-point plan for Bengali autonomy and political representation. He wrote Yahya that "they're not the Qur'an or the Bible," everything was negotiable.

This perked Yahya up a bit. He agreed to the visit.

Mujib didn't know that Yahya was already shipping thousands of troops to East Pakistan or that he'd picked an old friend to lead them,

General Tikka Khan. But Tikka was a blunt instrument, a "break in case of emergency" general, and Yahya still daydreamed of cheering crowds and his face on the rupee. Soaking up the international accolades about his election success, Yahya began to believe he could pull a statesman's rabbit out of his hat instead of setting Tikka loose. If he could task Mujib with getting the Bengalis in line, keeping all the kudos and power for himself, then all the better.

Yahya set up shop in Dacca's presidential quarters a couple of days later and invited Mujib over. Smelling an opportunity, Mujib accepted without hesitation. He tried convincing Yahya with straight-shooting army talk, sharing tall tales of when he cheated at poker on Indian trains, back before Partition. Yahya ate it up, telling his own rose-colored tales about battlefield glory.

After drinking and chain-smoking foreign cigarettes together for a day, Yahya thought Mujib wasn't so bad, all things considered. Maybe this was a man he could work with. Despite all the scheming that Bhutto had done to shut Mujib out, Yahya saw the chance to get the election business sorted out once and for all. They hammered out a handshake deal: Yahya would agree to all of Mujib's six points and he would be a ceremonial prime minister, under two conditions: that Pakistan stay unified and Yahya continue on as president.

After the meeting, Yayha looked uncharacteristically relieved. He told an adviser that it was all done but the transition: "It's going to be Mujib's government soon."

The summit's breakthrough looked so promising that Richard Nixon, who was meeting with Greece's prime minister at the time, bragged about Yahya's diplomatic acumen. He told his counterpart that the Greeks could learn a thing or two from Yahya about doing democracy.

Yahya left for Islamabad to tell Bhutto the good news. At first, Bhutto took it calmly, suppressing panic from creeping through his devilish smile. He nodded along as Yahya bragged about the agreement. Yahya didn't seem to realize that it left Bhutto out in the cold.

This time, Bhutto didn't yell. He didn't call Yahya a disgrace. Instead, he invited him up to his lakeside retreat for some well-deserved relaxation. But, Bhutto said, it would have to be secret. If word got out about it, the press would suspect something. Yahya agreed.

Safely tucked away from the public eye at his retreat, Bhutto wormed his way into Yahya's deepest thoughts and motivations. Bhutto talked and wandered around the lawns. They took his little two-man boat out into the middle of the lake. He talked while they loaded guns and peered down the sights. They even talked when they shot at fleeing ducks.

The chatter didn't score them a fowl dinner, but Bhutto hit a bull's-eye in Yahya's waffling psyche. Alone in the cabin, Bhutto plied Yahya with food and drink, reminding him night after night that Mujib would never settle for being just prime minister; he would surely betray them all. Bhutto forgave Yahya for being taken in by that silver-tongued politician. The devious and charismatic Bengali could be intoxicating, Bhutto said. That's what Bengalis were best at. He reminded Yahya of their postelection talk—of the importance of securing their country's legacy—and warned him again that having a Bengali leader would surely lead to Pakistan's dissolution.

Bhutto saved his coup de grâce for the final night. "Yahya, what if we made me prime minister? We would finally be the team we always dreamed of being. We would be unstoppable."

Bhutto had the magic ability to make even the most horrible things sound reasonable in a room full of skeptics. Now here he was, one-on-one with a man already inclined to give him what he wanted. Yahya didn't need much convincing by this point. All he needed was one last push.

"Yahya, you will be remembered as Pakistan's greatest leader. I am sure of it. But only if we handle this Bengal issue once and for all," he said. He offered to deal with the politicians and press so that Yahya could focus on what he did best: being a global statesman and overseeing the military.

"What should we do, Yahya? You're the military mind. How should we solve it?" Bhutto asked, laying bread crumbs in Yahya's brain that he knew would lead the army man to action.

For Yahya, the day in Dacca with Mujib already felt like a distant dream. Here he was, back with his own people, in surroundings that he knew and loved. He didn't quite trust Bhutto, but he knew Bhutto was right about Bengal. His head was swimming. How could they craft a permanent solution to these endless agitations?

Yahya knew that martial law wouldn't be enough. The Bengalis needed their spirits broken.

He told Bhutto about Tikka and the emergency plan they'd devised on the night of the election. They called it Operation Searchlight. The name didn't mean anything in particular; Yahya just thought it had a catchy ring to it. They'd adapted it from an existing worst-case contingency plan called Operation Blitz, which the army had put together in case of a government breakdown. And they'd already put several key pieces into place.

Bhutto was so thrilled that he offered to oversee the operation personally.

Yahya knew that an action this massive needed a mountain of men. He'd already had Tikka ship five thousand soldiers to Dacca. Now, he ordered fifty thousand more troops to East Pakistan.

He gave Tikka a special, essential task: Every detachment from Karachi to Dacca was to be sent off with the same indoctrination ritual. The soldiers first received white T-shirts and khaki chinos—to "blend in" to the civilian population. Then, in the terminal, Tikka and his minions gave rousing pep talks, with two imams in the wings. He told the junior cadets that he had inside information that East Pakistan's Bengalis were just pretending to be Muslims; in fact, most Bengalis were secretly pork-eating, conniving Hindus trying to steal Pakistan and make it a Hindu country. Given their reputation for bravery and piousness, Tikka said, these troops were specially chosen to fight for their faith and their country. It would be not just their job, Tikka explained, but their great honor to liquidate every last traitor.

The imams then chimed in that they had read and meditated on the scriptures and uncovered good news. In special cases like these, the imams said, Islam permitted the soldiers to kill nonbelievers without consequences. They could rape nonbelievers. They could even torture them. For there was no greater sin than blasphemy, and what were the Bengalis if not a blasphemous people, only pretending to pray to Allah and live by the Prophet's example? The imams said that not only was it honorable for the soldiers to wipe out these religious fakes but it was their solemn duty as good Muslims. After all, this was a holy war.

The speeches might have strained credibility for some, but who was an eighteen-year-old sepoy (the Pakistan Army equivalent of an American army private) to call out a famous general and two men of God? Tikka and Yahya knew that the army wasn't a place where you questioned superior officers if you hoped to do anything more glamorous than clean toilets the rest of your life. They leaned on that golden rule, infecting their subordinates' heads with the seeds of misinformation necessary to get them to do horrible things.

Tikka and the imams gave that same speech every day for six straight weeks to planeloads of young Punjabi and Balochi soldiers, outfitted in civilian clothes and bound for Dacca. While the soldiers' heads were filled with bile, their hands gripped new American guns, thanks to Nixon's arms shipments.

Yahya had just one more group to win over. On February 22, he assembled his top generals at President House. Everyone could see that the handshake deal with Mujib wasn't as ironclad as it appeared. West Pakistani media called Yahya weak for failing to finalize the transition, and Bengali media whipped East Pakistan into a frenzy by calling the inaction a coup. The impatient generals asked Yahya why he was depleting their resources, sending them to peaceful East Pakistan while their sworn enemy, India, was beefing up the Kashmiri border.

From the outside it looked like Pakistan was spiraling into chaos.

But Yahya wasn't going to lose control again. With Tikka by his side, Yahya told the surprised generals how everything was going according to plan. Yahya was never going to give Pakistan over to a Bengali, but he needed a good reason to strip Mujib of his victory—a reason that even foreign powers, like the United States, would support. Yahya knew that stonewalling Mujib would eventually force the Bengali to call for independence. Yahya was buying time so that when Mujib's rhetoric finally did tilt over into revolution, the military response could be justified, decisive, and permanent.

The time for politics was over, according to Yahya. These ungrateful Bengalis would learn to respect raw power. His plan was simple, easily articulated to the roomful of military men: "Kill three million, and the rest will eat out of our hands."

Yahya's handpicked generals nodded their ascent. These weren't squeamish politicians concerned about death and mayhem. These were warriors, men who had bled in battles every decade of their adult lives. Men who bonded over midnight tumblers of Black Dog at officers' clubs. Men schooled in a history where Bengalis were always on the losing side because they lacked a single fighting bone in their bodies.

For the generals, Tikka was the cherry on top. Now they were really stacking the deck. After all, Tikka had squashed the Baloch separatist struggle and those Balochis, the generals agreed, were *fighters*. These Bengalis were just fishermen and gossips. This was the Yahya who they'd assumed was lost to a world of diplomacy, drinks, and debauchery. Their Yahya—General Yahya—was back.

Standing around Yahya's ornate desk, the men planned their offensive with little figurines and topographic maps. Birds chirped love songs in the garden. Then, to eliminate any possible dissent from his own administration, Yahya dismissed his entire civilian cabinet.

26

Mohammad Hai and Sheikh Mujibur Rahman

Each night, the hordes descended. They arrived like apparitions, heard but not seen as they scurried around the floorboards. Squeaking. Gnawing. Scratching. The hordes were famished, and they had acquired a taste for flesh. Like a hive mind, they chewed in shifts through the cement and broken-glass minefield meant to stop them, driven by the smell of the squirming bodies within. They raced over bare human skin by the dozens, nibbling here and there. The sensations tormented the residents as they flailed at the intruders for hours. Then, when dawn broke, the hordes vanished back into whatever holes they could find.

The Manpura offices of HELP were under siege from a plague of rats. The cyclone wiped out the island's rodents, but a few specimens made it back by stowing away on commuter boats. With the island stripped of natural predators and rotting carcasses piled up everywhere, Manpura was a garden of Eden for vermin. The rat population grew to tens of thousands in weeks. The problem was that it peaked right when they'd eaten the last of the island's lifeless remains. Famished, they turned on the living in packs, infesting every house in search of a meal.

Within a few weeks, HELP decided that the best way to deal with the rodents was to issue bounties for every dead rat that people could deliver to the HELP offices. It wasn't clear whether or not the plan was working just yet, but Hai had bigger problems to deal with.

The BBC aired a documentary about Manpura a month before. It didn't matter that Hai hadn't seen it or even heard of it: The Pakistan Army had. The documentary juxtaposed the HELP camp on one side of Manpura with the army camp on the other. On the HELP side, Hai, Jon, and others kindly delivered mountains of goods in a calm, orderly fashion. Smiles abounded. On the army side, the video showed wailing, hungry kids and army officers screaming back at them in Punjabi, a language they didn't understand. The army gave almost nothing to the civilians.

The army was furious. They did the only thing they could: take retribution on the organization that made their efforts look so pitiful. Almost overnight, the paper HELP logos pinned on shirts around Manpura went from badges of pride to targets on volunteers' chests. Most quit the organization for fear of beatings—or worse. Hai kept his on but did his best to stay out of the army's way.

Hai was far too angry to be the army's lackey. Besides, Manpura's Bengali pirate radio station had started reporting a grim rumor that made the rats look trivial: The host claimed that Pakistani authorities ignored the data about the incoming cyclone and never bothered to update their warning systems.

They knew, thought Hai, *and they didn't warn us.* While it was true that his family heard radio reports about the coming storm, they all assumed they'd be fine just taking shelter in a sturdy house, like usual. Now he learned that the garbled warnings about getting to higher ground were part of a systematic failure perpetrated by racist West Pakistani officials. At sunset, his family's house almost touched the shadow of the three-story Manpura High School. They could have easily taken refuge there, along with a hundred others. If they had, he could have hugged his mother and little brother today. His dad would be teaching now, not staring vacantly at a water-damaged wall in their dark home.

The news spread like wildfire across Manpura. Dying from an act of God was one thing. Death from a government's callous and willful incompetence was something different. It felt like a call for retribution. While they stewed about how the government didn't lift a finger when they knew that a once-in-a-century storm was coming, the ferries transported horrifying stories about how army beatings were multiplying on nearly every island. Some claimed police imprisoned Bengalis for sport. Others said that soldiers raped young girls. Still other rumors told of rich Punjabi businessmen who treated Bengali villagers like slaves.

This time, Hai didn't have to imagine the worst elsewhere. Even on Manpura, Urdu-speaking soldiers abducted outspoken Awami League activists to ask about their organization. The mood was so tense that Malik went into hiding.

Mujib heard all the stories and used them in his speeches to show how West Pakistanis delighted in cruelty. Mujib was Hai's only ray of hope, and the same was true for many of his fellow survivors. Mujib said Yahya's stalling was unconstitutional and an egregious violation of democratic ideals. He said that Bengalis had earned the right to be equal citizens of Pakistan and that he would continue to fight for them as the rightful prime minister.

Despite the rhetoric, Mujib never gave up trying to close a deal behind the scenes. But he couldn't get a straight answer from anyone. Bhutto refused to return his calls. Mujib got desperate. His patience ran out when Yahya delayed convening the National Assembly where Mujib was supposed to officially take power. In response to the move, Mujib told everyone in East Pakistan to tune in on March 7 for what he promised would be the most important speech of his life.

Hai ran around the neighborhood, inviting everyone he knew to his front yard for a listening party. He borrowed a small battery-powered red radio for the big event. In Dacca, one million people gathered at the Ramna Race Course to hear Mujib speak in person. Awami League members, wearing all white, carried long bamboo sticks that looked like closet rods to facilitate a human corridor to the podium. Mujib passed through in a jeep convoy, waving like royalty as he made his way to the stage.

Mujib started slow and somber: "My brothers. Today, I appear before you with a heavy heart. You know how hard we have tried. But the sad fact is that today the streets are being splattered with the blood of my brothers. The cry we hear from our Bengali people is for freedom. A cry for survival. A cry for our rights." Hai felt goose bumps.

Mujib continued, getting louder and angrier with each line. He spoke of twenty-three years of Bengali bloodshed and subjugation by West Pakistan since Partition and about how every student, every able-bodied man, every youth should rise up and take their revenge against that lifetime of oppression.

Hai felt like Mujib was speaking directly to him through the airwaves. This was a blueprint for obtaining justice—for his mother's and little brother's needless drowning, for his father's destroyed soul. Hai's breaths got shallow as Mujib reached a crescendo, calling for physical emancipation from West Pakistan—by every man, in every house. He begged every last listener to "face the enemy with whatever you have." He warned Yahya, "We have given blood, and we will give more blood."

Hai punched his fist in the air. *Mujib understood!*

"The struggle now is the struggle for our emancipation; the struggle now is the struggle for our independence," Mujib said. "*Joi Bangla!*" The short phrase was loaded with meaning. While the simple translation was "Victory to Bengal," it was also the underground rallying cry for independence. This was the first time Mujib had ever said the phrase publicly.

The crowd in Dacca roared back: "*Joi Bangla!*"

Hai jumped up in his yard, joining the chant. "*Joi Bangla!*" He yelled the sacred words with his neighbors, and they all chanted it together, over and over again, while the radio, a stadium full of compatriots, and the entire nation cheered with them.

Over ten minutes, Mujib made the case for revolution and gave an ultimatum: If Yahya refused to make him prime minister of Pakistan by March 25, the Bengalis would declare independence, by force if they had to. A vicious energy pulsed through Hai's veins. He'd never felt anything like it before. He was ready to fight the next army man he saw and beat him with his bare hands if he had to.

Millions of Bengalis across East Pakistan shared the same feeling.

Hai walked away with his head high and brimming with patriotism.

27

Hafiz Uddin Ahmad

MULTAN, WEST PAKISTAN

EARLY MARCH 1971

Eight weeks after the election and three weeks until Operation Searchlight

As far as the West Pakistan papers were concerned, the agitation in East Pakistan was barely newsworthy. All anyone wanted to read about was the National Football Championship. Most just called it the National. The 1971 edition was being held at the Punjabi cultural capital of Multan, a city known for its Mughal-era mosques—and for hosting a revolt that heralded the end of British rule. Hafiz flew to Multan to bring the Army Team some desperately needed glory.

For the last decade or so, the Army Team hadn't made much of a mark at the National, a tournament where teams from all over the country's two wings played in a round-robin. The winner got bragging rights for a year and a small cash bonus. Over the course of the week, Hafiz hoped to score at least a few goals, and maybe even win a game or two.

Unlike when Hafiz played for the national team in Tehran, the army wasn't about to splurge on luxurious accommodations like single hotel rooms. Instead, they offered Hafiz quarters at the army cantonment and meals in the officers' club.

Hafiz looked around the spartan, musty bunks. He took a breath, inhaling the smell of men that only intensified in Multan's hundred-degree days. He glanced at a tournament schedule posted on the wall.

He'd gone from being a starter with thousands of fans screaming his name, to a ringer whose superior skill did little more than make an awful team a passably mediocre one. The international tournament circuit was effectively disbanded, and these piddling events were all he had left.

This year, the organizers did something new: They blocked any East Pakistan teams from competing for "security reasons." Hafiz was one of the only Bengalis at the entire tournament. He wasn't even made captain; that task fell to a lesser Punjabi player who happened to have a higher rank on his chest. At least Hafiz's teammates still worshipped him.

Somehow, Hafiz willed his team to a victory in the opening match. Maybe he could score his way out of this self-induced football purgatory. That night, he dined on chicken tikka and heavy, saucy curries in the officers' mess at a table all by himself. Other Bengalis might have complained at the Punjabi fare, but it was all the same to Hafiz. He stopped wolfing down his food when he heard the unmistakable notes of a Bengali-inflected English accent rise above the din.

Two officers, one from East Pakistan and one from West Pakistan, had launched into a different kind of sport. While nearly all Bengalis knew that Mujib had called for independence and fueled a revolutionary fervor in East Pakistan, few in West Pakistan thought it different from any other leftist blowhard rant. Newspapers wrote about the delays in the National Assembly, but the meaning of Yahya's legislative tactics was up to anyone's personal interpretation.

The Bengali stood up and pointed his finger. "Why has your Yahya stopped the assembly?"

"Mujib would destroy Pakistan. What choice does he have?" a Punjabi responded and got to his feet.

"Bhutto is a bastard."

Sensing a fistfight seconds away, more reasonable officers pulled them apart, but they were no closer to an understanding.

The higher-ranking officials chastised both officers for setting a

bad example of how military men were supposed to conduct themselves. No matter who held power, the role of the military was to uphold
the constitution and keep order in the face of the forces that would
tear a nation apart.

Hafiz nodded along. He didn't want to be involved in this sort of
fight.

Over the next week, the Army team came back down to earth.
Hafiz scored in every match, but they were bounced from the tourna-
ment by Pakistan Railways. Pakistan Airways, made up solely of West
Pakistani players, stood victorious in the end.

Hafiz tuned out the congratulatory podium speeches, with their
usual platitudes about talent and grace to God. His mind drifted to
his squad. They were tense, divided. The few Bengalis on the team
were clumped around Hafiz, and the Punjabis stood at the other end
of their space. The three feet between them felt like a mile.

Not again, thought Hafiz. Politics was getting between him and
the game he loved. Even worse, it was creeping into the army itself,
dividing officers along ethnic lines. Hafiz thought back to what the
major had said when he recruited him: The army was the one place
that was supposed to be above petty grievances and politics. Now hot-
heads all around him were acting like those student leaders who
broke up their game against the Soviets in Dacca.

Hafiz resolved to keep his head down and redouble his efforts to
stay above the fray. If his father could be a doctor and a politician at
the same time, surely Hafiz could help his fellow officers learn to keep
their political hobbies out of work and off the base. Even if the politicians of both wings of the country were at each other's throats, the
very least a man in his position could do was be professional.

28

Tikka Khan

As choruses of *Joi Bangla!* echoed back to Mujib from a million voices at the Ramna Race Course stadium in Dacca, a four-engine military transport plane landed across town. A polished black Mercedes idled alone at the end of the runway. The luxury sedan sported two small Pakistan flags, one attached above each headlight. The driver held the door to the backseat open.

While the propellers wound down, a stairway folded out of the plane's fuselage, and a solitary, middle-aged man stepped out and surveyed the lush and uncharacteristically vacant landscape. Tikka Khan's aviator sunglasses and the two dozen medals pinned to his chest reflected the afternoon sun as he walked down the stairs and into the waiting car.

Unaware of the passenger's identity behind the tinted windows, airport workers who pulled double duty as Awami League activists heckled the car as it passed through the airport gates. It wasn't personal; they taunted everyone who arrived on the military planes. Tikka glanced in their direction and made a mental note.

Officially, Tikka came to oust and succeed the East Pakistan governor. Even though the governor was Punjabi, Mujib and most other Bengalis liked him for his diplomatic impartiality, a trait that didn't fit with the upcoming operation. In order to stifle any dissent, it made sense to combine the military and state control of East Pakistan into one office. However, if Yahya fired the man without cause, it would look like he had planned the exact operation that he was planning. Optics were important. So before he sent Tikka, Yahya gave the governor one last chance to be a team player. He called him on the phone and told him, in detail, about the upcoming operation.

The governor listened in horror. He begged Yahya not to go through with it, pleading that it would lead to ruin. He said the operation would be a meaningless bloodbath that would crush any sense of political order in the divided country. The governor, who talked with Mujib daily, insisted that he was about to make a political breakthrough, and if Yahya would just come to Dacca they could solve things once and for all.

So Yahya fired him.

For the sake of appearances, he ordered the governor to resign, otherwise Yahya would blackball him from working anywhere in Pakistan. The governor penned a private resignation letter to Yahya the next day, writing "I am consequently unable to accept responsibility for complementing a mission, namely a military solution, which would mean civil war and large-scale killing [of] unarmed civilians and would achieve no sane aim. It would have disastrous consequences."

The man's opinionated letter fell flat. Indeed, Yahya prided himself on getting the last of the do-nothing, all-talk politicians out of the way. Everything was going according to plan.

Once Tikka was airborne for Dacca, Yahya finally returned Mujib's latest calls. Talks were off, Yahya said, and he'd ordered indefinite military rule in East Pakistan. Yahya taunted Mujib, warning him "not to take a step from which there would be no return." Of course, Mujib did just that during his March 7 speech. He urged all of East Pakistan to resist the regime, with violence if necessary, in order to meet Yahya's threat: "We cannot let it go unchallenged."

Tikka rushed from the Dacca airport to his first meeting, hosting a group of energized Awami League leaders who had just come from Mujib's speech. Unlike the old governor, Tikka had no time for niceties. He welcomed the men with a warning: "If Mujib talks against the integrity of Pakistan, I will muster all I can—tanks, artillery, and machine guns—to kill all the traitors and raze Dacca to the ground. There will be no one to rule. There will be nothing to rule."

His guests stood in shocked silence. Before they could open their mouths to protest, he shooed them out the door and called Radio Pakistan. He told the station head that if they replayed any part of Mujib's speech, he would jail their entire staff for treason.

Tikka changed quickly into a crisp blue suit for his next event, his swearing in at the high court. There, the chief justice—a regal, pompous seventy-five-year-old Bengali—refused to perform the ceremony on the grounds that Yahya had appointed him illegally. Instead, he held a press conference to explain how the courts were an essential backstop of democracy in troubled times.

Tikka noted the transgression, then took his polished black Mercedes back to the barracks, where he used the justice's speech for his own means. Instead of appealing to due process, he gave an invective-filled speech packed with lies to the soldiers, saying that the situation was even worse than they could have imagined. "The Awami League has committed horrendous acts of cruelty," he explained. "In Bogra, 15,000 non-Bengalis were murdered in cold blood. In Chittagong, thousands of people were killed and women raped. In Sirajganj, women and children were set on fire. The atrocities did not stop here. West Pakistani officers in the East Pakistan Rifles were murdered. Their wives were raped, [then] forced to get stark naked and serve food to Bengali officers."

Even though not a whit of what he had said was true, Tikka ordered all troops confined to the barracks, "for their protection." His Punjabi troops bounced off the walls, seething and ready to take revenge for the fictitious crimes.

Tikka promised them they'd have their revenge soon, and gave them one final directive before departing: "I want the land. Not the people."

Tikka rang up Yahya to inform him of the day's progress. The ecstatic president ordered the preparations for Operation Searchlight to proceed full steam ahead and told Tikka he'd be there next week to personally oversee the final details.

Meanwhile, Dacca's Bengalis erupted into mass demonstrations that some called peaceful protests. Others called them dangerous, provocative riots.

29

Hafiz Uddin Ahmad

His team's loss in Multan nagged Hafiz as he jogged through the terminal to catch his flight to Dacca. He felt impossibly far from home and was glad to be traveling back to East Pakistan. He cruised through security late and saw the gleaming yellow-and-green Boeing 720 with Pakistan International Airways stenciled on the fuselage above its four chrome engines. This aircraft, the crown jewel of Pakistan's civilian transportation network, was the critical link between West and East Pakistan.

Hafiz dashed across the tarmac, reaching the plane just before a stewardess in a green Punjabi salwar kameez and matching cap closed the door. He cast a sheepish smile her way, then quickly averted his eyes to search his boarding pass for his seat number. He looked down the aisle for an empty seat, scanning past row after row of passengers. All of them sported identical buzz cuts, white tucked shirts, and dark green slacks. Plainclothes soldiers. He'd never seen a civilian plane so completely full of military before.

Hafiz shrugged. It wasn't as though the higher-ups ever let the junior officers like him know what was going on. Maybe they were preparing for some military exercises. Still, he found it notable that none of the west-bound passengers uttered a single word of Bengali.

Once they touched down in Dacca, Hafiz caught a train to Jessore, where he'd rejoin his unit. He wasn't excited about telling his fellow officers that he'd lost yet another match even though the army's football team barely had any reputation left to tarnish. He'd rather be a hero than the guy who let down his service.

It was already past dark by the time the old colonial-era train pulled into Jessore station. A lone autorickshaw driver leaned against his vehicle under an amber streetlamp, hoping to snag one last fare.

When Hafiz said he needed a ride to the cantonment, the driver's eyes widened a bit and he shook his head reluctantly. "Please sir. They don't like Bengalis there. They will give me trouble," the driver pleaded.

Hafiz doubled, then tripled his offer for the ride. The driver shook his head. His life was worth more than that.

"They kill Bengalis, sir."

Hafiz frowned. This guy clearly let the rumors get to his head. It would take all night to walk to the camp, so he flashed his military ID and said that this rickshaw would be under the protection of a lieutenant of the Senior Tigers Battalion of the Pakistan Army East Bengal Regiment—an all-Bengali unit.

The tension across the driver's brow eased just a little; he hadn't realized that Hafiz was a soldier, let alone an officer. So he reluctantly agreed to take Hafiz for the increased rate. The small, bug-like autorickshaw sped through empty roads to the cantonment gate.

The soldier manning the booth peered into the vehicle.

"Identify yourself," the soldier said in Urdu.

Hafiz got out and walked up to the guard. "I am Lieutenant Hafiz Uddin Ahmad," he said proudly, expecting the soldier to salute and wave him on without delay. Perhaps he'd be embarrassed about questioning an officer's credentials.

Instead, the guard gave him a dirty look. He inspected the lieutenant up and down, scoffing at Hafiz's civilian outfit and Bengali manners, then told him to go back to where he came from.

Insubordination made Hafiz's blood boil. In the army, the chain of command was almost as sacred as devotion to God. *Who does he think he is?* Hafiz thought. Besides, with his coiled athletic frame, Hafiz had at least twenty pounds of muscle on the lowly guard.

"I am an officer. Show me the proper respect," Hafiz commanded.

The guard's eyes narrowed into reddened slits, and his hands gripped the .303 rifle in a manner that said he was considering raising it in Hafiz's direction.

The rickshaw driver cursed under his breath and turned to his passenger. "Sir, please, sir, let me leave you here for your argument. I have a family."

While Hafiz continued his stare-down, the driver grabbed the handle of Hafiz's suitcase and threw it onto the dirt. He gunned his engine, did a tight one-eighty, and sped back down the road.

This surprised Hafiz. *He didn't even take any money. He really thinks this man is going to start shooting.* Hafiz paused midthought and then, *Will he start shooting?*

There was just enough doubt in his mind that Hafiz reconsidered his approach. After all, Hafiz wasn't the one holding the gun. He suggested that the soldier ring his unit to sort it all out.

Notes of a Bengali accent cracked over the connection. The guard slumped a little bit at whatever he heard.

Within minutes, a jeep arrived from the barracks with an irate Bengali soldier behind the wheel. The guard reluctantly let Hafiz past but made a point of not saluting. Hafiz's driver told him that tensions were running high. In fact, just this week, half of Hafiz's regiment of seven hundred Bengali soldiers were shipped off to West Pakistan.

"Now there are only three hundred and fifty of us, and almost two thousand of *them*," the driver scoffed as they pulled up in front of the officers' quarters.

Hafiz tried to shake off the incident. This was the army. "Us" and "them" was anathema to their entire existence. Hafiz was sure that a superior officer would sort out the pissant guard's ill-thought insubordination in due course. Yet he couldn't help but think about the Punjabi and Bengali officers he'd seen fighting at the tournament.

The Bengali soldier grabbed Hafiz's suitcase and then leaned in close. "But it doesn't matter. We are going to teach those bastards a lesson someday," he whispered.

Now Hafiz was taken aback again. This was the same sort of nonsense the guard was spouting, but coming from the other side. Did all the men in his unit feel the same? It was his responsibility to keep his troops in line, and he didn't want any division between Bengalis and Punjabis. He hoped that giving them a quick reminder about their shared mission would clear the air.

It was late, though. He figured he'd sleep on it. Maybe things would be better in the morning. Nights always had a way of making things scarier than they really were.

Hafiz fell into a deep travel-worn sleep.

But all the morning brought were new orders. He barely had time to wring the sleep from his eyes before a messenger handed him a yellow piece of paper, ordering the rest of his battalion to ship out immediately to the Indian border for training exercises. He was to gather his men and depart within the hour.

Just like the army, he thought, cringing at the life of forced marches, rope climbing, and crawling in the mud that comprised the busywork of training a battalion of soldiers. He packed his kit and hefted the pack he'd carry for the next ninety-six hours. *At least we'll be too tired to start fighting with one another.*

Just about every Bengali on the base—except for Lieutenant Colonel Jalil, a battle-hardened sergeant named Abul Hasmem who everyone called T.J., and a few members of the office staff—had orders to join the maneuvers. A few fellow officers grumbled about the tasteless rations of rice and lentils with mustard oil that they'd have to eat on the road, after having gotten comfortable with the daily chicken and beef at the mess hall. Hafiz didn't care about the food, but he agreed that the sooner this training was over, the better.

Hafiz spied T.J. leaving the mess hall, wearing a pistol on his hip. He slapped T.J. on the back and grinned. Unlike Hafiz, T.J. never had any ambitions other than to be a career soldier; he was a real company man. His face was a patchwork of scars from 1965, the last time Pakistan went to war with India. That brutal sixteen-day conflict saw more tank and infantry clashes than any other engagement since World War II, and T.J. liked to remind everyone on the base that he single-handedly blew up an Indian tank, sending a dozen armor-piercing shots from a recoilless rifle into the enemy armor. The kill earned him a commendation for courage: the Tamgha-i-Jurat. The medal became his nickname: T.J. Now, whenever a Punjabi soldier drunkenly declared Bengalis cowardly by nature, Bengalis in Jessore could just point to T.J. and ask if any Punjabi on the base had stood up to a tank and won. While a few of them had similar medals, the point stood.

Since the war, T.J. had risen to the highest rank that an enlisted soldier could achieve. Some would even argue that, because he earned his spot the hard way, his words carried that much more weight among the rank and file than all the brass above him.

T.J. returned Hafiz's grin and wished him well on the busywork in the jungle. He'd keep the troops in line in his absence.

Hafiz and his Bengali cohort left the base in a line of jeeps and transports.

When T.J. turned back, he noticed a potbellied Punjabi officer walking through the East Pakistan Regiment courtyard. The officer barked orders in Urdu to confiscate all the personal radios on base. Leadership wanted communication with the outside world shut down. To T.J., this meant only one thing: He needed to hide whatever radios the skeleton crew of Bengalis had on hand and find out what the hell was going on.

News trickled in slowly. There was some sort of unrest in Dacca. A rumor spread that a young Punjabi sepoy fought with some villagers outside the cantonment. The villagers supposedly hacked him to death. Soldiers from the dead man's unit cast angry glances at the few remaining Bengalis. Later that evening, word went out on the base that there would be a funeral for the dead soldier in the village where he died. No Bengali soldiers were allowed to join.

None of this made much sense. The village was within sight of the cantonment walls. When T.J. looked in the direction of the so-called funeral from his house arrest, all he saw was a wall of flame and thick plumes of black smoke. *Why would they perform a cremation? Muslims bury their dead. Only Hindus burn them*, he thought. *That can't be right.*

He squinted his eyes. It looked like a soldier from his camp was dragging a woman from her thatched-roof house by her hair and ripping off her sari. T.J. saw the soldier pull her behind a wall. The staccato *pop* that hit T.J.'s ears a split second later eliminated any skepticism about what his eyes were seeing. He heard another gun-shot, then another.

It wasn't a funeral. It was a massacre.

"Those bastards. *Behanchod*, sons of dogs," T.J. cursed without any care about who was listening—or any superior officers watching his discovery.

T.J. left the viewing post and gave the few East Bengali Regiment men simple orders: "Keep your weapons. Don't give them up, even under a direct order. Shoot anyone who tries to take them by force." But there was just one problem; they had hardly any ammo.

Word spread among the Bengali contingent that, at some point, the two factions could end up facing off against each other, but they couldn't strike first. There were far too few Bengalis on the base to make any sort of coup d'état. Instead, they drew up quick plans for how they could resist the overwhelming force of Pakistani soldiers if they had to.

Completely cut off from communication, Hafiz and the rest of the Bengali regiment weren't due back for more than a week.

30

Yahya Khan, Tikka Khan, Sheikh Mujibur Rahman, and Zulfikar Ali Bhutto

DACCA, EAST PAKISTAN

MID-MARCH, 1971

Seven days until Operation Searchlight

"YAHYA IS WELCOME AS A GUEST OF BANGLA DESH."

Yahya read Mujib's quote in the *People's Daily* out loud in the backseat of Tikka's Mercedes as they left Dacca airport together for the InterContinental Hotel. He twisted the paper as if he were wringing a wet towel. In the car behind them were Yahya's advisers. And in the car behind that, were three comfort women that General Rani arranged for his stay.

Tikka hadn't been governor for a week yet, and Dacca was already a cauldron set to boil. The airport was on lockdown. The army stood confined to the barracks while rioters burned West Pakistani paraphernalia in the streets. Hecklers at the airport gates increased fivefold; as they passed, Yahya rolled down his window to make out what they said. He later wrote in a court affidavit: "The abuses hurled . . . were so filthy that even a foreign enemy would not use such phrases, like 'go back to West Pakistan, army dogs!' 'Go back, Yahya's dogs!'"

As Yahya and Tikka drove through upper-class neighborhoods, a startling scene zoomed by their windows. Almost every single house and apartment building flew a green flag with a red circle in the middle. Inside that circle was the yellow outline of the eastern wing of Pakistan all alone. It was the flag of a free Bangladesh. Yahya thought it looked like an amputated limb.

The motorcade lurched down the boulevards as Awami League activists chanted independence slogans at the intersections. Yahya didn't see a single national flag anywhere along his route. Even when they pulled up to the InterContinental, a big Bangladesh flag flew out front.

Yahya drove to army headquarters later that day. His political advisers peppered him with questions along the way. He hadn't told them anything about his secret strategy. They couldn't figure out why Yahya was so inactive as disaster unfolded all around them, or why he refused to entertain their plans to defuse the tension. One perplexed adviser said that "his plump face radiated health and vitality, there seemed to be no burden on his mind or conscience of the tragic situation." Every time they brainstormed a new strategy, he just smiled and stared out the car window. When they reached the barracks, he made them wait in the lobby.

That night at headquarters, Yahya and Tikka held a secret meeting with a few select military commanders. Yahya went first, warning them that Mujib was a threat to the integrity of Pakistan. "The bastard is not behaving," he told them. It was time to put Mujib in his place.

Tikka was up next. He drew a map of Dacca on a big chalkboard and outlined platoon movements and unit responsibilities. He pinpointed every target group in the city. Using intel gathered from his spies, he described the whereabouts, proclivities, and favorite haunts of every person on his exceedingly long list of enemies. Tikka circled Mujib's house on the board. He circled the entrance to Dacca University, as well as the Iqbal Hall dormitory, which he called the Awami League's youth headquarters. He circled dozens more locations with the white chalk. He circled neighborhoods of the politicians, of the poor, of the foreign journalists, and of the Hindus.

"Any questions?" asked Tikka.

The commander of the air force raised his hand. He didn't understand this operation at all. Those weren't military targets on the chalkboard. He didn't see how securing those locations achieved any strategic objectives. The proposed actions would only jeopardize lives. He suggested political diplomacy.

The room stank with an awkward silence. Yahya ignored the commander. He turned to Tikka. "You can get ready."

Yahya fired the commander of the air force the next morning.

That week, Tikka zigzagged by helicopter to military bases across East Pakistan, explaining the secret mission to the heads of each. He briefed the command in Jessore to plan for an operation that would cut off any spontaneous resistance by Bengali units. Leaving Tikka to handle the logistics from here on out, Yahya moved on to his plan's final step: the window dressing. He called Bhutto and told him that Dacca was set for his arrival.

Bhutto came to Dacca three days later. He'd been sending inspirational telegrams to Mujib all week about how they were about to lead Pakistan into a glorious new era. Bhutto told Mujib that only the two of them could save Pakistan and that they needed "to march forward hand in hand as brothers."

Mujib was so excited that he offered to host Bhutto at his house. He wanted to be there for Bhutto, like Bhutto had been there for him in the past. Not even Yahya knew that Bhutto had been slow-playing his mark for a decade now. It started when Bhutto was the first person Mujib met after getting out of prison for leading protests in 1962. Mujib said his wife could make them an exquisite meal and they could play poker until dawn.

But there was no time for poker today. Bhutto politely declined Mujib's invitation, saying that his security team wouldn't allow it but that he'd be just down the road at the InterContinental.

The visit started inauspiciously. Bhutto's plane made a crash landing at the airport after two of its four engines mysteriously failed. Bhutto made his way through the phalanx of insults at the gate, just like Tikka and Yahya had. But unlike Tikka and Yahya, he came with a detail of six huge Sikh bodyguards shadowing his every move. They wore all white, except for their red turbans, black knives, and cobalt submachine guns. Yahya would later yell at Bhutto for not being more subtle.

Bhutto had reserved the Presidential Suite at the InterContinental, but he got a bum's welcome. Employees and guests jeered at him in the lobby, pointing and yelling over his guards' heads. The desk clerk made himself scarce for the check-in procedure. When he finally found someone to give him the key to his top-floor suite, an OUT OF ORDER sign mysteriously appeared on the lobby elevator. It vanished once Bhutto trudged to the stairwell.

Bhutto was oddly oblivious to the insults. He acted as if he knew something the protestors didn't. Up in the room, he spoke to a reporter on the phone and said cryptically, "The cyclone may not have taken its full toll yet."

That night, Bhutto met with Tikka and Yahya to jointly finalize Operation Searchlight. In their final tweaks to the plan, they cut the provisions about arrests and trials that the initial planners painstakingly accounted for. There would be no need for those.

The next day, Tikka debriefed Hafiz's commanding officer. The military needed to handle the Bengali troops in just the right way once Operation Searchlight kicked off. Meanwhile, Yahya invited Mujib and Bhutto to his Dacca residence for talks. Mujib adored Bhutto's telegrams but was still upset with Yahya for backtracking on their agreement. Mujib anticipated a tense discussion, resulting in a compromise that delighted nobody but everyone could live with.

Instead, Mujib walked into an ambush. Over afternoon tea served on fine china—and shadowed by Bhutto's submachine-gun-toting Sikhs—the first thing Bhutto and Yahya told Mujib was that the six-point plan was off the table, as was Pakistan's prime ministership.

Mujib couldn't believe it. Had Bhutto just been gaslighting him this entire time? He tried to reset the discussions by appealing to Yahya's human side, reminding him what East Pakistan had been through. "I'm here to reach an agreement with you, Mr. President," he said. "So many people are dead from the cyclone, so many people are dead."

For Mujib, getting to an agreement was the only way they could properly honor the dead. He'd staked his reputation on it. He told Bhutto they had to find a way forward together—for his people's dignity as well as his own. After all, he'd just won a free and fair democratic election. The people had spoken.

Bhutto interjected, annoyed at Mujib for trying to pull their heartstrings, "How was I responsible for the cyclone, Mujib? Had I been the one to send the cyclone? Mujib, you have one more opportunity to prove your good intentions."

Bhutto told Mujib that the only way forward was if he gave up all of his key demands by March 25 at the latest, including the six points and his leadership of a united Pakistan. "If you refuse," he said, "I promise that martial law will be imposed in its classical role."

Playing good cop, Yahya then said that they still wanted to make Mujib prime minister, but they had to be convinced that the Bengalis cared about West Pakistan too. Yahya ran through a laundry list of excuses for why Mujib's other demands, like establishment of the National Assembly, hadn't happened. It was a security issue, Yahya said. It was a political issue too. What would minority politicians in West Pakistan do in an assembly like this? And there was also the legal angle to consider. We all know what happens when the lawyers get involved, right Mujib?

Mujib bit the tip of his pipe. He needed to get his thoughts together and calm his shaky nerves. He went out to the veranda for a smoke. Yahya went to the drink cart. Bhutto followed Mujib out the glass doors.

"Mujib, my friend! Let's talk bluntly out here. Besides, I think that this place is bugged."

Bhutto leaned in and whispered, "Don't worry! This is all an act. We still have our deal to run the country together once we get Yahya out of the way. You will lead the East, and me the West." He told Mujib that he could even rename the place Bangladesh if he wanted.

Mujib listened but kept his distance, unsure how much trust he should put in his old friend. It felt like another trick.

Tumbler in hand, Yahya barged out onto the veranda, interrupting the discussion. "Why are you two acting like shy newlyweds? That's no way for a honeymoon. Here, let's hold hands and be friends."

Yahya put down the whiskey and everyone held hands. Mujib bought the president's masterful performance. He agreed to keep negotiating while Yahya and Bhutto ironed out the logistics. They all agreed to start fresh in the coming days. Mujib walked out in good spirits.

After he left, Yahya turned to Bhutto. Something serious weighed on his mind. He complained that the plane he sent to fetch his vinyl rock-and-roll records from Islamabad hadn't arrived yet and that all of the TV shows in Dacca were terrible. Bhutto stared at Yahya incredulously, then left for his hotel room.

March 23 was Pakistan Day. It honored the birth of the nation as it was conceived in 1920 and then decreed into existence twenty-seven years later. Nixon sent Yahya a telegram with his heartfelt congratulations. Mujib accepted that the handover was stalled until March 25. Yahya assured him that this was the very last roadblock, and that an agreement was imminent.

Kept waiting for so long, the Awami League was ready to burn Dacca down. Loudspeakers blasted the Bengali national anthem, playing it on repeat on Pakistan Radio. The Awami League called it their Resistance Day. As expected, Mujib raised a Bangladesh flag at his house. The Soviet consulate in Dacca did the same, which no one had predicted. One boy even dared to tie a small Bangladesh flag to the gates of Yahya's residence. Yahya remained silent through it all, while his advisers tore out their hair in frustration. He tuned them out and clicked on the TV. It played the Bengali national anthem.

Mujib awoke on the morning of March 25 in an optimistic mood.

This was the day that Yahya and Bhutto promised they would settle the issue once and for all. Surely even they could see the passion for democracy in the streets. Mujib was ready to meet them halfway, or even three-quarters of the way, if he had to.

Yahya woke up optimistic too. Before going to the InterContinental, he made a detour to Tikka's headquarters. They went over the chalkboard in the briefing room one last time, calculating flight times down to the minute. Just before noon, Yahya left Tikka by saying, "It is tonight. Let's give them a whiff of grapeshot."

A smiling Bhutto invited Yahya and Mujib up to his InterContinental suite after lunch. It had a panoramic view of the city. Mujib felt something was off right away. Mujib brought a draft agreement, filled with concessions from the Awami League. It was almost everything that Yahya had said they would need in order to agree to a political resolution. Yet neither Yahya nor Bhutto seemed interested in negotiating or even reading it. They were standoffish. If Mujib didn't know any better, he would have thought they were bored.

Mujib tried to get them to recognize the urgency: "If we don't sign an agreement, there will be a revolt tomorrow." Another delay of Mujib's electoral and constitutional right to run the country, he said, would surely send Bengalis over the edge.

Yahya stared at Mujib's open, expressive face. He squinted into Mujib's eyes. "Very well! Go ahead and revolt."

That was it.

Mujib stormed toward the door. But before he could leave, Bhutto pulled him aside, promising that he'd talk with Yahya and calm him down. There would be a deal yet, Bhutto promised, but Mujib had to trust him to iron out a few last wrinkles. Punjabis were a proud people, he told him, and everyone had to save face after the past few months of upheaval. Bhutto promised Mujib that Yahya would call him that night with the details.

Mujib reluctantly agreed and went home to wait.

It was a pleasant evening. The temperature slightly under eighty degrees, no humidity, windless, not a cloud to be seen. As the sun set, Tikka's junior officers put out sofas and easy chairs on the lawn of the army headquarters, setting coffee and tea on a card table. Months of secret planning were complete, so Tikka threw a staff party to reward their hard work. Commanders even invited their wives and children.

Yahya's motorcade pulled up. His advisers opened the car doors, stunned to see an empty backseat. Yayha seemed to have vanished without a trace. Tikka told the bewildered men to relax, grab a drink, and have a seat on the lawn.

One general excused himself from the party early. It was time to get to work. His job was to remove witnesses. He rounded up the city's two hundred foreign journalists, aiming to detain them at the Inter-Continental and then deport them all as quickly as possible.

While the general sent out his roundup squads, Yahya squeezed his bulbous frame into the back of a Dodge Dart that headed in the opposite direction from the party, toward the airport. Mujib was still at home, waiting by the phone for his return call from Yahya.

The airport was deserted. Tikka canceled the evening's flights so Yahya would have the place to himself. A single unmarked plane, stocked with whiskey and soda—and half a dozen handpicked beautiful hostesses—idled on the tarmac. Yahya hustled into the plane, and they were airborne in minutes. His escape from Dacca went off flawlessly.

Well, almost flawlessly.

An Awami League activist stationed at the airport to monitor troop movements watched the president's plane ascend. He called Mujib, who put down the George Bernard Shaw book he was reading to pick up his black rotary phone. The spy said Yahya Khan had just flown out. Mujib finally realized that he'd been played.

He rang up the InterContinental, furious. "Bhutto, that son of a bitch has left Dacca."

Bhutto feigned surprise, but Mujib could finally see through the charade. It all clicked now. Mujib knew they were about to do something awful. Something evil.

He had to warn his people.

Mujib rushed around his house like a madman, wearing a maroon dressing gown over his pajamas. He ordered his staff to assemble his old radio transmitter before it was too late. He ordered his family to hide under the beds when they heard sirens in the distance and tanks rumbling in their direction. Mujib knew he only had a few minutes.

He switched on the reel-to-reel recording equipment just after midnight and gave a short, frenzied address to the nation:

> *The 75 million people of East Pakistan are citizens of a sovereign, independent Bangladesh. Every section of the people of Bangladesh must resist the enemy forces at all costs, in every corner of Bangladesh. This may be my last message. May God bless you and help you in the struggle for freedom from the enemy.* Joi Bangla.

Tikka listened to Mujib's address. Then he turned off his radio and opened the gates of hell.

31

Candy Rohde and Jon Rohde

THWUMP. Candy sat up in bed with a start. She looked around the dark room, making out the shapes of furniture in the moonlight. Everything seemed to be in place, but *something* shook their house.

THWUMP THWUMP. It felt like a giant in boots was stomping around in the jackal-infested swamp across the street.

"Jon. Jon." Candy shook him awake. "Something's happening."

THWUMP. BOOM. The explosion rattled the windows. BOOM. BOOM.

Candy raced upstairs to their second-story balcony and opened the French doors. Dacca was under attack. About a mile to her south, she saw smoke billowing up from Dacca University. Jon joined her, and they listened to the sound of bombers taking off from the military airstrip just up the road.

Candy and Jon stood on the balcony, watching tracer bullets light up the night sky, outshining the stars as they raced to the horizon. Machine-gun fire came from every direction. THWUMP. More explosions to the south. Jeeps and transport trucks sped past with their headlights off.

More gunfire, only it was louder now, coming from inside their posh neighborhood. They heard bullets whizzing by. Candy froze in place. She and Jon now found themselves in the exact combat scenario that they'd tried to avoid by picking Dacca when they were sitting at their kitchen table in Boston.

THWUMP. BOOM.

The explosions were closer. Candy leaned over the railing, squinting. Was India attacking Pakistan? Was it China? It felt surreal, as though she were watching a movie. She tried to decipher the battlefield.

"Get down, Candy!" Jon yelled, pulling her back inside and down to the floor as a building exploded on their block, sending concrete and dust everywhere.

The blast knocked out the electricity, so they fumbled around in the darkness. They crawled toward the kitchen to shield themselves from the tracers and mortars. It was the only room in their apartment that did not have an exterior wall or window.

Voices in the swamp outside yelled something in Urdu. Then Candy and Jon heard someone scream. Candy peeked around the kitchen door to try to see what was happening through the living-room windows. An American-made tank rolled by. Its chug-a-lug tracks tore up the new asphalt road.

Candy huddled with Jon under the sink, where they figured they were safest if a mortar hit their house.

Another scream from the swamp. It was too anguished to make out whether it belonged to a man or a woman. A burst of automatic gunfire stopped the human sounds. Then the tank started up again.

Candy and Jon clung to each other, both of them holding back tears. A military operation was in full force.

The shelling stopped after half an hour and Jon and Candy tried to calm themselves. For the moment, the tanks were rumbling away. Still hiding under the sink, adrenaline supplanted fear. Their minds raced for something to do that might help get them through the night.

How would they get out of Dacca if they had to? Their little VW

Beetle was outside, but it had barely a quarter tank of gas. And who knew if things were any better in other cities or in the countryside.

How would they defend themselves? The most threatening thing they owned was a dull kitchen knife that had trouble with tomatoes. Maybe they could use the empty flare gun that they took on HELP flights.

How could they help others? They had barely enough food in the pantry for themselves, and the US consulate was a mile away. Candy had seen the political tensions build up over the past few days as clearly as anyone else, but they didn't know if it was the army or the Awami League on the move—or if this battle was local, national, or international.

The sound of machine guns lulled, but the explosions didn't let up. Jon crawled back to the balcony to see if he could glean any intel. He pulled his head up to a catastrophe. All across the city buildings belched tongues of flame and black smoke so high into the sky that they blotted out the moon. Jon could make out at least a dozen fires. Barrages from rocket launchers, air strikes, mortars, and artillery increased every minute. He crawled back under the sink to relay the scene.

Candy understood now that this was the army's doing. The Awami League didn't have tanks or mortars, and everything to the north, near army headquarters, was quiet. If India or China went on the offensive, they'd surely bomb the barracks and airport. But right now only civilian targets burned. Nobody seemed to be shooting back.

Yahya was waging a war on his own people.

She thought of her friends. Bengali journalists. Bengali politicians. Bengali academics. All of them were in terrible danger. Plus, for the last few months, she and Jon rallied to the Bengali cause. If the army was massacring everyone, Candy wondered if their white skin would dissuade soldiers from killing them. In other war zones, it was often the only thing that saved foreigners like them.

Candy crawled into the living room to try the telephone, snaking her hand up the wall to grab the receiver.

It was dead.

THWUMP. BOOM. The tank barrel's cycle of launch and explosion piled shame on Candy's shoulders with each repetition. She and every other American expat in Dacca knew all too well that these were American weapons killing the Bengali people. Her own president was propping up a dictator. She pictured American bullets slicing through her friends, American bombers giving air cover to a massacre.

Candy and Jon went back to the balcony, damn the risks. She needed to bear witness to the slaughter. They watched the fires proliferate with each passing hour. Candy looked past the flames, to God. The moon and stars were as red as a furnace.

32

Yahya Khan and Tikka Khan

During Operation Searchlight's critical first hour, Tikka's shock-and-awe operation aimed to liquidate Dacca's soft targets—including universities, newspaper offices, police stations, government institutions, and known Awami League residences—before anyone had a chance to escape. The city was Tikka's body to torture, and the army was the scalpel he used to target the most sensitive spots.

Tikka's troops bolted out of the barracks around midnight in a frenzy, racing like animals to exact revenge for fictitious crimes. On their way out, Tikka urged them to "be more merciless than the massacre at Bukhara by Genghis Khan"—a siege where Genghis and his forces burned the city to the ground, killed any man taller than the butt of a bull whip, and raped women, one after another, in the town square until the city submitted. As field general, Tikka parked himself in front of his massive chalkboard map and a dozen rotary phones, each dedicated to a different field commander.

Tikka's troops started their operations with two target priorities: residential neighborhoods that housed large numbers of Awami League activists, and the Dacca University dorms. An Awami League spy in the army secretly recorded Tikka's radio communications that night:

OPERATIONS COMMANDER (OC): Work is proceeding smoothly. But the locality has so many houses that each has to be destroyed separately. Over.

TIKKA'S HEADQUARTERS (HQ): The M-24 tanks will be coming presently. We hope they will be helpful in destroying the houses. Jinnah Hall and Iqbal Hall seem quiet now? Over.

OC: We're quite jubilant about those two. Over.

HQ: Well done. Next, the Joi Bangla flag everywhere must be brought down. If the flag is flying atop any house, the owner must be punished. If any such flag is seen anywhere in the city, the consequence will be fearsome and terrible. Over.

OC: Got your message. Over.

HQ: If any barricade is seen, those in the locality will be punished. Raze all houses on both sides of the road. Repeat: both sides of the road. Wherever a barricade is seen, all inmates of the houses on either side of the road will be shot. Explain this clearly to all. Over.

OC: I am complying with the order. Over.

HQ: What about the *People's Daily*? Over.

OC: Reduced to rubble. Repeat: reduced to rubble. Over.

HQ: You have played wonderfully. Did you capture anyone? Over.

OC: No. Over.

HQ: Fine. Proceed according to plan. All the dead bodies should be whisked away before sunrise without anyone detecting. Over.

A mile north, at army headquarters, Tikka crossed targets off the chalkboard one by one. He ordered the full arsenal out on the streets: American M-24 Chaffee tanks, American jeeps, and American .50-caliber machine guns. He even sent up the F-86 jets that Nixon sold to Yahya the year before, just in case.

Tikka scowled when his hand moved over the chalk drawing of Mujib's house. Tikka and Bhutto leaned hard on Yahya to let them execute Mujib, but Yahya resisted. He reasoned that a broken Mujib might be useful down the line. Mujib was just so pliant, so willing to deal, and besides, the last thing Yahya needed was a martyr. Yahya ordered Mujib arrested instead.

After recording his midnight speech, Mujib put up a few barricades around his house. It took army rocket launchers five seconds to blow them to bits before the tanks rolled in.

> **OC:** Our boys have caged the big bird [Mujib]. Repeat: big bird is in the cage. Over.
>
> **HQ:** Hope you are having a nice time with your guest. Over.
>
> **OC:** I am thinking to give him some food. Over.
>
> **HQ:** Why worry about that? Over.

Tikka wasn't happy about letting Mujib live. After all, he was the Butcher of Balochistan, and he always wanted to improve his craft. To Tikka, that meant complete liquidation. He wasn't alone. Even Yahya's press secretary said that Operation Searchlight would be only the first step to "brainwash the people, wean them off their Bengali mores, and make them true Pakistanis . . . The Hindu influence must be eradicated root and branch, and the people who were misguiding the innocent and illiterate masses must be liquidated."

Yahya was pretty sure that Tikka could be counted on to execute his orders faithfully, but just in case, he directed Tikka's second in command to sneak Mujib out of the country before Tikka could draw and quarter him. Four soldiers handcuffed Mujib at his house and took him, at gunpoint, to the airport in a Toyota Land Cruiser. There, they strapped him into a seat, alone, on a cargo plane bound for Karachi.

Mujib was the only person that Tikka's forces captured alive during Operation Searchlight.

> **HQ:** If the Joi Bangla flags are spotted, administer the right medicine. Search every house, turn over every brick. Eliminate as you please. Annihilate everything. Over.

OC: I shall finish the task by eight o'clock. It will take time to gather all the dead bodies and whisk them away. Over.

One company of a hundred and fifty troops drove tanks through the Dacca University gates, firing shells at the buildings and emptying assault rifles at anything that moved. They split into two groups. One went after the students in the dorms, while Tikka tasked the rest to carry out more symbolic destruction. He ordered the university's grand banyan tree, the spiritual home of the Bengali language movement and shade-giver for infinite Bengali student debates, uprooted and chopped to bits. An American Chaffee tank made quick work of the thousand-year-old landmark.

Next, twenty soldiers ransacked Madhusudan Dey's canteen. They found its beloved owner huddling on the floor in a corner. They gunned him down without a word, then executed his wife, son, and two young daughters, simply for the crime of being Hindu. He died within arm's reach of his meticulous ledgers: a generation of documented goodwill to the Bengali people. As Dey bled out, the soldiers went on to the next building, killing students on sight. Throughout the executions the soldiers joked, "We sent them to Bangladesh!"

HQ: Tikka wants to know what kind of resistance you faced at Jagannath, Liaqat, and Iqbal Halls. Over.

OC: After we started automatic rifle operations, everything was silenced. From there, we proceeded to Iqbal. The enemies are silent. All good news. Over.

HQ: How many preys in the university? How many liquidated, wounded, or captured? Over.

OC: Three hundred or so. Over.

HQ: Very well. Three hundred liquidated, imprisoned, or wounded? Over.

OC: No, no. Finished off completely. The game is over. Over.

HQ: Well done! Very well done. This is the finest and easiest task. Go

on as you please. You won't be held to account for it by anyone. Let me
repeat, what you have shown has no parallel. Again, I would say well
done. Well done! You have given excellent news. Over.

With the main targets secured, some platoons went on extracurricular pursuits. Tikka emptied out the barracks, ordering his tanks to obliterate residential areas. He sent them to jeweler's row in cramped Old Dacca and the maze of slums where people slept eight to a room above the family shops, where the army leveled twenty-five blocks without warning. They fired mortars into the buildings. Another unit raided the Dacca University women's dorm, where they raped the girls to death on the roof.

From his balcony suite at the InterContinental, Bhutto sipped on a whiskey while he took in the searing panorama. Tanks surrounded the hotel, and Tikka ordered the troops to shoot anyone who tried to leave. The captain in charge wrote "PLEASE DO NOT GO OUTSIDE" on the community blackboard and parked it alongside four guards holding submachine guns at the entrance. Drunk British diplomats stumbled past them on their way in after a party, only faintly aware of what was going on.

Snacking on room-service chicken kebabs, Bhutto watched the carnage from above for three hours with friends and advisers. The suite was well insulated from the yells of the journalists on the floors below and protected by his intimidating Sikh bodyguards.

Bhutto's main adviser stood next to him. Together, they watched the army bomb the offices of the *People's Daily* newspaper across the street and assassinate the Bengali editors and journalists that survived the mortars. Bhutto nodded in approval.

The adviser felt torn. "Boss, I feel a great sadness. All this mayhem."

Bhutto scoffed. "A hundred thousand died in 1947 for Pakistan. Maybe the same number will die this time too. So what?" But Bhutto also fancied himself as Pakistan's greatest statesman, so he thought about just the right phrase to capture the moment, to get everyone to believe in patriotism again and forget Mujib forever.

Bhutto felt the spark of inspiration. He turned to his adviser. "By the Grace of God, Pakistan has at last been saved."

A couple hours later, Tikka strolled out of the operations room and onto the second-floor balcony as a red sun broke over the horizon. He cleaned his sunglasses with a handkerchief, put them back on, and surveyed Dacca's obliteration. Aside from the crackling fires, the city was as silent as a photograph. "Oh, not a soul there!" Tikka exclaimed with confidence. With joy.

Tikka felt a strong pat on the back. He turned, and Bhutto returned his broad grin. Bhutto said he saw the whole thing, and came over to promise Tikka that together, they would make Pakistan great again.

Tikka went back inside, where big white X's covered the names of alleged traitors and spies on the chalkboard. The base's mess hall overflowed with breakfast celebrations. Tikka passed a plate of oranges from Karachi around to Bhutto and his subordinates as they delivered their reports. A colonel confided that, after last night, his nagging sense of guilt simply evaporated; he could finally kill his countrymen without remorse or other vestiges of conscience.

Much of the rank and file beamed with pride, literally thumping their chests whenever they saw superior officers. The radio relayed bits of information about a possible mutiny in Chittagong, but nobody was concerned. One officer announced to the room, "The Bengalis have been sorted out well and proper for at least a generation," and everyone agreed.

Other soldiers compared body counts. One man bragged that he'd conducted 932 executions all by himself. Platoons of heavily armed soldiers recounted how they liquidated entire Hindu neighborhoods in a single night, butchering at least 10,000 people. Another unit gathered street children into tents and murdered every single one. The troops avenged tenfold every phantom crime they imagined the Bengalis committed.

In the first twelve hours of Operation Searchlight, Tikka's troops killed more than 25,000 unarmed civilians, as well as hundreds of Awami League activists who tried to put up an impromptu resistance with axes and farm implements. Bhutto's own calculations of the slaughter put 50,000 dead.

Tikka called Yahya in Islamabad with a status update. The president had slept soundly through the night while his troops did their bloody work. Ever the admirer of a job done efficiently and under budget, Yahya told Tikka that it was "a remarkable feat of military planning and execution. The world was amazed . . . I have nothing but praise for our planners." He was sure that other world leaders would be impressed with his ability to put down the budding insurrection so completely.

For Yahya, the best part was that almost no news leaked out of East Pakistan onto the world stage. The army managed to confine almost every foreign reporter in the country inside the InterContinental Hotel. Just three—one from the London *Daily Telegraph* and a pair of journalists from the Associated Press—had escaped the initial roundup. But even those men only managed another day or two in the field before soldiers arrested and deported them. The world would only know what Yahya released.

The official story was that the army had successfully put down a violent insurrection from Awami League terrorists. There had been some small skirmishes that Yahya ordered Tikka to "shoot his way through," but it was nothing that the nation couldn't recover from.

It was a lie, of course. But that lie impressed Richard Nixon and Henry Kissinger, who marveled at Operation Searchlight's efficiency. Nixon wished Yahya well and ordered the US government to maintain support of Yahya and his internal operations. Yahya even dashed off a quick telegram to China to assure them that, no matter what they heard, everything in Pakistan was under control.

33

Candy Rohde and Jon Rohde

That same morning, Candy stared out at the eerie red dawn. She and Jon spent an entire sleepless night watching mortar fire as screams and gunshots filled the air. Neither was sure what to do next. Should they make a run for the US consulate, where the consul general, a man named Archer Blood, would surely be planning some sort of official response? Or should they stay in hiding and somehow arrange for a ticket out of the country?

With the city still smoldering from American munitions, neither of them felt like running away. So Candy made the same choice she did after the cyclone: She decided to see if they could make a difference. They went downstairs, grabbed their bicycles, and unlocked the front gates.

Swerving through fresh tank treads that marred the asphalt, the couple cycled the silent streets. They traced the military's path from block to block, until they heard a sound that was somehow worse than the deathly quiet: flocks of crows feverishly cawing to one another about fresh sources of food. The shrill squawks rang down from the rooftops, echoing off the buildings.

Candy and Jon stopped outside the dark houses of every friend in the neighborhood and called their names. Only one answered, a fellow expat. He said he had seen three foreign journalists lined up for execution by trigger-happy sepoys. A colonel, who just happened to be passing by in a jeep, suggested that the soldiers go after less-prominent scalps instead. It was a stroke of luck for the journalists.

Candy and Jon looked at each other. The illusion that they had special protective status as white foreigners shattered in an instant. Any soldier whom they saw on the street could end their lives. They still had a choice: Rush home and bolt the door, or investigate this massacre? They agreed to press on. Their expat friend turned his shutters back down; he wasn't going anywhere.

They rode past one bombed-out shell of a building after another. Their favorite restaurants and cafés were now all burned-out husks.

Jon gazed into the still-smoldering interior of a restaurant when he heard engines just around the corner. The couple dashed behind a vegetable cart as a convoy of three army jeeps rushed past.

Once the jeeps disappeared into the distance, they ventured back into the streets and turned a corner. That's when they saw a body lying haphazardly in a ditch by the curb. They moved closer and realized it wasn't just one corpse; there were dozens. Men, women, children, the elderly—all, it seemed, gunned down at different times and dumped in a collective heap. Some were well-dressed, in expensive silk saris and suits; others wore only rags.

Candy and Jon worked up the courage to look into the faces, to see if they knew these people. Each body was a case study in ways that humans slaughter each other in war. A woman's corpse showed a bullet wound in the palm of her hand. The bullet's explosive force had torn half of her face and neck away. She died trying to ward off the bullet or, perhaps, begging the soldier for her life. Some people took bullets in their backs as they ran away. Others lay in a fetal position with single headshots. Candy gagged.

All around Dacca, army soldiers celebrated their victory over the defenseless population, delighting in enacting any cruelty their imaginations could muster. On one corner, troops played football with a victim's head. On another, soldiers beat a rickshaw driver to death for running a stop sign. Down the road, a third group erupted in cheers when they discovered two Bengali girls hiding in the trunk of a taxi—the teenagers were forced onto a transport truck going back to the barracks. There, an American consulate worker saw truckloads of prisoners arriving wearing the uniforms of the East Pakistan Rifles— the all-Bengali border-guard force—as he sat outside the gate. He then heard a single gunshot every ten seconds for thirty minutes. The soldiers executed the prisoners to forestall any organized resistance in the future. The trucks came back out of the barracks empty.

Candy and Jon didn't know if the massacre was over or just beginning, but they hoped that the apparent lull in mass murder would last at least a couple of hours. They went to Jon's lab to see if there was anything left of his life's work. On the way, they passed an area that used to be a small slum, but the slum was missing. Only blackened rubble remained.

They rolled up to the lab and knocked their kickstands down. One of Jon's Bengali colleagues rushed over to them.

"We saw the army men torch the houses," he said. "The people had no choice but to run outside. The army shot them even though they were screaming for mercy. So many people were killed."

Somehow the colleague managed to escape amid the massacre, but he needed someone who could protect him if the army reappeared. "Please. They will come back to kill us all."

Every Bengali in Dacca was a target.

Candy nodded at Jon. They told the man that they would shield him. They hoped that their house could be a safe zone and asked the man to spread the word that they would protect everyone they could. Then, they biked home to prepare the flat.

Two hours later, twenty-six people crammed themselves into Jon and Candy's little apartment. Candy emptied her cupboards for a meal, while Jon closed their shutters and peeked out the front gate, watching for soldiers. Inside, they shared a roast duck and a coconut-cream pie with the refugees. It was a delicious pairing under the circumstances, but nobody had much of an appetite. They told Candy about the night's horrors: how the soldiers laughed as they killed and how they promised to come back to finish the job. Everyone—Candy included—kept asking why.

All of the Bengali news channels had gone dead, but Candy could pick up international broadcasts on her shortwave radio. She wanted to know how the rest of the world would respond. She envisioned front-page *New York Times* stories and, eventually, Yahya resigning in disgrace. She turned the dial from station to station. There was a story about farmers in Europe going broke. Then one about the Boston Patriots changing their name to the New England Patriots. But nothing about the slaughter, other than some vague murmurings on BBC radio about a small military exercise in Dacca to quell a riot. Radio Pakistan played military marches and the Pakistan national anthem over and over.

Candy's heart sank. As far as the world knew, there was no slaughter in East Pakistan. This couldn't be possible. Where were the journalists?

Candy and Jon weren't the only ones who noticed the conspicuous lack of news. When Archer Blood, the top diplomat at the US consulate, heard about journalists being deported, he put out the word for anyone with a camera to document what was happening. He'd relay the evidence back to Washington, all the way up to the president himself if he had to.

News of Blood's request made it to the Rohdes' living room. This was something that they could do—document the slaughter before Tikka cleansed the city of evidence. Jon grabbed his Nikon and a lens from the wooden shelf in their living room. They had a single unexposed roll, which meant twenty-four chances to document a genocide. Jon cursed his thoughtlessness at not having more film on hand.

They boarded up their windows and told the twenty-six Bengalis not to answer the door, no matter what. A friend from the Ford Foundation, Stephen Baldwin, scored a ticket on the only plane allowed to leave East Pakistan that night, and he agreed to smuggle the roll out in his baggage. They fired up their trusty VW Beetle and headed to Dacca University, praying that they picked a route free of army patrols.

A man approached them the moment they rolled onto campus, trusting their foreignness. "It's horrible what they did," he said, leading the Rohdes to Jagganath Hall. The student dormitory bore pockmarks from gunfire all over its walls. The group walked slowly, speechless. They gazed at bloody handprints on the walls and pools of blood on the floors and in the stairwells. Everywhere red streaks traced the paths of soldiers dragging corpses just hours earlier. Candy followed one profusely bloody set of uneven bare footprints down a hallway. The tracks came to a sudden end in a bathroom.

Jon snapped a photo and wound the Nikon's silver metal dial.

The man led them to a burial site covered in the marks of tank treads. He said he counted a hundred and three corpses before they closed the mass grave. "Any door that wasn't locked, they shoved open and entered. We could hear our colleagues pleading with them and their wives sobbing and begging. But what could we do? We were too terrified to help."

The faculty housing hosted unspeakable scenes: children shot and bayoneted in their beds and pregnant women shot in the stomach, their fetuses birthed out of the gaping wounds. Candy and Jon documented the scenes, taking turns shooting and watching for troops.

On their way back to the car, two terrified old women came up to Candy. They asked a favor, something that the day before would have been nothing, but today would be a life-or-death request: Could they get a ride to the jetty? Secret boats were taking Bengalis across the river where they could escape into the countryside or even to India. But walking through the streets with soldiers everywhere meant certain death.

Candy herded the women into the back of the Beetle before Jon could say a word. But they had a problem. The fuel-gauge needle dipped almost to the R, meaning there was only one gallon left. There was no way to get more fuel. They needed to document the slaughter and drive back home. If they had to abandon their vehicle and walk, they'd never get the film to Baldwin in time for his flight. Jon wondered why they kept having such bad luck with gas, but Candy was resolved. She insisted that they had enough to make it to the jetty.

They transported the women, taking care to sneak them through an alley to the drop-off point, using the Beetle as a shield. They drove on to Old Dacca, passing jeeps and troop convoys that ignored them. The smell of charred flesh was everywhere. But it was strongest where little green Bangladesh flags fluttered in the air. Helicopters thumped overhead, while troops hung out of their open doors with weapons in hand. They fired indiscriminately into neighborhoods and at any groups of civilians trying to escape into the countryside. Bodies of Bengali policemen littered the street corners.

Snap. Candy's thumb wound the dial, putting the roll's next exposure in place.

They drove to the Old Town entrance, careful to elude a large troop buildup. By the time Candy and Jon arrived, the great Shankar Bazaar looked as though an erupting volcano had covered the neighborhood in smoldering gray ash. The night before, Tikka directed tanks to each side of the bazaar, ordering the regiments to fire every last shell they had into the homes of the Hindu conch-shell jewelers, sari shopkeepers, and fruit sellers. Then they poured gasoline around the entire bazaar and used flamethrowers on anyone who attempted to flee. The district went up in flames. Bodies and half bodies hung grotesquely from the tops of ruined walls and amid piles of debris.

Candy walked through the desolation in a trance. She stopped, fixated on a few jagged white shards sticking up out of the ground. Her eyes focused and tried to make sense of the curious objects until she realized they were the remains of conch-shell bangles, just like the ones she'd wanted Jon to buy for her a lifetime ago.

A young boy ran up, recognizing Jon somehow. "Doctor! I need a doctor!" he called, not waiting for a reply before pulling Jon's sleeve. Candy ran behind the with the camera.

Jon followed the child through a narrow gulley. They entered a courtyard in which sat a middle-aged man in a stained kurta. Blood spread into the soaked fabric across his midsection.

"When did this happen?" asked Jon.

"Just now."

Jon bent down over the man. His stomach was half hanging out. If they were in a hospital with a stocked operating room, it might have been possible to save his life. He looked at the man's wounds. There was nothing he could do. Not with a camera instead of a scalpel. Jon looked in the man's eyes. A dying man doesn't want to hear "if only." Jon held his hand and comforted him silently as the man's brown eyes shifted from fear and pain to acceptance.

A burst of machine-gun fire shook Jon out of his daze and back into the reality of a war zone. He and Candy said a too-quick goodbye and raced back toward their Beetle with the young boy, desperate to at least save his life.

A young teary Bengali couple leaned on the car when the Rohdes arrived. Their neighborhood had been torched and their family and friends murdered before their eyes. The couple begged for a ride to the jetty.

Candy and Jon knew that saying no meant signing their death warrant. But every successive trip compounded the risk that they'd run out of gas and be deported and unable to prove the genocide had happened . . . or that they'd be killed themselves.

Candy convinced Jon to make just one more trip. Jon couldn't get the thought of the middle-aged man's open stomach out of his mind. They had to do more for those who still had a chance to live, no matter the risk. He nodded gravely.

The noise of machine guns started up again somewhere inside Old Town. The group jumped in the car and they rushed away, weaving through the bloody streets to the relative safety of the water. The boy and couple were packed in the back, along with a few other Bengalis they picked up along the way. Ash from the boy's clothing whipped around the car. Candy and Jon could taste it.

The second drop went smoothly, but the white needle was now well below the R. Candy and Jon put all their faith in the belief that their car's reserve was more generous than the gauge depicted.

They needed to document the full scope of the murders if they wanted to prove that this was genocide, not some riot gone wrong. Jon drove to a Hindu temple, where the survivors told him hundreds of worshippers were slaughtered as they prayed for safety. Bodies littered the courtyard. Others hung from the fences, shot in the back as they tried to escape. The temple was on fire.

They heard gunfire. The army was still killing.

Jon used the roll's last exposure on a shot of the burning temple. Disaster struck as he wound the film: a company of soldiers spotted them from across the courtyard, about a hundred yards away.

"Stop!" a soldier yelled in heavily accented English. "Stay where you are!"

The soldiers were young, maybe nineteen. There wasn't an officer in sight. The troops sprinted in their direction, yelling at them to stop taking pictures and stand for inspection. At the very best, they'd take the camera. Candy refused to think of the worst.

But the Rohdes had a head start so they jumped in the car.

"Go, Jon! You've got to go! Go go go!" Candy yelled as Jon floored it in reverse.

The Beetle spun its wheels in the dirt, gaining just a bit of traction. Jon shifted gears and floored it again. They peeled out of the temple grounds in a cloud of dust, with the troops no more than an arm's length away.

Candy and Jon gulped for air and braced themselves for the gunshot that would shatter their window. But it didn't come. The needle was dipping farther past the R, but their little car still chugged along. Jon slowed down to conserve the last bit of gas. They coasted home just as the engine sputtered out.

They'd taken only two dozen photos, but it was enough evidence to show the world some of Yahya's slaughter. They gave Baldwin the roll of film, telling him to develop it as soon as he landed in Sri Lanka and then put it in the hands of every media outlet he could find. He was an eager and competent mule.

Soon the world would know everything.

But for now, all the world knew was that West Pakistan was celebrating like never before. People danced in the streets. Newspapers in Islamabad and Karachi lauded Yahya's success as a glorious achievement. Pundits marveled at how a simple soldier like Yahya had "mastered the political game so well."

That evening, Yahya gave a victory speech in which he declared that the Awami League was involved in a conspiracy to break up Pakistan, even in the midst of his own honest attempts at a peaceful transfer of power. He said he'd arrested Mujib on the charge of treason, banned the Awami League, and started a military operation to root out the other traitors who threatened their unified nation. As his voice rose into a crescendo of righteous anger, he declared: "This crime will not go unpunished!"

The insurrection was finished; Pakistan could go back to normal.

Meanwhile, Tikka itched to erase Bengali culture. He scrambled jets to bomb every radio station and newspaper in East Pakistan that was not already under military control. He sabotaged food supplies to trigger a famine. As far as he was concerned, civilians and traitors were all the same. That night, he rang Yahya to ask his approval for total liquidation. Yahya didn't pause for even a second before giving his affirmation.

Tikka wanted to act on another front as well. There were some nosy Americans milling about, with prying eyes and big mouths. Tikka had restrained his boys so far, but the foreigners were getting bolder, and the last thing anyone wanted was word getting out about Operation Searchlight before they'd had a chance to clean up.

It was time to stop treating the foreign spies with kid gloves.

34

Hafiz Uddin Ahmad

JESSORE CANTONMENT, EAST PAKISTAN

MARCH 29, 1971

Three days after Operation Searchlight

Hafiz and his men had no idea that the country was on fire as they marched back from the jungle near the Indian border. He didn't know that soldiers gunned down his friend Madhusudan Dey, the Dacca University canteen owner, along with his family. He didn't know that Pakistani troops rounded up his professors and murdered them on the football pitch behind his old dorm. And he didn't know that the army planned to liquidate every armed Bengali in the delta.

All Hafiz knew was that he was exhausted.

After more than a week of training, a Punjabi colonel annexed their jeeps and ordered the unit to march twenty miles back to the cantonment with all of their gear. Ordinarily, the end of exercises brought a chance to relax and bond after a few days of grueling labor. Adding a march onto the end of it felt like overkill, but the troops did as they were told. Hafiz let his men turn on the radio along the way, but no matter where they spun the dial, they only found static or an endless loop of the bombastic Pakistani national anthem. Only the military channels worked.

When the operator radioed the Bengali unit's position to the base, he got only terse responses in Urdu. A brigade commander said something over the air about organizing troops to respond to a clash between the East Pakistan Rifles and the rest of the army. The reception wasn't great. Hafiz asked for details. No one replied.

Was that a call for reinforcements? For a helicopter? I must have heard that wrong, Hafiz thought. *Lieutenant Colonel Jalil will know what to do.*

Once Hafiz cleared the gates, he checked to see if there were any new orders posted; he was happy to find none. The entire unit was covered in road dust and bone tired. His two hundred Bengali soldiers dutifully deposited their weapons in the armory, as usual, then locked its iron gate and collapsed in their bunks. Though they'd reached the base in the late afternoon, Hafiz was sound asleep within minutes of his head hitting his pillow.

He didn't dream.

Across the quad, T.J. and the rest of the Bengalis in the cantonment settled in to watch a movie: a forgettable romantic comedy. Punjabi officers stationed themselves at the doors as they turned the lights down and rolled the film. When it was dark, T.J. got up from his seat, careful not to let his pockets jingle too much. He snuck along the rows of fellow soldiers and handed out bullets that he'd surreptitiously stashed over the past week. Surrounded by Punjabis, the Bengalis all quietly loaded their pistols one bullet at a time in the darkness while the song-and-dance numbers flickered on the ratty screen.

Morning didn't do much to relieve Hafiz's fatigue. His muscles ached. He lurched toward the bathroom in the officer's quarters and splashed water on his face. The mirror revealed puffy, bloodshot eyes.

An orderly barged in as he dried his hands on an army-issued towel. Hafiz noted tears streaming down the man's cheeks.

"Sir! The arsenal is locked! The brigade commander took the key and said that Bengalis can't carry weapons anymore. We're disarmed!" Panic forced the man's voice into a higher register.

This made zero sense to Hafiz. Why would someone disarm the army? Could things on the base really have deteriorated so fast?

"They say that the Baloch Regiment is going to empty the armory within the hour," the orderly continued.

Whatever happened next, Hafiz was certain that it would be better if he was in uniform, so he picked out a shiny pair of shoes and a starched white shirt from his closet. If he was going to make a formal inquiry, it was best to look the part.

The only other junior officer in his unit, a whip-smart lieutenant named Anwar, fumed as he watched Hafiz do the buttons on his shirt. "We're not an army without weapons. The minute we reach the office, I'm going to throw down my belt at the commander's feet and resign. Bengalis cannot stand for this."

Hafiz smiled at his comrade and advised him to keep his cool. "It must be some sort of misunderstanding. These things have a way of working out."

They left their quarters together at a jog and were happily surprised that the other junior officers in their unit—all Punjabis—were just as concerned at the news as they were. They would confront Jalil together.

Hypervigilant since the village massacre three days before, T.J. had seen the brigade commander take the key from the armory to Jalil's office. T.J. watched for the slightest action that might give away what would happen next. He slipped behind the officer and followed him inside the command center, keeping enough distance to make his pursuit secret.

The commander looked angry. Sweat beaded on his forehead. His voice echoed through the concrete hallways with the air of a man who wasn't used to people questioning his orders. T.J. saw Jalil shoot up from his chair when the commander delivered an order in English, which T.J. could not understand. There was a flash of defiance in Jalil's eyes. The commander thrust his finger into Jalil's chest, and the lieutenant colonel sank back into his chair. Then the commander grabbed the nameplate off Jalil's desk, held it up in front of his subordinate's face, and threw it to the ground.

T.J. didn't need to understand the exact words being spoken to know what he'd just witnessed. It was a coup. He'd watched these same Punjabis murder innocent women and think nothing of it. He turned and ran back the way he'd come, planning to break down the armory door before the Punjabis knew what was happening.

Hafiz caught the flash of T.J. sprinting south as he walked into headquarters. He sensed something was going on and picked up his pace. When he and his retinue of junior officers reached Jalil's office, Hafiz tried to decipher the scene. His boss paced around the office, shaking his head. His nameplate lay on the floor.

"What happened, sir?" he asked. Maybe Jalil had just been demoted for a minor infraction of some sort.

"The brigade commander . . ." Jalil's eyes were beginning to water. "We are disarmed."

"What should we do, sir?" Hafiz asked.

None of this made sense, but they all felt a miasma of danger. Hafiz knew he had to stay sharp and calculating. He thought ahead to the next moves and applied his old striker tricks to read the room.

"So what shall we do now, sir?" he asked again, more force behind the words this time.

Jalil was no stranger to combat. He'd fought against India six years earlier, but Hafiz wondered if, now that he had a family, the lieutenant colonel had lost some of his mettle.

Hafiz searched Jalil's eyes for any sense of conviction, but found only the man's desolation. Then a strange calm fell over Hafiz. It was the same feeling he had on a football pitch when it was just him squaring off against a defender.

T.J. wasn't the only person dashing toward the armory. Word of disarmament spread among the Bengali sepoys. Everyone knew what it meant. Men, still in their underwear, streamed out of the bunks. Some had shaving cream on their faces. Only a few bothered with their boots. T.J. heard the soft crush of bolt cutters slicing through the metal chain that locked the iron gate to the armory just as he made it to the door. Other Bengalis, his brothers in arms, had beat him to the punch by seconds. Everyone acted on instinct alone. They knew their lives were on the line.

They stormed inside the armory. Most blindly grabbed from the rows of old British .303 rifles, Stens, bayonets, mortars, ammunition belts, and hand grenades—all the materiel that a unit could possibly need. Unlike the others, T.J. had already spent the last few days fantasizing about this moment. He knew exactly what he wanted from the armory and where he would go next.

He moved to the back of the room and pulled out a 7.62 millimeter machine gun. He pointed to two sepoys wearing only their bright white boxer shorts and told them to grab as many belts of ammunition as they could carry and follow him.

The first pops of gunfire rang through the courtyard. Half-dressed soldiers ran from the armory and fired their guns in the air. There wasn't any organization to the impromptu revolt. T.J. did not join the performance. There were only precious seconds before the Pakistanis organized their own response. Carrying the twenty-five-pound machine gun like a toothpick, T.J. flashed past a trench on the base's perimeter and dove into an irrigation ditch. From there, he crawled down a cement culvert that he knew drained directly into a field on the Punjabi side of the base. The position provided good cover and the high ground. A few days earlier, T.J. had dropped a few sandbags at the pipe's exit. Just in case.

T.J. mounted his weapon into firing position and fed in a belt of ammunition. His two sepoys arrived behind him with a few more belts of ammo. A platoon of confused Punjabi soldiers slowly formed ranks outside their barracks. T.J. saw an officer point toward the Bengali side and shout some sort of order.

T.J. had sights on the enemy. He squeezed the trigger.

Bullets pinged off the command center's concrete wall, shaking Hafiz's stunned officers out of their stupor. This wasn't just some bureaucratic mix up. People were actually firing weapons.

A mortar exploded in the central parade ground. Hafiz rushed to Jalil's window, hearing the tinny rat-tat-tat of a Sten. A major drenched in sweat crashed into the office. "The unit is in full revolt!" he yelled. "For the sake of Allah, please do something, Jalil."

Jalil just shook his head in disbelief. Almost in a whisper, he said, "Rebellion isn't possible in the Pakistan Army. It just can't be."

Bored by politics and always ready to assume that his country's problems would work out somehow, Hafiz never wanted to take part in a revolution. But those bullets flying outside weren't figments of some collective imagination. Every shot demanded he choose a side. Despite Jalil's protestations, his unit—an all Bengali unit in the sea of hostile Pakistanis—was in open revolt.

Hafiz spoke, his voice ground to gravel as he asked the question that he hoped would obliterate the blinders on his commanding officer's eyes. "Then why are they shooting?"

No answer.

Hafiz wasn't going to let this sad little officer decide his fate. He marched outside to face the situation for himself.

T.J.'s machine gun honored every trigger pull with brutal efficiency. Bullets streamed out of the culvert into the group of hapless soldiers. One moment they were planning a counterattack against the Bengali regiment; the next, clouds of their own aerosolized blood inked the air. They fell like rag dolls. One man clutched his guts. Another seemed to be gasping for oxygen with a fresh bullet hole through his lung. A few managed to scramble their way to cover.

T.J.'s mantra was "Kill before being killed." He delivered long-overdue payback, not only for the rapes and murders in the village next door but also for the years of constant derision by his Urdu-speaking comrades in arms. They called him a coward. They called him weak and said that his beloved Bengali language was "womanly." They never cared that he gave his own blood for Pakistan. Today, whether he survived for hours or mere minutes, he would be honored to bleed for Bangladesh.

Exiting the offices, Hafiz saw Bengali soldiers running through the grounds in various states of undress, wearing steel helmets with half-buttoned shirts and boots but no pants. Some of the men were shoeless but carried ammo belts and grenades.

Choruses of "*Joi Bangla*" followed gunfire aimed at no obvious targets. One man ran out of the armory clutching a mortar. He immediately set it up and started launching shells at random. Sure, some of the Bengali rank and file might have daydreamed about a revolt, but in this moment, it was clear that no one had actually made a plan for what that resistance might look like. No one was in charge.

The shocked Pakistanis were regrouping, and the chances of a bloodbath were high. There were only three hundred and fifty Bengali soldiers against more than a thousand Pakistanis in the cantonment. It was only a matter of time before the army overran the Bengali positions. Pakistani companies were already moving into position and returning fire from two sides. Everyone knew that the penalty for mutiny was death, so there was no point in surrendering now.

A bullet ricocheted off the cement column next to Hafiz. As he ducked for cover, one unbuttoned sergeant caught sight of Hafiz's officer uniform and dashed across an open field in his direction. The man dodged a mortar round along the way, arriving breathless and shaken.

"Sir, what should we do?" he asked.

Hafiz tried to process the scene. He felt the immense weight of the moment. Jalil was not the warrior he once was and would not be emerging to lead the Bengalis.

"Sir, I want to say one thing," the sergeant said. "Can you listen with some patience?"

Hafiz nodded.

"I have fought in this unit for twenty-five years. But we are in a fix now. None of us knows what will happen."

"What do you want me to do?" asked Hafiz.

"You are a Bengali officer, and we—your brothers—are rebelling against Pakistan. Who will lead us if not you?"

"But Jalil is our commander," Hafiz protested.

The man shook his head. "Commanders lead."

Responsibility for what happened to this underequipped and undertrained regiment would either fall on Hafiz's shoulders or the regiment would be exterminated. They had seconds left to organize a resistance. For all he knew, this was the only Bengali unit in all of Pakistan in revolt. If he fought and lost, they'd execute him on the spot. If he followed Jalil, he might live a little longer, but what of his men? Would he be remembered as the celebrity who cowered in the face of conflict? As a traitor to Pakistan? As a martyr for Bengali independence? Or as something else entirely?

Hafiz steeled himself. The months and years before this moment— Yahya drunkenly insulting cyclone survivors, the partisan cheers of Bengali fans in the stadium in Dacca, the savage insults of Punjabis who thought his people were less than human—came into focus.

The Pelé of Pakistan made his choice. He would lead his men with honor, for a cause worthy of his life.

He was a mutineer; he was a Bengali.

He would take command.

Hafiz followed the sergeant to a spot under a mango tree where Bengali troops had taken cover. All of the men were terrified, though some did a better job of hiding it than others. One responded to a mortar round by emptying an entire magazine from his Sten at nothing in particular.

Hafiz raised his hand to silence the man's weapon. "From now on, this war goes on my orders. From now on, no one fires unless you're certain you're going to spill someone's blood. This is a life-or-death struggle."

The men stopped firing. They had their leader.

T.J. grinned as enemy soldiers attempted to drag the body of their fallen officer back to cover. He'd laid a trap built on the universal human weakness of empathy: a wounded man transforms into bait for anyone who lets their emotions get ahead of them. Maybe the soldiers didn't know where T.J. had set up his machine gun. Maybe they thought their officer was shot by a roving band of Bengali rebels, instead of falling like a piece of cheese on a carefully prepared mouse-trap. Not that it mattered to T.J. The two Punjabi soldiers fell dead to the ground next to their leader. Then he pulled his machine gun back from the cement pipe's aperture and crawled out of sight. There was no telling how long he would have to hold this position, so he looked at the ammo box, which was already half empty. He'd have to tell the two men who followed him here to go back to the armory for more.

Starting a rebellion in a military cantonment had pluses and minuses. On the positive side, Hafiz's rebels already had defensive positions. Trenches lined the perimeter of the Bengali regiment, and the maga-zine had enough ammunition and weapons for several hours of sus-tained combat. On the negative side, the rest of the Pakistan Army had similar defensive positioning, triple the men, and even more am-munition.

To succeed in this rebellion, they'd need to fight like guerrillas, not like a standing army. That meant escaping their grim situation to regroup on more favorable terrain. Large concentrations of Pakistani soldiers covered the north, east, and south from their current posi-tions. The only way out was to flee across a dry rice field to the west. Hafiz was reasonably certain that locals in the village there would help cover their retreat, but he had no idea that Pakistani soldiers had attacked the village just a few days earlier.

The route had other, more obvious risks. A light Pakistani detach-ment covered their exit with machine guns. Running through the open field would be suicide for many, if not all of his men.

Hafiz conferred with three other junior officers, and they all agreed that it was better to fight now and die than to be hung as cowards later. He sent one of them to organize fighters to the north. Another would look after the south, while Hafiz strategized and tried to think his way out of the deathtrap that they were all in together.

The distorted sounds of the base's PA system somehow pierced through the din of battle: "Listen, young men. None of you will be harmed if you just lay down your weapons and stop firing."

Hafiz recognized the voice; it belonged to a Punjabi he'd eaten with a few times in the officers' mess.

"He's lying. Make every bullet count," Hafiz shouted to his men.

He ran back inside headquarters to stop the propaganda. Inside, Jalil and the other officers who chose to wait out the conflict talked urgently over the phone to the Punjabi commander on the other side of the cantonment.

Hafiz took the phone from Jalil and immediately recognized the voice of his former superior, a man with decades of experience waging war on India.

"Stop this madness. We are stopping the attack. Tell your boys to stop firing," the commander ordered.

"That's not possible, sir. If you are so peaceful, then tell me why your men are trying to break through our lines," Hafiz replied in smooth English.

"Listen, young man, this is not a football match. What is your intention?"

"No. It's not a game," Hafiz said.

He slammed down the receiver and told the handful of Punjabi officers to clear out of his headquarters. This was now the Bengali command post, and they weren't welcome anymore. Hafiz ordered his troops to let them live. As far as he was concerned, if they weren't carrying a weapon, then they weren't in the fight, even if they might be enemies tomorrow.

The next six unrelenting hours witnessed a cacophony of mortar explosions, bullets ripping apart flesh, and screaming men. The Pakistanis knew they couldn't safely rush the Bengali trenches, so instead, they focused their mortars on the magazine. There was an explosion as the armory went up in a ball of fire. Hafiz and his men had only the weapons in their hands and the ammo on their backs. He needed to get all two hundred of them across open ground. Now. It was three o'clock in the afternoon with the sun still high in the sky.

Lieutenant Anwar moved his men to the north of the field, and Hafiz sent light machine guns to the south. The two officers gazed out over the rough soil. Little clouds of dust floated above the earth here and there. A Baloch Regiment peppered the field with hundreds of bullets. Anwar suggested that they wait until dark, but Hafiz knew this wasn't an option. His left flank was taking more fire, an indication that the Pakistanis were preparing to invade. He squinted at the field, mentally calculating how many of his men would die if they tried to make their way across it.

He pointed toward the village. Hafiz gave the order.

Four of the men crouched next to Hafiz in the trench prepared to make the first charge. Each carried a heavy load of munitions and guns, which was all they would have available to them should the Pakistanis give chase. Hafiz nodded and said, "Allah protect you."

The men launched themselves over the barrier, and the Bengali trenches erupted in covering fire. Anwar and his machine gunners sent a ceaseless stream of bullets toward the Pakistani lines. Hafiz pulled this tactic—the "fire and move" method—straight from military-academy textbooks.

But it wasn't perfect. Hafiz watched anxiously as the field turned into a rain of deadly fire. One of the four went down. No one turned back to rescue the fallen man; it wasn't possible. He died slowly in front of Hafiz's eyes.

May Allah have mercy on the martyr's soul, Hafiz prayed. *Every one of us shoulders the same risk.*

Thankfully, the other three made it safely across. Now all of the men knew it was possible. Hafiz pressed forward with his plan. He ordered groups of four men over the barricade every few minutes. After an hour, the Bengali trenches stood mostly empty. At least a dozen men bled out in the field. They would be mourned later. The Pakistanis were closing in.

Hafiz remained in the trench with a skeleton crew, but before he could attempt his own escape, he needed to do one thing. He ran back, against the flow of his retreating soldiers, to the command post. Pakistani soldiers took cover by the shell of the armory. Soon, they would be on top of him, but he couldn't leave Jalil behind. He found his commanding officer still in his office. He hadn't moved.

"Please come with me, sir," Hafiz said.

"Where will you go?" Jalil asked. His voice rang hollow; he was incapable of courage. Then his real reason for staying became clear. "My wife and children are on the base somewhere. What would become of them?"

They both knew the answer. It didn't need to be said.

Hafiz tried one last time. "If this is war, then Bangladesh needs officers like you."

Jalil looked up at Hafiz. For a second, his eyes glimmered with hope. Just hearing the word "Bangladesh" could do that right now: a dream not dared before today.

A Pakistani major entered the room, advancing on Jalil with an open set of handcuffs. Jalil opened his mouth to speak and then shook his head at Hafiz.

Hafiz brushed past the enemy officer with ease as he turned and left.

He ran to Anwar's position as Pakistani troops gained ground.

"Jalil?" asked Anwar hopefully.

Hafiz said nothing.

They looked out across the field that they would have to cover and the dead bodies of their brothers. It was about two hundred yards. They were the only officers left. At least one of them had to make it. They would cross together and hope that the Pakistanis wouldn't follow them to the village—at least, not today.

Hafiz signaled for covering fire. His men shot from behind the mud walls that marked the perimeter of the village. Hafiz, Anwar, and the last ten Bengalis made a run for it together. Hafiz heard the relentless sounds of machine-gun fire. He couldn't tell what was coming his way and which bullets were part of his men's diversion. He ran with a full backpack, in a sprint honed from more than a decade on football fields.

Halfway there, a line of dust exploded in front of him. A gunner marked his position, but as long as he was alive, he could keep moving. He was nearly there. His eyes locked on a small, elevated mound of dirt used to keep water on the paddy. He dove forward as hot metal pierced the air around him.

He rolled forward and over the mud wall, and let out a small cheer. He patted his body for holes—maybe the adrenaline masked a wound—but there weren't any. There was no blood, no injury whatsoever.

Hafiz turned over to congratulate Anwar, but his fellow officer wasn't beside him. He peeked back over the mud walls. Anwar was fifty yards away. He shuffled forward, grasping his belly. Blood welled up though his mouth and onto his uniform. The Bengali lieutenant collapsed in the dirt, alone on the field. He died less than a minute later.

Hafiz said a prayer for his brother in arms. Not knowing what sort of resistance might greet them in the village, the Pakistanis held their positions. The battle was over for today. Hafiz made his way to the center of the group of huts and found a hundred villagers carrying sticks, machetes, scythes, and homemade shotguns. They'd come from all around the countryside, rallying to the soldiers' cause. They raised their weapons into the air for him and his men. They shouted, *"Joi Bangla!"*

The pent-up emotions of the day all welled up at once. Tears streaked down Hafiz's cheeks. Tears for his friend Anwar, for the mutiny, for Jalil's family, for his own family, for all of it. A villager lopped off the top of a coconut and handed Hafiz the cool drink. He gulped it down greedily.

A few days earlier, in the port city of Chittagong, Major Ziaur Rahman of the East Bengal Regiment (everyone called him Zia) waged a desperate battle against West Pakistani forces with five battalions of Bengali soldiers. Zia's command fled from the center of the city to an industrial area to the east where he was able to get hold of a radio transmitter:

> This is Swadhin Bangla Betar Kendra. I, Major Ziaur Rahman, at the direction of Bangabondhu Mujibur Rahman, hereby declare that the independent People's Republic of Bangladesh has been established. At his direction, I have taken command as the temporary head of the Republic. In the name of Sheikh Mujibur Rahman, I call upon all Bengalis to rise against the attack by the West Pakistan Army. We shall fight to the last to free our motherland. By the grace of Allah, victory is ours. *Joi Bangla.*

A nearby Japanese merchant ship picked up the message and Radio Australia rebroadcast the declaration, letting the world know that Bangladesh was in a fight for its independence. The Pakistan Army attacked every Bengali military unit, paramilitary force, and police regiment in East Pakistan. Thousands died in the first hours of fighting as units like Hafiz's rose up spontaneously in rebellion.

A few hours after he fled from Jessore, the broadcast reached Hafiz's desperate group of rebels too, giving them their first flicker of hope. Hafiz's unit was just one of dozens of ragtag groups of mutineers spread thin across East Pakistan's marshy river systems. The rebels were disconnected and without any concrete orders, directives, or central military organization. But none of that mattered because they all knew one incontrovertible fact: The fight for Bangladesh had begun.

35

Candy Rohde, Jon Rohde, and Richard Nixon

"Goddamnit, Henry! What is he doing over there?" Nixon asked, annoyed. Yahya was the only man who could secure Nixon's meeting with China, and this Dacca business complicated things. Archer Blood, the US consul general in Dacca, had just announced in a diplomatic cable to the entire State Department—a cable that became known as the "Blood Telegram"—that Yahya was committing a genocide. He wanted Nixon to come out and support the Bengalis, the damned fool.

Nixon was furious. Genocide was a hard thing to defend. Kissinger reminded Nixon that they couldn't publicly support what Yahya was doing. If either Congress or China got wind of their support, the CHINESE CONNECTION was as good as dead. So they had to prop Yahya up clandestinely. They had to play down the violence, too. If Yahya got deposed, it was game over. The Nixon administration had to thread the needle.

Kissinger and Nixon formulated a strategy. Officially, they'd pretend that the genocide didn't exist. They'd suppress all evidence claiming otherwise. Then they'd find some fixers adept at working in the shadows to get Yahya enough weapons to ensure total military supremacy. For his part, the Chinese premier Zhou Enlai told Yahya that events in East Pakistan were a "purely internal affair" for Yahya to solve as he saw fit and "without foreign interference."

Nixon then sent World War II ace Chuck Yeager, the first man to break the sound barrier, over from Vietnam where he met with Pakistan Air Force officials to help strategize bombing raids. Yeager thought it was barely worth his time. He surmised there was no way the Bengalis could ever defeat the well-disciplined Pakistan Army.

Yahya was doing his best to blitz through the Bengalis, but he needed a favor from Nixon. He'd kicked out the journalists, but there were a few Americans on government contracts causing trouble. Cholera lab workers, charity heads, even priests were talking to the press with eyewitness stories, complicating his propaganda effort.

Nixon understood. He ordered every American working in East Pakistan evacuated to Iran via Karachi. Once there, the Shah could monitor everyone who knew anything about what was happening in Dacca. And what was happening in Dacca was Tikka's latest agenda item: A door-to-door mop-up operation to clear out the Bengali resistance.

Jon watched from his balcony as four young sepoys searched each house on their block. Just behind him, Candy and twenty-six terrified Bengalis occupied every last inch of their two-bedroom apartment. To Jon and Candy, they were friends, neighbors, intelligentsia, maids, old men, and children. To the soldiers, they were just Bengalis. No other distinction mattered.

Jon's mind raced as the troops finished up next door and came to the front gate. *I have to protect these people*, he thought. *I have to protect Candy.*

Jon knew that opening the gate was a death sentence for the twenty-six Bengalis. Trading the Bengalis for their own safety was out of the question, and he refused to think about what the teenage soldiers might do with Candy if they shot him to get inside.

Jon took a risk. "You may NOT enter," he ordered them. "We have diplomatic immunity."

The young soldiers didn't react. They seemed totally unimpressed with the claim, though they probably had no idea what the phrase even meant. Then two of them pointed assault rifles at Jon's head. Two others pointed barrels at the gate's cheap padlock. Jon wouldn't budge.

"I'm warning you!" Jon bluffed, willing his voice to remain steady and authoritative, despite his growing terror. "Take one step forward, and you will cause an international incident!"

The soldiers glanced at each other, as if to say *So what?* Their guns remained pointed at Jon.

"This is US government property. If you come in here, there will be a massive response from the USA. You will be putting Pakistan in great danger if you take one more step."

Finally, this seemed to give them pause. Nobody was willing to risk embarrassing Tikka, in case the wild-eyed white man was telling the truth. They'd be as good as dead themselves. The soldiers lowered their guns, warily. Best to get a superior officer's approval first.

"We'll be back," one said. The soldiers jumped into their jeep and sped away.

Jon leaned on the gate, trying to calm his racing heart. The Bengalis knew that he'd bought an hour at best. They packed up their meager belongings and steeled themselves to make the dangerous hundred-and-thirty-mile journey westward to India—a several-day walk in the best of times, now two weeks punctuated by hiding behind trees and in ditches. They snuck out of the house in pairs, creeping as best they could through Dacca's nicest neighborhood on their way out of the city.

That night, Candy turned on the radio like she always did, waiting for the BBC update. Surely the photos they'd taken must have gotten out by now. She imagined breathless reports on the evening news back home in America and calls for justice filling the streets.

Her heart sank when, once again, the shortwave didn't offer any news or sense of outrage about what was happening in East Pakistan.

For the first couple of days after they'd sent out the film, Candy managed to convince herself that a delay was normal—that the reporters were probably just busy writing and fact-checking—but each morning and night that she clicked on the radio and heard nothing, her hopes dimmed. Their gambit must have failed.

She didn't know it, but the photos that they'd taken to document the atrocities by the Pakistan Army never made it out of Dacca. Their friend Stephen Baldwin from the Ford Foundation hid the cannister inside the lining of a black Samsonite briefcase, along with a list of the names of dead professors at the university and how they died. A Punjabi soldier pulled him aside for a search, just as he was about to board his plane. It didn't take much effort to find the roll of film and the list. The soldier turned to the courier, looked him in the eye, and exposed the undeveloped film to light. He crumpled up the celluloid, threw it and the list into a wastebasket, and escorted Baldwin onto the plane.

Evidence of the massacre disappeared. The army cleaned up the streets with military precision, scrubbing away any trace of genocide. According to the authorities, the burned-out husks of buildings were just the aftereffects of Awami League–induced riots.

When the soldiers returned to Jon and Candy's house two days later, they weren't interested in some random Bengalis. Instead, they came with Tikka's orders for every foreigner to pack up their belongings and clear out of East Pakistan within twelve hours. No one got to leave with more than a suitcase. Even pets had to stay behind, so Jon spent most of his last day in Dacca putting down their friends' dogs and cats so they wouldn't be eaten on the streets.

Islamabad-based US ambassador Joseph Farland assured everyone that the evacuation was for their own protection, and that while the decision to leave was technically voluntary, anyone who stayed would be thrown into a Pakistani prison. The choice was theirs.

Candy sat with Jon on the bumpy airport bus as it picked up passengers around the neighborhood, its windows clumsily blacked out. Most of the evacuees stared in silence at the horrible images passing by through gaps in the paint. Candy was elated to see her friends Marty Chen and her husband onboard and alive too. They shared horror stories of the previous days as they rode together.

A massive lightning storm hit the moment they arrived at the airport, knocking out power to a good chunk of the city. Guards rushed them into the foreigner VIP waiting lounge and forced everyone to buy full-fare tickets to Iran. The rain couldn't drown out the din of thousands of frightened Bengalis outside, begging for an airlift away from certain death. The faces of those desperate souls lit up with each flash of lightning.

Candy fumed at the injustice. Jon whispered to others in the lounge that maybe one of them could make a break for it in Karachi.

Soldiers herded the group onto the plane. Once the doors closed and the engine rumbled on the tarmac, the reality of their escape and a sense of collective duty to bear witness about what they'd seen swept through the passengers. Jon, Candy, Marty, and the rest of the deportees shouted "*Joi Bangla,*" waving miniature, handmade Bangladesh flags that someone smuggled aboard, as the plane ascended through the raging thunderstorm.

An hour into the flight, Jon, Candy, and several of the other passengers schemed while a scattering of people who appeared to be Punjabi businessmen drank their whiskeys and watched the foreigners with suspicion. There was a stroke of luck when the pilot announced that the plane would refuel in Colombo, Sri Lanka, on the way to West Pakistan. Safety protocols dictated that the crew would have to open the doors, which meant that one of the Americans could to sneak out and contact the media. They didn't have hard evidence anymore, but they could speak freely to anyone who might listen.

Jon volunteered to escape. Candy backed him up.

When they touched down in Colombo, the fuel truck and stair cars came over. Jon was ready to make his move. The problem was that each stair car had an armed guard blocking the plane's doors.

Jon stood up, willing to risk it.

Then a few of the businessmen got up, set aside their untouched whiskeys, and drew guns out of hidden holsters. They were plainclothes military. Two took positions ahead of Jon in the aisle and two more guarded the rear exit.

Jon screamed to be let off the plane. Other passengers chimed in claiming diplomatic immunity. These soldiers weren't that naïve. Jon slunk back into his seat and the plane refueled for the next leg to Karachi.

When they landed six hours later, Ambassador Farland greeted them on the same tarmac where just two months ago Tikka and the imams brainwashed soldiers into committing genocide. The passengers on the plane, most of them high-ranking US government employees, yelled at Farland about what they'd witnessed during the massacre. The ambassador told them that they shouldn't trust their lying eyes and that whatever they had seen in Dacca had some other, more reasonable explanation. They were too emotional.

Farland's wife tried to calm the women. She told Candy that the hard part was over and that she was safe now. "Don't worry about the horrible things you thought you saw," she said. "A good steak and a tranquilizer will cheer you right up."

The ambassador and his wife greeted each furious disembarking passenger with the same incredulity—and the same offer to tap into the embassy's private tranquilizer stash.

"The West Wing will never let East Pakistan go," the ambassador's wife said to Candy in what she thought were diplomatic words of wisdom.

Candy knew better.

"It's too late now," Candy said. "You'll see what happens."

A few days later, Candy and Jon lay side by side on cushioned, reclining folding chairs. Their bare feet could almost touch a pristine pool. It felt all too surreal—too artificial. Beyond the pool lay the blinding beach and glistening ocean waters that gave the five-star Karachi Beach Hotel its name. After what happened on the tarmac, the ambassador quarantined the evacuees into suites, with orders to not leave the compound.

That very afternoon, Jon slipped through the cordon and made his way to the Indian consulate. There, he told the Indian consul about the massacre and every last tank, plane, and troop movement he could remember. Jon spilled his guts as fast as he could so that he could get back for the dinner roll call, their next head count.

Jon knew that India might use this intel to prepare for war. To be honest, he hoped they would. Somebody had to stop Yahya.

While the staff spied on Candy's conversations by repeatedly "forgetting" food orders and swatting flies, she plotted how to tell the world about what she had seen. All around the pool and on manicured lawns, the Americans shared stories about what they'd experienced, putting together the pieces of Operation Searchlight. It was the first time that Candy started to get a clear picture of what was happening.

They didn't have evidence, but they were still witnesses. So they drafted a letter to Jon and Candy's senator, a man named William Saxbe. It began: "The law of the jungle prevails in East Pakistan, where mass killing of unarmed citizens, systemic elimination of the intelligentsia and annihilation of the Hindu population is in progress."

Meanwhile, Archer Blood used Candy and Jon's earlier testimony to him to update Nixon about the growing genocide. Disturbed, Kissinger told Nixon that they had to find some way to get rid of that "maniac in Dacca." Nixon agreed and fired Blood a week later.

Everyone knew that angry letters weren't enough. The next evacuation to Iran was "for their safety," but the deportees recognized it for what it really was: a muzzle. The ambassador assumed that the wives would stay with their husbands but made one critical error when he neglected to order couples onto the same flights.

Candy saw an opening. She packed the letter for Senator Saxbe and bought a one-way ticket on the next flight to Washington. She and Jon said a quick goodbye in the hotel lobby, careful not to give the spies—Pakistani or American—any reason to think that something momentous was about to happen. Perhaps because she was just a "diplomat's wife," no one asked her any questions. Jon promised he'd find some way to make it to Washington.

Candy opened the taxi door and slid into the backseat. She was going to take the fight right to Nixon's doorstep.

36

Mohammad Hai

MANPURA ISLAND, EAST PAKISTAN

APRIL AND MAY 1971

Nine men grunted softly and swung their sticks toward imaginary targets. There was just enough moonlight to see that they weren't nearly in unison.

"Again! Harder!" their leader whispered, as loud as he could without raising unwanted attention. The men brought the sticks back to their shoulders. Some lofted broom handles. A few others bore shovels.

The group attacked again, and their improvised weapons thudded back to the ground.

The Bengali resistance's Manpura regiment was not quite battle-ready. In fact, this was their first training session. Hai and Malik cobbled the group together out of their friends and family. Like Hai, they'd all heard Mujib's March 7 call for resistance. Like Hai, they had nothing to lose. Malik was the oldest at nineteen; the youngest was fifteen.

Hai and Malik approached candidates in secret, no more than one or two each day. With Manpura under a total media blackout, aside from a West Pakistan propaganda channel, they had only the slightest inkling that their spontaneous fighting collective was one of thousands popping up all over the East Pakistan countryside.

They also had no clue what they were doing.

Hai knew that good fighters needed training. He remembered pictures from his schoolbooks that made him think that walking in a straight line together was somehow important. Malik had an uncle who went through boot camp and liked to tell stories. Eventually, Malik convinced his uncle to show the ragtag army how to aim a rifle even though he didn't have ammunition. This was what the island could muster in terms of resistance—organic and homegrown, sporting less than a fool's chance of doing any damage on their own.

News of the massacres in Dacca made its way to the island via the ferries about a week later. While most Bengalis worried that the army would expand operations everywhere, a few people saw a chance to profit. On Manpura, the chairman's supporters had gotten suspiciously friendly with the army colonel. These cronies feasted on imported food—bread, tea, exotic meat, and other delicacies that regular people in Manpura couldn't get for any price. And it was clear that the perks of collaboration weren't for everyone. Once, one of the chairman's lackeys made the mistake of sharing some of his bounty with a Hindu friend. A junior officer pinned the man down and bit him all over his body as punishment. Nobody shared with Hindus after that.

The collaborators got their own name: *razakar*, the Urdu word for "volunteer." In Bengali, it took on a new meaning: traitor.

The teens lined up in front of a tin shack near the beach with the moonlight reflecting off their bare backs. Hai knew the shack intimately. He'd spent a dozen days under its roof with Malik over the last month. They raced to hide there any time Punjabi patrols swept Manpura for Awami League supporters, which seemed to be almost every day. The patrols used whatever documents they could find to root out the traitors, including the Awami League's own Dacca youth sign-up ledgers. Thanks to their whimsical Dacca University weekends, Hai and Malik were marked men.

They repeated their improvised routines ad nauseam, jogging in place with the sticks above their heads, and swinging the sticks like police batons. Recruits on each end of the line shot glances down the path keeping watch for any insomniac soldiers or *razakars* who might wander in their direction. They trained with a deadly seriousness, knowing that the army had purged the words "trials" and "prisoners" from its vocabulary. Gunning down a few nobodies carried so few consequences that soldiers barely found executions worth mentioning to their commanding officer.

Sneaking out at night to throw some sticks around might boost the Manpuran youths' morale, but Hai knew it wasn't going to overthrow a professional army backed by a global superpower. They needed real weapons, real training, and real money to pay for it. The question was: How would they get it? Hai and Malik brainstormed a series of bad ideas—everything from storming the local barracks, to spying on army movements from a distance, to robbing a bank in Dacca. Nothing clicked. Sweaty and exhausted, Hai went back to the tent that he'd set up in front of his house to sleep for a couple of hours.

In the daytime, everyone saw Hai as a dutiful HELP officer, as difficult and dangerous as that was becoming. The operation was seriously flagging with Candy gone, the army watching them like hawks, and the chairman's son commandeering their international donations for his own needs. Even if Candy and Jon were on Manpura, there would have been little they could do to keep the organization fully afloat. But Hai remained steadfast. He raised supplies from what little was available on the island in the way of charity.

When that ran out in early May, he took a boat to Dacca to pick up some of the last goods that HELP still had there. It was his first trip to Dacca since Operation Searchlight, and when the boat pulled up to the jetty, Hai felt like he was setting foot in a foreign country. Two dozen soldiers with submachine guns poked around the boats, looking for any reason to make a scene. Anyone doing anything "subversive" earned a bullet. Anyone who ran away, fumbled over words during an interrogation, or failed to give everything they owned to the army was as good as dead. The city was a pastiche of panic and fear.

Hai tried as best he could to remain inconspicuous. He hired a local ox-drawn cart to move the shipment through Dacca's streets, trying to look like a city student instead of a fisherman from the delta. Thankfully, most army men couldn't tell the difference.

But being inconspicuous was hard when there was almost no one else on the streets. The usually bustling market was almost vacant. There weren't any Awami League signs this time; their slogans had all been scrubbed away. The few people Hai saw darted off before he could ask them what was happening in the city.

Only the army was out in full force. It felt like every time Hai turned a corner he came to another checkpoint. After picking up the goods, prepaid by HELP, there were some Hindu friends he wanted to check in on. Hai knew it was dangerous, but he needed to see some friendly faces. Maybe they could tell him something about the local resistance.

When he arrived, he found their front door lolling open on its hinges and the house vacant. *Strange.* He called out to his friends but heard only silence. Hai peeked through cracks of the house's two boarded-up windows and saw papers strewn about on the floor as if someone had left in a hurry. A chill crept up his spine. This felt wrong. He thought he glimpsed dried blood on the walls.

Dacca wasn't safe. Hai hurried out and returned to the ship. He unloaded his cart in front of a guard post made of sandbags and run by Urdu-speaking soldiers. They gave Hai suspicious, disgusted looks. One soldier interrogated the ship's captain, poking Hai's boxes with a knife and threatening to take the entire shipment to the barracks. The blade cut through a burlap sack. It came out with only a dusting of flour. The soldiers didn't need food. They cursed the captain and let them both go.

Hai stared at the Red Cross box in his hands while the soldiers laughed and pushed around the dockworkers. Distributing supplies to villages, only to have the soldiers massacre members of the relief effort, felt like a lost cause. Hai remembered a bit of his Urdu from school, so he half listened to their taunts as he waited to put the box on the ship.

Then he heard something that caught his full attention: "Those East Bengal Regiment bastards can run off to India, but we will get them in the end."

Hai shuffled his feet toward a Dacca HELP employee. "Is that true?" Hai whispered as the ship prepared to embark.

The employee told Hai there was a rumor that a few Bengali military units had revolted and managed to escape. They were regrouping in India for a counterstrike. Word was they needed fighters to join the civilian resistance. They called themselves the Mukti Bahini, literally "freedom force," a catchall term that included any person from an army man to the lowliest fisherman willing to fight for a free Bangladesh. The Dacca employee warned Hai that it was secondhand information that someone said they heard from All India Radio, but Hai felt it had to be true.

The moment Hai landed back on Manpura, he told Malik the rumor while they unloaded boxes. Malik kept trying to interrupt the story with news of his own: He had managed to tune in to a pirate radio station that the resistance ran for an hour a week, which said that fighters were training in India and anyone could come. They weren't alone. They knew that they had to go.

Of course, the trip would be dangerous. The army and *razakars* were killing anyone they pleased. Trusting the wrong person at any point of the journey would mean not only torture but probably death as well. There were practical concerns too.

"Hai, where are we going to get the money for it?" Malik asked. "I don't have a single rupee to my name, and neither do you. We can't walk to India."

They mulled it over. This couldn't be just another half-baked plan. Mujib, if he was alive, was counting on them.

With more troops landing in Manpura every day, Hai didn't have the luxury to ask people leisurely and carefully if they wanted to finance the revolution. Troops did door-to-door searches, taking whatever they wanted from the already destitute population. Soon, nobody would have anything left to give, even if they wanted to. He needed to spread the word, quickly and quietly.

Eventually, Hai thought he'd figured out a foolproof way to do it. "Malik, everyone knows about our cyclone relief work. What if we asked the people we're already helping?"

Hai could ask the aid recipients in the HELP line while he gave them their rations. It would be dangerous; many of Manpura's *razakars* were Bengalis just like Hai. They were classmates and his neighbors. Some were even former Awami Leaguers who'd joined because they didn't want to be caught on the losing side. Traitors were omnipresent and invisible. If Hai asked a *razakar* by accident, they'd probably slit his throat and ban HELP from Manpura. So he could only ask people he was sure about.

For the next week, Hai lived a double life on the aid line at Manpura High School. At every interaction, he made a split-second decision about the trustworthiness of the face in front of him, playing Russian roulette by gut instinct alone. Was this person a friend or an enemy? He pulled the trigger over and over, for excruciating hours. Malik did the same at his relief post at the junior high next door.

That first day, Hai picked correctly more than three hundred times. He made coded requests and handed blankets to supporters. It didn't go very well at first. Most people said no. Some didn't understand the question. A few slunk away from Hai, wondering if *he* was a *razakar*, trying to trap them into saying something incriminating.

Eventually, Hai found his footing. The message went out to enough people that the message started spreading organically. Hai set a secret midnight meeting place for donations. He and Malik changed the meeting location each night, but new donors kept coming, spreading the news to like-minded family members and neighbors.

What Hai and Malik hadn't realized until then was that a fire for freedom burned behind facades of hunger and helplessness. Once donors learned their boys were heading to war, they handed over whatever the cyclone hadn't taken away. They gave their life savings, in bits of gold and wadded-up bills of dirty rupees.

In less than a week, they'd collected 20,000 rupees: enough to buy three houses and a dozen cows. Hai counted and recounted the pile of cash, making mental notes of what the bills could buy. It was enough to get over the border, pay for training, and maybe even return with a small arsenal. He sifted through the notes, which all boasted the picture of Pakistan's founder, Muhammad Ali Jinnah.

There wasn't a moment to lose. Hai and Malik told the other would-be fighters that they would all take the next boat off the island to begin their journey to India, at five in the morning. Hai didn't share details with anyone else. The army was interrogating and torturing the parents of boys who went off to fight in the resistance, which meant that his father would be in harm's way. The more his dad knew about Hai's plans, the more dangerous it would be for all of them.

So before dawn, Hai looked down at his sleeping father and said a silent goodbye. He prayed that he would see him again. Then he snuck out of his house and walked down the dirt path to the jetty, carrying only a small backpack and the cash tucked in his waistband.

Hai and Malik, along with eight friends, boarded a commuter boat to the mainland, the first step on the hundred-and-twenty-mile journey to the border—a journey that Malik's contacts assured him got progressively harder the farther they were from home. The young men knew the risks but were in high spirits nonetheless. Hai swallowed his terror at walking into a war and felt a rush of pride. He was fulfilling his destiny, just as Mujib asked him to. This was revolution. With Manpura's life savings stuffed in his belt, Hai felt as if he held the fate of the island in his hands.

Bobbing through the waves, the young men talked about the future. Hai dreamed of coming back a hero with a gun in his hand. Malik dreamed of liberating the country and kicking out the hated Punjabis once and for all. The duo dreamed of restoring democracy while their boat sailed past pile after pile of coastal cyclone debris. Silently, Hai fantasized about darker things too: revenge, shooting a soldier, killing a *razakar*, making them all pay.

The teen posse sat in a circle at the bow of the boat and softly sang the Mukti Bahini anthem together, over and over, as the boat pulled away from Manpura:

> *The day belongs to the army and the night to us.*
> *The sunshine belongs to the army and the rain to us.*
> *The cities belong to the army and the countryside to us.*

37

Yahya Khan, Tikka Khan, and A. A. K. Niazi

DACCA, EAST PAKISTAN

APRIL AND MAY 1971

Muddy tire tracks crisscrossed the lawn at Governor House, leaving the exquisitely manicured grass and exotic flower beds a torn-up mess. Within the ground's iron gates, a dozen cars with diplomatic plates parked wherever they could. Drivers dozed behind the wheels in the ninety-degree heat, waiting for their bosses—a who's who of Dacca's foreign power elite.

Enjoying the relative coolness inside the redbrick colonial building, Tikka Khan ordered the ceremony to begin. He wore full military regalia, complete with a saber and polished war medals on his chest. Tikka loved nothing more than a freshly pressed uniform on his body. It made him feel like a true professional. This ceremony would cement him as East Pakistan's civilian governor.

Tikka wanted the foreign press, who were sitting on one side of the small church-like room, to witness his ascension to power. He filled the remaining benches with a few dozen stone-faced army subordinates. Diplomats from Poland, America, Nepal, Japan, Australia, and Burma debated in the foyer about whether they should drink Tikka's tea and eat Tikka's biscuits after they'd witnessed the slaughter he'd started. Otherwise, they could walk out in protest. Only the Chinese delegation happily took their seats. Then, after they remembered how Tikka dealt with dissent, the rest reluctantly took their refreshments, sat down, and fanned themselves with their programs.

Just as he did a month earlier, Tikka asked the septuagenarian Bengali chief justice to administer the oath of office. The pair sat down together at the main table while the cameras clicked and tape recorders whirred. The judge wasn't as fiery as he'd been before Operation Searchlight. He cowered before the soon-to-be-governor. Per the old British tradition, the judge wore a powder white wig. Tikka wore sunglasses, even though the ceremony was taking place indoors. The judge signed the handover documents while pretending to ignore the implicit threat of what would happen if he didn't. An imam blessed the signing and prayed for Tikka's long and just rule.

Then Tikka kicked everyone out with their Darjeeling tea still steaming on the serving platters. The time for diplomacy was over. The dozen drivers wrangled their way off the lawn as a dozen bosses simultaneously issued orders to get the hell out of there. Tikka had a scotch and watched them negotiate their way around each other.

Tikka returned to his barracks and issued his first law as governor. He called it "Collective Responsibility." The policy said that any village that raised or hosted a Mukti Bahini fighter bore collective responsibility for that fighter's actions, and that the army could then punish the entire village with the death penalty. It applied even if the fighter had left a decade ago and not a soul there even knew his name. In a speech to promote the move, Tikka announced that the few thousand rebels who'd taken up arms against the military would get "compassionate treatment" if they surrendered, but "any fascists failing to avail themselves of this opportunity will be destroyed completely."

Fighting a war against a few thousand guerrilla fighters in a population of seventy million required exceptional on-the-ground knowledge. So Tikka formulated a second policy to reward Bengalis who spied on their own communities with land and lucrative government positions. He called upon the *razakars* to join so-called peace committees and to deliver intel to the military about enemy actions. Any *razakar* could execute an alleged Mukti Bahini fighter, no questions asked.

It was a good way to glean intel, but it was also a great way for entrepreneurial types to settle old scores. Tikka distributed the orders to every army post and municipal office in East Pakistan.

Yahya stayed in Islamabad when Tikka officially took office. Operation Searchlight's afterglow was waning, and he was in a bind. Kicking all of the foreigners out of East Pakistan had backfired. Now there was a global media backlash as journalists alleged a cover-up. The story wasn't everywhere yet, but people were talking—and it wasn't always on the side of a unified Pakistan.

The Associated Press reported a pleasingly pro-Pakistan headline: "West Pakistan Hits Rebels." But the *New York Times* warned of attacks on civilians and exposed the American connection in an article titled "U.S. Continues to Aid Pakistan Army."

Bhutto remained a loyal mouthpiece, telling European journalists, "World opinion should [be] unambiguously on the side of Pakistan. Here is a country doing its fundamental duty to preserve its national integrity. The attitude of the British and the American press has been, to say the least, deplorable."

Yahya pushed his Propaganda Ministry into full service too. They told *Time* magazine that "a deep conspiracy has been hatched by the Indo-Israeli axis against the integrity of Pakistan and the Islamic basis of her ideology." Tikka joined in, calling all reports in the foreign media "concocted stories" written by "brainwashed" journalists. Yahya and Bhutto started day drinking whiskey together at President House, commiserating about how unfair it all was.

Yahya wanted to make sure that everyone in West Pakistan knew of his unparalleled success. He ordered a full-out media blitz. Newspapers in Islamabad and Karachi declared victory, running headlines like "All Normal in the East" and, more simply, "LIQUIDATED." Yahya promised that he would never hand power over to Mujib. Aside from a minority of constitutional-scholar nay-sayers, few West Pakistanis seemed to mind the crackdown's brutality or the fact that Yahya broke his promise to deliver democracy. Perhaps they, too, had just as little interest in a Bengali prime minister as Yahya or Bhutto did. Yahya preached about how Bengalis were fake Muslims and said that he sent West Pakistan troops in as holy warriors to protect the faith. The public lapped it up. Most West Pakistanis thought the BBC and other foreign sources were lying on behalf of India, so they tuned out the misdeeds.

Indeed, while he was happy to get rid of as many Bengalis as possible from East Pakistan, millions of them had migrated to India, and the enormous refugee camps on the border were becoming a political issue inside the neighboring country. But India also saw tantalizing strategic opportunities in breaking up their mortal enemy. Indira Gandhi, India's prime minister, set up military camps along the border to help train and arm the Bengali resistance. It was anyone's guess if the 1965 war was just a prelude to a much bigger continental conflict.

Meanwhile, the US-China discussions were on the verge of collapse, even as the CHINESE CONNECTION folder filled up. Mao didn't trust Nixon, and Yahya had to focus all of his efforts on getting them to commit to talks.

Yahya leafed through his folder each morning, trying to find the right diplomatic strategy to connect the two world leaders. If he could make the China meeting happen, Nixon promised to look the other way on East Pakistan, give Yahya more weaponry, and "see to it that the United States Government does nothing to embarrass President Yahya's government" by mentioning the slaughter. China promised the same. Mao thanked Yahya profusely in every letter he shuttled back and forth. Nixon even told Yahya, "You are making a personal contribution to international understanding and world peace."

It was nice to hear, but the platitudes didn't get Nixon and Mao any closer to sharing a room. The Chinese were stalling. If negotiations went on too long—and the additional arms never made it to Pakistan—putting down the revolutionaries might be impossible.

Yahya didn't have time for that. He feared he'd lose control of the country in months, if not weeks. Having to answer questions about East Pakistan to the press or his own military was exhausting. It sapped his strength and attention. Even General Rani's women weren't clearing his mind like they used to.

Yahya needed a buffer from the massacre he'd started—someone he could publicly delegate the mess in East Pakistan to, someone who relished being the media's lightning rod. Yahya liked Tikka, but Yahya's hardliner advisers grumbled that he was soft. Tikka was a good strategist, they said, but he seemed to feel that the hard part of the mission was over and the rest was just mop-up. Only a few weeks in, the man was more obsessed with organizing military units than with actually delivering the coup de grâce.

As the army moved into the countryside, where 85 percent of East Pakistan's people lived, Yahya needed a blunt instrument now—someone just as hungry to kill as Tikka, yet also willing to be the public face of Operation Searchlight. Problem was, most of Yahya's generals balked at mowing down more unarmed Bengalis. It just wasn't good for their images. Yahya ran through the top twelve names on his list. They all turned him down.

But Yahya knew a guy. He was a real go-getter, one of Yahya's old students at the army college and Tikka's old World War II buddy in Burma. He was even a hero of the 1965 war, who had taken out Indian tanks in Kashmir. He wasn't the most senior or most disciplined officer in the ranks, not by a long shot. But he was ambitious. He'd pestered Yahya for more responsibility ever since Operation Searchlight, volunteering to spearhead rural operations. His name was General A. A. K. Niazi. Everyone called him the Tiger, a nickname earned after he tracked, stalked, and killed twelve Japanese soldiers in the Burmese jungle. He had a reputation as a sex-crazed, arrogant, dirty-joke-telling, socially awkward idiot. In other words, he was the perfect man for the job.

On April 10, Yahya shipped the Tiger to Bengal.

He made an immediate impression. At Niazi's first joint briefing at the barracks, a lieutenant came in, his arms stuffed with papers and maps. He unrolled the bundle on the table, then started to brief the general on the state of the operation, using the maps to highlight troop movements and locations.

Niazi, sharply dressed with a red carnation on his lapel and matching red pocket handkerchief, shushed the man after just a few words. "Hey, don't worry about the war, my friend. We'll manage that. For now, just give me the phone numbers of your Bengali whores."

Other officers in the briefing shook their heads. The rumors about his reputation looked to be spot-on.

Tikka invited Niazi to introduce himself. The smiling general made his way to the front of the room like a man ready to run it, clean shaven, his black hair slicked back and parted a few inches above his right ear. Twenty years of debauchery had taken their predictable toll, but Niazi's broad shoulders and strong chin still managed to project strength from his paunchy body. Like Tikka, Niazi loved wearing a chest full of medals whenever he got the chance.

When he arrived at the lectern and turned around to look at his audience, Niazi's smile vanished. He saw two Bengalis in the back. They were the only two Bengali officers left in East Pakistan. He started his speech, glaring at them the entire time.

"I am here to change the race of this bastard nation. Bengalis are enemies of the people. And I will let my soldiers loose on the women." He then pointed at Tikka. "You have made the troops feminine. I will make them men again."

Tikka scoffed and left the briefing.

Next, Niazi moved on to logistics. Tikka had already commandeered all of East Pakistan's cyclone relief supplies for the troops. Even Jon's Cholera Research Lab boats now ferried troops up and down the delta. Niazi stood in one for a photo op; he didn't even bother to take off the USAID logos on the sides.

Niazi sneered at other aspects of the operation too. "What have I been hearing about a shortage of rations? Are not there any cows and goats in this country? This is enemy territory. Take what you want. This is what we used to do in Burma."

One of the two Bengalis in the back stood up to confront the Tiger. He was a major, a couple of ranks below Niazi. He told the newly installed general to take back his words and that he was every bit as Pakistani as they were. What's more, they were fighting the traitors together. The Tiger glared back at him, then stormed out of the room.

The next morning, the Bengali major was found dead in the toilet. Niazi filed the report himself. He said it was a tragic suicide by gunshot, committed by a man who'd had his gun taken away during Operation Searchlight, with a bullet in his head that nobody in the barracks heard fired. Niazi refused to give the body back to the man's family.

The Tiger settled in quickly. He gleefully interrogated returning platoons with a single question: "What was your score last night?" Every unit got one point for each rape or murder of a Hindu.

Replying "zero" earned a demotion. He wrote orders to cleanse East Pakistan of all Hindus, and he loved to join in on the patrols. In a typical operation, *razakars* gave the army tips about which neighborhoods housed Hindus or Mukti Bahini, handing over notes with names and addresses. The collaborators' notes were detailed and specific. But the Tiger couldn't read Bengali. Nor could anyone else in his cohort.

So they just killed everyone in the neighborhood, by the hundreds. And more *razakar* tips flowed in every day. The army rarely found weapons or incriminating information. They weren't concerned with the details.

One local commander told the *New York Times*, "You do not go around counting the bodies of your enemies, you throw them in the rivers and be done with it."

Now that soldiers had free rein to commandeer anything they wished, the barracks looked like distribution warehouses, stuffed with looted television sets, refrigerators, typewriters, watches, gold, and air conditioners.

Then the Tiger started a diabolical new terror front. He told the troops to rape as many women as they could to breed out East Pakistan's Hinduness. He set aside a building in the Dacca barracks and filled it with hundreds of Bengali sex slaves. Some girls were as young as eleven years old. Tikka thought it was a great idea and ordered the women to be naked at all times. He claimed it was for their protection, but it was also so they wouldn't hang themselves with their saris at the end of each shift.

The directive leaked to the media. Tikka responded that his soldiers had raped only four women. He obtained this figure by driving around Dacca in his jeep with loudspeakers asking women to come to him with their grievances. Bhutto told the Italian media that it was forty women at the absolute most. Niazi said that the figure was zero and that the only women the army slept with were prostitutes who were so delighted to see real men that they gave sex away for free. Later studies estimated that army troops raped 250,000 women in the spring of 1971 alone.

Tikka and Niazi knew that what mattered to their boss was the completeness of the task, and Yahya's orders were clear: Neutralize the threat and cleanse East Pakistan so thoroughly that another Bengali resistance couldn't happen for a thousand years. That translated to each man going to even crueler extremes. Tikka opened an extermination camp on Dacca's outskirts, on the old Pakistan National Oil Company compound. By day, the army herded Dacca's Hindus and suspected Awami League sympathizers into the vast complex of riverside warehouses. Each night, they tied them up in groups of eight and made them wade out into the river together. Then they lit the captives up with spotlights and fired from the rooftops. The river's current did the rest.

Everything about this thrilled Yahya. Tikka and the Tiger made an efficient and ruthless team, constantly trying to one-up the other in their efforts to eradicate East Pakistan of political and ethnic impurities. The Tiger lit a fire under Tikka to keep up his murdering spirit, and Tikka gave the Tiger logistical and strategic guidance to help spread his sadism across the countryside.

They all shared the same vision: to solve the Bengali problem so completely, so thoroughly, that no politician could ever mess it up again. Yahya gave a few interviews, where he talked about how his "maximum austerity program" would lead to a "maximum economy" in East Pakistan in no time.

There were, however, unintended consequences. For example, the trains stopped running in East Pakistan because they killed all the railroad workers, and there was nobody left who knew how to drive a train.

By May, after six exhausting months of cyclones, elections, and uprisings, Yahya finally felt that East Pakistan was tamed. He opened the CHINESE CONNECTION folder and leafed through the communications. So far, most of the notes between Mao and Nixon contained platitudes and vague promises, but they weren't much closer to accomplishing their mission than before Operation Searchlight started. Yahya resolved then and there that it was time to get the deal done.

He picked up the phone and called the Chinese ambassador in Islamabad.

38

Hafiz Uddin Ahmad and Mohammad Hai

THE INDIA-PAKISTAN BORDER

Summer 1971, a few months after Operation Searchlight

Call it mutiny. Call it rebellion. At this point, Hafiz didn't bother with semantics: he was at war. He sat in his barracks, a hastily converted concrete farmhouse in India, somewhere just over the border from East Pakistan. The sounds of men training with bamboo sticks filtered in through the open doorway as his counterpart, a major in the Indian Army, went over a supply manifest of arms and munitions that the Indian government was secretly sending to Mukti Bahini forces.

Until Hafiz arrived in the village outside the Jessore Cantonment, he feared that his two hundred Bengali soldiers were all that stood against the full power of the Pakistan Army. But they weren't alone, not by a long shot. On the night of Tikka's offensive, five hundred Bengali police officers in Dacca defended themselves with ancient .303 rifles, while the Pakistan Army mowed them down with machine guns and artillery. The Bengalis didn't last long, but the distress call they sent out from their radio room gave enough warning to Bengali police and military units around East Pakistan to stage their own resistance before the army could finish them off too.

That one broadcast saved thousands of soldiers' lives and spurred thousands more to mutiny. After Major Ziaur Rahman—a mustachioed, ambitious military man that most everyone just called Zia—announced Bangladesh's independence in his own radio transmission, he formed a new battalion and called it Z-Force. Hafiz thought that had a nice ring to it, like a real commando team.

T.J. was one of the last men to escape Jessore; he'd crawled out of a drainage ditch in the dead of the night. Word eventually leaked out that the Pakistan Army executed every Bengali sepoy left inside the cantonment walls—about a hundred men. Hafiz had no idea if they'd executed or just imprisoned and tortured Lieutenant Colonel Jalil. He feared the worst.

It had taken Hafiz a few months to really understand the scenario. His unit was too small and undersupplied to attack Pakistani positions directly. At first, they stayed close to the Indian border. Hafiz led a small skirmish near a place called Benapol, but nothing much came of it, except for Hafiz earning a promotion to captain.

The resistance started to organize itself and the group from Jessore broke apart to fill out gaps elsewhere. Next, Captain Hafiz crossed the border to contact Indian Army handlers for help. It felt strange, at first, to work with people he was trained to think of as enemies, but since both the Pakistan and Indian militaries inherited their structure from the British, everything had a familiar ring to it. No one was sure what the Indians were planning, but Hafiz figured they might help liberate Bangladesh for their own strategic ends. The Indians brought him to a training camp outside the city of Tura, where thousands of volunteers flocked to join the resistance.

The volunteers arrived with an endless stream of horror stories. There were boys who had seen their mothers raped and murdered and teenagers who fled when the army set their villages ablaze and gunned down anyone fleeing the infernos. There were men with dark, hollow eyes who wouldn't speak. All these ragged souls wanted to do was fight; they'd give their lives for an ounce of revenge. These were the men whom Hafiz would transform into a modern fighting force. These were the men of the revolution.

The Indian Army major who was going over the manifest showed Hafiz a box of grenades. In the time that they had, not every man would be able to learn to fire a rifle, but anyone could learn to throw a grenade. If they sent back hundreds of revenge-seeking freedom fighters with a handful of explosives each, some of the missiles might land in the right places.

Hafiz walked outside the camp in Tura where monsoon rains instantly drenched him to the skin. Nearby were immense Soviet-made artillery pieces covered in tarps to keep them dry. While most of the small weapons that the Mukti Bahini fought with came from Indian factories, the planes and artillery originated in the Soviet Union—a reminder that foreign powers were eyeing the contested soil of Hafiz's homeland too.

Training couldn't wait on weather. Besides, every Bengali was used to the seasonal deluge. He issued orders to a line of mostly shirtless, rain-slicked men in white pajama pants and cloth dhotis. He inspected them for obvious signs of illness, shaking, or malnutrition. Only one in twenty would make the cut for military training. The rest would be on their own. Hafiz singled out the three tallest applicants for rifle training. He figured that, all things being equal, the strongest recruits could carry the most gear into battle. The rest would learn to throw grenades. Some would cross back across the border on their own personal revenge missions.

For the next two months, Hafiz trained cohorts of twenty and led them back across the border to liberate whatever they could of Bangladesh with small attacks and retaliations that might, one day, mature into a full-scale military invasion. Hafiz liked Zia, his new commanding officer. He was charismatic and courageous. Hafiz saw him as a true soldier's soldier: honest, matter-of-fact, and willing to sacrifice whatever was necessary for the cause. Zia undertook every action with utter seriousness. Hafiz swore that he would follow whatever orders Zia sent him, even those that meant certain death. If his father was still alive, he hoped he'd be proud of him.

———

About two hundred miles away on the eastern side of East Pakistan's border with India, Hai chewed a gravel-and-rice concoction one delicate grind at a time. He tried to avoid chipping a tooth. At least there weren't many maggots in this bite. After eating only one meal a day for the last two weeks, Hai, Malik, and three comrades weren't about to get picky. Hunger was an old friend now, a point of pride as they saved Manpura's money for guns instead of wasting it on food. Hai's stomach rumbled against the money strapped to his belly.

As he saw it, every chew mattered. Cracking a tooth on a hasty bite meant pulling it out with pliers—and no painkillers—lest infection set in. Infection meant an agonizing death in a country that lacked the most basic medicines. Sometimes the hole left behind got infected anyway. So, dizzy from hunger but determined to stay alive, Hai chewed slowly.

The finish line was in sight. Their resistance party was camped out less than a mile from the Indian border at a place called Boxanagar, and this was their last meal before they made a run for it. They could see lush Indian hills in the distance. For the first time since they'd left their village, they'd had a chance to pray with an imam that day. They'd overheard the announcement from the nearby town's loudspeaker and joined the evening service from afar. With God on their side, all they had to do now was wait until darkness to cross over.

They'd used up quite a bit of their luck to get to this point. They hitched rides on buses and rickshaws early on, but with the army monitoring the mainland's washed-out roads, they covered the last half by foot through fields and jungles. The army had gotten wise to the resistance's movements. West Pakistan ringed East Pakistan with troops to stop Bengalis from sneaking out to India for training, effectively walling up the country.

Hai's group originally planned to cross to the west, along with the fifty thousand refugees that fled each day to Calcutta, not only running from the genocide but also desperately searching for clean water because their village wells were ruined after the cyclone. On that route, troops pulled every able-bodied man they spied out of the procession. Any man without a family got interrogated. Most were never seen again. So Hai and his friends changed tack, opting instead to cross into India's northeastern state of Tripura.

When he was growing up, Hai loved the monsoon, but he cursed it now. The downpours soaked his only clothes, which never dried out. He smelled like mildew. The worst part was the clouds. The team moved under cover of darkness whenever they could. With no compass, no map, and no stars or moon to guide them—and only dense jungle in every direction—they got lost most nights. It cost them precious time as the army tightened its vise. They still sang the Mukti Bahini anthem, but the words were losing their magic.

Hai and Malik were making progress, but barely. A big group of teenage boys traveling together was like waving a giant Mukti Bahini flag, so they split into two groups. They planned to meet up each night but lost each other for good after only one day apart. Hai and Malik had no idea if their comrades were still alive.

Before Operation Searchlight, they could have simply asked a local for directions, but now every sleepy small town was a battlefield. Able-bodied kids who were asking how to get to India were only going for one reason: to join the guerrilla camps. As in Manpura, anyone could be a *razakar*; but unlike in Manpura, everyone on the road was a stranger. If Hai asked the wrong person which direction was east, they'd all die.

It was Russian roulette all over again.

Hai figured that at least he was developing a sixth sense for this sort of thing. He took a calculated guess that not too many grandmas would be *razakars*. In each new town, he would look for an old woman pumping water or sorting rice and strike up a conversation. Grandmas were the village sages—utterly invisible to an army looking for targets but aware of everything that happened around their homes. They called Hai and the others "son," just like his own grandma had. The gesture warmed Hai's heart and steeled his conviction. Sometimes, a woman would invite them to rest on bamboo mats. Hai and Malik used their sandals as pillows. It was infinitely better than the nights outside in the rain and tiger-infested jungles.

One such night, a venerable old woman told Hai about a secret code phrase that people in neighboring villages used to signal that they were in the resistance: "We're going home to our mother." It sounded silly, but it saved their lives. Just before reaching the border, a farmer ambushed them while they crept across his field. The man thought the scruffy group were *razakars* out to rob or kill him. He jumped out, swinging a scythe as he tried to slice off their heads. Unarmed and lying in the mud, Hai and Malik yelled, "We're going home to our mother!" The farmer stopped midswing, paused, then held out his hand. Instead of killing them, he invited the group inside for tea and biscuits.

Their last hurdle—getting over the border itself—was within reach. Hai could almost taste the army rations. He imagined trading in his torn clothes for military fatigues. He couldn't wait to prove to the commanders how brave and loyal he was. However, crossing the border was the hardest part. Everyone had heard rumors that the only way to safely cross was by paying a trafficker. The team made discreet roadside inquiries to find one.

Hours of asking passed without success. Nobody would help, but a few warned that they needed to make their move fast. More troops were coming from Dacca and soon crossing would be impossible. One man they met had been a mule for weeks, but he refused their request, saying he almost got killed the day before when the border patrol started shooting. It was just too dangerous now, he said.

Soaking wet, Hai cursed his luck. If the godforsaken rain had held off a week, they would have gotten here in time. A new army checkpoint was only a couple hundred feet ahead of them. It was a simple shed, with a two armed guards, but it felt like a fortress. Malik got desperate, offering fistfuls of cash to every potato farmer and firewood collector that he passed.

Hai pulled Malik back and told him to be more careful. They couldn't let their plans fall apart now. Their argument heated up. They yelled at each other as a woman carrying a baby in a basket walked by. She stopped and asked what they wanted. Hai guessed a mother with a newborn couldn't be a *razakar*. He tried his luck, saying they needed a guide to India.

"Follow me," she said, "and take her in your arms. If anyone asks, you are my brothers."

She handed Malik the baby and guided them through the checkpoint to her house, talking her way past the skeptical but lazy soldiers. She made gravely rice while they played with the baby.

Hai and his friends had gotten lucky again. The woman had been helping resistance fighters get across for a month. Hai didn't ask why she took such risks. It wasn't necessary. Everyone had a story of pain and suffering. They all had a reason to resist. She warned that they still had to traverse a village full of *razakars* and soldiers. Just last night she tried to help another group cross over, but they got gunned down at the border. Their bodies were still outside as a warning to anyone else who might try. Still, if they had the courage, then dawn was the time to go. The army was quiet then.

Malik shook his head. He worried they'd lose their last chance if they waited that long. Hai sided with the woman. Malik stormed out of the hut.

Hai followed, trying to calm him down. Hai put a hand on Malik's shoulder. But Malik brushed it off.

"Tomorrow morning will be too late, Hai!" Malik said. "We have to go now!"

Hai was sure the woman was right. After all, she lived here and had helped countless others get across. Hai decided he'd go at dawn.

It made Malik livid. Their argument flared again, this time drawing dangerous attention. Everyone tried to calm them both down. A neighboring boy came up to Malik and called him a *razakar*, pointing at his beard. He was probably too young to even know what the word meant.

Malik snapped. He slapped the boy, hard. "How dare you call me a *razakar*! After how far we came to save you!"

The boy crumpled in the dirt, wailing. More people showed up to see what the commotion was. Malik ran off into the darkness. Hai wanted to yell for him to come back, but he couldn't; it was just too dangerous. Throwing up his hands, he went back inside with the last member of his group: a man named Latif.

Hai awoke at dawn to the loudspeaker's morning prayer. He prayed he'd see Malik later that day. He hadn't even had a chance to give him any money. He would not make that mistake again. He peeled off a few notes for himself and gave Latif the wad of cash. They dressed and left, thanking the woman for her hospitality even though she wouldn't help them cross, and apologizing for making a scene. Hai realized later that he never asked her name.

A minute after they hit the road, a bicycle rickshaw pulled up beside them. The driver was maybe fifty years old, beaten down by life, with a long gray beard and unkempt, muddy hair. Playing his personal game of Russian roulette again, Hai asked the driver if he could get them across. They would pay handsomely. The driver said he knew just the place. It was about five miles down the road and vacant—a blind spot that only locals knew about.

Another stroke of luck. Hai felt the wind rush over his wet hair as he sat down on the rickshaw, calmed by the occasional dinging of the cycle's bell as it weaved in and out of people and animals on the road. It started pouring again, but it didn't matter this time. They breezed past the few troops they saw without a second glance. Hai hummed the Mukti Bahini anthem to himself.

They coasted into a border town, where they found a few blocks of densely packed houses and alleyways. It must have bustled before the war but now was boarded up. The driver pulled into an alley and parked. He asked them for partial payment before going any farther. Latif pulled out the wad from his waist, revealing the vast sum of yellowed, wet cash. The driver studied it as Latif peeled off a few notes, while Hai looked toward the border, mentally preparing himself for the danger to come.

"What is this? These notes are ruined. Give me some other ones," the driver demanded.

Latif peeled off a few more.

"No, no. Come with me. We'll find a shop to exchange them." He pointed at Hai. "You wait here."

The driver took Latif toward a maze of alleyways. Hai ate a biscuit as he watched them turn a corner.

Suddenly, Hai heard yelling and stomping coming from a block away. It was an army ambush.

"Traitors!" a voice called. "We know you're here! Come out, and we'll spare your lives!"

"There's one here! Come quickly!" the rickshaw driver yelled, tugging at Latif's shirt to hold him in place, while Latif tried to pry the money from the driver's hands. Paralyzed, Hai couldn't believe the scene unfolding in front of him.

The army rushed toward the noise. Latif gave up on the money and ran for the jungle.

"Run, Hai! He's a *razakar*! He stole our money!"

Hai snapped out of his stupor and bolted in the opposite direction, through the driving rain, and into the jungle. Stumbling over slick roots, he ran until his lungs cried out for mercy. Soon the patter of the rain drowned out the sound of yelling. Soaked and hiding behind a rotten tree trunk, Hai took shallow, hard breaths. There wasn't anyone behind him anymore. But there wasn't a trace of Latif either.

Hai sat on a root, shattered. He had escaped with his life, but everything else that mattered was gone. He looked toward India in the east. He had no idea if Malik was dead or alive, no way of finding out, no money to get across the border, and no more window of opportunity to cross. Plus, the army was chasing him now, and the *razakars* knew what he looked like.

Manpura lay to the southwest. A trip home was just as dangerous as the one he took to get here. Even if he made it back safe, he would have nothing to show for it. What would he tell his neighbors? His father? The island's investment went bust. He'd be branded a coward. He felt as impotent as he did while clinging to that palm tree in the face of a cyclone that took his entire family. He felt like a failure all over again.

I could just vanish, Hai thought. It would be easy. He could go west to Dacca and start a new anonymous life in a factory. People did it all the time. Or he could pluck tea leaves up north in the mountains. The thought sent waves of shame washing through his soul. It suffocated his thoughts and choked out his resolve.

Suddenly he heard sounds in the jungle. It was the army, closing in on him, fast. The time to think was over.

He started running.

39

Candy Rohde

"Why are they so far apart?" Thomas Morgan squinted at the atlas, utterly stumped. There was an East Pakistan *and* a West Pakistan? He stabbed his index finger at India. "And what is *that* doing in between them?"

Candy groaned inside. Time for another geography lesson. She gently explained to the chair of the House of Representatives Foreign Relations Committee that his finger was pressing down on India and that they didn't like Pakistan all that much. More than that, East Pakistan and West Pakistan were at war.

Morgan nodded appreciatively. He'd been the chair of the committee for a decade. Candy didn't mind dolling out education; blank slates were receptive audiences. So she told the story of the stolen election and the genocide, and of the American weapons fueling an ongoing civilian slaughter. Most of the representatives and senators she spoke with were shocked. For many, it was the first time they'd even heard about it. Just after Operation Searchlight, Nixon cited executive privilege and effectively banned the US State Department's own reports on the situation.

Candy left Morgan's office and jotted down notes from the meeting on an index card, with "THOMAS MORGAN (D)-Penn" scrawled across the top. She planned to fill out a card for the important representatives like Morgan—and all one hundred senators, too.

Candy came to Washington with one goal: to get the United States to stop funding and arming West Pakistan. The Bengali diaspora beat her by a month, arranging small protest marches and fasts in front of the White House, but few paid attention. Candy hoped that she could amplify their message by penetrating the offices by way of her social status and natural networking abilities. She didn't mind that she had next to no chance of success; no legislative branch had ever curbed a president's foreign policy in this way. Then again, Candy didn't care about history.

Each morning, Candy walked to the Senate office buildings from her friend's house in Georgetown, armed with her stack of index cards. Lobbyists were rare in the early 1970s, and security at the Capitol was more or less based on the honor system. So Candy just walked through their front doors and asked for a chat.

Most of the senators, ninety-nine men and the lone woman, were sympathetic to the plight. A few, like Edward Kennedy, already knew about the genocide. Others needed a crash course. Candy tried to find common ground on both sides of the partisan aisle. She told one southern senator that Bengalis ate rice, just like his constituents, and that supporting their cause might make for a great export opportunity.

In the meantime, Jon was still stuck in Tehran, forbidden to leave, along with the rest of the US government staff members originally stationed in East Pakistan. They weren't allowed to speak to the media or even write to American journalists with their stories. The American embassy in Tehran would only forward letters addressed to family members, and Jon's letters to Candy got extra scrutiny. Jon knew that any letter directly addressing the genocide was destined to get "lost" or otherwise buried.

However, he had an idea. The embassy staff didn't seem to read or even open the letters he sent to his mom in Cape Cod, so he started

Hafiz Uddin Ahmad played hundreds of games in Dacca Stadium, capacity 36,000, over his career.
(RASHID TALUKDER/DRIK PICTURE LIBRARY)

Cornelia (Candy) Rohde and
Jon Rohde in Dacca, 1968
(COURTESY JON ROHDE)

President Yahya Khan and President Richard Nixon along with their wives Fakhra
Khan and Pat Nixon at a state dinner in Lahore, West Pakistan, August 1, 1969
(NIXON LIBRARY/NATIONAL ARCHIVES)

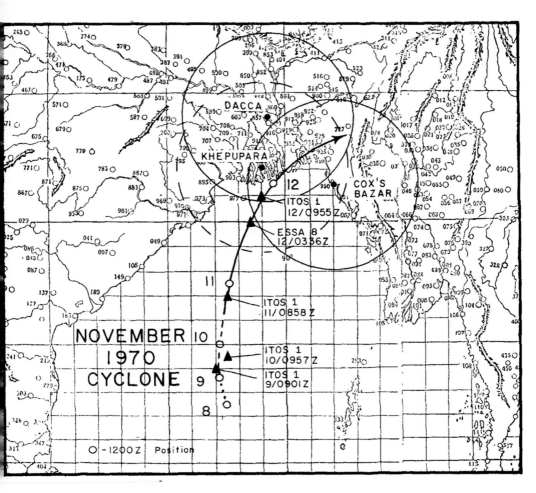

The path of the Great Bhola Cyclone captured by both the ESSA-8 and ITOS-1 satellites. The cyclone's eye passed directly over the island of Manpura, East Pakistan.
(EAST PAKISTAN WATER AND DEVELOPMENT AUTHORITY/WORLD BANK)

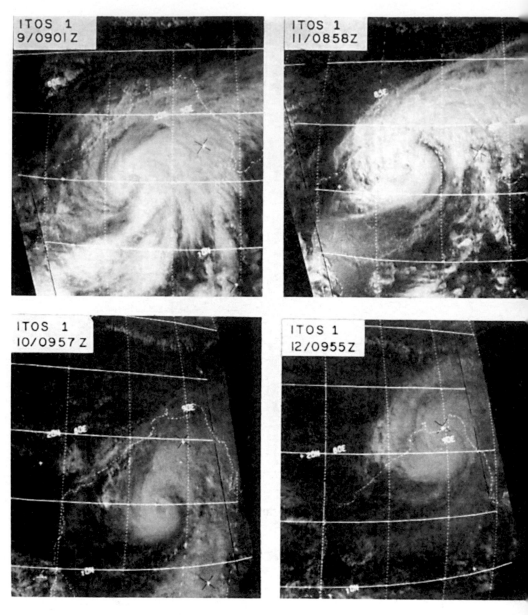

Imaging from the ITOS-1 weather satellite showed the approaching cyclone that created a storm surge of more than 20 feet and killed an estimated 500,000 people.

(NATIONAL WEATHER SERVICE)

President Yahya Khan (center with cane) visits Bhola island where Lt.
Hafiz Uddin Ahmad (far left in beret) and Lt. Col Jalil (third from left)
bury the dead in the wake of the cyclone. November 21, 1970.
(ALAMY IMAGES/KEYSTONE)

Candy Rohde
discusses logistics
with Jon Rohde
before delivering the
first cyclone relief
supplies to Manpura
through their
organization HELP.
(COURTESY JON ROHDE)

After traveling to Dacca to understand how the cyclone warning system failed, Neil Frank returned to America where he became the director of the National Hurricane Center. Pictured here in 1985 after helping usher the NHC into a computerized future. *(COURTESY KHOU 11)*

Hundreds of cyclone survivors wait for meager rations, largely supplied by international donors and distributed by HELP. East Pakistan, 1971. *(RAGHU RAI/MAGNUM PHOTOS)*

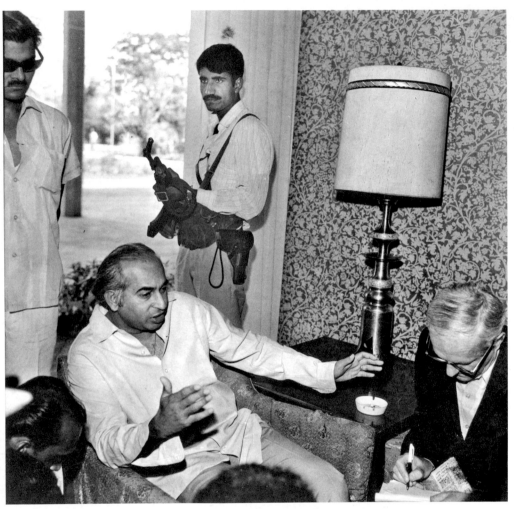

The morning after a brutal military crackdown, Pakistan Peoples'
Party (PPP) leader Zulfikar Ali Bhutto holds a press conference amid
tight security at Dacca's InterContinental Hotel. March 26, 1971.
(RASHID TALUKDER/DRIK PICTURE LIBRARY)

A large refugee camp at Salt Lake, India, extends into the distance. Over six million people fled East Pakistan for India during the war. 1971. *(RAGHU RAI/MAGNUM PHOTOS)*

With tents and tin shacks scarce, refugees seek shelter in concrete culverts during the annual monsoon after fleeing to India. 1971. *(RAGHU RAI/MAGNUM PHOTOS)*

Mukti Bahini fighters march into contested territory in East Pakistan. November 1971.
(RAGHU RAI/MAGNUM PHOTOS)

Beatles' guitarist George Harrison and sitar legend Ravi Shankar hold a press conference announcing their benefit concert and album to aid victims of famine and war in Bangladesh, known as The Concert for Bangladesh. *(ROCK NEGATIVES/MEDIAPUNCH)*

Refugees from East Pakistan awaiting food and medicine at Salt Lake. Money raised by The Concert for Bangladesh album eventually funded Oral Rehydration Salts (ORS) treatments that Jon Rohde helped develop and deliver to refugees. November 1971.
(RAYMOND DEPARDON/MAGNUM PHOTOS)

Mukti Bahini
fighters carrying
Indian weapons
cross a river in East
Pakistan as they
return to fight their
Liberation War.
*(RAYMOND DEPARDON/
MAGNUM PHOTOS)*

Indian troops and Mukti Bahini fighters stand over an injured Pakistani soldier. 1971.
(RAGHU RAI/MAGNUM PHOTOS)

Photographers and reporters await the *USS Enterprise* after a mission in Asia in 1972. The nuclear-powered carrier survived a standoff with Soviet nuclear submarines and missile cruisers less than a year earlier.
(U.S. NAVY/NATIONAL ARCHIVES)

Lt. General Jagjit Singh Aurora (center) who commanded Indian Forces accepts the surrender of East Pakistani Lt. General A.A.K. Niazi (right) at the conclusion of the Liberation War, December 15, 1971.
(RAGHU RAI/MAGNUM PHOTOS)

After the war, the Mukti Bahini executed thousands of accused traitors (*razakars*) in the newly independent nation. In this photo, a Mukti Bahini leader beats an accused *razakar* in front of the press before stabbing him to death with a bayonet. *(DRIK LIBRARY/WILLIAM LOVELACE)*

Sheikh Mujibir Rahman addressing over one million people in Dacca upon his return in January 1972 after nine months in detention in West Pakistan. In this speech he charted the path forward for a liberated Bangladesh.
(MARILYN SILVERSTONE/MAGNUM PHOTOS)

President Richard Nixon and Premier Zhou Enlai toast to the reopening of relations between the United States and China. The so-called CHINESE CONNECTION could never have happened without Yahya Khan's matchmaking. February 25, 1972. *(NIXON LIBRARY)*

Soccer star-turned-soldier Hafiz Uddin Ahmad
in Dhaka holding a portrait of himself in uniform.
(CARNEY/MIKLIAN 2021)

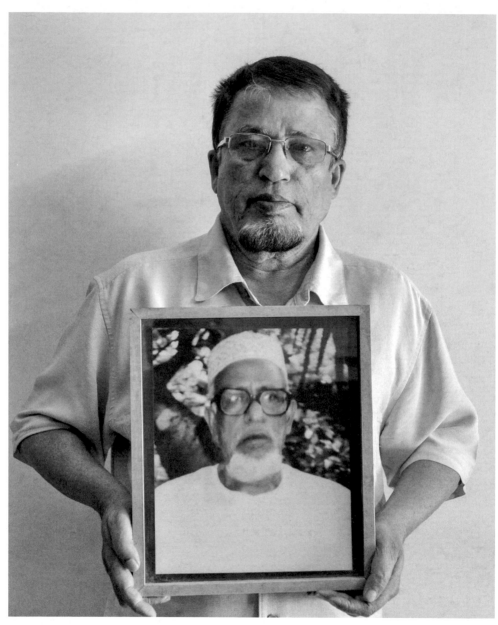

HELP-aid-worker-turned-Mukti-Dahini fighter,
Mohammad Hai holds a photo of his father.
(CARNEY/MIKLIAN 2021)

filling the envelopes not with heartfelt wishes to eat a home-cooked meal again but with evidence of massacres. He collected firsthand accounts from every employee stuck in Tehran with him, documenting the scope of the attack, its brutality, and its genocidal nature. He sent letters to her daily, bulging with horrific tales.

Each time Jon's mom got a letter from her son, she carefully copied the contents in triplicate and sent them out to three people: her senator, her representative, and Candy. Candy used the evidence in her meetings as proof not only of the genocide but also of the American support for it. With Nixon preventing the State Department's analysts from doing any real work, the senators counted on her information pipeline.

Candy's index cards filled up with neat notes, summarizing each senator's pressure points. But while senators were supportive to her face, few lifted a finger after she left their office. Her best hope lay in Frank Church, a Democrat from Idaho. He had lived in Calcutta during World War II, where he served as an intelligence officer, supporting Tikka Khan and the rest of the Allies in the Burmese theater. He'd never forgotten the Bengalis' warmth and generosity.

Candy lurked around Church's office nearly every day, cajoling him to bring a debate to the Senate floor. While Church was amenable, even his patience wore thin. He told Candy he'd vote for something if it ever came up, but he wasn't going to squander what little political capital he had by taking the lead on it. After all, there weren't many Bengali constituents in Boise.

Eventually, one of Church's congressional aides sat Candy down for a talk. He'd seen her in the hallways, shuffling her cards, and took pity. Her biggest problem, he said, was that she drastically overestimated the congressional work ethic.

"Look, Candy, if you want legislation, you will have to write it yourself," he told her.

Candy was sure he was joking. She had no background in law or legislation. Random citizens didn't just write amendments. Did they?

"Why are you looking at me like that?" he asked. "Use this desk right here."

Candy sat down at the desk that would be her temporary new home. It was parked next to a big autopen machine that assistants powered by foot, like a sewing machine, to sign Church's name on constituent letters. She banged away at the typewriter day after day, writing and rewriting each line like it was computer code, then rereading it carefully for potential loopholes.

Three weeks later, she had a draft bill ready. If it passed, the United States wouldn't be able to arm or fund Pakistan in its war against the Bengalis. Church would support it on one condition: She'd need to find a Republican senator—someone from Nixon's own party—for a cosponsor.

Candy realized that she'd swapped one problem for another. The bill laid out in no uncertain terms that Yahya and other West Pakistanis were war criminals. The senators she showed it to squirmed. Pakistan was a loyal Cold War ally, and with the United States already bogged down in the Vietnam War, America needed every international friend it could get. It was a tragedy, sure, but why start a tooth-and-nail battle with Nixon over a cause that harmed America's strategic interests? They had to save those fights for things like health care, things that mattered to everyday Americans. Besides, how could anyone be sure that what Candy said about the massacres was true if even the press was having trouble reporting from East Pakistan?

Nobody wanted to stick their neck out. Candy redoubled her efforts, camping out at Senate offices from early in the morning to late at night, along with the offices of congressmen on the Foreign Affairs subcommittee.

Meanwhile, Jon and the other Americans finally got clearance to come back from Iran; perhaps the Pakistani government was under the impression that a couple of months off had cooled their will to protest. He arrived in Washington on June 2 and eight days later he'd already managed to speak in front of the Senate. Kennedy arranged it.

He said that people would trust him over Candy because of his medical background. Candy overlooked the slight as Senate aides escorted her to the chamber with a group of twentysomething women, all of whom where there for the sole purpose of delivering coffee to their bosses.

Jon gave vivid testimony, speaking passionately for ten minutes. Some senators pretended like they were hearing the news for the first time, as if they hadn't been blowing Candy off for weeks. Now they stood up and fumed at the pulpit. This was an outrage, they said. How dare Nixon keep this from them, they said, and how were they only finding out now?

Jon won over the Democrats, but those in Nixon's party were skeptical. They tried to poke holes in his testimony. One aged senator began: "Doctor, you've told us about all the bad things that happened with our military aid, but that was only $35 million this year, compared to the $50 million in humanitarian aid we committed! Doesn't that mean anything to you?"

"Senator, yes, it does. That tells me it's cheaper to kill people than keep them alive." Jon pulled a photo out of his briefcase. He'd been praying some senator would be dumb enough to bring this up. Jackpot.

"Look at this," he said, holding out a picture of a UNICEF van. The Pakistan army had retrofitted it, mounting a machine gun on the roof and cutting out the sides to fit a dozen armed soldiers so that they could fire in all directions. "This is where your $50 million in aid money went."

The senator glanced at the photo without comment and set it aside. Jon's gotcha moment didn't have the impact he'd expected.

Jon answered the rest of the questions, but as the hearing dragged on and the senators gradually lost interest, one thought kept running through his head: *My God, they really don't care about the Bengalis at all. Why?*

After the hearing, Kennedy assured Jon that his testimony mattered and promised to fight the good fight and do whatever it took.

Word filtered down to Pakistan's embassy in Washington about rabble-rousers trying to scuttle some essential deals. Pakistan ambassador Agha Hilaly was close with Kissinger and started making his own calls. Hilaly was the only man on the planet whom Yahya trusted enough to give a few precious details about the CHINESE CONNECTION.

Hilaly reminded senators that Pakistan was on the front lines of the global war against communism and a loyal friend to the United States. True, there were some missteps in East Pakistan, but that was over now. Sometimes people like Jon got carried away when they first saw how the world really was. And Candy? Well, she was just a woman. Of course she'd be hysterical. Senators nodded into their receivers.

Hilaly also rang up Robert McNamara, the architect of the Vietnam War and then-director of the World Bank. Distressed by Neil Frank's brief and the unfolding chaos, Peter Cargill, the Bank's South Asia head, sent a new fact-finding team to East Pakistan. The horrified team wrote an incendiary internal report, arguing that the World Bank should stop all operations for fear that they were helping the army. When nothing happened, a whistleblower leaked the report to the press.

McNamara couldn't hide his outrage. Not at the findings but at the leakers. He ordered the mole outed and punished. He then wrote Yahya to apologize for the embarrassment and assure him that all World Bank projects in East Pakistan would go on as scheduled. Hilaly handed the letter to Yahya personally.

Hilaly didn't mention to the senators or the World Bank that Nixon was in the middle of a covert arms deal designed to ratchet up the carnage in East Pakistan. Two freighters full of weapons and jet and tank parts were setting sail to Pakistan from New York via Baltimore. The shipment was a clear violation of the arms embargo, so Nixon hid it from Congress. Inside the ship were all the weapons and ammunition that Yahya needed to crush the revolution. Hilaly managed the details and entrusted two Pakistan embassy men who had the highest level of national security clearance to sneak the ships to Karachi.

What Hilaly didn't know is that one of the men was a mole for the resistance and a conscious objector to Pakistan's atrocities. The mole photocopied the cargo manifests and Nixon's signed letter of approval. He sent it to the only person he knew of who cared, the person his boss wouldn't shut up about.

The next morning, an unmarked manila envelope appeared on Candy's desk. Nobody knew who'd dropped it off. Candy tore it open and scanned the first few pages. Minutes later, she started looking up contacts for reporters at the *New York Times*.

The story ran the next morning on the front page: "U.S. Military Goods Sent to Pakistan Despite Ban." It detailed weapons shipments that were misclassified as "auto parts," "wooden boxes," or simply "parts" on the manifests to evade sanctions.

All holy hell broke loose.

Kennedy yelled at everyone he could think of, desperately trying to stop the freighters before they left port. He called up union heads and longshoremen working on the docks, and he told them to get out in canoes and park themselves in the shipping lanes if they had to.

After two months of talking to pleasant brick walls, Candy now had senators begging for an audience. She got her first Republican to support the bill, William Saxbe from Ohio. Church was true to his word and agreed to cosponsor. Kennedy was on board. Ten more followed by noon.

As the freighter captains tried to figure out how to get past some oddly muscled, canoe-paddling activists blocking their way out of Baltimore, the House Foreign Relations Committee was about to put Candy's bill—which mandated a total halt to all economic and military aid to Pakistan—to a vote. If it made it through, then the House and Senate would vote, in turn, to make it law.

A few hours later, Nixon paced back and forth in the Lincoln Sitting Room of the White House. *Goddamnit, Kissinger should have been here an hour ago with news. What is the holdup?*

Minutes passed before Kissinger burst through the door, gasping for air. The man never ran, and he had to put his hands on his knees to recover before he placed an unopened letter into Nixon's sweaty palm.

Nixon ripped it open, his face tense and twisted.

They read it together, standing side by side over the note. They tried not to rush their eyes to the bottom of the page while a gaudy golden clock ticked and tocked on the wall.

All the tension melted from their faces. They broke out in smiles. Kissinger looked triumphant. They were as giddy as schoolgirls.

The note was a handwritten update from Yahya. A Pakistani foreign service officer just flew in from Islamabad with the note sewn up in his suit. There'd been a breakthrough. Yahya convinced the Chinese to host Kissinger as a first secret step toward normalizing relations. And they wanted to do it in two weeks.

Nixon sat at the desk and they wrote a quick confirmation. They sent it as fast as possible, as if the Chinese might change their mind if they had a chance to think twice. Nixon made one demand: that Yahya remain their intermediary for secrecy's sake. They sealed their response and the officer sewed it back into his suit for the return flight home that night.

By God, they'd done it! Nixon ambled over to the liquor cabinet, pushing aside the Johnnie Walker and other assorted half-full brown bottles. This called for something special.

He settled on an elegant bottle of Courvoisier, a special gift from his wife that he'd been saving for the right moment. He popped it open and gave himself and Kissinger a healthy pour.

Nixon raised his glass in one hand and Yahya's letter in the other. "This is the most important communication that has come to an American president since World War II. Let us drink to generations to come who may have a better chance to live in peace because of what we have done."

Meanwhile, the committee voted. Thomas Morgan, the committee chair whom Candy had patiently explained South Asian geography to two months ago, bulldozed the bill through in a quick vote. She cheered and danced. Jon never felt more patriotic. Surely, the House and Senate would act quickly now that they knew hundreds were dying every day. Maybe the freighters would turn back even before they hit international waters.

Their hope in the American political system wouldn't last.

Despite entreaties by Kennedy and others to vote immediately, a group of serious Republicans and concerned Democrats united to table the bill and think it over for a while. Congress went on summer vacation. They'd take up Candy's bill in a month or two. Until then, it was dead in the water.

Nixon never worried about it. He'd had enough votes in his pocket from the start—a coalition of anti-communists and representatives tied to defense firms—to gum up the works. Sure, it was a loss on paper, but the bill wasn't close enough to passage to threaten his plans. A mere proposition couldn't stop ongoing shipments, and Nixon had four full weeks to ram through all the weapons Yahya needed before Congress came back from vacation. Plenty of time.

Candy and Jon ruminated on their friend's Georgetown couch. Months of warning, screaming, doing anything to stop this insane mass killing ran head-on into the slow-as-molasses pace of bureaucracy. Even the proof of genocide couldn't stop Nixon. It was the Cold War, and America's national security trumped every other possible concern. The United States wouldn't turn on its allies, no matter how strong the case.

Two weeks later, the freighters docked in Karachi without further incident. In the end, no longshoreman in a canoe wanted to play chicken with a freighter.

———

Two weeks later, an urgent telegram from one of HELP's Bengali coordinators in London arrived by courier to Candy's desk. The organization was in ruins. Worse, everyone associated with it had to flee East Pakistan. The army branded anyone who wore a HELP badge an enemy of the state: from the administrators down to the armband-wearing distributors. The military stole HELP's every last aid packet, bag, boat, and shirt.

A few lucky souls were able to smuggle themselves to Europe, but the vast majority of Candy's hundreds of employees had no such escape hatch. They had to go by foot like the rest. Reports trickled out of India about new horrors unfolding on the border. Terrified Bengalis fled to India on foot through a hundred-mile gauntlet of trigger-happy soldiers.

To get there, refugees walked past fields of dead bodies that the army dropped on the outskirts of towns. They trudged past babies who sucked on their dead mothers' breasts, desperate for one last meal. Past the mosquito swamps. Past the despair of wailing fathers, unable to stop their families from wasting away. Past the silent toddlers, too weak and dehydrated to cry. Past crematoriums, churning out ash twenty-four hours a day.

If they made it, the reward at the finish line was a wretched cup of cholera-laced rainwater, served under a leaking tarp. The refugees fought for even that, crammed shoulder to shoulder among an almost incalculable mass of ten million other desperate, starving souls who fled to escape the army's butchery and a cyclone that had destroyed their land. It was the largest refugee crisis in history.

Even if the United States was the villain, Candy could still try to do something. Anything.

Candy and Jon booked a flight to Calcutta.

40

Yahya Khan and Henry Kissinger

Henry Kissinger moaned in agony.

Squatting on a luxurious toilet in President House, the US secretary of state had just arrived in Islamabad from India. He'd picked up a nasty stomach bug at a state dinner thrown by Prime Minister Indira Gandhi, a leader whom both he and Nixon liked to call "That Bitch."

After about half an hour Kissinger waddled back down the hall to the living room, where Yahya set a lavish feast in his honor. Officially, this was Kissinger's second and final stop of a South Asian tour aimed to help set America's regional diplomatic priorities. Unofficially, the journey would open a back channel between China and the United States. It would be the first time a US official would visit China in more than two decades. The plan was simple: Kissinger would fake a stomachache, and Yahya would magnanimously offer his mountain villa for him to recuperate out of the public view. That would be enough time to disguise the covert trip to China.

Kissinger held his bowels as they gurgled and pressed their own agenda. Apparently, they didn't get the memo that the sickness was supposed to be a ruse.

"How is your stomach, Dr. Kissinger?" Yahya boomed out to the room as he entered. Kissinger thought that Yahya was overdoing his performance. Yahya winked at him in return.

"You simply must rest at my summer estate for a few days. It will do the body wonders."

"Thank you, Mr. President, but I'm sure I will be fine here."

"No, no, Dr. Kissinger, I absolutely insist." Yahya was practically yelling now. He wanted to make sure nobody missed the excuse. "The heat of Islamabad will impede your recovery. Furthermore, in a Muslim country, it is the host's and not the guest's wishes that are decisive."

Kissinger shrugged for effect, as if he was agreeing that maybe this was the best course of action.

Yahya then led a toast to the American's health.

As the dinner wore on, Yahya got loose. He just couldn't help himself. His audaciousness burst forth in an attempt to impress. It made Kissinger wonder if he'd been right to entrust Yahya with the most delicate operation in the free world.

After ordering another round of wine and whiskey, Yahya launched into a long rant about East Pakistan. The foreign media was making up the most awful sorts of stories about what the army was doing. Worse, they were attacking his incorruptible, unimpeachable character. They called him a monster, could you believe it? Some papers promoted grotesque cartoons, making him look fat and hairy! It was all so uncivil, just too disrespectful.

He had to set the record straight for his exalted guest.

"Everyone calls me a dictator," Yahya said, then pointed at one of his generals. "Am I a dictator?"

"No, Mr. President, of course you are not."

Yahya pointed at the next man. "Am I a dictator?"

"No, sir. That's preposterous."

Yahya went around the table, soliciting responses from the entire dinner party. They all assured Yahya that he was not, in fact, a dictator.

Finally, Yahya asked Kissinger, "Am I a dictator?"

"I don't know, Mr. President, except that for a dictator you run a lousy election."

Yahya roared with laughter. He bragged late into the night about how badly Pakistan would annihilate India if they tried to invade.

Kissinger wasn't so sure. Yahya's East Pakistan offensive was so blatantly outside the rules of warfare that even Kissinger, an über-hawk, publicly told him to tone it down. Maybe Yahya could let the United Nations take care of some refugees, he explained, or appoint a token Bengali figurehead, instead of allowing Tikka and Niazi to outdo themselves in cruelty. Otherwise, Gandhi might get involved. She wouldn't really have a choice.

Yahya blew it off. He reminded Kissinger about the historic superiority of Muslim fighters against Hindus. Besides, with the United States behind them now, the Indians would never dare.

Kissinger said that they might indeed dare. The rest of the dinner party sat in stony silence.

Kissinger pressed on: India had just bought an airport's worth of top-of-the-line Soviet jets and tanks. Plus, India's army was twice the size of Pakistan's.

Yahya roared again, his jowls shaking in delight. He told Kissinger to study a bit more history before prognosticating about the subcontinent. After all, Pakistan had the world's most brilliant military minds.

Kissinger's guts convulsed in pain again. He excused himself to the guesthouse for bed without finishing the conversation.

Three hours later, Kissinger woke to a stern knock on his door. A red VW Beetle idled outside; his airport taxi was right on time. Kissinger threw on a hat and dark sunglasses and left President House at three-thirty a.m. sharp. He contorted himself into the back of the car, flanked by two Secret Service guards, while his body double drove off for the mountains. All radio traffic about the operation used the code name "Polo" for Kissinger, in honor of Marco Polo and his trip to China seven hundred years earlier.

Darkness still enveloped the airport when Kissinger's car arrived.

Yahya's personal pilot waited in a Boeing 707, along with a skeleton crew. The car rolled to a stop inside a steel hangar dotted with armed guards. Kissinger and his Secret Service detail climbed out of the car and walked up the stairs. Once inside the plane, he'd be totally cut off from outside communication for three days. He removed his sunglasses and scanned the skyline, soaking in the moment.

Halfway up, Kissinger made out the silhouettes of two figures just inside the plane's door. He held his breath and adjusted his hat. He wanted to make a dignified first impression when he met his very first Chinese communist.

But his bodyguards acted first. They whipped out their pistols like cowboys, ready to make a kill shot, just in case communism happened to be contagious. Kissinger froze. He had never touched a gun in his life, and now, his bodyguards' weapons were mere inches from his ears. Mao's officers smiled over the gun barrels, disarming the moment. Firefight averted, the 707 took off in total darkness.

Yahya woke with a hangover, but his spirits improved when he learned that the drop-off had gone without a hitch. This mission would change the world. Yahya's last two months were a blur of ten-hour working days and six-hour drinking nights dedicated to micromanaging every last aspect, down to the make and model of the car that Kissinger would take to the airport, to ensure that nothing could possibly go wrong. And, indeed, nothing had gone wrong.

Yahya felt like that was cause for celebration. He ordered his advisers to prepare an epic party, sparing no expense. He wanted Shakespeare and singing. Dancing and poetry. Tonight, everyone would enjoy a hard-earned reward. He called General Rani and told her to make sure the guests matched his expectations.

While the party planners buzzed, Yahya occupied his afternoon with a task that needed particular attention. He'd neglected it for months because of the CHINESE CONNECTION, but there was finally time to give it the seriousness it deserved. Yahya ordered in two key advisers for a long-overdue update. It was important to make the right choice, the advisers said. It was a delicate situation. They debated if the problem was simply an invasive species that couldn't live peacefully with anyone, and if there was any way to force the two groups to live together without killing each other. Yahya squinted out the window. The advisers presented Yahya with three choices.

Yahya decided. He would populate the bird-viewing pond outside his window with Australian parrots. The cranes and swans would go in the pool instead as they were more compatible with each other. The landscapers complimented him on his excellent foresight before leaving to implement his directive.

Yahya finally felt like a real leader, the ultimate Man of Action. Without an opposition party, the government ran like a well-oiled machine. That evening, he sauntered into his celebration. Half the guests were a who's who of the governing elite—generals, politicians, and advisers—while the other half were musicians, actresses, sycophants, and socialites courtesy of General Rani. Yahya invited his son, Ali, too, now that he was nearly nineteen years old. It was never too soon to show Ali how business really got done in Pakistan.

Ali gazed around the room, entranced by the revelry and opulence. He was used to partying with the sons and daughters of the country's elite; actually being in the same room as the real power was something different. Nearby, Rani and Bhutto chatted like the old friends they were, while Yahya milled about with assorted eye candy.

Then Yahya stopped dead in his tracks. A sari-clad Bengali woman recited Byron for the growing crowd. She spoke the poet's lines confidently, with the authentic British accent that Yahya had long aspired to perfect. Smart women turned Yahya on. She was in her mid-forties, plump and regal. Just his type. She effortlessly switched from Byron to Shakespeare, commanding the crowd's attention with her grace.

That was all Yahya needed to know he was in love.

Across the room, Ali watched her, equally awestruck.

Her name was Begum Hussain, a Bengali living in West Pakistan. Yahya called her Black Beauty. Though born into high society, she'd somehow married a lowly Bengali police officer and had four children. Ostracized from her family for the perceived slight, she clawed her way back into the elite through the force of her intellect and refinement. Indeed, her ability to project a dignified British upper-crust air was perhaps the only thing that saved her from the fate of her Bengali compatriots. She was at the party by sheer coincidence. Yahya added her husband to his security detail a few months before; the only reason he got the job was because Yahya wanted to put a token Bengali on his team, to show the media and whoever else asked that he wasn't prejudiced.

He walked over to give Mrs. Hussain a dose of presidential charm. By the end of the night, the two were scheming to send her husband to Austria as an ambassador, alone. Hussain's cop husband would be thrilled with the promotion.

Ali jealously watched the two of them giggle and flirt. Then he watched as they left the party together, before he'd even had a chance to say hello.

Two days later, Yahya cleared out the cobwebs with a quick swig of Black Dog. The swill calmed his nerves. His tryst had lasted fifty-six straight hours, and the only reason he broke it off was because Kissinger would be back any minute.

No news from his ambassador in Peking was probably good news, but there was no way of knowing for sure until he saw Kissinger's face. The only hiccup that he'd heard about so far was that Kissinger's body double got sick all over the mountain guesthouse after eating half a crate of overripe mangos. Considering Kissinger's stomach-bug alibi, Yahya felt Allah himself was on his side.

Kissinger snuck back via the VW Beetle to President House just after lunch. He was grinning from ear to ear, holding a copy of Mao's words translated into English in one hand and a photo album of his trip in the other. That was all Yahya needed to see to know the mission was a success. They'd done it. Yahya hopped around like a schoolboy, asking Kissinger to relive every moment.

Kissinger got along famously with the Chinese, and now a meeting between Nixon and Mao was in the works. Even better, Kissinger's trip succeeded in its mission of total secrecy; nobody had discovered the ruse. Kissinger called it one of the greatest feats in the history of diplomacy and international relations. And Yahya got his greatest wish: Just as he'd promised, Kissinger confirmed for Yahya that the United States and China would offer Pakistan their full support if India ever dared to try and go to war over East Pakistan.

They sent a telegram to Nixon:

WE HAVE LAID THE GROUNDWORK FOR YOU AND MAO TO TURN A PAGE IN HISTORY. THE PROCESS WE HAVE STARTED WILL SEND ENORMOUS SHOCK WAVES AROUND THE WORLD. IF WE CAN MAS-TER IT, WE WILL HAVE MADE A REVOLUTION.

Still high from the victory, Kissinger took Air Force Two back to America and wrote Yahya a parting note of thanks:

I SHALL ALWAYS REMEMBER YOUR GENEROSITY WHEN YOU IN-SISTED ON SETTING ASIDE THE MASSIVE PROBLEMS THAT YOUR COUNTRY FACES, CONCENTRATING INSTEAD ON MY VISIT TO PE-KING. YOUR EFFORTS HAVE MADE INDELIBLE CONTRIBUTIONS TO THE FOREIGN POLICY OBJECTIVES OF THE UNITED STATES, AND I BELIEVE, THE GOAL OF PEACE IN THE WORLD.

Yahya sat alone at his desk, reading the note proudly. He breathed a sigh of relief. Military support from the United States and China meant that Pakistan's future would never be in question again. His own legacy was secure. He'd crushed every conceivable obstacle to dust.

He placed the note in the back of his bulging CHINESE CON-NECTION folder: the very last contribution.

Tumbler in hand, Yahya flipped through the forty-nine documents one last time—the photocopies, the carbon papers, the dictated notes, the cyphers, the letters and handwritten scribbles that filled the CHINESE CONNECTION—then put the folder in a desk drawer. Kissinger later said it was the last happy day of Yahya's life.

41

Hafiz Uddin Ahmad

Hafiz flexed his bare six-pack and scratched along the ground with a scythe. He was naked, except for a farmer's lungi, a pistol, and a set of iron shears carefully concealed in the folds of the waistband. *The perfect disguise*, he thought. Costumed like a laborer, he cast a sideways glance at a barbed-wire military perimeter. Behind it: a Pakistani bunker.

Hafiz and a handful of scouts arrived outside the hamlet of Kamalpur a few days earlier, along with a hundred and fifty Mukti Bahini fighters. They'd trained in the Indian jungle for six weeks, and now it was time to go on the offensive. This small outpost sat between the Indian border and Dacca. Hafiz's Indian handlers wanted it out of the way if and when Indira Gandhi green-lit the Indian army's invasion. They hoped it would be the first real victory in a young war and a way to show the Pakistanis that this small group of rebels was a force capable of more than cutting supply lines and making a nuisance in tiny engagements, that it could confront the Pakistani military.

The problem was that they had no intel on the outpost itself and, therefore, no idea of its weak points. Nearby farmers worked fields just outside the wire without raising suspicion. Maybe if they could look the part, his fighters could glean useful information. Hafiz smiled at the other men in his group, admiring how convincing their costumes were. In another life, he would have made a sharp-looking farmhand.

With the scorching late-July sun beating down on their brows, the scouts approached the bunkers and could make out the silhouettes of khaki-clad soldiers behind the gunmetal. Hafiz and his men inched forward, intent on making a few cuts in the razor wire that might help during the attack. Hafiz studied the fortifications—concrete bunkers reinforced with heavy tree trunks and several rows of wire. It wasn't good news. He wasn't sure how his men would fare in a protracted battle.

He gripped the handle of his sheers and worked up the nerve to get even closer when a farmer—a real farmer—waved in his direction. The man shook his head as vigorously as someone could inside the sightlines of Pakistani machine gunners.

"Brother, get away from here. You're going to get us all killed," the farmer said in upbeat Bengali, hoping that the troops inside wouldn't make out the local language.

Hafiz puckered inside as his faith in his costume met harsh reality. No matter how good he thought he looked, neither Hafiz nor his men actually passed for farmers. The soldiers in that bunker had been staring at the same faces for months and were always looking for excuses to shoot Bengalis simply on suspicion of being part of the Mukti Bahini.

Now someone was moving inside the bunker, paying more attention than was comfortable. Hafiz motioned to his men with a hand signal that told them to slink back out of sight. They made their way back to their lines with their lives, but the recon failed. They'd have to attack blind.

Before the sun rose three days later on July 31, Hafiz knew that the attack on Kamalpur would mark a new phase in the Bengali rebellion, one way or the other. He radioed Zia, asking for another week to prepare and do proper recon. Negative. The attack had to happen today.

The plan was a simple pincer movement aimed at dividing the enemy forces. Hafiz commanded Bravo Company and took up a position in the north, while a brash young captain named Salauddin Mumtaz led Delta Company's charge from the east. Before they separated, Hafiz saw that Salauddin had opted to carry a megaphone with him into battle instead of a rifle.

"What's that for?" Hafiz asked.

"How will the Pakistanis know they can surrender if I don't tell them?" he replied with a smirk.

Hafiz couldn't help but crack a smile at the thought of his comrade popping out from behind a tree to demand that the bunkered men lay down their weapons and give up.

Hafiz laid on his stomach next to his radio operator and kept his eyes trained on Kamalpur's distant fortifications. It rained after he got back from his scouting trip, and the ground was still muddy. The captain angled his watch to catch the moonlight. They were going to attack at first light: 4:45 a.m. His watch read 4:40.

Luckily, they weren't alone. A little way back, the Indian army had set up mortars and Soviet artillery to help cover the attack. The Indians promised to hold their fire until they heard combat; this way, Delta and Bravo companies could traverse as much ground as possible with the element of surprise and rely on the big guns to keep the Pakistanis from taking precise shots.

Hafiz lay in the mud of the Bengal jungle, mere minutes from facing down gunsights from the very army officers who would have once called him a friend.

Hafiz's watch clicked to 4:44, and he took a deep breath.

Then he heard a whistle. Something hurtled over his head. Explosives detonated near the Pakistani position, but not directly on it. The Indians had fired early. *Dammit.* Hafiz didn't have any other choice but to charge, leading a hundred and fifty boys into battle for the first time. And without the element of surprise. They had no idea what they were headed into.

Captain Salauddin's own order to charge crackled over the wireless. The two units had to cover ground fast, before the Pakistanis started to fire.

His men shouted, *"Allahu akbar."*

"Joi Bangla!"

The entire force converged on the fortifications. A hundred and fifty men fired in the direction of the enemy.

From somewhere in the middle of the charge, Hafiz could see that almost every single man in his unit was aiming too high, sending their ammunition fruitlessly into the ether. *Why is it so hard to train men to shoot at the enemy?* he seethed.

Seconds later, the bunker's dark windows erupted with the rapid-fire machine guns. Three men collapsed in front of Hafiz in the first salvo. He and his men pushed on to the outermost tangle of razor wire and cut what they could.

Ten yards in front of him, he saw a puff of black smoke and a hot white flash. One of his men stepped on a land mine in the no-man's-land before the bunker. Another man exploded a second later.

Hafiz squeezed the trigger of his rifle, taking aim at the enemy machine-gun placement. Even though he had next to no chance of actually hitting someone behind the fortifications, he hoped that the distraction of his bullets pinging off their concrete walls would at least make it harder for the Pakistani soldiers to pick off his men.

It wasn't working.

Mortars and bullets crashed around him. He tried to reach Salauddin on the wireless. Only static.

And yet, while men died in all directions, his force continued to make forward progress.

Hafiz somehow made it to wall of the bunker. He wasn't sure how he'd survived this long. Someone threw a grenade in, neutralizing the first line of the Pakistani defense. But as Hafiz climbed over the fortification, he saw that it was just one of several similar fortifications before the interior of the base. On the other side of the bunker was another stretch of barbed wire. The next machine gunner was already hard at work ending the lives of the attacking force.

"Delta Company, come in!" he shouted into the wireless set. He hoped that his counterpart had made miraculous progress and could help Hafiz's own pitiful situation.

He waited for a moment. Nothing. He had to assume that Salauddin was already dead.

Hafiz looked out at the doomed Bengali soldiers who pushed forward despite the deadly fire. Every minute that ticked by meant another dead soldier. *Only a freedom fighter could give his life so willingly*, he thought.

Hafiz wouldn't give up. Not yet. He moved toward the second line of bunkers. Barely three steps into his charge, his radio operator stepped on a land mine; the blast took his leg off just above the knee. The man bled out in seconds.

Hafiz pulled up his weapon to return fire but was surprised to see that his hands were empty. The blast that killed his radio man had sent a piece of shrapnel through the stock of his rifle, and his weapon all but disintegrated. Somehow, amid the cacophony, he hadn't noticed.

He didn't pause to think about what would have happened to his body if his rifle hadn't blocked the flying metal. Instead, he peeled the wireless off the fallen soldier's back and appointed a new radio operator. The new operator managed to reach Salahuddin's wireless. An unfamiliar voice crackled back: "Delta Company's captain is dead. What are your orders, Hafiz?"

Did they dare continue forward in the face of certain death? Was it better to spare the lives of his soldiers on the field to fight another day, or to try to take a bunker that they surely wouldn't be able to hold?

Before Hafiz could decide, another mortar exploded just a few feet from where he crouched. Splinters of hot metal shot through his hand and shoulder and sent him careening backward into a ditch.

It took a moment to clear the fireworks from his eyes. Blood gushed from some unseen wound and turned his uniform a deep shade of purple. He crumpled to the ground, and with the last of his energy, told his radio man to order the retreat.

Men continued to fall as the two companies pulled back. Of the hundred and fifty who began the charge, thirty-five men died in just under two hours of fighting. Seventy returned wounded. Salauddin's corpse stayed behind, rotting in grim repose on the enemy's barbed wire.

Too wounded to retreat under his own power, Hafiz's eyesight blurred from the pain. He saw his men falling, one after the other, in what seemed like slow motion. They were corpses before they even hit the ground. The revolution crumbled all around him.

He ached to see the Pakistanis pay for the rape and murder of his country. But there was nothing he could do now. Blown off his position into the ditch, he didn't even have a pistol at hand to fire a final futile shot.

Hafiz let the darkness take over.

Ravi Shankar, George Harrison, Richard Nixon, and Henry Kissinger

MADISON SQUARE GARDEN, NEW YORK CITY

AUGUST 1, 1971

Concert for Bangladesh

Ravi Shankar methodically plucked the seven top strings on his sitar, drawing twanged melodies out of the four-foot-long instrument. Surrounded by marigolds and burning incense, Shankar paired the heavy top strings with notes from the airy twelve bottom strings, making complex sounds that a guitar could never attain. Barefoot, sitting cross-legged on a large antique rug, and draped in an exquisite white kurta, he was the world's best-known sitar player and a musical deity in his home of India.

Shankar paused for a moment; the packed Madison Square Garden crowd cheered wildly. He smirked like he was remembering a joke. He'd toured the United States for a few years now and gotten used to the flower-power hippie crowd trying to find God by mixing his live music with drugs.

He finished adjusting his instrument and took the microphone. "If you appreciate the tuning so much, I hope you'll enjoy the playing more."

To be fair, a sports arena was a pretty odd place to showcase an instrument best suited for intimate rooms or beneath banyan trees.

Still, Shankar couldn't resist gently mocking their musical ignorance. They cheered again, their marijuana haze easily deflecting his barb. Shankar played on as his sharp, lingering notes reverberated through the cavernous steel rafters and echoed away into oblivion. Backstage, George Harrison, Eric Clapton, and Ringo Starr waited their turns to perform.

This was the birth of a new phenomenon in American music: the rock-and-roll charity benefit concert. The idea was as simple as it was unorthodox: leverage the power of celebrity musicians to draw attention to an under-recognized human rights issue and raise money for organizations working in the field.

Two months earlier, Shankar paced around his Spanish-style villa in the heart of Hollywood. He'd followed the horrors in Pakistan, like every other overseas Bengali, and felt a kinship with the Pakistani Bengalis from just across the border of his own home in Calcutta. As the most famous living Bengali in the world, friends, gurus, and countrymen all asked him to help. Could he play a benefit at the local temple? And one at a high school too? Shankar agreed time and again, but the pitiful handfuls of money, one three-hour show at a time, couldn't possibly move the needle when ten million were starving to death.

Then Shankar's friend George Harrison called. He was coming to Los Angeles to work on a film score and would love to get in a sitar lesson or two. Shankar and Harrison had been friends ever since the Beatles ventured to India in 1966. John Lennon, Paul McCartney, and Ringo Starr soaked in the subcontinent like typical tourists, hitting up spiritual hotspots to taste transcendent religious bliss, only to have it evaporate by the time their plane touched down in London.

But Harrison was different. He spent the next four years diving ever deeper into Indian mysticism. He flew around the world to seek out temples and ashrams, rereading the Bhagavad Gita and *Autobiography of a Yogi*, and studying at the feet of gurus, babas, and swamis. With music part and parcel of his spiritual journey (not to mention copious amounts of LSD, weed, and cocaine), he'd sought out India's most famous musician.

The moment Harrison heard Shankar play, he said, "I felt I wanted to walk out of my home that day and buy a one-way ticket to Calcutta. I would even have left my wife behind."

The feeling wasn't exactly mutual. Shankar had never heard a Beatles song in his life. Harrison told the Bengali musician he played sitar on their megahit "Norwegian Wood." When Shankar listened to it later, he told a *Rolling Stone* journalist: "To tell you the truth, I had to keep my mouth shut. I couldn't believe it. It sounded so terrible."

Still, Shankar loved Harrison's earnestness. Harrison loved that Shankar was one of the only people who never asked him for anything. They became fast friends.

And when Harrison came by Shankar's house that summer day in 1971, Shankar asked his first-ever favor. "George, this is the situation, I know it doesn't concern you, I know you can't possibly identify . . . but would you help me?"

Shankar mailed Harrison newspaper clippings of the atrocities that had been written by journalists who snuck back into Dacca to document Yahya and Tikka's genocidal path, but he didn't know if Harrison cared enough to read them. Shankar hoped they could do a fund-raiser together. With luck they might get $25,000.

Harrison sat back and squinted, calculating the request.

Maybe I went too far, Shankar thought. Now he looked like just another hanger-on hoping to milk a Beatle. Harrison had ended friendships for less.

Harrison snapped back to attention. No, a fund-raiser was no good. They needed something bigger, another Woodstock, but one where every artist would play for free and every penny would help East Pakistan's refugees. They'd make an album and a movie. They'd raise millions.

A musical revolution was born. They called it The Concert for Bangla Desh.

Harrison rang up his friends: the world's biggest rock stars. Getting a visa for Mick Jagger would be tricky after he'd been busted for marijuana possession. Bob Dylan was Harrison's idol, but he'd stopped performing live in 1966. The Beatles broke up two years back, and they were barely on speaking terms. And Eric Clapton was a heroin junkie, madly in love with Harrison's wife, Pattie. Harrison asked them all anyway—and dozens more. He made the calls on his rotary phone, from dawn until dusk, for six straight weeks.

For the show, Harrison and Shankar agreed they'd start with a traditional Bengali music set, then bring on the rock. Harrison hired an Indian astrologer, who picked out the most auspicious date: August 1, 1971. Conveniently, it was also the only open date on the Garden's calendar on such short notice.

Shankar reached a blistering crescendo under the hot amber lights. Tabla, sarod, and tamboura players matched him, beat for beat, and doubled their tempo. Joni Mitchell, Crosby, Stills & Nash, The Who, and Grand Funk Railroad swayed along in the front row. Behind them, 19,500 fans itched for Shankar's long set to wrap while they waited for the main event.

Shankar tore through the last few dozen notes at 140 beats per minute, grinning from ear to ear. The crowd broke into wild applause. Then Shankar bowed, picked up his ten-pound sitar, and strolled backstage as the audio-visual team flicked on a documentary. The movie aimed to shock. Thousands of screaming fans hushed themselves to silence while absorbing nauseating images of crows picking at rotting corpses on the outskirts of Calcutta, Bengali mothers wiping biting flies off toddlers too weak to protest, and cholera victims dying in ditches.

The film's credits rolled with a plea to give to UNICEF and Harrison took the stage. He scanned the crowd nervously, white electric guitar in hand. The cord got wrapped around his foot. He had no idea if the show was going to be legendary—or just a legendary debacle. He wore a white suit with a red Om embroidered on the lapel in Sanskrit, a red button-up shirt, and a full Jesus beard and hair. He shook off the cord and strummed the opening bars of one of his biggest post-Beatles hits, "Wah-Wah." Ringo delivered drums right on cue.

Emotions rose as they played a series of massive hits, one after another, including "Jumpin' Jack Flash" to honor Mick Jagger, as well as some Beatles' tunes sung live by a Beatle for the first time in several years. A mustachioed Clapton floated his way onstage, dressed in a navy blue sports coat and jeans. He accessorized the outfit with a bloodstream packed to the gills with opioids.

Clapton wedged his lit cigarette into his guitar's headstock and launched into a duet with Harrison. Together, they did the first ever live performance of "While My Guitar Gently Weeps." Clapton later said he was ashamed because he was so high he could barely walk, let alone play. The crowd was too enthralled at the sight of George Harrison and Eric Clapton riffing together to care.

Now they were rolling. Harrison wrapped up "Here Comes the Sun," then took a quick sip from a Coca-Cola can resting on the monitor. He glanced offstage and breathed a sigh of relief. A man with a simple guitar at his side and a harmonica strapped to his neck waited for his turn onstage. He'd just biked into the arena, appearing like a divine apparition.

"I'd like to bring out a friend to us all, Mr. Bob Dylan!"

The crowd erupted. Dylan had gone recluse at the height of his popularity five years earlier and wasn't listed on the roster. He brought tender soul to his renditions of "A Hard Rain's A-Gonna Fall" and "Blowin' in the Wind," channeling the Great Bhola Cyclone through his song selections.

The concert was just one of dozens of public outpourings in support of the Bengali cause during that summer and fall. West Pakistan imprisoned a pregnant woman from Philadelphia for illegally crossing from India to East Pakistan to deliver saris. A Dutch man stole a famous Vermeer painting and tried to fence it for millions of dollars in order to give the sum in relief aid. Children in thirty thousand schools across America fasted for a day so that they could donate their lunch money to the cause. Activists built a refugee camp out of sewer pipes in front of the UN, about a mile and a half northeast of Madison Square Garden. They tried to shock the diplomats and ate the same single daily meal of rice and lentils that refugees did, while Allen Ginsberg read poetry.

In Paris, a former French special forces officer took a pistol and a briefcase bursting with colorful wires up to the cockpit of a Pakistan International Airways plane bound for Karachi. He hijacked it, demanding twenty tons of medical supplies for the Calcutta refugee camps. During the tense standoff, the French Red Cross brought the supplies as requested. Commandos disguised as airport workers loaded the crates, then captured the skyjacker. Though he only carried a toy gun and some wires, he still got five years in jail for the stunt. Nevertheless, the French Red Cross delivered the goods to the refugee camps as promised.

Yet none of those protests captured the imagination quite like the Concert for Bangladesh. It launched a geopolitical issue into America's collective psyche in a way that no concert ever had before. Harrison closed the show with a brand-new song. He called it "Bangla Desh." The lyrics were a simple plea to his millions of fans to help a suffering people. Harrison and the rest of rock's biggest stars left the stage, pumping their fists to raucous whistles and whoops.

Clapton said, "This will always be remembered as a time that we could be proud of being musicians. We just weren't thinking of ourselves for five minutes."

Shankar agreed: "It was a miracle, really."

At the after-party, Keith Moon demolished a drum set and hotel room in celebration, as they all reveled in a job well done. The live concert album sold millions of copies and won a Grammy.

The morning after the concert, Richard Nixon welcomed Henry Kissinger into the Oval Office for a debriefing. Transcripts of their conversations would eventually come out during the Watergate hearings.

NIXON: Tell me about Pakistan. I see the Beatles are out raising money for them. You know, it's a funny thing, the way we are in this goddamn country. We get involved in all these screwball causes.

KISSINGER: Who are they raising money for? The refugees in India?

NIXON: Refugees, yeah.

KISSINGER: Is it for India or Pakistan?

NIXON: The goddamn Indians.

KISSINGER: Well, we've given them seventy million dollars. No one knows how they're using the goddamn money, because—

NIXON: You're giving it to the government?

KISSINGER: Yeah.

NIXON: Well, that's a terrible mistake.

KISSINGER: Well, they don't let any foreigners into the refugee area. Their record is outrageous.

NIXON: Well, what about Pakistan?

KISSINGER: Well, we moved in a hundred million dollars' worth of food, which is in the port. We've had a task force working on it. The big problem now is to get it distributed. The UN has sent in thirty-eight experts.

NIXON: What can we do though? What are you going to tell the Indian ambassador? What the hell can you tell that son of a gun?

KISSINGER: I'm going to tell him, "I just want you to understand one thing. If there is a war in the subcontinent, we are going to move against you, one way or the other."

NIXON: Right.

KISSINGER: And if you think you can afford to throw yourself completely into Soviet arms, go ahead and do it.

NIXON: That's right. Tell him the president wants him to know that in the event that they decide to go to war in the subcontinent, and side with the Soviets, then they have chosen. And much as I will regret it, we will have to take another position—and will.

KISSINGER: Right.

NIXON: And he'll have a fit. And you can sort of play this, you say: "Now, Mr. Ambassador, you know how I personally feel." Give him a little bullshit about how much you love the Indians.

KISSINGER: If there's a God, he'll punish me.

NIXON: We've got to fight like hell. At least the Congress, thank God, is gone. We've got three to four weeks.

KISSINGER: Yahya will probably attack India now.

NIXON: I fear he will commit suicide.

KISSINGER: No, he will fight. Just as Abraham Lincoln would have fought.

ACT III

THE RECKONING

42

Hafiz Uddin Ahmad

TURA AND CALCUTTA, INDIA

AUGUST 1, 1971

Hafiz blinked through a haze of painkillers, grit, and dried tears. The bright white room and stiff antiseptic mattress told him that he must be in a hospital. A cheap ceiling fan spun lazily above; he sensed its faint breeze on his cheeks. Eventually, he made out a small brown shape by the side of his bed. Straining his eyes, the blur transformed into a boy. He couldn't have been more than fourteen. The child gripped a glass of water and stared at Hafiz's bandages.

"Where are you hurt?" The boy spoke in a rural Bengali dialect.

Where doesn't it hurt? Hafiz thought. Jagged pieces of metal skewered his torso and hand. Had the pieces hit an artery, he never would have woken up. The explosions left his body so badly shaken that every joint screamed out in pain, but he knew that pain was a good sign—a sign that he'd survive and heal. He was lucky.

Hafiz took a deep, grateful breath. Then he exhaled and took a second look at the boy. A white bandage with a red spot at the tip truncated the boy's arm at the wrist.

"I think I'll make it." Hafiz winked. He asked about the kid's injuries.

"It's nothing, sir. I went out to lay a mine in the road across the border, but something went wrong. I lost my hand." The kid was matter-of-fact about it. Almost proud. These were just the things that happened in war.

It wasn't the worst horror that Hafiz had witnessed these last months, but it was still hard to see. Tears came back to his eyes. He tried to tell himself that they were tears of pride, for the willingness of a child to sacrifice himself for Bangladesh.

Later that afternoon, surgeons dug around for shrapnel inside Hafiz's body. It was a hit-or-miss affair, and they rarely got everything in cases like these. The good news was that none of the pieces punctured any major organs. The doctors predicted that he'd be back to the front in no time. As they tugged the Pakistani- and American-made metal out of his flesh, half a world away the Concert for Bangladesh was in full swing.

It took Hafiz three bedridden days in the hospital before he felt good enough to walk. He learned that two of his men risked their lives to drag his comatose body back to safety. They were among the last men to retreat. Hafiz felt impossibly lucky—a luck he didn't deserve.

He requested a discharge from the hospital and hobbled his way to a training camp on the outskirts of town, where the Mukti Bahini were busily replacing their casualties. There, he met Major Zia Rahman, the leader of his battalion and the man who urged every Bengali military unit to resist the Pakistan military at all costs over the radio in the first days of Operation Searchlight. Zia took the Kamalpur defeat hard, furious at the needless loss of life. The major fumed when he learned that the Indians ordered an artillery barrage without waiting for proper reconnaissance or the sounds of gunfire. That error alone may have doomed the assault.

In his makeshift office, Zia assured Hafiz that he wasn't upset with him. "You need to rest your body and your mind after a battle like that," Zia said. He suggested that Hafiz visit Calcutta.

Hafiz resisted the suggestion at first. He wanted to be with his men; a holiday felt wrong. But Zia was adamant.

So later that day, Hafiz boarded an Indian Airlines flight into an entirely different world. Forty-five minutes later, he disembarked in Calcutta, the spiritual center of Bengali culture. Hafiz couldn't believe that only a couple of years ago he spent entire days consumed in pulp stories about this city's gritty and alluring underbelly—or that, until just a few months ago, he was a loyal Pakistani soldier determined to fight their sworn enemy of India. It seemed reasonable back then that the only way he'd ever actually see a major Indian city would be from behind a gun sight.

But as Hafiz wandered around the cultural epicenter, he witnessed something even stranger: The city welcomed him with open arms.

Up was down and down was up. His former enemies were now his friends. Some of his former friends were now his enemies. The city was full of resistance soldiers and refugees, and everyone wanted to help him with whatever he needed. Contacts in the resistance loaned him a Toyota, and he scored a bedroom in the home of Aly Zaker, a prominent actor living in Calcutta in exile. Hafiz had seen Zaker onstage in Dacca but never met him in person. Now Zaker used his talents to read the news on Independent Bengali radio, which broadcast his famous, familiar voice to the interior of the liberation movement.

When Hafiz arrived, Zaker's family looked over his wounds. They'd hosted many fighters and were relieved that this officer's injuries weren't life threatening. They also desperately wanted to know when he thought Bangladesh would finally achieve independence.

His mind raced back to the failure at Kamalpur, how they had left the bodies of his friends tangled in barbed wire on the battlefield. What could he say? Surely it was not just a matter of time. Freedom would come at the expense of more Bengali lives. There was no other way.

It seemed that all the leaders of the Bengali resistance came through Calcutta that week, and they all asked Hafiz how Kamalpur could have happened. Even General M. A. G. Osmani—the overarching commander of all Mukti Bahini operations—dropped in. Hafiz ignored his body's cries and snapped upright to salute him. The general led masterful resistance movements in sectors all across East Pakistan.

Everyone knew that if the Bengalis had any chance, it would be through this man's military acumen. Osmani criticized Zia for forcing a suicide mission before they were ready. Never mind the damn Indians, he said, the consequences were Zia's to own up to.

Osmani placed a fatherly hand on Hafiz's shoulder. "Thank God you are alive." Osmani gave Hafiz a few months' worth of pocket money. It was all the wealth Hafiz had in the world.

Though he didn't fill Hafiz in, Osmani was putting the finishing touches on a plan to attack Pakistani naval targets and reverse the war's momentum. In the previous months, the Mukti Bahini had conducted a largely ineffective monsoon offensive with small, sporadic attacks across East Pakistan. The battle of Kamalpur was the first major engagement against the Pakistani army, but even though it was a resounding defeat, it was a sign of things to come. India was building up large forces on the border of East Pakistan, and many people believed they were simply waiting for the drier winter weather to start an all-out offensive. If the Mukti Bahini crumbled before that, the Indian forces wouldn't have the much-needed support on the ground to prepare the way for the attack.

Earlier that summer, Bengali submariners on a Pakistani boat, the *Mangro*, almost carried off a mutiny while docked in France. The plan fell apart when Pakistani naval intelligence caught wind of the plot. One man died, but the remaining twelve mutineers escaped to Geneva. When the submariners made it back to the resistance, they convinced Osmani that the Pakistan Navy would be easy prey for commando teams. Their intelligence informed Osmani's offensive against ports across the delta. Osmani dubbed it Operation Jackpot.

Hafiz left the meeting a bit more optimistic, but everything was still so surreal. Just a few days ago, he was fighting for his life. Now he could feel history come alive at every turn. He threw on some gray trousers and a collared shirt and took off for a wander, zigzagging through MG Road, Park Street, and College Street. On Theatre Road, he recognized Tanvir Majhar, a top Bengali cricket player he'd known in Dacca. The man waved from across the street.

"The great Hafiz Uddin!" the man exclaimed. They met with an embrace, athlete to athlete. "The resistance could use you in the stadium!"

Hafiz cocked an eyebrow and thumbed his busted hand. What could he mean?

Majhar told him that most professional Bengali football players fled to Calcutta and now played exhibition games to raise money for the resistance. He was now their manager. Having a stud like Hafiz could double the take at the gate.

"You should see the crowds!"

They took his jeep to a house tucked away off Sudder Street. Inside was an all-star lineup of Bengali football talent: Pintu, Nurunnabi, Imam, Ainul, Kayakobad, Pratab, and Taslim. Hafiz smiled so broadly that his cheeks hurt. He'd played with these men on the Pakistan National Team, at Dacca Stadium in front of tens of thousands of screaming fans. Pintu was with him in Iran, when dozens of women hounded them for autographs. They'd eaten with Ravi Shankar together. After fleeing from Jessore, Hafiz figured he'd never see any of them again.

While East Pakistan languished under a news blackout, the Indian press ran unfiltered stories about the genocide. They had good reason: After so many lost everything in the cyclone, the army's massacres forced millions to flee to India. They festered underneath canvas tents, in culverts, or in makeshift shelters cobbled together with little more than leaves, worn-out sari material, and branches. India spent immense sums every month just scrounging up food.

Indira Gandhi warned Nixon that her country couldn't keep bearing the costs of social upheaval in East Pakistan and that if the influx of refugees didn't stop, it could start a war. To hedge her bets, she signed a mutual defense agreement with the Soviet Union.

Nevertheless, the Bengali plight garnered sympathy across India, and the football players emerged as important tools in the fight to keep those feelings high. They barnstormed across India and became symbols of the Bengali cause.

"You wouldn't believe it, Hafiz! They fly the flag of a free Bangladesh at every stadium!" said one of the men.

The players looked at him expectantly.

The offer was obvious, as was the question: Why not leave the war behind? Hafiz could travel across India, a hero of the resistance, and he would never have to see one of his friends shot and killed again. It was at least worth hearing them out.

They talked late into the night. The resistance desperately needed money to go on fighting. He could play football again and still be part of the freedom struggle. Thousands of tickets meant arms, ammunition, and training for the fighters who risked their lives on the front lines. Eventually, they stumbled to bed. Hafiz crashed on a mattress on the floor of the guesthouse. He looked at the ceiling, feeling the draw back to simpler times—that rush when tens of thousands chanted his name.

He closed his eyes. It was so easy to imagine the crowds and feel their roars. Surely his father, if he was even still alive, wouldn't be praying for him to return to the front.

Then Hafiz thought of the young boy he'd met in the hospital, with the stump for a hand. He thought of the ghastly scenes in the refugee camps. He thought of his fellow officer Salauddin's corpse suspended in the air on enemy barbed wire, a megaphone in the dirt below him. He probed his own wound as he drifted off.

Hafiz woke up late in the morning from his first undisturbed sleep in months. It felt selfish. His brothers in the jungles weren't sleeping like this, safe from raids and mortars. They weren't wolfing down English breakfasts on white tablecloths at the Grand Hotel. Hundreds of the men he'd trained were without their leader, while he lived it up like a tourist. Like a celebrity.

Hafiz emptied his wallet of whatever he had left from Osmani's bonus, donating it to the footballers' cause. Penniless, he hopped into the back of an old jeep, hitching a ride to the border. Death might be knocking at the door, but Hafiz had a war to win.

43

Mohammad Hai

MANPURA ISLAND, EAST PAKISTAN
SEPTEMBER 1971

"On the ground, you scum! Get lower than a dog!"

Hai went horizontal. The routine changed a bit each day, but this part was always the same. Facedown and await orders.

"Now crawl!"

Hai and the others slithered together toward the exit of the cramped room. They wore stained white tank tops and pajama bottoms. The man with the gun barked out orders, blocking the door. Hai obeyed. He shuffled forward on his elbows and knees, making sure his butt stayed down.

It was Hai's nineteenth birthday, and this was the best present he could imagine.

Two months ago, he ran from Pakistani border guards and made the long, humiliating journey back to Manpura. He arrived without the money he'd received from friends and family. Meanwhile the island was a shadow of its former self. Without aid coming in from HELP or the military, people were again on the brink of starvation. The social upheaval amplified the ravages started by the cyclone. Cholera spread throughout what remained of East Pakistan's population and few people had any hope for the future. The people of Manpura pinned their hopes on Hai and the rest of the erstwhile freedom fighters, but Hai couldn't even offer them news about the other boys' fates. It was hard to look anyone in the eye. Then, last week, everything changed.

Malik ordered the boys to stand and take a five-minute break. He'd just come back from India, where he'd had a six-week crash course courtesy of Indian special forces and Bengali Mukti Bahini commandos. The entire affair happened in secret. He was one of ten teens handpicked out of a group of five thousand who'd crossed into India for military training. The commandos taught him how to set a land mine. How to fire a rocket launcher. How to aim a machine gun so that the weapon's kick didn't send bullets streaming over the enemy's heads. How to plan a guerrilla raid. And how to crawl undetected through the jungle.

Above all else, they taught Malik military training tactics that could turn a fisherman into a fighter. He would be a virus set to replicate his training to the countless youths who would rather pick up a gun than wait for the Pakistani military to root them out. Now Malik imparted the same tough-love training that the commandos taught him. Hai was Malik's most eager recruit. This was a chance at redemption.

When Malik arrived at the jetty a week before, Hai didn't recognize the bearded, disheveled man with sun-blackened skin. The traveler unloaded a few heavy crates and looked around, as if willing a way to announce himself. Then he saw Hai and yelled out.

Hai froze—was the figure a *razakar* from the border still hot on his heels? It took him a second to recognize the voice. Malik! They shared a long hug, apologizing to each other for the stupid way they'd left things. They loaded up a tricycle cart, struggling to deadlift the crates onto the flat wooden box above the back wheels.

On the way to town, Malik told Hai about sneaking over the border. He walked all night with *razakars* in pursuit and snaked through mud-filled fields to find an opening to India. The *razakars* shot wildly but gave up rather than deal with the slippery bog themselves. Just across the border an Indian family congratulated Malik for his journey and offered him coconut water. The next morning he ate a massive breakfast of lentils, jackfruit, and pumpkin, then waited on Hai and the rest of the group. No one came. By nightfall he feared the worst.

Hai wished that he'd not listened to the woman that evening and instead followed Malik. Now Malik was a fighter and Hai was just another teen lacking any tools to fight the chairman and the *razakars* who kept a stranglehold on the island.

But with Malik back, maybe the island could make a stand. Maybe Manpura could earn its salvation.

At Hai's house, they carried the crates in, setting them down next to the family safe. The hodgepodge of wooden boxes came in various shapes and sizes, each one imported by a Mukti Bahini fighter from India under risk of immediate execution. Some had innocuous markings on the side, like PARTS, or VEGETABLES. All of them were heavy. Malik closed the door and drew the blinds. He grabbed a shovel and used it like a crowbar to open the first crate. The steel of fifty Indian-made assault rifles modeled after Soviet AK-47s reflected the room's dim light. Malik pried open the second box and revealed enough ammunition to keep a platoon of soldiers fighting for weeks, or maybe even months if they were careful.

Hai picked up a gun, gauging its weight. He'd never held a weapon before. This was true power. The power to take a life. The power to take revenge. He was ready to storm out of the house that instant.

Malik laughed at his friend, placing his hand on the barrel and pressing down slightly to calm the show of exuberance. Then he showed Hai how to load the gun by slotting in the magazine just so. The guns were simple and rarely jammed, making them the perfect weapons for poorly trained freedom fighters. But aiming it and hitting something would still take practice.

It only took a day or two to find willing recruits and, while the training left them exhausted and panting for breath, every one of the would-be freedom fighters relished each moment. Through the thrill of the training, Hai had to admit to himself that Malik had changed.

It might have started when Malik broke his leg, squandering any hope for a football career, but now there was something almost cold-blooded in his attitude. Where Hai wanted to fight for the freedom of his country and bandied about lofty ideals, Malik instead talked low and calmly about killing Punjabis. He delivered sermons on the army's atrocities around the country, about the massacres in Dacca and the necessary brutality of their own response. The war language also seemed to mean telling dirty jokes about wives and mothers after training sessions. Hai winced at the jokes. Any mention of mothers or family still gave him flashbacks to the night of the cyclone.

Over the next few weeks Malik amassed a small arsenal of about five hundred rifles through secret Mukti Bahini supply lines and crafted a mission to protect Manpura and Bhola islands. In India he'd learned how to raid an enemy position, but that experience didn't exactly teach him how to coordinate a multi-island defense. How would a teenager protect more than two thousand square miles of territory, all the while escaping the notice of army patrols and *razakars*?

Malik needed to defend the islands, swamps, and riverways against thousands of West Pakistani troops and their gunboats, airplanes, and heavy artillery. Every week shipments sailed around the bottom of India and came up through the Bay of Bengal and into the delta. It was the exact same path the cyclone had taken.

In short, Malik had a logistics problem. One that was almost impossible to crack.

But Hai had tackled similar problems before. Six months ago Hai wouldn't have had the first clue where to begin. But the longer he thought, the more he realized that distributing aid and managing an arsenal weren't really so different. They had a limited amount of resources that had to spread out evenly among a vast population. The trick was getting the right resources in the right places at exactly the right time.

Malik's orders from his Indian handlers were clear enough. No one expected him to lead a commando raid with his friends against a well-trained army battalion. That might work in the movies, but in real life it would just be a pointless slaughter. Instead, his orders mimicked those given to hundreds of other Mukti Bahini cells around the country. Slow down the enemy where you can, protect your village, and try not to get caught. No kamikaze attacks on the front lines due to misplaced heroic dreams.

One could think of the one hundred thousand Mukti Bahini soldiers as a swarm of mosquitoes. The invisible guerrilla forces would give just a touch of resistance at a time. But they would give it at every turn, at every village, on every road. They would harass the enemy at every juncture, but not be so forceful as to warrant a full-scale counteroperation. A thousand little speed bumps all over the country, delaying things by a couple of hours each time, would give the commandos and regular Indian and Bangladeshi forces the month they needed to have an edge on the battlefield.

Hai grabbed a piece of paper and a pencil and sat down with Malik, using a gun crate as a makeshift table. He sketched out a map of the islands from memory, marking possible strategic strengths and weaknesses. It reminded Hai of Candy's HELP maps, pinpointing areas of need and distribution launches. Malik would train the recruits and organize the missions. Hai would distribute the guns and ammo. They moved their base of operations to the next island over: Bhola, the island that had become the de facto moniker of the Great Bhola Cyclone. It was the most logical point from which to organize the resistance—with better connections to the mainland and more avenues for distribution.

Hai frowned while looking down at the map. It covered an area the size of a small US state. Getting the strategy wrong meant losing lives. There was no way around that. The pressure was enormous. With HELP, if Hai failed to get food to one village in favor of another, starvation at least afforded a little wiggle room. Starvation killed slowly.

But now, if the army uncovered their cell, death would come in an instant.

Hai studied his paper again. Then filled it with arrows, tick marks, erasures, and small grids scattered around the blobs that represented islands. Malik figured he could muster up a thousand fighters from his old Awami League contacts and the people like Hai who'd tried and failed to make it across the border. Hai placed these future units around the paper at strategic choke points like game pieces, taking advantage of hidden sandbars and other bits of inside information that outsiders couldn't know.

The plan was set. Hai and Malik studied each other. Everything so far had been done in secret and under the cover of night. Now they were the most exposed men on the island. It would only be a matter of time until word of their actions reached the traitors in the chairman's office. Fighting out in the open meant there would be no way back into the shadows and no return to their old life.

They had nothing to lose, aside from their lives. With no idea if their leader, Mujib, was even still alive, they were ready to fight to the death. For him, and for their country.

44

Candy Rohde and Jon Rohde

CALCUTTA, INDIA

OCTOBER 1971

Candy bounced around in the Land Rover's front seat as the 4x4 crawled along the mud road. Thousands of emaciated bodies parted like water in front of their vehicle, re-forming themselves behind it after the vehicle passed through. The truck's suspension whined at the bottom of each deep pothole. The driver had to be careful. One errant jerk of the wheel could send them careening into a group of refugees— the very people Candy came here to help.

Of the seventy million people who lived in East Pakistan before the war, at least twenty million of them were forced from their homes. Half of those ended up in India's refugee camps, which meant ten million suffering and starving people. Salt Lake, an impromptu tent city of two hundred and fifty thousand, located a mile east of Calcutta, was the biggest and most needy of the lot.

For months now, fifty thousand people a day crossed over to India— one nearly every second. The vast majority were women and children. The very relentlessness of the procession demoralized short-staffed relief workers. They were perpetually running out of food, medicine, shelter, and hope.

The main escape road from East Pakistan to Salt Lake was an endless trail of cholera-ridden people on the brink of starvation. Most all were barefoot, pulling their legs through each step as mud gripped their feet. Some had open wounds from army beatings. Mothers and fathers who should have collapsed thirty miles back had to choose: Carry both babies or only the least sick one? The dead and dying were taken as far as starved pencil-thin arms could carry them, but for tens of thousands, it wasn't enough. Vultures and wild dogs welcomed the plague feast, picking at roadside carrion as the procession passed through.

The car lurched to a halt just in front of a corpse abandoned in the middle of the road; nobody had enough spare energy to move it. The driver gingerly backed up and found a route around. Candy studied the scene, unsure of the best action to ameliorate the unfolding tragedy. The 4x4 lugged a token package of experimental medicines in the back for the field hospital that Jon had set up in the camp. But no matter how magical the cure that the boxes contained, they would be woefully inadequate for the task ahead.

Once Jon and the other doctors managed to triage the worst cases and stop the most acute traumas, what would happen to these people next month? Or next year? And even more profoundly, what sort of independent nation would arise out of the ashes of a refugee camp?

On the other side of Salt Lake, toward East Pakistan, the migration took on a different character. Yes, the refugees still arrived looking for a place to bed down and maybe, if they were lucky, a hot meal. But now, in the relative safety of India, there was a new and more horrible line, roughly a half mile long. Hundreds of women stood in a queue, each holding a tightly wrapped white cloth package in her arms. Each package weighed no more than ten pounds and measured no more than two feet long.

The women's faces were vacant, broken, and without tears.

Candy's 4x4 crept forward for what felt like an eternity. Some women wore red-and-white bangles—symbols of marriage and fertility—while others had only their rags that passed for saris. Every woman held her package like lives once depended on it.

Finally Candy made it close enough to see the front of the queue, she found a middle-aged Indian bureaucrat at a clunky desk that had no business being outside. He sat under an umbrella and poured over a long, thick ledger, with one thin line allocated for each woman.

Once she made it to the front, every woman followed the same routine. She handed the bureaucrat a small piece of laminated paper, and he examined it for pertinent details. He'd nod approval, then she'd hand him the package and cut the laminated ration card in half. Only after he declared it all in order did he allow her to take the corpse of her child and move on.

From there, the line separated into two. To the left, Hindu women went to the crematorium to burn their babies according to Hindu principles. To the right, the women gave their babies to the gravediggers, who buried them with Islamic prayers. This was the trade that every woman accepted: to get a proper burial, she had to forfeit the child's government ration card and the meager amount of calories that the card afforded. Women who didn't have the ration cards to properly register their children's deaths sometimes used a hot coal to burn their babies' mouths for a symbolic cremation or, alternately, dug roadside graves by hand.

The truck didn't pause to contemplate the scene. It rolled past the camp entrance, past Mother Teresa's tent and similar do-gooder operations, all the way to Jon's tarp hospital. Candy thanked the driver and climbed down to grab the box. Jon rushed out when he heard the truck, then ripped open the package like a kid at Christmas. The medicine almost spilled onto the mud.

"It's working!" Jon said. He rushed inside with the precious resources. He'd spent months thinking about the child in Manpura whom he'd first met when he got off the boat and how hard it was to get her to drink milk. The same scene repeated hundreds of thousands of times in camps up and down the Indian border. Tens of thousands more would die unless they could figure out a better way to deliver calories. Just taking the time to explain how to open a can, let alone show what was inside, meant the difference between life and death in some cases.

Jon kept coming back to the idea he'd scribbled down on broken cinder blocks that spring on Manpura: a single drink that could give starved bodies the most important vitamins and minerals all in one shot to prevent imminent death. He just needed to buy time for each body to recover and more aid to arrive. This could be a game changer in the midst of a cholera epidemic, when the disease overwhelmed the body with diarrhea and most patients died from dehydration and lack of electrolytes.

Jon rang up colleagues around the world. A few others had been thinking along the same lines. In 1964, the US Army treated two cholera patients with oral glucose and saline. It was enough to keep the patients alive while their bodies passed the infection. The problem was that the exact balance of ingredients was finicky; unless it was just right, it didn't work at all, and it had never been tried on a massive scale.

Jon's plan was to make a simpler product that didn't require a laboratory setup to measure it out. He worked with American, Indian, and Bengali colleagues to come up with an easy-to-produce formula for oral rehydration salt. The ORS replenished essential minerals lost through diarrhea, vomiting, and other effects of diseases like cholera. It would also be a quick fix for those on the brink of starvation, replacing lost salts and vitamins so that the body would stop attacking itself. It gave patients enough energy to be able to eat. Jon's task was to try to understand exactly how ORS worked in real-world conditions and how to improve the formula even further.

Jon was on the front lines of one of the most urgent clinical trials in human history, with millions of lives at stake. So far, the results were dramatic. He gave it to children who sat lethargic in the dirt, with sunken eye sockets and ears extended from starvation and dehydration. Their cold, clammy limbs didn't have the strength to wave away the flies, and they licked their lips incessantly as they tried to find any moisture at all. Previously, every child he'd seen like this had died within a day or two; other camp doctors wrote them off, focusing instead on those with better odds of survival.

Now, when Jon poured the liquid down these children's throats—or gave intravenous lines to those too weak to swallow—the life returned to their eyes within hours. They found enough strength to eat a chapati or a handful of rice. It felt like a metamorphosis. The simple mix of ingredients, combined in the right way and designed so that the body absorbed it as quickly as possible, saved lives before Jon's very eyes. Camp mortality dropped from 30 percent to 3 percent in just thirty days. Jon and his colleagues had discovered the holy grail for cholera survival.

Jon rushed to the telegraph office. He hammered out a telegram to every funder he could think of. They had to ramp up ORS delivery as quickly as possible; this would help relief efforts get ahead of the illness before the epidemic took thousands more lives. He made sure that ORS was the first thing that new arrivals got when they crossed the camp's threshold.

Miracle in hand, Jon had another idea. He knew that there were no doctors and no medicines being administered in East Pakistan, but the cholera epidemic was just as widespread and deadly there. So he approached the teens who were not quite tall or healthy enough to get picked for the Mukti Bahini; thousands of them milled about Salt Lake, dejected and bored. He offered them a mission: What if you could go back home and save lives instead of taking them? Jon would train them to make the magic ORS formula, and they could administer it around their villages to keep babies alive. More than one thousand boys and young men jumped at the offer. Every morning, he gave lessons to a few dozen freedom fighters-turned-doctors and handed them a plastic bucket with markings to measure out the right dosage. Every afternoon, a few dozen teens left the camp and snuck back over the border, buckets in hand. He eventually expanded the ORS program to more than a hundred thousand helpers.

While Jon tried to get refugees through the most acute phase of survival, Candy had her mind fixed on the next, equally pressing problem. How do you form a new, independent nation out of the deprivation of a refugee camp? After Yahya murdered the intellectual class, the students, the artists, and the bureaucrats, who would lay a foundation for a new society?

Candy pitched an audacious idea to the International Rescue Committee. She proposed starting schools in the camps and hiring refugees as teachers to give vulnerable children an opportunity to forget their surroundings and immerse in study, even if for only for a few hours a day. The camps shouldn't just be waiting rooms, Candy argued; they needed to help create a future. The funders couldn't believe that no one had thought of it before. Just like when she'd founded the largest civilian relief effort in history, Candy's new project was the future. And the grants flowed in.

Candy started tent schools with the money. First she searched out former teachers among the refugees, then added to their ranks inexperienced people willing to try it, too. She gave them curriculum instructions, a few dozen teachers at a time, and supervised the distribution of what meager supplies they had.

Candy's HELP experiences enabled her to expand the program beyond anyone's imagination. Within one month, she established more than a thousand micro-schools, giving over one hundred thousand children the chance to learn.

Meanwhile, foreign journalists streamed through the camps. Their front-page articles decimated Yahya's "all is normal" public relations push. Perhaps with Kissinger's comments about needing to give the press a bit of misdirection still in his mind, Yahya ordered Tikka and Niazi to put up a new front for Pakistan's public image. The bright idea? Welcome centers for refugees who wanted to come back across the border. They put up colorful banners on charred walls of dozens of villages that the army obliterated two months before. With stories of the ongoing slaughter still coming into the camps every day, almost nobody went back. To fix that inconvenient truth, Yahya hired a group of "professional refugees" to appear whenever a foreign reporter wanted to see the camps.

It didn't fool anyone, and the army's scorched-earth plans continued unabated. They burned anything that wasn't immediately profitable. Letters from whistleblowers documenting atrocities piled up in the unchecked InterContinental mailboxes of journalists who were long gone from Dacca.

Eventually, the drumbeat of headlines out of India became too horrific for even American politicians to ignore. Fresh off his legislative defeat, Edward Kennedy took a fact-finding trip to Calcutta. He trudged through the monsoon rains and watched children die at his feet. He called it a genocide. Kennedy returned to America a changed man. While Candy built schools, Kennedy promised that he would stop at nothing to pass her bill. He would put his career on the line for it if he had to.

45

A. A. K. Niazi and Tikka Khan

DACCA, EAST PAKISTAN
OCTOBER 1971

"Ay Behanchod! Idhar Aao! Goli khao!"

A six-year-old girl sang the words as she skipped alone down the streets of Dacca. She'd heard the new Punjabi forces say it so often that she picked up on what certainly sounded like an important phrase. The new arrivals didn't speak any Bengali, and many of Dacca's residents had to figure out the meaning from the context, which usually included an officer jamming a gun into their faces.

"Ay Behanchod! Idhar Aao! Goli khao!"

She repeated it each time she passed someone, in that singsong way that little kids do. Maybe she was walking to a market or to find fresh water. It was probably the only phrase of Urdu she could speak.

The phrase meant: "Hey sisterfucker! Come here. Eat a bullet."

In the seven months since Operation Searchlight launched, Tikka and Niazi transformed East Pakistan into a horror zone. While Tikka directed thousands of police to lock down Dacca, Niazi hunted the Mukti Bahini in the countryside. More than forty thousand *razakars* drew up target lists and went down them one name at a time.

Tikka spent his days at the torture and execution center at the old Pakistan National Oil Company warehouses. He saw his job as not just one of military strategy but one focused on permanently breaking the Bengali spirit. He surmised that the most effective way to keep Bengalis under his thumb forever was to completely remove any sense of a social structure. He must eradicate intellectuals, bureaucrats, artists, and anyone else who might contribute to Bengali culture. He'd scorch the earth so that even if Bangladesh did find freedom, it wouldn't have the people it needed to build a functional nation. This meant summary executions, arbitrary torture, ethnic cleansing, and leveling entire towns if the army suspected that even a single resident did something wrong. As one diplomat put it, "Tikka says 'collective punishment' the way you or I say 'good morning.'"

That summer, Tikka tortured seventeen thousand Awami League members to death along with their families. He wasn't looking for secrets; he simply wanted to deliver death. He ordered troops to paint a large yellow H on the homes and shops of every remaining Hindu. It was a tactic he'd learned during World War II from the Nazis when they rounded up Jews. It was a tactic he'd tested in Balochistan. He sold the daughters of activists into prostitution. After his men finished torturing and murdering prisoners, sometimes he'd dismember them and arrange the body parts into grotesque sculptures to show to their compatriots before he tortured them too.

In the countryside, Niazi's passion for raiding started to wane. So many of his enemies vanished into the jungles that his so-called cleansing trips didn't produce the numbers they used to. He wanted more action. He begged Yahya to let him invade India and kill every refugee he found along the way. "I am in their heart. They are on the run. We are cleansing them."

Yahya ignored the request. Why couldn't he just handle things, and complete the task at hand like a good soldier? Why did everyone need a babysitter all the time?

Niazi wished he was back in Lahore, where he sold promotions under the table to rich officers during the day and emptied his wallet each night at the brothels. Bored in Dacca, he decided to make a simulacrum of his old haunts. He set up a brothel complex for himself and his subordinates. Then he filled military planes with contraband

and smuggled the goods he'd looted in Dacca back to Karachi and Lahore.

For all intents and purposes, outside of the military bases and government offices, Dacca was a ghost town. Nobody dared venture on the streets and risk arbitrary execution or rape. Most every rooftop sported a green-and-white Pakistani flag.

But one place stood out like an oasis of normality. The InterContinental Hotel weathered every disruption the war threw at it. When the Mukti Bahini blew up Dacca's power plant, the InterContinental's banks of diesel generators chugged into action. When World Bank and United Nations teams brought aid contracts worth hundreds of millions of dollars to Dacca, they signed them in partnership with army officials at the bar. Despite the carnage that surrounded it in every direction, men could still get business done in the upscale hotel. Even Niazi closed his import-export deals there.

But the InterContinental held a secret that none of the officials and foreign dignitaries ever suspected. Behind its laundry-room doors, inside its room-cleaning carts, and within its food-service stairwells, the InterContinental was also the Mukti Bahini's communication headquarters.

A few months into the war, the Mukti Bahini had a problem. They could talk to supporters via bootleg radios, but the lack of range and encryption limited any two-way communication. Every time they transmitted a signal, the Pakistan Army had a chance to intercept their plans. They needed a secret base in the center of the country to process reports. The InterContinental became that switchboard almost by accident.

The man who kept the laundry room's books joined the Mukti Bahini early on. Army officials housed their girlfriends in the hotel and had a habit of using hotel phones to communicate their orders back to the base. They also tended to leave classified documents on their desks when they went down to dinner.

The bookkeeper's crew had no problem eavesdropping on conversations. At dinnertime the bookkeeper headed up to their rooms to poke around for incidental tidbits. It was all too easy. He packaged the intel into concise summaries and coordinated information across the whole battlefront with the hotel's perfectly intact phone system.

The InterContinental's bowels were the last place in East Pakistan that Tikka and Niazi thought to look for insurgents. But the InterContinental was a microcosm for secret resistance groups from all over the country. In the face of unmitigated aggression, everyone had reason to join the fight. Broke vagabonds carried bags of vegetables and bomb fuses across checkpoints; fishermen covered the top of grenade crates with seasonal fruit. The army never really knew who the enemy was, so they got in the habit of simply liquidating villages all at once. But indiscriminate killing meant that there wasn't a real way to uncover the resistance's structure when everyone who knew anything died in the initial onslaught.

As the summer monsoon wound down, army troops wasted time searching hundreds of boats, trucks, and boxes based on *razakar* tips, while unsuspecting grandmothers strapped contraband to their bodies. Army morale in the countryside sank like their moldy desert combat boots did into the monsoon swamps. They couldn't ramp up the cruelty to get what they wanted; they'd already played that card. Every attack they made only seemed to build the resistance against them, not break it.

With their days focused on their favorite extracurriculars, Tikka and the Tiger couldn't sense that the tide was turning against them. Only a real scare could shake them back to full attention.

46

Mohammad Hai and Malik Mahmud

Hai squinted through the gunsight and tried to lock in the target. It was a hopeless shot, but he thought if he just concentrated hard enough, and got a bit lucky, he might will a miracle. He pulled the trigger. The gun barked out into the darkness.

The twenty or so bullets landed harmlessly, zipping in the water and then arcing over the Pakistani gunboat a hundred yards away. The boat didn't seem to mind. It just continued chugging away up the delta.

A couple of other fighters opened up. Rat-a-tat-tat. Another harmless volley, though this time at least a few bullets clanked off the boat's metal hull. A spotlight clicked on from the deck. A couple more rounds. Finally, they got their attention. The boat stopped its chugging and its siren whined to life.

"Yes! *Joi Bangla!* Now let's get out of here!"

They were close enough to hear the turrets clinking their gears in their direction. Hai and the others ran back inland as the spotlights swung back and forth along the empty shore. Two quick BOOMS erupted from the antiquated antiaircraft guns. The shots landed far away in a field. The gunboat would take at least half an hour to finish its combing operation, file its reports, get all the men settled down, and chug back up to speed again.

Mission accomplished.

Hai and Malik's nightly trips down to the beach were mostly just reconnaissance missions around the islands of Bhola and nearby Manpura. Though sometimes when they had escape routes they didn't mind harassing the Pakistan Army just a little bit. They, along with about a hundred and fifty other Mukti Bahini fighters, worked in twelve-hour shifts, monitoring army troop movements and sending reports up the chain of command. Malik told the regional commander, who radioed central command, who then passed the news to Osmani and even the Indian Air Force and Navy if it was good enough.

About once a week, they'd spot a Pakistani gunboat moving troops and supplies up to Dacca. They'd fire a few rounds at each one as they passed, careful not to use up too much ammo. If they fired too much they wouldn't have enough for the next gunboats. Or worse, the captain might make a change of plans and deploy to the island.

Tonight, the Pakistanis just fired blindly onto the beach. After an hour or two, the boat would be on its way upstream again where freedom fighters on the next island would repeat the routine.

The mosquitoes of the Mukti Bahini sucked precious time away from the Pakistani reinforcements, an hour at a stretch.

As the fighting wore on, a few other men in the group acquired Malik's taste for dirty jokes. They bragged about the girlfriends they'd score when it was all over and what they'd do to a *razakar* if they caught one. But most were like Hai, keeping the conversations focused on the next mission. They all wondered if the war would ever end or if liberation was just a light at the end of a never-ending tunnel. And if it did come, would any of them be alive to see it?

The next morning Hai banged his head on the desk at his provisional headquarters. It was half out of frustration and half just for the free wake-up call. He'd locked himself in a windowless basement, alone with his thoughts and the submachine guns stacked in neat rows against the walls.

His ledger had whole sections crossed out and then re-inked. The numbers just weren't working out. As in the HELP days, his job was to try to make half of what was needed go twice as far. Only this time it was guns, not food. Working on no sleep for the last three days, he drew a map of the islands from memory, placing little tick marks in strategic coastal spots that represented small weapons caches. There was never enough to cover everywhere; he'd have to make his best guess.

The mildewing concrete headquarters of the local water board was a perfect place to hide the massive stash of guns. The nine-story building was a municipal maze that nobody in their right mind would spend any more time in than they had to. While the bureaucrats toiled above, Hai stewed below, in what he hoped was out of sight of any particularly nosy worker bees. It was also the highest point on the island, with a roof ideally suited for lookouts.

During the daytime, Hai guarded the gun room. At night, he allocated weapons and conducted guerrilla patrols with small teams. They avoided open confrontation, knowing that outright combat was suicide. They didn't dare provoke the gunboats during the day. In the sunshine, the army had a habit of firing at every fishing boat they saw. Then they'd gun down any fishermen who tried to swim away from their doomed craft.

Hai had a little radio at his subterranean desk, but he hadn't turned it on in a month. The only channel that he could get put out nonstop West Pakistan propaganda. Even the pirate rebel radio stations went silent after army intelligence started to triangulate their signals. Announcers droned on about how the resistance was about to collapse and that all Mukti Bahini traitors would be dead within weeks. Hai gave up listening for any real news months ago.

The strange thing about running a military cell in a municipal building was that when Hai wanted to get lunch, all he had to do was disappear among the office workers. He asked a buddy to watch the stockpile while he blended into the crowd. He was anonymous.

Even so, the walk into town didn't feel quite right. It was normal for civilians to make themselves scarce during a guerrilla war, but Hai and Malik had noticed that even in the daytime, when army patrols were nowhere nearby, citizens could barely keep the sense of dread from creeping across their faces. The problem, of course, was that while the army wore uniforms, *razakars* could be anywhere—or anyone.

As Hai ate his lunch beneath a tree in the town center, he thought about the bullets his team fired harmlessly against the steel gunwales of the patrol boat. The mosquito actions might serve a broad strategic purpose, but he still yearned for something more.

Malik arrived, also on his freedom-fighting lunch break. He seemed restless and had a story to tell.

"Hai, I've got to tell you about someone." Malik was shaking as he started talking in a whisper. Hai leaned in. It was a story about a cruel, despicable man responsible for the deaths of hundreds of people.

His name was Tonir, and he was the head of a so-called Peace Committee the next town over. Tonir was a powerful Bengali landowner who became a *razakar* after Operation Searchlight. He had so much influence that people didn't even use the town's real name anymore—they simply called it Tonir Haat, roughly translated as "Tonir's Town" in Bengali. Never a particularly kind man, Tonir promised everyone that he became a *razakar* only to help protect the town and its people. In truth, he only cared about protecting himself and his money. And in time, his village learned about the depths of his depravity.

Malik launched into the tale of the surprise that awaited Tonir's dinner guests. "Remember how hard it was to get to India, how we prayed to Allah for help every night?"

Hai nodded, of course.

"They say that Tonir sits in his village square waiting for groups like ours to pass through, regular boys looking for directions or food on their way to India. He welcomes them and greets them like saviors.

"He says to them '*Joi Bangla!* Victory to Mujib!' and compliments them on their courage to stand up for Bangladesh. Then, the bastard, he says he can't fight himself because he needs to look after the village." Malik spat on the ground, disgusted. "He buys them tea and says, 'Come, come! Have a home-cooked meal before your long journey ahead.' And then they walk together to his house. Of course, the sisterfucker, he signals to his spies along the way that he's caught some new prey."

Malik continued, rapid-fire: "He takes them out to a country house he stole from a freedom fighter, and then announces there's a feast. Lentils, goat, vegetables, rice, curries. Tonir says, 'Don't worry, this is a safe place, leave your weapons in the other room.' They say that Tonir has a silver tongue. But he's a snake—saying that he's just a simple villager. He tells them to relax. That they're safe now.

"Tonir seats everyone around big piles of steaming food. Remember how hungry we were, Hai? That unripe fruit we ate? Think how we would have felt. And that bastard Tonir tells them to eat their fill. When everyone else is stuffing their mouths, Tonir finds some excuse to leave, like he has to take a piss. So he heads out into the jungle. Only by then his spies have sent soldiers, they're lying out back. They rush into the dining room firing through the windows and doors. Bang, everyone's dead. He kills all our brothers in cold blood but is too cowardly to pull the trigger himself.

"And then Tonir shows up again, but now with a big wad of cash from the Punjabis. Tonir pays other people to wipe up the blood, throw the bodies in the water, and patch up the bullet holes in his walls to set the trap for the next group of our brothers."

Hai's blood boiled as he listened to Malik's story. The worst part wasn't the gore or Tonir's evil but how plausible the whole thing was. There was a *razakar* like Tonir in every village.

"He terrorizes the whole island and the army loves him. Every time one of those big officers comes through, Tonir dishes up more local boys for them. He even burns houses and villages with our Bengali brothers still inside. The traitor gets rich and everyone's too afraid to do anything."

How could a fellow Bengali betray his people so completely? Fighting the army was one thing. But traitors like Tonir hurt in a special way. This was a man who symbolized everything that was evil in the world.

Someone needed to take revenge. Revenge for the Bengali people. Revenge for Hai's lost family members. For the island itself.

Hai listened to Malik's story and nodded. They could do something.

47

Yahya Khan and Richard Nixon

WASHINGTON, DC, AND ISLAMABAD, WEST PAKISTAN

DECEMBER 3, 1971

Yahya stood on a wobbly wooden stage, pleading with the savage crowd. Their eyes lusted for death. The scratchy twine noose pressed tightly against his flabby jowls.

"Hang him!" Bhutto yelled. The crowd cheered. Yahya felt his knees turn rubbery.

"Hang him!" Indira Gandhi yelled. More wild cheers.

"No! We must kill Mujib, not me! Mujib is the traitor!" Yahya tried to yell over the crowd. The noose constricted his throat and vocal cords, dampening the pleas. Nobody heard.

"Hang. Him! Hang. Him! Hang. Him!" The crowd was deafening. The executioner moved his hand to the trapdoor lever.

"Noooooooooooo!"

Yahya thrashed himself awake, breathing hard and soaked in a cold sweat under the bedsheets. He looked at the clock: three-thirty a.m. It was always around that time when the nightmares started, right as the whiskey and pills lost their potency. Yahya drifted in and out of consciousness in a fugue state most nights, never really sure if the terrors were hallucinations, visions of the future, a nervous breakdown—or all three.

At least he had his Black Beauty to comfort him. Yahya hired Mrs. Hussain as his President House interior decorator and gave her a guesthouse on the presidential grounds to live in with her kids. He gave her a security detail that matched a foreign minister's. She was never more than a one-minute walk away.

But even she wasn't enough. In the last two months the war started to go sideways for Yahya, and his sleep suffered. The Mukti Bahini was getting more effective with their constant harassment, and Pakistani forces feared that India was poised for a strike of its own. After all he did to connect the United States and China on a historic new journey to openness and, presumably, strategic alliances, Pakistan hadn't yet seen a whiff of Nixon's promised rewards other than a single boat of supplies and spare jet parts.

In their weekly phone calls Nixon was always kind, even upbeat that the situation would change soon. After one call Nixon warned Congress from his winter White House in Key Biscayne, Florida, that they had to give Yahya a quarter of a billion dollars of aid immediately. But it all seemed like posturing. Indeed, Edward Kennedy finally got Candy's bill passed through the Senate Foreign Relations Committee, which forbade Nixon from sending more weapons or aid of any type to West Pakistan. Yahya's dreams of cashing in on the favor to score planeloads of state-of-the-art military weaponry—or humanitarian aid he could trade away to a third country for the same—were fading fast.

Yahya needed a way to turn it all around. He saw as well as anyone that drifting along would lead to ruin. Maybe Bhutto would find a way to usurp the presidency. Or maybe an assassin might find him in the dead of night.

Meanwhile, Nixon was rambling on about Indira Gandhi, saying that he and Kissinger were sure that India and the Soviet Union had made a secret plan to take over South Asia. Pakistan was really just one piece of a larger global picture. And if the Soviets wanted to flex their muscles, then the United States was going to flex right back.

Nixon screamed at some poor low-level staffer who dared to come to the Oval Office with a peace deal crafted by the State Department.

"We aren't going to do it. Never! Goddamn it! I told those people! They know how I feel about India. Now, understand: I don't like the Indians! And let's remember the Pakistanis have been our friends in these late few days and the damn Indians have not been." Kissinger egged him on, saying that people even came up to him on the street in Cincinnati to tell him how much they hated the Indians.

Yahya and Nixon commiserated over how unfair everything had gotten lately. They scoffed at India training Mukti Bahini boys with impunity and worried about Soviet weapons coming into East Pakistan just like they had in Vietnam. They were even more annoyed that the United Nations was unwilling to lift a finger. It was a violation of international law!

Yahya sensed an opportunity. What if they turned the tables and used the violations as justification for a surprise attack? Someone could teach Gandhi a lesson she'd never forget, and put Pakistan back in its rightful place as South Asia's one true regional power. Any Pakistani leader who could pull that off would be worshipped alongside God himself. An outright war would mean that the United States would have to choose a side. Then Yahya would have a real superpower ally and maybe even American boots on the ground.

But the new direction hadn't stopped his nightmares. Each night, they got worse. He started to fear that they were premonitions.

Tikka drew up the plans for an attack, proposing that they do a surprise bombing raid of all eleven of India's main military airstrips during Friday prayers to neutralize Indian air superiority and make the land war a quick one. It would be like a Nazi blitzkrieg.

While Yahya still believed the Pakistan Army maxim that one Pakistani solider was equal to ten Indian ones, he remembered Kissinger's warning that India bought ships full of state-of-the-art Soviet tanks, missiles, and MiG fighter jets. Pakistan had rammed most of its rickety post–World War II American-made weaponry into East Pakistan, so there was little to stop India from making a devastating counterattack on their cities in West Pakistan.

Yahya paced around President House. He glanced at Tikka's plans on his desk from a distance, trying not to get too close to them for fear he'd get excited and call the strike that day. He had a drink, unsure if he was really ready to pull the trigger.

"Not yet," he mumbled to himself.

Tikka's scorched-earth approach was a strategy for a man who had nothing to lose. Instead, Yahya sent Bhutto to the United Nations in New York with evidence that India was interfering in Pakistan's internal affairs. Maybe once the world saw Indira Gandhi's treachery masquerading as a relief effort then everyone would finally see his side.

It was a more measured approach, the approach of a general. Yahya felt his body relax when he made it. With his mind cleared he decided to see Mrs. Hussain. He rang her guesthouse.

But she wasn't there.

Where could she be? Yahya wondered. He hated when his women weren't at home. It set his mind wandering. He ordered his security staff to track her down.

A little while later the head of his security detail told Yahya, delicately, that she'd booked a suite at the Islamabad InterContinental Hotel. And she wasn't alone.

Yahya grabbed a pistol. *How could she? That Bengali snake.* He checked the chamber to make sure it was loaded. He ignored the security head yelling about who she was with. The yelling woke up his wife from across the residence.

Yahya raced from President House to the five-star hotel with the pistol in his hand. He arrived just before dawn. The night manager saw the infuriated president and could only stammer the suite number. Yahya rushed upstairs and banged on the door, screaming for the scoundrel sleeping with his mistress to face him man to man.

The security chain slid open and the lock clicked. The door opened revealing his son, Ali. It was often said that father and son had the same taste in women. Ali had even started procuring services from General Rani's harem over the past few months. Yahya had paid it little mind, boys that age needed a release. But now Yahya recoiled, horrified. His efforts to groom Ali had gone all wrong. They actually had the taste for the *same* woman.

Yahya screamed at Ali. Ali screamed back. After everything Yahya had done for his son, all the spoiling and gifts, he repaid his father by stealing his most precious property. Yahya raised the gun and pointed it at his son's head, ordering him out of the suite. Ali refused to go. Yahya's hand trembled.

Hussain tried to intervene between the father and son, pleading with Ali to go.

Yahya debated pulling the trigger right then. But he controlled his rage just enough to avoid murder. Instead, he disowned Ali, telling him he wasn't welcome in President House ever again. Indeed, if he ever saw the boy again—even casually—he'd have him imprisoned for adultery.

Ali withdrew down the hallway with his life. Yahya went inside, sliding the security chain back in place.

An hour later, a drained Yahya returned to President House. His wife, Fakhra, was waiting. She paced around his office, furious. After leaving the suite, Ali went right to her and told her everything. Yahya tried to tell his side of things, tried to tell her how disrespectful Ali had been, how he would never tolerate such blatant insubordination. Yahya explained that he had no choice but to cast Ali out of the family forever.

Fakhra Khan had had enough.

She laid in to Yahya, telling him that the family squabble was disastrous for the whole nation. Worse, he and Ali, with all their blasphemous drunken cavorting, made her look like the biggest fool in Pakistan.

Yahya was still holding the gun, gripping it steadily now despite the ocean of booze in his blood. But he didn't scream back. He didn't hit her, like so many of his comrades would have for such brazen insolence. Instead he swallowed his anger. Perhaps it was because deep down he knew she was right. He walked back on his promise of sending Ali to prison. But now he could only look on his own wife's face in disgust. He told her to leave him alone. Then he retreated to his office.

Yahya sat back in his chair. He squinted daggers outside at the chirping birds in his pond as dawn broke. It was not the time for songs.

Yahya put the gun down on the desk, next to Tikka's plan for attacking India. He glanced at the papers, then did a double take and studied them more intently. Tikka had named it Operation Chengis Khan. Yahya nodded as he scanned through the document. He placed the gun softly back in the open desk drawer.

Yahya picked up the phone and ordered the attack.

48

A. A. K. Niazi and Yayha Khan

DACCA, EAST PAKISTAN, AND ISLAMABAD, WEST PAKISTAN

DECEMBER 3, 1971

American-built B-57s and F-86s launched from airfields in West Pakistan and dropped hundreds of American-made bombs all across northwestern India while A.K.K. Niazi sat down to a plate of chicken tikka and bubbly, crispy stacks of naan.

The air force modeled the attack on Israel's offensive in the Six-Day War against Egypt, Jordan, and Syria. In that brief conflict Israel launched two hundred combat aircraft and all but eradicated the opposition in a few hours. The Pakistani strike force of just fifty planes hit eleven targets across India, striking as far inland as the home of the Taj Mahal in Agra as well as airfields in Rajasthan and Punjab. Pakistani artillery batteries shelled Indian Army positions along the western border. Unfortunately for Yahya, Pakistan's imitation of over-whelming Israeli airpower fell far short of the mark. Casualties were light. India had moved the bulk of its air force inland a week earlier. Most Pakistani bombs exploded without doing any real damage.

When all was said and done, Indira Gandhi felt a deep well of gratitude to Yahya Khan. She had been giving a speech at a million-strong political rally in Calcutta when the bombs began to drop. After she heard the news she told an aide privately, "Thank God, they've attacked us." India's own military preparations had been ticking forward since the first refugee camps sprang up. But unwilling to risk the ire of the international community, Gandhi held back. Yahya's attack offered her the moral high ground. Truth be told, she hated the Pakistanis just as much as they hated her.

Gandhi calculated strike plans on the tense flight to Delhi. They all knew that the Pakistani Air Force might try to shoot them down to decapitate the Indian leadership. After her safe landing, she bolted to the war room in what one general remembered as an "almighty rage."

The next day Gandhi delivered a war cry to the Indian leadership at the Lok Sabha. "We meet as a fighting Parliament," she began. "A war has been forced upon us, a war that we did not seek and did our utmost to prevent." With that declaration, war had expanded from East Pakistan to all of South Asia. Indian troops and Mukti Bahini fighters surged over the border.

Less than twelve hours after Yahya launched his attack, Niazi finally realized that they were in real trouble. The attack fizzled. Pakistani operational superiority over the Mukti Bahini was paper thin. With Indian support enemy forces would break through their defenses in weeks.

Niazi really had only two choices: rally the front lines by committing to the old maxim that a Pakistani solider was worth ten Indians, or call a cease-fire before they all got slaughtered. While the general liked to bluster about Pakistan's military fortitude, India's army vastly overmatched Pakistan's in both equipment and sheer troop numbers.

Worse, just a few weeks earlier Yahya aimed to change the tide of the war by firing anyone he could blame for his own poor leadership. He removed Tikka from his position as governor, said a few choice words to the media about how Tikka couldn't finish the job properly, and replaced him with a septuagenarian dentist. At the time Niazi celebrated. It meant he won the cruelness competition. Now he realized it meant he was the only one around with any real operational experience, surrounded by men who weren't capable of doing anything more than saying "Yes sir!"

The dentist-turned-governor came to seek advice from Niazi, but found a terrified Tiger hiding his face and sobbing at his desk. Niazi kept order like a schoolyard bully—trusting terror to keep the population in line. But now the tables had turned, and he knew he was outmatched. Their only hope was that Yahya really was the military genius he'd claimed to be, with a spectacular trick up his sleeve. So the Tiger and the Dentist sent him a desperate telegram:

FOR *PRESIDENT OF PAKISTAN*: IT IS IMPERATIVE THAT THE CORRECT SITUATION IN *EAST PAKISTAN* IS BROUGHT TO YOUR NOTICE. TROOPS ARE FIGHTING HEROICALLY BUT AGAINST HEAVY ODDS WITHOUT ADEQUATE ARTILLERY AND AIR SUPPORT. REBELS CONTINUE CUTTING THE REAR AND LOSSES IN EQUIPMENT AND MEN ARE VERY HEAVY AND CANNOT BE REPLACED. THE FRONT IN *EASTERN* AND *WESTERN SECTOR* HAS COLLAPSED. LOSS OF WHOLE CORRIDOR *EAST OF MEGHNA RIVER* CANNOT BE AVOIDED. *JESSORE* HAS ALREADY FALLEN. FOOD AND OTHER SUPPLIES RUNNING SHORT. EVEN *DACCA* CITY WILL BE WITHOUT FOOD AFTER 7 DAYS. WITHOUT FUEL AND OIL THERE WILL BE COMPLETE PARALYSIS. NO AMOUNT OF LIP SYMPATHY OR EVEN MATERIAL HELP FROM WORLD POWERS EXCEPT DIRECT PHYSICAL INTERVENTION WILL HELP. IF ANY OF OUR FRIENDS IS EXPECTED TO HELP THAT SHOULD HAVE AN IMPACT WITHIN THE NEXT 48 REPEAT 48 HOURS. IF NO HELP IS EXPECTED I BESEECH YOU TO NEGOTIATE SO THAT A CIVILIZED AND PEACEFUL TRANSFER TAKES PLACE AND MILLIONS OF LIVES ARE SAVED AND UNTOLD MISERY AVOIDED. IS IT WORTH SACRIFICING SO MUCH WHEN THE END SEEMS INEVITABLE. IF HELP IS COMING WE WILL FIGHT ON WHATEVER CONSEQUENCES THERE MAY BE.

Yahya crumpled up the telegram and threw it across the room. The war had just started! How was it possible that they wanted to give up so quickly? Nixon and Mao promised backup, but that plan required more time. A week. Two, tops. A coalition of Cold War powers would surely step up and rally to his defense. All he needed was for the Indian army to overextend itself just enough to find itself surrounded by the military forces of all the world's great powers. They would decapitate Gandhi's army and make her a global laughingstock. He just needed to buy the Tiger some time.

Yahya drew up what he thought was the perfect stall. He'd send Bhutto to the United Nations to give a big show about how Pakistan was trying to broker a cease-fire, while he secretly assembled a joint Pakistan-US-China strike force. There was no question that both countries would help. They promised, and now it was time to cash in the favor.

He wrote back to his worried war chiefs within the hour.

> FULL SCALE AND BITTER WAR IS GOING ON IN THE *WEST WING*. A VERY HIGH POWERED DELEGATION IS BEING RUSHED TO *NEW YORK*. PLEASE REST ASSURED THAT I AM FULLY ALIVE TO THE TERRIBLE SITUATION THAT YOU ARE FACING. YOU ON YOUR PART AND YOUR GOVERNMENT SHOULD ADOPT STRONGEST MEASURES IN THE FIELD OF FOOD RATIONING AND CURTAILING SUPPLY OF ALL ESSENTIAL ITEMS AS ON WAR FOOTING TO BE ABLE TO LAST FOR MAXIMUM PERIOD OF TIME AND PREVENT A COLLAPSE. *GOD* BE WITH YOU. WE ARE ALL PRAYING.

Niazi read over the communique, shaking his head in disbelief. The tears started again. He locked himself in his quarters and ordered his staff to stay away.

49

Hafiz Uddin Ahmad

BANGLADESH LIBERATED ZONE

DECEMBER 6, 1971

Hafiz sensed victory. Soon his ragtag band of freedom fighters would have a chance to exert a bit of revenge. Just a few hours after the invasion started, his unit arrived at the site of a recently destroyed Pakistan Army position called Atgram. Losses were heavy for both the Indians and the West Pakistanis. With reprisal attacks multiplying as the Pakistan Army withdrew, their soldiers preferred to die on their feet rather than surrender.

While the Indian soldiers recuperated, Hafiz wandered over to see the wreckage for himself. He came across an army scout shaken by something he'd found. The scout led Hafiz to a loose dirt pile about fifty feet long with scraps of sari cloth poking out from the moist clods. It was a mass grave: clear evidence of the atrocities that the Pakistan Army left in their wake.

Over the next hour Hafiz's men uncovered twenty bodies; everyone had their hands tied behind their backs. Two of the corpses bore fresh gunshot wounds, but the rest were eerily unmarked. They'd been buried alive. Hafiz found survivors hiding among the nearby houses. They recounted how just hours before the Indian Army's attack, the Pakistani soldiers forced these people to dig the grave and lay down inside of it. They shot resisters. Everyone else simply got covered in dirt. They suffocated hours before the Indians arrived.

Hafiz gazed down at the bodies until he shook with rage. But he couldn't stand there forever. Orders filtered down from above that he needed to bring his men into position outside a government enclave called Chargram that was a mile or so away.

They marched out to a place where he could see three white concrete buildings. A villager said at least a hundred Pakistani soldiers had taken refuge there and planned to make a last stand. He and his men hunched behind an irrigation berm and he looked at the buildings through a set of army binoculars. Every now and then he could make out the rounded shape of a metal helmet peek out above a windowsill.

It was close to noon when Hafiz's wireless set crackled with the familiar voice of Z-Force commander Zia Rahman, transmitting from a secure location a couple miles behind the front: "Hafiz, the Ghurkas lost officers at Atgram, and now refuse to move forward. This is the time for the Mukti Bahini to show their strength. You must take those buildings." Zia needed a win. The major ached for a battle victory to call his own.

But Hafiz's stomach dropped at his commander's words. The empty rice paddy between his position and the first concrete structure offered almost no place to hide from the enemy fire. Two well-placed machine guns could cut down his entire company.

This was going be another Kamalpur. Another deathtrap.

His mind screamed out in protest. *Sir, you have so many other officers under your command, why not ask one of them?* But for some reason those words never made it to his lips. He grabbed the receiver on the wireless set and simply said, "Yes sir."

Hafiz squinted at the buildings until the reflective glare from the sun blurred their edges. He ran scenarios in his head: A frontal attack. A pincer movement. An artillery barrage. But all he saw was suicide. He'd never see his country get its freedom. This is the problem with being a soldier. Someone always has to be the last person to die in a war.

There weren't any good options, and the clock was ticking, so Hafiz ordered the most audacious attack in his arsenal—a full-frontal assault. He hoped that the enemy wouldn't expect it precisely because it was so suicidal. He ordered his men toward the imposing buildings. The only advice he could offer was: "Remember, boys, ammo is your friend." They charged ahead. Hafiz prayed that enough soldiers would survive to take the position.

The plan was doomed from its inception. The Pakistani soldiers were smart enough to hold their fire just long enough so that Hafiz's entire company was in the open before they let loose a torrent of bullets.

Metal screamed over his men and the entire attacking force hit the ground in unison. The enemy's line of site was so clear, and their fire so constant, that Hafiz couldn't even raise his head to get a look at the buildings to see where it was all coming from. Men near him whimpered in terror. The only thing that kept any of them alive were a few one-and-a-half-foot high berms in the middle of the rice paddy that farmers used to move water around the land. Hafiz laid flat on the ground behind one as bullets plinked into the dirt all around him.

He was pinned. And he couldn't do anything but wait for his enemies to run low on ammunition. But the enemy showed no sign of slowing down. Just then, Hafiz's wireless set cracked to life and he heard Zia's voice asking for an update. Hafiz relayed that they were all alive but trapped.

"You don't have any casualties, why aren't you moving forward? Over."

Hafiz peeked above his berm and immediately ducked down as another bullet zipped into the dirt a few feet from his head. He picked up the transmitter and gave his senior officer a piece of his mind.

"No casualties yet, but give me some time. I'll attack in the morning to satisfy you. Over and out."

Then Hafiz switched off the set, not interested in hearing another order to charge into certain death. He was going to succeed or die trying before he switched that set back on. Instead, the company waited for six excruciating hours under the scorching sun until darkness fell over the field. They withdrew to a village nearby when the enemy couldn't see them anymore.

That night Hafiz looked over the weary faces of his men by the light of a kerosene lantern. All things considered, they'd been surprisingly lucky. Only two men were actually wounded in the assault, and no one had died. But taking the heavily defended position wouldn't be easy.

"I won't lie to you," he said, laying out the impossibility of the task ahead of them. "In every war soldiers must give their lives for causes that are greater than themselves. This is probably our time. At Kamalpur many of our brothers gave their blood back to the land. We are going to attack in the morning. You have seen what we are up against. I fully expect that every one of us will die." His soldiers looked at him with exhausted, bloodshot eyes, unsure of what to say.

Hafiz continued: "But here is the question we must ask ourselves: Who should liberate Bangladesh? Will Indians give us our freedom? Or do we have a role in the birth of our own country? Tomorrow we will either capture that position or give up our lives. Either way, we are soldiers for Bangladesh. Our country."

A few seconds passed in silence. There was no whooping or rushing back out to the battlefield. This speech was nothing less than Hafiz asking each and every man to weigh his own place in history. Each man would make their own sober calculation to die for a country that did not yet exist.

Then one soldier, fighting back tears, stood up and raised a rifle skyward.

"*Joi Bangla*," he said in a level voice, like it was the answer to a complex math problem.

"*Joi Bangla*," said another, just a little louder.

But they never rose to a cheer. Instead, the men hugged one another and knew themselves for dead. Some no doubt prayed to Allah that showing such courage in the face of evil would earn them passage through the gates of heaven.

Hafiz decided to stage the attack just before dawn. If they had any luck, the Pakistanis would expect them to take a few days to regroup. Their best hope was to try to recapture the element of surprise. This time, Hafiz wouldn't call on the Indians for artillery backup. If they could just get close enough to the buildings without starting a firefight, they'd have a chance of penetrating the perimeter.

They tried to sleep. Few succeeded. Just before the sun arced above the horizon the men emerged like shadows from the village huts. They crouched low as they began a silent march out of the woods. The closest of the three buildings lay a few hundred yards away. They crossed the rice paddy, the same site that held them captive from incessant enemy fire just a few hours earlier. The three buildings were all silent. So far so good.

Gunfire erupted when they were a hundred yards from the walls: They'd been spotted. A single light machine gun opened fire from a window. Bullets spurted into their loose formation. The attack urged Hafiz and his company into a sprint.

"*Behanchod!*" Hafiz roared the insult in Urdu as he fired several rounds from his pistol at the window.

Hafiz's imperfect cover was just good enough to help his company clear the remaining ground in seconds. They all splayed themselves against the wall of the closest building, reaching their target without losing a single man. Hafiz broke down the door. Inside, ten paramilitary youths immediately raised their hands to surrender. They were teenagers, not even wearing army uniforms.

Hafiz studied the young faces of what was supposed to be a professional force and realized that this wasn't the regular Pakistan Army. He disarmed them and put the captives in a corner of the room.

But the building itself told another story. Hafiz looked around and saw dozens of crates of ammunition, explosives, and well-maintained arms. It was an entire arsenal—enough to keep the army in place for weeks or months. The paramilitary troops cowered below Hafiz's imposing form. One boy was brave enough to open his mouth.

"They knew you were coming. They said the whole Indian Army and Mukti Bahini were coming to take revenge for what they'd done."

His attack yesterday was enough to set the army on the run.

Hafiz blinked and recalled his night of terror. The Pakistanis were crumbling under the slightest pressure. At this rate, the resistance could control Dacca in a week. Hafiz walked over to the radio operator and decided it was time to turn the wireless back on.

"Bravo Company reporting," he said into the black handset.

Seconds later Zia clicked in, as if he'd been sitting by his set all night long. "What is happening? I've been hearing gunshots all morning. And why the hell is your radio off?"

"I have captured the objective, sir."

There was a pause.

"Say again? Repeat," said Zia, in disbelief.

"I have captured the objective."

"But you never called for artillery." Zia couldn't conceive of a victory without it.

"It was a surprise attack."

Another pause. The larger enormity of what this meant was starting to sink in.

"Well, congratulations! You have done a great service to the struggle. But, maybe more important, now the Mukti Bahini has a victory of our own. We won our own ground without the help of the Indians." Zia said he'd send a relief force and that Hafiz should secure the area.

Hafiz took an hour to assess the victory. He examined the cache of weapons and prisoners and reconned the entire building. In one bunker he found broken bangles and sari cloth. It was the room where soldiers raped village women. He felt the same anger he'd felt standing over the mass grave the previous morning.

Hafiz walked out into the eerily silent courtyard in the center of the small enclave of buildings. It was a dusty parcel of land with a large flagpole stuck in the middle. As the orange sun ignited the horizon,

Hafiz did a double take. Three men were tied to the pole with gags in their mouths. Hafiz approached and noticed a note on one of their chests. The men had tears in their eyes that seemed to plead more intensely with every step he took toward them. They murmured under the gags, but Hafiz wasn't ready to hear what they had to say just yet. He kept his hand on his pistol as he read the note, scribbled in English:

These are traitors. Sort them out.

Razakars. Traitors. Profiteers. Scum.

Hafiz eyed the men again. He cared little for why, exactly, the army might have left them behind. Maybe they'd outgrown their usefulness. Maybe it was a peace offering for mercy in case Hafiz captured the army men later. Or maybe it was simply because no one likes a traitor.

As an officer, Hafiz had a duty to treat prisoners of war humanely. But not everyone in the Mukti Bahini followed such a strict moral code. As he walked away from the sobbing men at the flagpole, Hafiz told the local freedom fighters that they could deal with the *razakars* however they liked. He wouldn't lose sleep over their fate.

50

Yahya Khan and Richard Nixon

Every hour, the Mukti Bahini and Indian Army advanced on Dacca, side by side. They'd made it a third of the distance from the border to the capital in just five days, liberating every village along the way. Some villagers used the table-turning to torture and execute suspected *razakars*, killing more than a hundred thousand West Pakistani supporters in reprisal attacks.

With Niazi holed up like a hermit, the Dentist was flying blind. In his first act as de facto commander of the eastern wing, he floated the idea of surrendering to a few diplomats. He gave Yahya an ominous update:

ONCE THE ENEMY HAS CROSSED THE *GANGES* FURTHER RESISTANCE WILL BE FUTILE UNLESS *CHINA* OR *USA* INTERVENES TODAY WITH A MASSIVE AIR AND GROUND SUPPORT.

The governor asked Yahya if he could surrender to the United Nations. All Yahya had to do was say yes and, just like that, the war would be over. India promised to abide by anything the UN passed. Yes, the loss would be humiliating, but Pakistan would live on. The Dentist awaited Yahya's order, hoping that Yahya would save some soldiers' lives before the Indian Army took Dacca.

Yahya had to act fast. But he knew that any cease-fire would lead to a coup. He needed to rally the troops with a gesture that would get everyone from Niazi down to the most insignificant sepoy ready to give their lives for the cause. He needed to make India look so bad in the process that Bhutto could make a convincing case, buying time as the diplomats debated solutions.

Yahya's idea was as genius as it was ghastly. As Bhutto's plane taxied into the gate at John F. Kennedy Airport, Yahya green-lit a covert mission to bomb an orphanage in Dacca and plant evidence within the rubble that fingered the Indians.

That day Yahya incinerated two hundred children. Then his surrogates led journalists to the site and filled their notebooks with righteous indignations. This was the Indian war machine slaughtering innocent children while they played.

And somehow the ploy worked. In the confusion that followed, the Indians paused their offensive to determine if, indeed, they *had* done it. Yahya's gamble bought him just the time he needed.

At his winter White House in the Florida Keys, President Nixon wanted to take control of the situation. For the past few days he'd screamed at his advisers that the beacon of the free world couldn't stand by neutral as Indians invaded their neighbors. Now was a time for action. Kissinger saw it in even grander terms.

"Mr. President, this is a Soviet-India power play to humiliate us. It's nothing less than Indian-Soviet collusion, raping a friend of ours!" Henry Kissinger matched Nixon's emotional intensity, fearing that yet another country might fall like a domino to Soviet ideology. For his part, Nixon had a bad habit of getting wasted and scheming to nuke America's enemies, whoever they happened to be that week. This week, Nixon was paying attention to India.

"Get tougher, goddamnit!" Nixon wanted India sanctioned. He wanted an economic embargo. He yelled a new demand at Kissinger nearly every half hour. Kissinger obligingly yelled it down the chain of command. Terrified of getting fired, the advisers and bureaucrats stopped offering advice. Nixon was never going to be swayed by nuanced fifty-page assessments anyway. Who needed analytics when Nixon had his guts to guide him?

He would escalate at all costs to force the Indians to back down.

Meanwhile, Yahya stopped sugarcoating the situation in their calls. He told the president and his secretary of state that the Pakistan Army was disintegrating by the minute. Now was the time, Yahya said, for Nixon to return the favor built up over the last two years which he'd documented so meticulously in the CHINESE CONNECTION.

Nixon hated India at least as much as he liked Yahya. And both Nixon and Kissinger were ardent proponents of the domino theory, a Cold War philosophy that if any country switched to a communist or leftist government, it would set off a chain reaction by which the Soviets and their allies would take over the globe as countries fell like dominoes.

In their eyes, a liberated Bangladesh would have Mujib for a leader. And he was as red as they got.

Nixon and Kissinger scowled as they mulled over their options. Any half measures, like giving Yahya more weapons, were too late now to stem the tide. The Vietnam War raged just a few hundred miles away and putting boots on the ground in East Pakistan was all but impossible. Nixon certainly didn't need *two* proxy wars.

They kept coming back to an idea. It was dangerous. Kissinger convinced Nixon that they only had one card left to play: Get the Soviet Union so scared of the possibility of global thermonuclear war that the USSR would force India to pull back before the crazy Americans did something that nobody could come back from. They'd bring the world to the brink of annihilation.

With the Mukti Bahini closing in from the north, east, and west, it was only a matter of time before Pakistan folded. If any one of them made it to the city, the war would be lost. It was now or never.

Kissinger egged Nixon on, celebrating the choice before he'd even finished making it. "It's a typical Nixon plan," he told the still-wary president in the Oval Office. "I mean it's bold. You're putting all your chips into the pot. At least we're coming off like men."

Nixon decided. He picked up the phone and put the order in. The most powerful vessel in the American fleet, the *Enterprise*, was coming for Dacca. Elated, Yahya rushed to send a telegram to the Dentist with the good news.

FOR *GOVERNOR* FROM *PRESIDENT*: VERY IMPORTANT DIPLOMATIC AND MILITARY MOVES ARE TAKING PLACE BY OUR FRIENDS. IS ESSENTIAL THAT WE HOLD ON FOR ANOTHER THIRTY-SIX HOURS AT ALL COSTS. *UNITED STATES SEVENTH FLEET* WILL BE VERY SOON IN POSITION. ALSO FRONT HAS BEEN ACTIVATED BY *CHINESE*. GOOD LUCK TO YOU.

The *Enterprise* was about to save the day. Bhutto wired Yahya that the Americans and Chinese were in position for a joint strike on Indian forces. The network of alliances would draw the world powers together to back his cause. With victory all but a formality, Yahya had an overpowering urge to celebrate. So he threw a President House champagne party, inviting all the generals and their wives to reward them for a job well done.

51

Captain Ernest Tissot and Rear Admiral Vladimir Kruglyakov

THE BAY OF BENGAL
DECEMBER 10, 1971

The USS *Enterprise* sliced through the Bay of Bengal's placid night waters. It was the largest nuclear-propelled aircraft carrier ever constructed and the flagship of the Seventh Fleet. Whenever the United States needed to remind a country that America was, indeed, a superpower, that's where the *Enterprise* went.

This time, the Big E, as its sailors often called it, sailed from Vietnam. Three months earlier its air wing destroyed 198 North Vietnamese aircraft in one raid and didn't take a single loss. Since then, it had flown hundreds more missions with a similar exemplary record. It parked off the coast of Cuba during the missile crisis. It was the sort of ship that could win a war all on its own. At a thousand feet long, its hangars could hold ninety planes. Its nuclear reactors could power the ship for up to ten years at sea without ever having to come back to port. It was all but unstoppable.

At the helm was Captain Ernest Tissot, a World War II, Korea, and Vietnam hero with an exceptional record who always obeyed the chain of command, no matter how dangerous the order. Five thousand sailors kept the vast war machine running. Its magazine held one hundred nuclear gravity bombs, each one up to twenty times more powerful than the bombs dropped on Hiroshima and Nagasaki. Flight crews could load weapons and send them airborne in less than thirty minutes from the moment the captain issued the order. The *Enterprise* carried enough firepower to obliterate every major city in South Asia.

Flanked by two quick-strike missile destroyers, the *Enterprise* sailed up the Bay of Bengal at a measured fifteen nautical miles an hour, about the same pace as the Great Bhola Cyclone one year earlier. An American nuclear-attack submarine shadowed the carrier group somewhere below the surface. The flotilla set a course to within a few dozen miles of the *Mahajagmitra*'s final resting place.

The world paid attention when the *Enterprise* set a course for someplace new. Military radios crackled to life all along the Strait of Malacca when the ship passed Singapore and Malaysia on its way to the Bay of Bengal. Nixon didn't need to announce the deployment for Soviet intelligence to sit up and recognize there was a new front in the struggle between superpowers.

Ostensibly, the story was that the *Enterprise* was en route to evacuate about twenty Americans from Dacca. But everyone knew that was just a cover.

A communications officer shoved a recently decrypted message into Captain Tissot's hand. It was a direct order from Nixon via the secretary of defense. Nixon authorized Tissot to destroy all Indian communications if the Soviets provoked the carrier group. The *Enterprise* would prepare for war.

Five hundred miles south of their position, a Soviet attack force churned in the carrier group's direction at full speed, having already gone two thousand miles from Vladivostok in the last week. Guiding the flotilla from a destroyer whose name translated to *"Excited,"* Rear Admiral Vladimir Kruglyakov closed the distance fast. The Soviet fleet included a missile cruiser and two Foxtrot-class submarines, both equipped with tactical nuclear weapons. The flotilla had enough firepower to vaporize any ship they encountered or, for that matter, a city, if they got close enough.

The Indian Navy tipped off a BBC journalist that the *Enterprise* was entering the Bay of Bengal and took him out on an airplane so he could see it for himself. After the flight, the reporter rushed back to the Grand Hotel in Calcutta to telex the news to his home office. The Grand Hotel was the de facto press headquarters for foreign correspondents covering the Liberation War after they'd been kicked out of Dacca.

The BBC newsman knew the scoop was too important to keep to himself. He shouted into the lobby that the *Enterprise* was on its way to strike India. Everyone knew the ship's capabilities and what it meant for the conflict. The United States was in the fight, and this might be the flashpoint into a global nuclear war. The opulent marble room fell silent as everyone took in the news and then erupted it into a cacaphony. Sipping tea on a lobby couch on a rare day off, Jon and Candy Rohde heard the announcement, and their hearts sank. Once again America was on the wrong side of history.

The anger, frustration, and overwhelming sadness of the last year came out in waves, and Jon's tears spilled onto the hand-carved teak sofa. Candy held him tight as reporters rushed out of the lobby to file the breaking news.

Rear Admiral Kruglyakov swallowed hard when he read his most recent decoded orders from central command. The Soviet naval commander in chief ordered him to stop the *Enterprise* from advancing, by any means necessary. The American Seventh Fleet must not come within striking distance of India's military bases. This meant that if the Big E and its escorts sailed just a hundred more miles northwest, Kruglyakov must vaporize them. The standoff between Soviet Foxtrot submarines and American airpower had precedent in the Cuban missile crisis just nine years earlier.

The submarine commander brought the crew to high alert. The change in plans bounced around the polished steel walls in the language of red flashing lights, keeping silent cover beneath the surface of the sea. A mechanic on the bridge asked, "Where are we going, Captain?"

The commander ignored the blatant breach in protocol. It was no time to be pedantic.

"We're going to war."

Kruglyakov would start World War III if he had to. Any Soviet commander would. The protocols dictated that he must follow the last order he received unless the central command notified him otherwise. The tricky part was that when his attack submarines were five hundred feet underwater—nearly 100 percent of the time when on military operations—Kruglyakov couldn't communicate with them from his command post, so every dictate he gave had to account for that eventuality. The submarine commander couldn't contradict orders from Moscow and every moment risked a chain reaction that would spiral out of his control.

It was a grave responsibility, but the autonomy of submarine captains was also a critical Cold War deterrent. The subs could still fire their weapons if the Soviet Union was already smoldering after a nuclear attack. Supposedly, this meant that global thermonuclear war would be less likely to happen because no world leader would be insane enough to start lobbing nukes if that meant their own mutually assured destruction.

And that was why Indira Gandhi couldn't believe what was happening just off the Indian coast. She was dumbstruck that the United States was really willing to end life on the planet in order to prop up a genocidal regime. She worried that the Soviets had overplayed their hand and their Bay of Bengal submarine ploy was little more than a high-stakes bluff. The Indian secretary of defense K. B. Lall captured the feeling: "They must have gone absolutely mad. Such things simply don't happen! The Americans must be totally out of their senses."

The Soviet subs dove to a depth where they could no longer communicate with the outside world. The commander's orders mandated him to launch his arsenal if the unstoppable *Enterprise* sailed too close to an arbitrary line off the Indian coast.

52

Zulfikar Ali Bhutto, Yahya Khan, and Henry Kissinger

NEW YORK CITY AND ISLAMABAD, WEST PAKISTAN

DECEMBER 12, 1971

Half a world away, Zulfikar Ali Bhutto was giving the performance of his life over an opulent breakfast at one of the world's most luxurious hotels. Before leaving Pakistan, Bhutto had Yahya make him the deputy prime minister. It was just a nonsense title, Bhutto claimed, but one that would lend his message at the United Nations more gravitas. Yahya agreed without a second thought.

Bhutto met Henry Kissinger at the Waldorf-Astoria in New York. The title, Bhutto explained to his intrigued breakfast mate, was a harbinger of change in Pakistan. Everyone in Pakistan knew it was just a matter of time before Yahya was gone, Bhutto said, probably mere days. Bhutto was ready to pick up the pieces, and he was reaching out to select allies to let them know that he was loyal and trustworthy.

What Bhutto didn't tell Kissinger was that without an international coalition to back him up on the day he betrayed Yahya, he'd be as good as dead too. Bhutto buttered up the secretary of state while the waiters discreetly served coffee and croissants.

Bhutto played the conversation like a virtuoso. "Elegant, eloquent, subtle, I found him brilliant, charming, of global stature in his perceptions. In its hour of greatest need, he [could] save his country from complete destruction," a mesmerized Kissinger remembered. He was astute enough to see that Pakistan's future—if it even had a future—would run through Bhutto. Never one to harbor lifelong loyalties himself, Kissinger swapped Yahya for Bhutto as his preferred partner in Pakistan in less time than it took for his coffee to get cold.

"But Bhutto," Kissinger warned, "tough rhetoric and bluffing alone won't save Pakistan."

Bhutto reeled in his big fish nice and slow. "Henry, I know the facts as well as you, and I'm prepared to do whatever [is] necessary, no matter how painful, to save my country." Bhutto warned Kissinger that Indira Gandhi was itching to level all of Pakistan.

"Look. There's no secret where the President and I stand. We want to cooperate with those who want to save West Pakistan." Kissinger felt a tinge of regret about stabbing Yahya in the back so coldly, but there was just something about Bhutto that gave Kissinger a good feeling. This was a man he could work with.

Bhutto and Kissinger came to a deal. The Big E would chug northward, twisting the screws on the Soviet Union ever tighter. Kissinger said that the journalists wondering if America's leaders had lost their minds didn't understand the cold calculations of brinksmanship like he and Bhutto did. Kissinger explained that if the Soviets thought that the Americans *might* actually nuke India, then everyone would slow down their military operations, which would buy time for Bhutto to regain control over the situation. After it was all over, Bhutto would lead Pakistan, with American backing. The men shook hands and wished each other well.

With that, Bhutto walked out of the Waldorf-Astoria. Kissinger had to catch a plane back to Washington. Bhutto decided to walk the few blocks to the United Nations, where he had a peace deal to sabotage. The impeccably besuited Bhutto wore a devilish smile as he strolled down Manhattan's gray, windy streets.

As the last partygoers stumbled out of President House in Islamabad at around three in the morning, Yahya still believed that he'd effectively won the war and saved his country. He rang Bhutto in New York, where it was six p.m. Both men were dead drunk. The call got weird. Out of nowhere, Bhutto said that Yahya's dancing and drinking would be his ruin. This confused Yahya: Wasn't everything going great?

Bhutto slurred something about a dinner he had to get to and hung up. Yahya passed out.

In truth, things weren't going that great at the United Nations. Bhutto had managed to scuttle the first round of cease-fire deals, but the sneaky Polish and meticulous Italian delegates wouldn't give up. Worse, the Indians realized that stalling might be a great way to help the Mukti Bahini get to Dacca, so they gave a forty-eight-hour non-stop speech to run out the clock on a cease-fire proposal by the Security Council as the liberation fighters advanced. Bhutto didn't tell Yahya that if he'd simply kept his mouth shut, the UN would have already forced the Indians to withdraw.

Later, Yahya spent his sober hours telling his generals to relax. The United States and China were bringing massive armies, but they just needed more time to get everything organized. It would take one more day, two tops. Desperate officers in Dacca called Yahya's office every hour, begging for guidance. When would the Chinese bring reinforcements from the north? When would the Americans start bombing? Troops were dying every minute, strategic points fell every hour.

"Soon," Yahya said, over and again. "Soon. Soon."

53

Richard Nixon

WASHINGTON, DC

DECEMBER 14, 1971

A black telegraph machine with unbreakable cryptography gathered a thin layer of dust on a nondescript Oval Office end table. It looked a bit like a cash register without a drawer. Incoming messages emerged from a small spool printer in the top case. None had come through in years.

This machine was the Moscow–Washington Direct Communications Link, also known as the Hotline, or the Red Telephone, despite being neither red nor a phone. Just a few months back, both sides agreed to use the Hotline only if there had been a nuclear accident or there was threat of imminent nuclear war. Simply using the machine sent an unmistakable signal: Pay attention, now. Nixon and Kissinger decided to try it out. Their opening volley to the Soviets was a threat.

```
WE HAVE WAITED FOR YOUR RESPONSE TO RESTRAIN INDIA WITH-
OUT REPLY. I HAVE NOW SET IN MOTION CERTAIN MOVES THAT
CANNOT BE REVERSED. I CANNOT EMPHASIZE TOO STRONGLY THAT
TIME IS OF THE ESSENCE TO AVOID CONSEQUENCES NEITHER OF
US WANT.
```

Nixon called the secretary of the navy and ordered the Big E to proceed deeper into the Bay of Bengal. As Kissinger later said, "It became urgent to convince them that we meant business." Nixon would employ the entire American nuclear arsenal at his disposal if the Soviets refused to force India and the Mukti Bahini to retreat. Then he directed his attention to the Indian diplomatic corps.

Kissinger wished he could see the look on Indira Gandhi's face now. "After this is over we ought to do something about that goddamned Indian ambassador here going on television every day and attacking American policy."

Nixon agreed. "Why haven't we done something already?"

"He says he has unmistakable proof that we are planning to land troops in the Bay of Bengal. Well, that's okay with me."

"Yeah, that scares them."

"If we don't do anything, we'll be finished," Kissinger said, effortlessly planting the seeds of escalation in Nixon's mind.

"So, what do we do if the Soviets move with them? Start lobbing nuclear weapons in? Is that what you mean?"

"Well, if the Soviets move in, that will be the final showdown. So that carrier move is good."

"Why, hell yes!"

Convinced they had the upper hand, Nixon and Kissinger awaited what would surely be a groveling apology from the Soviets on the Hotline.

54

A. A. K. Niazi and Yahya Khan

ISLAMABAD AND DACCA, EAST PAKISTAN

DECEMBER 14, 1971

The Tiger raged up and down the street like a madman in front of the InterContinental. "Dacca will fall over my dead body!" He beat his chest with his fist. "They will have to drive a tank over this!" He tried to get the reporters covering him to join in chants of "Crush India!" and "Long Live Pakistan!" They demurred. A decrypted message arrived just half an hour earlier:

```
YOU MUST HOLD OUT UNDER ALL CONDITIONS. THE GREAT BLOW
FROM THE NORTH AND THE GREAT BLOW FROM THE SOUTH WILL
SOON BE DELIVERED.
```

The Tiger thought he was rallying the troops by example, but looking down at the spectacle from above, the Dentist and the rest of East Pakistan's government knew that their time in power was coming to an end. They barricaded themselves in suites at the InterContinental to ride out the rest of the war. A rumor circulated that if Dacca *did* fall, a court in Geneva would try them all for war crimes. The Dentist and his ministers drank away their sorrows alongside foreign correspondents who hoarded the hotel's last bottles of average scotch.

The journalists had turned the InterContinental into their own little fiefdom. They manned the doors, patting down the incoming

Pakistani officials for contraband after the regular guards vanished. They held an all-night poker marathon by candlelight in the basement, pausing only for BBC radio bulletins that they listened to without putting down their cards. Photographers sat in folding chairs on the roof, waiting to capture the explosions when India bombed another barracks. Every few hours, they'd fish shrapnel out of the swimming pool.

The InterContinental was a green-zone oasis that everyone from politicians, to the Red Cross, to the police, to the United Nations and the Mukti Bahini respected. Whenever a foreigner or Pakistani official crossed the threshold into the lobby, war activities were strictly off-limits. Regular Bengalis were less lucky. The guards outside the front of the hotel had gunned down at least five people seeking safe haven just in the last week.

The Mukti Bahini were just fifty miles out when they got word that the *Enterprise* was on the way. Their new objective: Take Dacca as fast as possible.

As would-be liberators marched on the capital of East Pakistan, back in Islamabad Yahya's psyche swung wildly, lurching back and forth from euphoria to despair. Yahya hadn't slept in a week and couldn't resist the siren call of tranquilizers to settle his nerves. It didn't help that the war had made it to West Pakistan. For the last seven days Karachi had been on fire. The Indian Navy lobbed shells into the port city as Indian fighter jets set fuel tanks and tankers ablaze.

For the last eight hours, he'd tried calling every Chinese diplomat and military contact he had. All the People's Liberation Army had to do was show up with force in North India and the whole affair would be over. Why couldn't they see that? Where was the northern front? Nobody would pick up the phone.

This was bad.

And it didn't help that Kissinger and Nixon were being cagey.

America kept promising a big show of force, but Yahya hadn't heard a thing about troop movements from Vietnam. No one in the East Pakistan government returned his calls. On top of that, a petrified Niazi told Yahya he could hear the rebel bullets now and was sure they were coming for him.

Yahya fished the latest UN cease-fire proposal out of a stack of papers next to his telex. It was an utter humiliation: a defeat in all but the most pedantic face-saving phrases about "integrity" and whatnot.

Yahya sighed, staring at the document and lamenting his legacy. The invasion failed. His selective genocide of Bengalis failed. The India gambit failed. His friendships, his power, his family, even his mistresses had all slipped through his fingers. The only honorable thing left was to accept defeat gracefully. He was still a soldier after all, with an unbreakable loyalty to his country. He rang Bhutto in New York to tell him the bad news.

Bhutto picked up. He was sober this time, and about to go to the UN General Assembly floor to chastise India. Yahya said he had the peace proposal in his hands. Bhutto laughed. It was such a joke, wasn't it? Bhutto asked Yahya how forcefully he should reject it. The phone line was silent for what felt like an eternity. Finally, Yahya spoke.

"I think it looks good. We should accept it."

Bhutto was incredulous. His months of meticulous planning were about to be undone by an idiot's weakness in the face of the unknown. If they accepted the UN peace deal before Dacca fell, then Yahya might look like a statesman, not a failure. Bhutto needed Yahya's complete humiliation for his plan to work. Bhutto needed him broken.

But Bhutto couldn't turn down an order to accept a peace deal from his country's leader, either. Treason was still treason, even in Pakistan. Thinking fast, Bhutto came up with an idea.

"What? I can't hear you."

"We should accept it, Bhutto."

"What?"

"Accept the deal!"

"What? What?"

The UN operator who'd patched them through and was listening on the line jumped in on the conversation. "I can hear him fine."

"Shut up!" Bhutto slammed down the phone and walked out of the building.

Even a bad military strategist can see when there's no way out. Throwing more lives into the face of a vastly superior enemy would barely slow down the approach. Dacca was lost. Yahya sat in silence, mulling over the choice that wasn't really a choice anymore. Give up or double down again, this time by betting the lives of tens of millions more citizens.

The people would forgive him. They had to. They always had.

At 1:32 a.m., alone at President House, Yahya threw in the towel. He sat down at the encrypted telex and clicked out a typo-filled message to Niazi. He was so drunk he forgot to turn on the encryption.

FOR *GOVERNOR* AND *GENERAL NIAZI* FROM *PRESIDENT*. YOU HAVE FOUGHT A HEROIC BATTLES AGAINST OVERWHELMING ODD. THE NATION IS PROUD OF YOU AND THE WORLD FULL OF ADMIRATION. I HAVE DONE ALL THAT IS HUMANLY POSSIBLE TO FIND AN ACCEPTABLE SOLUTION TO THE PROBLEM. YOU HAVE NOW REACHED A STAGE WHERE FURTHER RESISTANCE IS NO LONGER *HUMANLY* POSSIBLE NOR WILL IT SERVE ANY USEFUL PURPOSE. YOU SHOULD NOW TAKE ALL NECESSARY *MEASURES* *TO* *STOP* *THE* *FIGHTING* *AND* *PRESERVE* THE LIVES OF ALL ARMED FORCES PERSONNEL ALL THOSE FROM *WEST PAKISTAN* AND ALL LOYAL ELEMENTS.

The Mukti Bahini were at the Dacca city limits. They broke into a fierce firefight with the last line of the Pakistan Army forces, the final obstacle before they could enter their capital as liberators.

Niazi read Yahya's message at five a.m. and started the morning with a panic attack. Losing on the battlefield meant fleeing Bengal for Karachi. He could handle that just fine. But if the United Nations came in, that meant war crimes investigations, international inspectors, and a criminal court. They'd put him in prison for decades.

No, that wouldn't do at all. Niazi had to accomplish two things before it all came crashing down. First, he'd offer to surrender to the United Nations, to India, to the Americans, even to the Mukti Bahini if he had to, in exchange for amnesty for any and all acts he had committed during the war.

Second, if Bangladesh achieved independence, Niazi, with Yahya's blessing, wanted to make certain that the new nation would begin its life as a cripple. The last thing Pakistan needed was another powerful enemy country in South Asia. Niazi told what remained of his army to stop defending the city and instead drive around Dacca to liquidate every Bengali intellectual they could find.

The army abducted novelists, engineers, artists, actors, anyone left in the city with an advanced degree and any other public figure of note. They threw them into buses with blackened windows and butchered them in a potter's field. As one reporter wrote: "They cut out the heart of a heart doctor, the eyes out of an eye doctor; they chopped off the hands of writers and tore out the throats of singers." Niazi's men dumped more than two hundred famous bodies in a shallow mass grave on the outskirts of town. They didn't bother to fill it in with dirt; they wanted to send a message.

Next, Niazi burned down the Central Bank. His men threw the bank's gold and silver into the Bay of Bengal, perhaps to make it look like a robbery. The new country would have no intellectual class, and it would be bankrupt too. Then Niazi waited in his office for his reckoning, knocking on the city's outskirts in the form of thousands of armed Bengalis seeking revenge.

55

Rear Admiral Kruglyakov and Richard Nixon

THE BAY OF BENGAL
DECEMBER 15, 1971

Soviet rear admiral Kruglyakov was uneasy. As he stood on the bridge of his missile cruiser about two hundred miles due west from the USS *Enterprise* in the Bay of Bengal, he worried about what he might be forced to do. A few hundred feet beneath the surface, two Soviet subs under his command reached their position, somewhere near the intersection of the 92nd meridian and the 13th parallel. Kruglyakov's orders from Moscow were simple: Destroy the *Enterprise* if it passed an arbitrary set of coordinates, using their nuclear arsenals if necessary.

Kruglyakov's fleet stalked in the deathly silence, waiting for the Big E to arrive. The Americans crept closer by the minute, on a course for Dacca. They showed no signs of stopping.

Kruglyakov's missile cruiser parked just out of the *Enterprise*'s radar range, but the Big E was poised to sail right over his subs. They hovered on their red line, lying in stasis. Kruglyakov ordered total radio silence to avoid detection, but it also meant that they had no way to communicate with Moscow should his sub captains make a rash decision.

At the Big E's current pace, Kruglyakov calculated he would need to launch his torpedoes in about sixty minutes.

Before he dropped contact with his underwater fleet, Kruglyakov made a risky bet. Just as the Tiger was reading Yahya's surrender telegram, Kruglyakov's commanders brought their subs to surface in case the *Enterprise* was about to advance beyond the point of no return. The admiral's reasoning for the advance orders was simple: How could his flotilla be a deterrent to war if the Americans didn't even know they were there, or didn't understand the Soviet significance of the red line in the sea?

Problem was, Kruglyakov's subs were sitting ducks above water. It wasn't like they could just dive back down to secrecy if the Americans spotted them. Stopping the carrier group from crossing one arbitrary line risked starting a completely new provocation.

Still, if Kruglyakov was going to blow up the world's biggest aircraft carrier, he needed to make damn sure there was no other option. Moscow hadn't ordered him to surface the subs, but they hadn't formally ordered him *not* to surface them either. Only a lunatic would do that—it had no tactical merit. Kruglyakov used the gray area to communicate his intention to the Americans.

The two subs climbed fast, hulls creaking under the rapid pressure change. The plan was to park the subs right in front of the *Enterprise* before it could cross the line, waving a Soviet flag to mark it as their territory. Officially it was a friendly gesture in international waters. Unofficially the message was as plain as day: We were here first, so back off.

The subs broke the surface just before dawn. A watchman manning the periscope on one of the subs yelled out in terror: "A city is coming towards us!"

The city was the USS *Enterprise*, so close that it dwarfed the two nuclear torpedo–equipped subs. Alarms went off inside the Soviet vessels as they armed their weapons systems. They formed a pincer directly in the path of the oncoming Americans.

There was no going back. Kruglyakov sailed the *Excited* toward the *Enterprise*, so that his destroyer, missile cruiser, and subs made a wall on the line of no return. Captain Ernest Tissot was within his rights to vaporize the entire Soviet flotilla for the provocation. The submarine captains were so close they could see the command staff on the *Enterprise*'s bridge through their binoculars.

The *Enterprise* stopped its forward movement and dug in for a standoff. By the end of the day Soviet and American destroyers, cruisers, and minesweepers flanked the *Excited* and the *Enterprise*, more than a dozen vessels in all. The Bay of Bengal was set up like a live-action game of Battleship.

The Soviets intercepted Tissot's communication back to the commander in chief of the Pacific fleet: "We are constantly being monitored, we were too late with the deployment, there are a lot of Soviet ships, and their commander is acting impudently."

Nixon had Tissot's message in his hands within the hour. How could the Soviets have beaten them to the punch? Worse, he got intel that Niazi was about to surrender, but confirming the move proved impossible. When the US ambassador to Pakistan called up Yahya to find out what was happening, saying it was a matter of life or death, the Pakistani president was too drunk to speak and hung up the phone without conveying any useful information.

Nixon was flying blind. But he had to stand tough. Kissinger warned him: "I consider this our Rhineland."

Getting nervous, Nixon agreed: "Once we go balls out, we never look back." They needed to do anything they could to stop Dacca from falling, even if it meant launching missiles into India. "Hell," Nixon said, "we've done worse. The point about the carrier move, we just say: look, 'these people are savages! The United Nations cannot survive and we cannot have a stable world if we allow one member to cannibalize another.' Cannibalize, that's the word, I should have thought of it earlier. You see that really puts it to the Indians. The connotation is [that they're] savages. To cannibalize, and that's what the sons-of-bitches are up to." He reiterated his orders to the *Enterprise*. Full steam ahead.

Tissot prepared to execute the orders. The Soviets had no intention of moving.

As the standoff escalated, Nixon and Kissinger debated strategy in the Oval Office. "If the Soviets move against [the *Enterprise*] in these conditions . . ." For once, Kissinger seemed to be at a loss for words. He continued gravely: "If they succeed we'll be finished. We'll be through."

China was still a wild card and it was anyone's guess what they would think about US involvement. Nixon feared that no matter what the final result, this debacle might scuttle his delicate negotiations to open up new trade opportunities.

Kissinger agreed, thinking out loud that if they did anything to irritate the Chinese, "our China initiative is pretty well down the drain."

It was decided: They'd stay the course, like men. They waited for the next telex.

The Big E crept up on the imaginary red line.

Now Kruglyakov was under direct orders to destroy the *Enterprise*. Tissot was under direct orders to stop India from taking Dacca. The men stood on their respective ships, within sight of each other like a couple of old-fashioned gunslingers, waiting for the clock to strike high noon, their fingers inches from the trigger. Except in this case their holsters had nuclear weapons instead of revolvers. Kruglyakov armed his K-31 missiles. Tissot armed his own weapons. Both men prayed that something in the geostrategic calculus would change, fast. Someone had to flinch.

Kruglyakov sent a final message to Moscow. It was precise and brief, but anyone reading between the lines would know he was praying for an order that would stop this madness: "I have targeted and locked on the *Enterprise*."

Tissot and Kruglyakov stood tense on their respective ships, unmoving. Everyone knew how to react to an escalation, but nobody knew quite how to make a move to reduce the tension that wasn't a humiliating withdrawal.

With the Americans and Soviets deadlocked, pointing torpedoes, missiles, and cannons at each other across the dozen ships, it felt like only a matter of time before a chain reaction would start a war over a part of the world that neither Soviet nor American leaders cared the slightest bit about only twelve months earlier.

Just then, Tissot got a message from the US Pacific commander. Dacca had fallen; the war was over. Just after sunset on December 15, the Mukti Bahini broke through the army's last line of defense. Minutes later Kruglyakov got the same message from his superiors.

Tissot breathed a sigh of relief. Kruglyakov did the same. His gamble apparently had paid off. The rival commanders disarmed their nuclear missiles. There was nothing to fight over anymore.

56

A. A. K. Niazi, Richard Nixon, Zulfikar Ali Bhutto, and Hafiz Uddin Ahmad

Niazi woke up on the morning of December 16 after a surprisingly good sleep. No gunfire echoed through the streets of Dacca. No mortar fire. No airstrikes. No mass executions. But that didn't mean it was quiet. Once the Indian Army and Mukti Bahini stormed the city, Bengali citizens emerged shocked and blinking into a new reality: freedom. Niazi told his Indian counterpart, Lieutenant General J. S. Aurora, that he'd like to surrender around noon. He set up a fancy lunch table that included a display of his own battlefield awards and a plate of samosas.

Niazi passed the time before the signing ceremony by cracking dirty jokes to disgusted subordinates. He didn't care. His amnesty was in the bag. The Indians even promised him an escort to the airport.

At the ceremony, Lieutenant General Aurora, a Sikh in a neatly appointed turban, scrutinized the Pakistani general's signature on the official documents. The Indian general asked Niazi to surrender his weapon as a sign of respect and to show his desire to never take up arms against India again. Niazi had hidden his own gun in his quarters and gave Aurora a broken revolver instead.

Then Aurora sent Niazi to his plane; the general's car passed through a Mukti Bahini mob that futilely smashed at the windows with their fists and rifle butts. Without further incident, the Indians airlifted the Tiger to Islamabad.

That evening, Yahya was supposed to address the nation about the terms of surrender. But there was a problem. He'd locked himself in his room ever since his last call with Bhutto. Advisers banged on the door for hours until Yahya finally opened it. He'd been wearing the same pajamas for days and could barely stand up. His sour stench overpowered the cohort. Not knowing what else to do, his security head shoved the speech into the hands of a twenty-one-year-old Pakistan TV announcer and ordered him to read it live. Like everyone else in the country, the announcer was so used to Yahya's slurring cadence that he had to stop himself from mimicking it as he presented Pakistan's defeat to millions.

Captain Tissot set the *Enterprise* on a course back to Vietnam. Rear Admiral Kruglyakov turned the Soviet fleet back to Vladivostok. As it happened, that meant sailing side by side. The two captains navigated their flotillas out of the Bay of Bengal, keeping a wary distance as they followed the same sea route through the Strait of Malacca before parting ways at Singapore to their respective destinations. Just before the two fleets left visual range, the *Enterprise* raised a string of nautical flags onto its mast. The message read "Happy Voyage."

News of the surrender reached Hafiz in the town of Sylhet after he'd just captured fifty members of the Pakistan Army. His mind wandered into the open future. Maybe he'd return to Dacca as a different kind of hero, doing his part to rebuild the country. Whatever the future might hold, now was a time to celebrate.

Hafiz and his men joined in a chorus of *"Joi Bangla."* Then he issued an order that he never expected. It was the exact opposite of the very first command he gave to his men in Jessore during the rebellion. He ordered his men to fire into the air. He emptied his pistol at the sky and his men followed suit. They fired until their weapons clicked empty.

The revelry continued for several minutes before Hafiz heard the urgent voice of General Zia over the wireless.

"I thought we won? Are we fighting again?" asked Zia.

"There is no one left to fight," Hafiz said back over the radio, laughing. "This is the sound of freedom."

Down in the Bay of Biscayne, Nixon answered the phone the morning after the surrender.

"Mr. President?" came Kissinger's voice.

"Henry! I just got out of the water." Nixon was soaking wet in his swimsuit.

"Isn't that great. You certainly need it. It looks like we are in business. The Paks have accepted the cease-fire. Yahya has accepted it now too."

"So, the Paks are satisfied, the Chinese are satisfied, and the Russians. That is fine."

"We have come out of this amazingly well and we scared the pants off the Russians. One shouldn't give somebody who drops a match into a fire credit for calling the fire department."

"Right."

"We can tell the media they were planning to attack, but not say how."

"You ought to make the point that if we hadn't used our influence as strongly as possible, it never would have come out the way it did. I think that is the point."

"Your whole strategy came out brilliantly."

"I should think everyone is happy."

Nixon had only the one day at the beach before he flew back to Washington to host Bhutto at the Oval Office. The mood was upbeat. Bhutto impressed Nixon with the way he handled the United Nations, and the two leaders agreed that it was a shame how Yahya had let them all down. Bhutto said he was on the cusp of making a much more favorable peace deal. They all knew that Yahya's career was over. And Nixon couldn't think of anyone better suited to take his place than Bhutto.

They looked forward to working together. Nixon and Bhutto shared a few laughs. Nixon offered millions in aid in the months and years to come. He hoped that India "would just let you build your 'live and let live' society down there . . . knowing that you've suffered a lot."

"You're helping all nations build their own destinies, Mr. President."

"That's right. All we want to do is help others help themselves."

The smiles were contagious. Nixon wrapped up the meeting by talking about his tough election ahead. Bhutto offered his services: "Mr. President, I can be an excellent campaign manager for you in '72." The room erupted in laughter. They shook hands warmly, and Bhutto headed for the door.

"Oh oh, wait, I forgot to give you this." Nixon rushed over to his desk and handed Bhutto a package.

"This is for Yahya. We give each other gifts every year. It's a set of presidential cuff links and a presidential towel. Christmas can be a lonely time, and I want to make sure he has a Merry Christmas. From president to president."

"Certainly, Mr. President. I will see that he gets it."

On his way back to Pakistan, Bhutto gave an interview at the London Heathrow transit lounge. He was confident that Pakistan's return to democracy would lead to brighter days.

"The people of Pakistan elected me as their chosen and undisputed leader a year ago. Power should have been transferred to me then, so that we could have made a political settlement in the East." He blamed Yahya for all of the violence and chaos that followed.

Bhutto wished the British people a Merry Christmas, and left to become president of his suddenly much smaller country. Somewhere between Washington and Islamabad, Yahya's presidential cuff links and towel made their way into the trash.

57

Mohammad Hai and Malik Mahmud

UNDISCLOSED LOCATION, BANGLADESH

DECEMBER 17, 1971

Hai inspected the hastily built cage, constructed from bamboo stalks and rope aligned in a lattice pattern. He tested the improvised bars to be sure they were secure. Then he contemplated the prisoner. Just a few inches away, on the other side of the bamboo, tears ran down Tonir's cheeks. He begged Hai to save his life.

Earlier that day, Malik learned that Tonir, the *razakar* who had betrayed Mukti Bahini fighters time and time again, was hiding in one of the many farmhouses he'd commandeered in the countryside. The tipster said that Malik's men would have to act fast. He was only there to grab his gold and flee to India, just like thousands of other *razakars* who suddenly found themselves exposed after the army surrendered. Malik recruited ten men, and they sped to the farm in a transport truck before Tonir could get away.

Malik's men fanned out around the perimeter of the ten-acre property. Once they covered every possible exit they crept in silently, weaving through cornfields and chili plants. The house was as silent as a grave.

When Malik broke through the last corn row he found Tonir resting in a throne-like dining-room chair in the middle of the yard. He looked as if he somehow knew that the end was near and he wanted to fill his lungs one last time with the smell of his soil: the land he'd earned by selling the blood of his fellow Bengalis. It was his last moment as king.

Malik put a gun to Tonir's head. Tonir laughed, nodding down to a piece of paper in his hand. Then he looked Malik in the eye.

"Here is a blank check. I'm a very rich man and you can be too if you let me live. Just fill out your price. Then I'll be on my way."

Malik slammed the gun butt into Tonir's face, spraying blood over the check. Then his team dragged Tonir to the truck and loaded him in the back. Tonir still didn't seem too worried. Instead, he bragged about the Mukti Bahini fighters he'd helped kill, and how it was just a matter of finding the right person to take his check. He'd bought himself out of worse jams than this.

If he'd had his way, Malik would have executed Tonir right there in the field. But he had a feeling it would be best to talk it over with Hai and the others first.

It was only after they incarcerated Tonir in Hai's bamboo cell that something changed. Hai let the villagers have a look at the captive. No one looked at him in fear or averted their eyes, not anymore. He saw the faces of people whose houses he'd burned down. They spat at him through the stalks. They screamed in his face. One man grabbed Tonir through the bars and smashed his smug face against the bars until it was bruised and bloody. They wanted Tonir to bleed. They wanted him to suffer.

That's when Tonir broke. He blubbered and wailed. He begged. He saw his own dismal future.

Hai looked at the mess of a man kneeling in front of him. When they were alone, Tonir tried the same pitch with Hai that he had with Malik, offering him money, land, anything Hai could dream of. The offers carried a more desperate tone now: more pleading than proposing. Tonir was one of the richest men on the island. He told Hai he could have it all, every last rupee, if he just untied a single stalk. Tonir started rambling, recycling the same desperate offers that young Bengali men had made to him when the army dragged them away to their deaths.

"I didn't do half the things they said I did," Tonir cried.

Hai stared at Tonir. He fixated his gaze deep into Tonir's glassy wet eyes. The Qur'an spoke often of forgiveness. It also spoke of vengeance. Should he kill Tonir, or show him mercy?

Alone with the *razakar*, Hai leaned against the opposing wall and reminded himself that the war was over. Sparing Tonir's life would show that the Mukti Bahini were gracious and honorable victors, willing to heal the nation through reconciliation. Bankrupting Tonir was still a punishment. The man would live out his life in poverty. And the money could do some real good and buy cows for everyone he knew. The Mukti Bahini could give everything that Tonir owned back to the communities that he'd ravaged. They'd turn the blood money into something good and noble.

But Hai felt a darker impulse too. His righteous anger had festered and grown for a year. Tonir was a *razakar*: the worst of the worst. Hai thought of the chairman's son who'd ruined HELP just to curry favor and the stories of *razakars* all over the country. Everyone knew what Tonir did. This was Hai's chance for vengeance, and Tonir deserved to die.

Hai fantasized about unloading all of the pain that had accumulated from the cyclone until today into Tonir's body. Hai wanted to kill this man more than anything. This traitor. This rapist. This Judas who profited from death and torture. The man who killed freedom fighters and Hai's Awami League brothers. This man who killed Bengalis.

Hai thought through the options, over and over again. All the while, Tonir wailed for benevolence.

Hai felt a sudden flashback to what his mom had said so many times while he did his homework on their kitchen table. "Use your brain, Hai. It's the only way out." He imagined her looking down on him now.

The captive wrapped a hand around a thin bamboo shaft. Hai's decision would define how he'd let the agony of the last year determine his future. Would he give in to rage, liquidating an enemy in cold blood now that he had the power?

Still, part of him knew that vengeance wasn't the answer. Despite his pain, Hai wouldn't be a savage that killed for sport. He wouldn't continue the cycle of violence into a newly born Bangladesh. Mujib was probably long dead by now, and the least they could do would be to honor the spirit of his March 7 speech. The best thing he could do in the new country was offer up a future built on Mujib's higher ideals: a future that they'd fought for. He'd give Tonir justice.

Righteous justice.

And if that meant Tonir had to die, then so be it. After all, it wasn't his decision to make. Hai would deliver him to the village where Tonir had done his bloodiest work and see what the people of Bangladesh wanted to do with the man. There, the judges and jury would be the mothers of the girls he raped. The brothers and uncles of the boys he tortured. The parents of the teens he ratted out.

They're the ones who had earned the right to decide Tonir's sentence, not me, Hai thought. Tonir would face hard justice, not blind vengeance.

Hai turned his back on Tonir and went to Malik. Tonir watched his last chance to live walk away.

Three hours later and ten miles away, Tonir faced charges of treason in an impromptu court that Malik arranged. Any member of the public could attend.

There weren't any lawyers. Instead, they planned to list Tonir's crimes to the people, and let them decide on his punishment together. On just a few hours' notice, a thousand people showed up in the town square for the evening trial. Malik's men tied Tonir's arms behind the central flagpole with twine, and wrapped more around his feet.

Malik read out Tonir's crimes to the crowd. These were the stories he'd collected from victims and their relatives. It was a nauseating, repetitive list of betrayal, rape, and accessory to murder. There were dozens upon dozens of charges. Malik read the names of the dead. He proclaimed that these people would be remembered forever. These were martyrs for Bangladesh.

Tonir looked out at the crowd and knew there was no hope. Whether or not his crimes matched the list in Malik's hand, the survivors of the Liberation War were the survivors of genocide. Complaining that he hadn't been given due process wasn't going to save him. The best he could hope for was a quick death.

Malik asked Tonir if he had any defense for his crimes.

Tonir blubbered half-heartedly for mercy, one last time. The crowd jeered.

"People of Bhola!" Malik yelled, quieting them like a ringmaster at a circus. "People of Bhola. Now you will decide the fate of the *razakar* Tonir. Will he live, or will he die for his crimes against the people? Who here says he should be punished with DEATH?"

"Death! Death! DEATH!" The jury of survivors chanted in unison. If anyone wanted mercy, they asked for it silently. Malik didn't bother to ask for a second opinion. This was the people's justice.

Tonir launched into a new round of wailing when he heard the chant. Hai watched him writhe on the pole and felt no remorse.

Malik cut Tonir down, and dragged him out back through a ditch. Hai and a few others held back members of the crowd who wanted to see Tonir tortured. They had a right to it. They wanted him to suffer. They needed to see it.

But Hai told the crowd no. They had to be better than the army or the *razakars* if their new country was going to make it. They had to be honorable, even against their worst enemies. There would be no torture. It would be quick—quicker than the murders Tonir committed. Hai held the line while Malik and Tonir disappeared with three other Mukti Bahini fighters down to the riverbank about a hundred feet away.

A minute later, they reached the end of the path. In the darkness, two men held Tonir down on the ground by the arms while a third shined a flashlight on his torso. Two quick rounds from a semiautomatic rifle ripped into Tonir's chest, and one more bullet tore through his skull for good measure. They kicked his corpse down the gentle slope. It splashed into the same water that claimed so many lives during the cyclone. The same great life-giving river where Hai caught his helicopter catfish downstream a lifetime ago.

Hai heard the shots from the town square. An avalanche of cheers erupted from the crowd. Hai took a deep breath, and exhaled. He heard Bangladesh's future in the sound of the gunfire and the exaltation of the crowd.

58

Candy Rohde and Jon Rohde

CALCUTTA, INDIA

DECEMBER 19, 1971

Jon pinched the large, pressurized syringe in one hand and carefully cradled a little girl's forearm in the other. She squirmed, afraid of the foreign doctor. Jon whispered some encouraging words in Bengali, and plunged the needle in. She cried out. Crying was good. Jon had learned to love the sound of a child's healthy cry. Then he gave her a few quick drops of vitamin A and sent her and her mother on their way.

"That's the last of it." Jon flipped the empty box of vitamin A drops into a bin. The refugees were returning home and this, along with more than fifty thousand cholera vaccine doses, would help keep their fragile immune systems intact for the journey back across the border and maybe even for brighter years to come. Jon's oral rehydration salt treatments had already saved tens of thousands of lives. Even better, relief groups showed interest in using them worldwide whenever and wherever there were people in need. For the first time since before Operation Searchlight, Candy saw light in Jon's eyes.

"Let's pack up. The truck's leaving in a half hour," he said to her.

Candy and Jon were helping to close down the Salt Lake refugee camp. She smiled warmly in his direction. Their work didn't feel quite finished, but their time was over nonetheless. Boston City Hospital was calling. So was the Newton school district. It was time to go back to America.

There was another reason Jon was walking on air. A week ago they had discovered that Candy was pregnant. They packed up the last of their school and hospital paraphernalia and said goodbye to Salt Lake. They gathered the bureaucratic documents, certificates, manifests, academic papers, and letters of thanks that were strewn about their respective desks. They each had only a small suitcase but allowed themselves space for the souvenirs. Then they threw their little bags into the back of the 4x4 and hopped in.

The couple navigated the short distance to Calcutta's airport through a sea of barefoot men, women, and children. This time most of the children could walk by themselves.

The thousands and thousands of survivors, unbroken in spirit, were starting their own long journeys. They walked back together on the same muddy paths they had trod upon months ago. They were walking home.

59

Yahya Khan and Zulfikar Ali Bhutto

Three days after Dacca fell, Yahya stumbled through a general's living room at a child's sixth birthday party. Smoking a big, thick Cuban cigar, he slalomed his body around the upholstered chairs and teak coffee tables. Eyes followed the cigar's glowing ring as people prepared to get out of the way of an erratic swing of his arm. Technically, it wouldn't be correct to say that he was hungover after his weeklong bender as he hadn't yet stopped drinking.

Yahya was jovial, floating in that intoxicated sweet spot where the world's problems had melted away and all that's left was a burning desire for camaraderie and entertainment. He was also feeling good because he made up with Ali that morning. They agreed never to let women come between them again. To prove his love, he bequeathed Ali his precious CHINESE CONNECTION folder, as a symbol of the greatness that the Khan men could achieve.

But now, Yahya wanted to put on a show. He took a big drag off the cigar so that the embers glowed cherry red. He broke into a smile and touched the lit end to a nearby balloon. POP.

"Thus finishes Bhutto!" Yahya laughed as if his joke was the best one he'd heard in weeks. He wasn't paying attention to the other guests to see if they reacted. He squinted, scanning for another balloon. POP.

"This is the end of Mujib!" His own uproarious laugh filled the room.

One by one, Yahya vanquished his balloon enemies. When the last demons were gone, he looked around for the day's lover, a formerly A-list but now C-list singer. He grabbed her and whisked her into his subordinate's bedroom while the man of the house watched, dumbstruck.

The birthday girl's father promised that he'd find her more balloons as soon as Yahya left the party. Nobody was quite sure what would happen next with the future of Pakistan, but the subordinate didn't dare enrage Yahya in case he weathered this crisis. The father turned up the music, to calm the kids and drown out sounds carrying over from his bedroom.

Outside, the mood was less carefree. Egged on by Bhutto's underlings, large crowds gathered in Islamabad chanting "Death to Yahya Khan!" Another mob burned a Yahya effigy and torched a house they thought he owned. Wives of fallen soldiers stormed the gates of President House, throwing their marriage bangles over the wall to signify their disgust at how callous Yahya had been with their husbands' lives.

After two decades of walking through political minefields and setting more than a few mines himself along the way, Bhutto was ready to make his final move. Later that day, he returned from New York and went directly to President House to relieve Yahya of duty and take over what was left of Pakistan. Too drunk to speak in full sentences, Yahya didn't quite comprehend what was happening.

Bhutto put Yahya under house arrest in a remote desert cottage and forbade him to leave or communicate with anyone but his wife, son, and Bhutto's handpicked military handlers. Keeping Yahya there, instead of sending him to a real prison, avoided the messy trials and publicity that Yahya could use to tell his side of things. And just like that, Yahya, the founder and father of Pakistan's gleaming white capital, was unceremoniously banished from the city he built.

That night, Bhutto drank a bottle of champagne alone at President

House and then delivered his first presidential address. He promised the people hope after darkness. "My dear countrymen, my dear friends, my dear students, laborers, peasants, those who fought for Pakistan. We are facing the worst crisis in our country's life, a deadly crisis." Bhutto always could hold his liquor better than Yahya. There was no trace of slurring in his eloquent elocution. "We have to pick up the pieces, very small pieces, but [from them] we will make a new Pakistan. A prosperous and progressive Pakistan. A Pakistan free of exploitation." The speech was wildly popular. As they had done for Yahya two short years before, journalists sang Bhutto's praises at the Rawalpindi Club and in the broadsheets the next morning.

Bhutto's first communique went to Nixon. The morning after the speech, he wrote like a war correspondent living through a battle that existed only in a parallel universe:

YOUR EXCELLENCY, THE NEWS FROM DACCA IS GRIM. REPORTS SPEAK OF INHUMAN ATROCITIES AND MASS MURDERS OF INNOCENT PEOPLE IN A PART OF PAKISTAN UNDER INDIA'S MILITARY OCCUPATION. I AM ADDRESSING THIS EARNEST APPEAL TO YOU ON BEHALF OF THE PEOPLE OF PAKISTAN AND ON MY OWN BEHALF TO PREVENT FURTHER CARNAGE. OTHERWISE, THAT PROVINCE MIGHT SOON BE ENGULFED IN A WIDESPREAD BLOOD-BATH.

Bhutto's message landed in Nixon's lap while the White House spin machine was in full swing. Nixon and Kissinger chatted about it in the Oval Office as they patted each other's back for averting World War III. They decided that their own reckless nuclear brinksmanship forced the Indians to reconsider fictitious plans to invade West Pakistan and made the Soviets pull back nonexistent plans to start a global war. It was equal parts face-saving and self-delusion.

Nixon and Kissinger toasted each other as heroes and for their own coldhearted yet brilliant strategic calculations. Bhutto, their new ally, was in place, and Indira Gandhi was too preoccupied with helping ten million refugees return to their new country to invade what was left of Pakistan. The president and his secretary of state were sure they had pulled a rabbit out of a hat.

"Congratulations Mr. President. You saved West Pakistan." Nixon couldn't wait to tell the world. Kissinger always did have a knack for stroking fragile men's egos.

Meanwhile Bhutto was wrapping up loose ends. First, he ordered Pakistan TV to run exposes on Yahya's harem and other unflattering details of his life. The public's disgust was so great that it started a groundswell of support for a more Islamic country, one that would shun corrupting Western influences like alcohol, music, and modernity. The idea spread like a virus, not just in Pakistan but also in neighboring, equally corrupt Iran and Afghanistan. Bhutto encouraged pro-Islamic protests when he realized they made a handy scapegoat whenever his own half-baked policies went awry.

Entering the presidency as a civilian surrounded by generals, Bhutto knew he had to shore up support with what was left of the military and show that he was the iron man the country needed. To do that, he made himself foreign minister and defense minister in addition to president.

Next, Bhutto arrested General Rani at her InterContinental suite and charged her with smuggling contraband items like dinner sets, tape recorders, records, foreign liquor, and contraceptives, to keep her from telling the country the real story. But when the police took her in they accidentally arrested her clients: Bhutto's interim press secretary and naval adviser, who both happened to be in her suite when the cops rushed in. Bhutto quietly freed the men the next day. He let Rani stew in solitary for another few months.

Then Bhutto tracked down Tikka. As it happened, the best thing that Yahya ever did for Tikka's career was ship him to Karachi before the end of the war, where he was free of the shame and stink of a military defeat. The Butcher of Balochistan gained a new nickname: the Butcher of Bengal. Bhutto remembered his Operation Searchlight promise, promoting Tikka to four-star general and giving him a new secret task.

Bhutto told Tikka that it was the most important mission in the country's history, and the new president promised the world that Pakistanis would invest so heavily in the program that the citizens might have to eat grass to fund it. Bhutto named Tikka the first head of Pakistan's new nuclear weapons program. Having nukes, Bhutto believed, would ensure that India would never dare embarrass Pakistan on the battlefield again. Bhutto would be the father of the Islamic atomic bomb. This would cement his legacy as Pakistan's greatest leader and maybe even get his face on the hundred-rupee note.

There was just one more loose end that Bhutto needed to tie up. It was a job he yearned to take care of personally, one he'd fantasized about for months. He had to make sure it was done right. After a year of disasters, there couldn't be any more screwups.

Bhutto picked up the phone and called the secret jail that held the prime minister of Bangladesh.

60

Sheikh Mujibur Rahman and Zulfikar Ali Bhutto

DECEMBER 25, 1971
UNDISCLOSED LOCATION, PAKISTAN, AND LONDON, ENGLAND

Mujib sat on the stone floor of his dirty, dark jail cell and thumbed through his Qur'an. The only shaft of light came from a single window, perched three feet above eye level. Mujib read the scriptures just like he had every day for the past nine months. His only other worldly possession was a pouch of damp tobacco.

The only person Mujib had spoken with during his incarceration was the tight-lipped guard outside his cell door. He wasn't the talkative type. Since the Pakistan Army pulled him from his house, Mujib hadn't heard a radio broadcast, seen a newspaper, or even read a letter from his family. Mujib didn't know about the resistance, the Liberation War, or the extent of the genocide. He only knew what happened in his cell.

Mujib heard several sets of footsteps coming down the hall. He recognized the sound army boots made by now. One week earlier he'd heard similar-sounding boots and then the sound of metal shovels in dirt. When he asked what was happening, the guard said they were digging a trench to hide in, in case the jail got attacked from the air.

But Mujib knew better. They were digging his grave.

He steeled himself for the end. The footsteps stopped in front of his door.

I am ready for execution, Mujib thought. *Nobody can kill a man who is ready to die.*

An iron key slid into the lock, opening the door, revealing a shadowy figure in the threshold. Mujib recognized the devilish smile.

"Bhutto! I'm so glad to see you! Have they imprisoned you too?"

Bhutto laughed. "No, Mujib, I am the president of Pakistan."

Mujib laughed along, then fell silent when he realized that Bhutto was serious. The guards at his side weren't Bhutto's jailers; they were his henchmen. Mujib recoiled, backing toward his bed. He grasped at his Qur'an. Trembling, he placed his hand on the book's cover and swore: "I am a good Muslim, Bhutto."

Bhutto laughed again. "No Mujib, I'm here to save your life! Yahya tried to have you killed many times, but I overthrew his dictatorship. Together, we can bring democracy back to a united Pakistan."

Mujib couldn't believe it. Bhutto offered his hand in peace. Mujib took it, warily. They walked out of the jail together. Bhutto welcomed Mujib to his car like an old friend. Mujib staggered toward it; he hadn't stepped outside his cell in nine full months.

Bhutto drove them to his secluded countryside bungalow. He started a roaring fire and held Mujib's attention with a roaring yarn. Over the next week, Mujib and Bhutto spoke for hours in front of the fire. Bhutto told him of Yahya's evils, and how Bhutto had put himself in the way of Mujib's execution time and time again.

"Mujib, you owe your life to me," Bhutto said every day as he wined and dined Mujib. It took a week, but eventually Mujib started to believe him.

Still, Mujib wanted some sort of independent confirmation before he would talk politics earnestly. Bhutto was ready with a customized misinformation campaign. He ordered the main West Pakistan papers to cover their front pages with stories of Bhutto's heroism and commitment to autonomy for East Pakistan. He gave Mujib the papers, the first he'd read in nearly a year. The papers didn't mention the genocide or the war.

"You see, Mujib, Pakistan and Bangladesh are simply quarreling brothers. Now let us unite again, for the quarrel is finished." In the interest of compromise and brotherhood, Bhutto agreed to Mujib's six points, and said that he would support Mujib's role as co–prime minister. Mujib had no way of knowing if his once friend was telling the truth, he was just grateful to be alive. Still shell-shocked from imprisonment, Mujib took the deal, getting everything he had asked for on March 24, 1971. Pakistan would stay united under Bhutto.

Bhutto was delighted. He threw Mujib a regal state dinner to celebrate. But there was just one more show he needed to put on. Bhutto knew that no handshake deal could survive Mujib learning the actual truth about Bangladesh. So he planned a spectacle to convince Mujib that East and West Pakistanis were indeed brothers and that they loved Mujib and Bhutto equally. The West Pakistanis were going to save Mujib's life.

After two weeks in the bungalow, Bhutto admitted somberly to Mujib that he was on trial for treason. The penalty, of course, was death. But this wasn't a regular trial, Bhutto explained. He'd convinced Pakistan's chief justice to stand aside and instead let everyday people decide Mujib's fate at a public gathering. Bhutto assured Mujib that a real criminal trial in a Pakistani court would undoubtedly lead to execution. The evidence was simply overwhelming. But Bhutto believed in the people. He was rooting for Mujib to win.

Bhutto drove Mujib to a nondescript village for the show trial, accompanied as always by his Sikh bodyguards. The day before, Bhutto had planted a thousand of his diehard supporters in the village and told them just how to act.

The trial started mere minutes after they arrived. A magistrate read out Mujib's crimes: Sedition. Treason. Threatening the unity of Pakistan. Mujib thought carefully on how to respond, how to win over the hearts of West Pakistanis. The magistrate announced that the dozen counts of treason each carried a death sentence. But then men in the crowd started yelling.

"Save him!"

"Mujib, a true Pakistani!"

"Mercy! Freedom!"

The cheers swelled into a crescendo of support for the Bengali leader. The cheers drowned out the magistrate's words and Mujib didn't even need to speak.

The magistrate dismissed all charges. The crowd roared with joy. Mujib wasn't sure what he had witnessed. It was all too surreal for words.

Less than half an hour after it started, the trial was over and Bhutto escorted Mujib back into the car. They drove to the airport where he would board a plane to London.

"The Pakistani people have saved your life, Mujib. You must remember to keep them in your hearts, and thank Allah that you have a friend as great as I to look out for you. The people in London will tell you all sorts of lies, but remember this: The threads that bind East and West Pakistan together are strong as steel."

Mujib nodded. He and Bhutto rode the rest of the way to the airport in silence. Bhutto wished Mujib well as he got on the plane. He smiled his devilish smile all the way back to the car.

Eight hours later an unmarked Pakistan International Airways plane rolled to a stop at the VIP terminal of London's Heathrow airport. A single passenger climbed down the plane's steps. Mujib blinked in bewilderment as British officials and a few Awami League advisers-turned-refugees greeted him on the tarmac and whisked him to a luxury West End hotel suite. Overwhelmed by the opulence, he wandered from room to room, sniffing the flowers and flopping down on the couch each time he passed by one.

Mujib stared out through the big glass windows like a child, transfixed at the London traffic. He didn't even know if his wife and kids were alive.

At the press conference in the hotel ballroom later that day, Mujib tried to shake off the cobwebs of solitary confinement. His last memory of East Pakistan was his abduction during Operation Searchlight, and he'd been in a total news blackout since then. He knew nothing about the refugees, the millions dead, the Mukti Bahini, or how close the world came to nuclear war. Bhutto's lies swam around in his head, mucking up his understanding even further. Advisers tried to brief him in the car to the hotel, but they didn't have time to fully inform their dazed leader. Now, dozens of reporters peppered him with questions on how it felt to be the new leader of an independent Bangladesh.

Mujib smoked his long black pipe at the press conference, savoring the first taste of quality tobacco in what felt like forever. He said Bangladesh had an exceptionally bright future. It would be the "Switzerland of Asia," a paradise of wealth and political neutrality. He took long draws on his pipe between questions, both for the pleasure of it and to allow some time to collect his thoughts. His famous thick black hair now gray, Mujib said the British had a duty as former colonialists to help Bangladesh grow, and Bhutto was going to be an essential partner in that effort. He wished Bhutto good luck, proclaiming him the "Mujib of Pakistan."

This didn't quite sit right with the people asking the questions. Something was off. A friendly journalist dragged Mujib off the stage before he could dig his hole any deeper.

Mujib's mind had been frozen in time on March 25, 1971, and he simply didn't have the capacity to process all of the war's details let alone respond. Bengalis fought and won an entire war for their freedom while he languished in a dirty jail cell. Even though every Bengali held him up as the true hero of the conflict and their rightful leader, Mujib hadn't experienced the war in the same terms as tens of millions of his countrymen.

He boarded the next plane to Dacca, ringed with advisers who desperately tried to get him up to speed before he made any bizarre statements to his own people.

61

Hafiz Uddin Ahmad

DACCA, BANGLADESH

JANUARY 9, 1972

Hafiz scanned each face that squeezed against the chain-link fence, one by one. Managing a boisterous crowd of thousands was nearly impossible, but his battle-hardened demeanor convinced the people in front of him to stay put, at least for now. Eight months before, thousands of Bengalis pushed up against that same rusty barrier, desperate to board any aircraft they could. Today they craved a chance to welcome a man home.

Guarding a runway might have sounded pedestrian, but today it was the military's most sought-after position. Thousands of Mukti Bahini fighters wanted a chance to be part of the victory celebration, but only a select few earned the honor of protecting Mujib's life. Just three weeks after Yahya and Niazi's surrender, *razakars* still skulked in the shadows, and most military planners thought an assassination attempt was likely when Mujib landed. Hafiz managed to score the gig only because of his war record.

He studied the faces for miscreants. But all he saw were smiles. Only joy.

Hafiz couldn't help from beaming himself. He knew they'd won their freedom because the entire population came together in a united struggle. This wasn't just a victory for people like him who fired bullets but for every farmer, banker, artist, intellectual, rickshaw puller, fisher, teacher, and weaver who shared in the suffering and the struggle. Now this new nation of Bangladesh had a chance to fulfill a generation of dreams.

It was glorious.

"He's here! He's here!" Eagle-eyed spectators announced the dark speck in the air coming from the west before anyone actually heard the engine's roar. Thousands rushed the chain-link fence like it was a Beatles concert, eventually bending it into submission. They sprinted out onto the runway. Mujib's right-hand man looked out the plane window and thought that it looked like an ocean of human heads.

As Mujib's plane landed, Hafiz and other officers formed a human chain to ring the runway. They pushed back well-wishers and foreign press in what felt like equal numbers. Some circumvented the order by climbing to the top of an airstair trolley. The blue-and-silver British Air Force plane finally got a clear path and landed on the bomb-scarred runway without incident. Then the real rush started.

With tears in his eyes, Mujib made it only a few feet down the red carpet to the terminal before thousands of cheering supporters blocked his progress. Outnumbered a thousand to one by the crush of well-wishers, Hafiz and the rest of the military force gave up on crowd control. Instead, fifty thousand students made a human wall to protect Mujib themselves.

Mujib climbed atop a jeep to get through the crowd and the driver navigated the throng. Nearly a million citizens of Bangladesh took to the streets to guide him home, shouting *"Joi Bangla"* all the way. Covering the event, NBC said that the return of the "George Washington of Bangladesh" led to "an emotional outburst in that emotional part of the world."

Hafiz spied the shockingly gray locks of their previously black-haired leader as his head bobbed among the crowd, keeping his senses sharp as he got into his car to deliver the most important speech of his career—a speech that needed somehow to unite the country for an impossible new mission. In the coming year this man would have to forge a prosperous and egalitarian nation after nearly every last office, rail line, road, bridge, school, and tractor had been destroyed.

Hafiz followed the throng for at least a mile, trying to pick his way toward the race course. As he got nearer to the site of the speech, the crowd got so thick that it came to a dead stop. His formal duties done, Hafiz stood in the gridlock for almost half an hour, hoping to be able to see the speech in person. It was impossible. Eventually he gave up and returned to the officers' mess at Dacca Cantonment to catch it on the radio with his men.

He arrived just in time. Inside, officers and sepoys who had fought together in the war gathered in a room full of the military regalia of a unit that could trace their lineages back to when the British first colonized India. It was a room built for celebration. Badges on the walls celebrated victories against sultanates, commendations for heroism in colonial conflicts, photos of heroes in both world wars, battles fought against India on behalf of Pakistan, and, now, hastily placed plaques of gallantry during the Liberation War. The military tradition started a proud new chapter.

The soldiers toasted to victory, over and over. The celebrations quieted down only when Mujib's voice broke through on the radio. The men listened with rapt attention. Mujib said he looked toward a bright political future of Bangladesh, but there were huge challenges ahead. He called for unity and for forgiveness for those who might have picked the other side during the fight but wanted to support Bangladesh now. The men nodded in the spirit of the moment.

After the first ten minutes or so, one junior officer noticed something a bit odd. He remarked softly, "Why hasn't he mentioned the fighters?" Indeed, Mujib hadn't acknowledged either the Mukti Bahini or the deprivations that all Bengalis faced together. Instead, he focused on the bright future. The junior officer grew upset. He wanted recognition.

Hafiz and most of the other officers brushed it off. They figured it was just an oversight. Surely Mujib understood the sacrifices they'd made by now, even though he'd been a prisoner of war for almost the whole year. Besides, the challenges facing the new Bangladesh were justifiably on his mind. It was one thing to win a war and quite another to build a country from scratch with few resources—and even fewer international allies.

For the first time in nearly a year, bicycle rickshaws roamed the alleyways and boulevards, ringing their bells as they looked for passengers. For the first time since Operation Searchlight, women dared to go out in public. What remained of the old government staff left the InterContinental under escort and was sent back to Karachi.

A few days later, Mujib tried to make up for the oversight. Now fully briefed on the enormity of the year's events, he gave a conciliatory press conference at Dacca's InterContinental Hotel, saying, "I come back with no hatred in my heart for anyone. I only wish for justice over injustice." It was time to move on, Mujib said, and he promised to be the strong leader the country needed. Smiling, he breezed through reporters at the InterContinental's parking lot, carrying two pomegranates in his left hand. Feeling fit for celebration, he bought himself the country's first Cadillac. He also appointed himself prime minister, minister of defense, home minister, and minister of information.

Hafiz, like most of the soldiers coming home after months of war, didn't pay the self-appointments much mind. What mattered now was that for the first time in generations, maybe centuries, a Bengali ruled in Bangladesh. Besides, maybe he needed to consolidate power to be effective. There was so much to be done, so much to build, that maybe this was the strong display of decisiveness that the country needed. Surely democracy would thrive once Mujib put the country back together. Hafiz saw no point in spending energy bickering about every tiny detail. The less that politics got in the way, the better.

62

Mohammad Hai and Malik Mahmud

DACCA, BANGLADESH

JANUARY 22, 1972

Liberation Day

Hai sat cross-legged on the floor of the wooden boat, watching Manpura's shoreline slowly shrink to nothing. Five hundred guns were stacked neatly next to him. The pile of weaponry included light machine guns, heavy machine guns, rifles, and pistols, but no ammunition. What wasn't used up during the war got spent firing at the sky in celebration.

Hai had collected the guns from friends and comrades all over the islands and was sailing them up the Meghna River to Dacca for a historic ceremony that would signify the end of one era and the beginning of another. The official surrendering of arms was the cathartic end to a wartime mentality. It was time to build a future Bangladesh, not dwell on the violence of the past. Hai hoped to see Mujib again. Maybe he would have a chance to tell the new president how they made it through the darkest times of the war.

Malik was annoyed, shooing away curious passengers who wanted to touch the stockpile. This was only the first small step in rebuilding a society that had suffered near-universal physical and psychological destruction.

There was no welcoming party to greet them, no parades lined up for the brave fighters when the boat docked at Dacca jetty. Just a few fishmongers and vegetable sellers milled about and unloaded their cargo from the countryside. So Hai and Malik found some crates for the guns and loaded them onto a couple of rickshaw carts.

The handover ceremony would happen tomorrow at Dacca Stadium—the same place where Hafiz played in front of thousands of cheering fans. Hai heard that Mujib himself was going to be there. He was over the moon. As part of the exchange program, Mukti Bahini fighters from outside Dacca all found rooms in the Dacca University dorms.

Hai and Malik stayed in Iqbal Hall, the site of one of Operation Searchlight's worst massacres. The hall had been vacant since that day and Hai saw bullet holes in the walls everywhere. Despite the reminder of the violence, he felt a funny feeling: hope. It overwhelmed him. He would help their new country build itself up to greatness.

Hai and Malik partied that night with Mukti Bahini fighters from all over the country. Their cries of "*Joi Bangla*" echoed off the half-destroyed walls. The joy of independence outweighed their pain and loss. Hai lay awake in bed, imagining what he might say to Mujib when they met.

Hai had finally made it to Dacca University, his lifelong dream, although the circumstances were almost impossibly different from those he had imagined before the cyclone. His mother would have been thrilled to see her son walking through the campus. He said a prayer for her, promising her, and himself, that he would apply to the political science program in her honor. He prayed for his father too, who still lay in a near comatose state on Manpura.

Students were beginning to trickle back to campus. In a few weeks Senator Edward Kennedy would come to Dacca University and plant a new banyan sapling in the spot where past generations of students summoned political sermons and the spirit of revolution. That same week, George Harrison's album *Concert for Bangla Desh* came out in stores around the world.

The Mukti Bahini lined up at dawn in front of the dorm. They didn't have to stand at attention, but it felt right. Hai had the two carts full of guns beside him, and they started marching together toward the stadium. They pushed the weapons through the city streets.

It was a short walk to the stadium, and they arrived early. Hai handed out a gun to each of the other Mukti Bahini fighters who showed up to stand with him. There were about a hundred in their group now. Neither Malik nor Hai had seen Dacca Stadium in person before. It felt massive, gargantuan. More than thirty thousand people could watch a game there.

They'd pictured it in their heads, of course. It was the site of some of their greatest childhood radio memories. Hai and Malik thought back to famous plays by Hafiz when he scored for the Mohammedan Sporting Club against teams from Karachi. The two friends tried to one-up each other to see who could remember the all-time best football moment on these hallowed grounds. Hai walked through the tunnel onto the grounds, gun in hand. He even *felt* like a hero.

A thousand Mukti Bahini formed a ring inside the track. Mujib stood at a podium by the main grandstand and thanked the men one at a time. A huge pile of guns lay next to the podium, ten feet tall and thirty feet wide. Mujib was only about a foot off the ground, but the fighters were in awe at his towering presence. Hai wanted to ask Mujib if he remembered that emaciated boy from the Manpura jetty who was standing in front of him today.

The line crept along at a snail's pace, but Hai didn't notice. Two hours went by in a flash as he soaked in the atmosphere. Finally, it was his turn at the front. Mujib stood inches away. They both looked much older than when this all started.

Hai held the gun with two hands and kneeled down at Mujib's feet. His outstretched arms revealed the jagged scars he'd gotten holding on to the trunk of the palm tree in his family's yard. Mujib bent down and picked up the gun.

Hai opened his mouth to speak. Mujib looked him in the eyes and nodded.

Hai closed his mouth and nodded back. He realized that he didn't need to say anything at all. Mujib knew exactly what men like him had sacrificed to make this new country.

Hai and Malik took their places in the crowd while the remaining fighters surrendered the last guns. When it was all over, Mujib addressed them.

"I could not give you arms, but I still asked you to resist the enemy. I am proud of you." The typically booming Mujib spoke quietly. His voice quivered while tears rolled down his cheeks. "Today you have made history by surrendering your arms. You have created an example for others to follow. I salute you."

Together, the ten thousand patriots sang the national anthem under a cloudless sunny sky for the first time.

63

Neil Frank

Neil Frank squinted into the skies, transfixed. It was eighty degrees on this late-January day. Fine white sand clumped to his trousers as he shifted his butt around, sprinkling occasional grains into his rolled-up shirtsleeves.

"Neil!" a voice called out. Frank was too absorbed for it to register.

He traced the cumulus and nimbus cloud patterns as they danced on the stage of an azure sky. Even after everything, Neil still loved studying the apparitions in action and trying to predict where they would move next. The puzzle pieces were right up there for anyone to see. For anyone to solve.

"Neil!" The skies demanded his full attention. It wasn't going to rain for days. He smiled as his bare forearms soaked up the rays.

After Frank returned from Dacca, he realized something horrifying: The Gulf coast and eastern seaboard were nearly as unprepared as Bangladesh if a Category 5 storm hit at high tide. And 1971 was an active year—that fall, five different hurricanes hit the United States in a six-week span. By 1974, Frank would become the National Hurricane Center's director, taking over from Gordon Dunn. Many vulnerable coastal communities and barrier islands had no idea what the Category system even meant or what a storm surge was, and they had no warning systems and no plan at all of what do if they were in the middle of a storm. Worse, hundreds of thousands of people moved to the coasts each year, totally unprepared for the danger.

This was his home turf. And he'd just witnessed the worst-case scenario. Frank knew he had to act. He barnstormed thousands of miles, from southern Texas around the Florida panhandle up to Virginia, racing to collect data and build warning systems in case the next swirling cloud mass between the Caribbean and Africa was the Big One. He adapted storm-surge models into NHC hurricane forecasts for the first time, and designed a system to simply and directly inform the public what was coming, how seriously they should take it, and what to do. Frank's work formed the foundation of United States hurricane action plans that have warned the American people for over fifty years.

Frank helped move the NHC from what seemed like an alchemy-based organization to a hard-science paradise. They used statistical modeling in hurricane tracking for the first time, and bought a secret weapon: a state-of-the-art mainframe with a brand-new terminal interface. The eight-thousand-pound machine took up an entire room, and the quantum leap in computational power meant that the NHC could forecast forty-eight or even seventy-two hours out instead of just twelve. Frank knew that those newfound hours could mean the difference between five dead or five thousand. He made the NHC a satellite field service station too, so they'd never again get images a week late from the growing number of satellites that followed the ITOS 1.

Frank couldn't bear to return to Bangladesh, but he never stopped trying to improve their cyclone preparedness. He helped the country get its first-ever radar weather station. After he filed his report, the World Bank launched a multimillion-dollar Bangladesh cyclone project to develop better warning systems, more sophisticated forecasting models, and, most important, to build twenty-foot-tall concrete cyclone shelters on every populated island. Storm surges like Bhola's would never be so deadly again.

But back on Miami Beach, Frank still couldn't tear himself away from the sky. The nut he just couldn't seem to crack was how to make sure that leaders cared enough about their own people to act when it mattered. He replayed the general's comment in his mind over and over, the one about Bhola solving half a million of their problems.

If we could just take the politics out of the equation, he thought, *we could solve this thing*.

"Neil!" His wife, Velma, gave his shoulder a gentle shake. "I've been calling you. Come dip your feet!" Their little girl toddled through the waves, squealing in delight.

The giggles snapped Frank back to reality. He glanced at his Rolex. "Sorry, time to get back."

Lunch break was over. Frank put his black suit jacket on over his starched white shirt and hopped into his car. He'd parked on the beach, just a few feet from the water and a few more from the rows of dump trucks importing sand from other parts of Florida. In the mid-1960s, Miami Beach's climate suddenly changed, surprising nearly everyone in the city. Without human intervention, the namesake beaches that drew millions of tourists would vanish into the sea.

Frank dropped off his family before driving on to the NHC. It might be a late night, he warned Velma. He had a puzzle to solve.

64

Richard Nixon and Zhou Enlai

BEIJING, CHINA

FEBRUARY 23, 1972

With Kissinger dutifully at his side, Richard Nixon strolled into the President's Guesthouse in Beijing just after lunch. Dressed in a gray suit with a tightly knotted black-and-white-checkered tie, Nixon beamed. This was the moment he'd worked toward for years: a grand display of the success of secrecy. He walked up to Prime Minister Zhou and shook his hand vigorously. The men embraced while cameras whirred against a pale yellow back wall.

Later, while they sat on an embroidered couch draped with round white lace doilies, Nixon told Zhou how much his wife, Pat, loved the exotic acupuncture demonstrations the prime minister had arranged that morning. Nixon then teased Kissinger for being too lazy to climb the Great Wall. Dressed in his own simple gray Communist Party suit, Zhou laughed along.

Everything was coming up Nixon. He felt invincible. So much so that just a few weeks before, Nixon started a new top-secret scheme: to wiretap the Democratic National Committee headquarters at the Watergate building. If he could sneak a whole man into China, surely planting a little tape recorder in an office would be a snap.

Zhou and Nixon lost themselves in philosophical musings about the state of the world. They reflected together on the past two years, about all of the delicate clandestine steps that had to break just right to bring this meeting to pass.

Zhou felt a touch of melancholy. He was grateful to the man not in the room, a man who surely imagined himself grinning alongside them on this day. "Although he did not show much statesmanship in leading his country, both of us owe something to Yahya, for bridging the link between our two countries."

Nixon nodded solemnly. "He was a bridge." Cameras clicked incessantly, capturing for posterity one of the twentieth century's most improbable diplomatic breakthroughs.

"Yes. There's a Chinese saying that to tear down a bridge after having crossed it is not good."

Nixon agreed. "One doesn't burn down a bridge which has proved useful." Zhou gave a wry smile. Thanks to Nixon's eagerness, his and Mao's decade-long plan to make China a respected country and open its economy to the world had finally come to fruition.

"I have also taken note of certain incidents. We found that when your navy ships were moving toward the Indian Ocean, [the Soviets] also very quickly sent nuclear subs down from Vladivostok to the Indian Ocean."

"Your intelligence is very good."

Zhou went back to the missing man. "President Yahya was probably a good man, a man of good intentions, but he didn't know how to lead an army or how to fight. But there is some reason to say good words about him. We should not forget, and we cannot forget that when a man makes a contribution to the world, we should remember him."

Nixon nodded again. Then he paused, deep in thought. "Maybe we have some disagreements, but, as we both have emphasized, this world can be a better and more peaceful place."

The two new friends toasted to each other's courage, and to their countries' new friendship. They left the residence in their respective motorcades, to unite again twenty minutes later to watch a Ping-Pong exhibition.

Later that week, Nixon called Bhutto to emphasize that he shouldn't hang Yahya for treason, and to make sure that his exile accommodations were comfortable.

After all, it was the least he could do for an old friend.

AFTERWORD

The Gathering Storm

More than half a century later, Bangladesh continues to struggle to escape the shadow of its horrific birth. In 1971, Mujib landed at the helm of an almost stillborn nation. Half a million people died in the Great Bhola Cyclone, making it the deadliest storm in human history. A further three million perished in the genocide that targeted not only Bengalis but also indigenous groups, Hindus, Christians, the disabled, and other religious and cultural minorities. Moreover, targeted assassinations of the educated elite, career bureaucrats, lawyers, police, and artists meant that Mujib couldn't draw from the well of Bengali talent he needed to begin his nation-building project. Within a year a famine swept the countryside, taking millions more lives. Still holding a grudge for its embarrassing defeat, the United States exacerbated the famine by withholding food aid. And within a few years even Bangladesh's relationship with India soured.

In his efforts to put the country on track, Mujib concentrated his own power in an authoritarian turn that quickly backfired. The Awami League fractured into left- and right-leaning branches. In 1972, a group of Liberation War veterans assassinated Mujib in his home in an attempt to establish their own military government. Some speculated that the assassination was actually a secret CIA operation. Whatever the case, this led the two camps to a series of reprisals and further assassinations. After an interim government, Ziaur Rahman, Hafiz's commander in the Liberation War, led yet another coup and took over the presidency. He remained in office until he was assassinated in 1981 in Bangladesh's third coup in eight years.

Since then Bangladesh's leaders have alternated between three groups: two multigenerational political dynasties and the military. They all have an unfortunate habit of corruptly siphoning off enough cash until they are overthrown by one of the other groups and the cycle repeats. Military tribunals of genocidal perpetrators (including Bengalis who massacred Hindus and Punjabis in retaliatory attacks) are still pending five decades later. They are also subject to incessant political tampering, since many *razakars* maintained their local political power even after independence.

Regional tensions remain fraught, as ever-larger cyclones batter Bangladesh's coast. Worried that the next Great Bhola Cyclone will bring a wave of Muslim climate refugees to its borders, India built a 2,545-mile wall around Bangladesh, giving border guards shoot-to-kill orders for anyone who tries to cross. In New Delhi, Indian politicians promise that the wall will stop any and all "climate refugees" from entering. As if to punctuate the point, in 2011 Indian soldiers killed a fifteen-year-old Bangladeshi girl who was trying to cross the border for her wedding. Pictures of her corpse twisted up in the barbed wire atop the wall became a symbol for the ongoing injustice. To date, no soldiers have been held accountable for the crime, or for hundreds of others like it. Meanwhile, climate scientists predict that one-third of Bangladesh will be underwater in two generations. Fifty million people will be displaced from their homes. A country that contributed almost nothing to the climate crisis will have to bear its most significant fallout, boxed in on all sides by neighbors who would rather see it drown.

Make no mistake: This is a book about climate change. Hundred-year storms like the Great Bhola Cyclone might feel like once-in-a-lifetime anomalies, but climate change is accelerating their frequency into once a decade or, in the worst projections, annual events. They crash into fragile political systems just as surely as they do coastlines.

They trigger chain reactions that build into ever greater catastrophes as one dangerous situation collides with another. Dozens of countries like Bangladesh are at high risk of armed conflict. Cyclones like the one that hit East Pakistan in 1970 can be the spark that sends a country over the edge. Of course, climate change probably didn't cause the Great Bhola Cyclone, rather it's a harbinger of what climate change will bring in the future. The problem isn't just that each specific storm is a roll of the dice for societal and perhaps political destruction depending on intensity; those odds haven't changed. The real problem is that due to climate change the dice are being rolled more often, in more places, and generating more powerful storms, each and every year. And the Great Bhola Cyclone was a threshold moment for the globe. Aside from the human toll, the killings, and the rise of new international aid paradigms, in its aftermath the conflict carried the potential for escalating all the way to a nuclear apocalypse.

Megastorms won't be the only thing that drives climate conflict. Droughts, floods, desertification, and other shocks to fragile environments can all trigger political and economic upheavals. For example, in 2018 Central American farmers were pushed off land that was no longer arable, and were unable to settle in violent local cities. They joined what then-president Donald Trump called the "migrant caravan": four thousand displaced people seeking an opportunity simply to live productive lives again. Experts estimate that two million climate refugees from Central America alone will attempt to enter the United States by 2040. That's two new climate caravans every month for the next two decades.

The stakes are higher—and more immediate—than even most climate-change advocates realize. Our global climate future means not just flooded beach houses in twenty years and more expensive groceries next decade, but an increasing likelihood of selective genocide and even global international war. Analysis from peace research scholars shows that disasters are increasingly used to leverage political aims, using the same blueprint that Yahya Khan did after the Great Bhola Cyclone.

The path is nauseatingly familiar: A disaster strikes a country that is already under strains of political tension. Leaders of that country, whether out of malice or indifference (or both), give a half-hearted disaster response. It inflames tensions between different parties or ethnic groups, or along other dividing lines. The ruling party blames the aggrieved for the tensions in order to justify further suppression. Then, war erupts. Sophisticated quantitative modeling gives strong evidence for how local politicians used the 2017 drought in Sudan, the 2004 Sri Lanka tsunami, and the 2016–2020 drought-flood cycles in Afghanistan and Somalia, among others, to increase the intensity of wars or even justify them in the first place.

But the future is not predetermined. In issues of war and climate, holding politicians to account at critical junctures can mean the difference between heartwarming tales of humanity coming together or a genocide. It's tremendously challenging to penetrate the noise of information overflow on topics as wide-ranging and combative as the relationship between natural disasters and social conflict.

The book you have just read examines this complex terrain through the experiences and perspectives of the people who lived through the Great Bhola Cyclone and its aftermath. Their stories shed light on how global, regional, and climate events play out in human lives in seven ways.

First, the process from disaster to conflict can be long, but the time frames of those who track storms and their fallout is short. **Neil Frank**, like most storm and disaster experts before and since, had no professional avenue to track the political impact of a storm. His job mandated that he move on to the next storm as quickly as possible. In East Pakistan, Frank discovered how Yahya and his advisers planned to use the storm as an excuse for violence, and he knew that the general's words were every bit as ominous as ITOS 1's images. But he was just a hurricane tracker. He had no structure in place to help others put together these pieces, and no whistleblower network to help him take concerns up the chain of command. Even fifty years on, we're just starting to build these structures.

Second, in the messy world of postdisaster aid and reconstruction, well-meaning agencies often willfully ignore bad deeds by governments in order to maintain their access. Sometimes they even provide cover for horrific misdeeds by believing that their aid work is "too important" to risk. **Candy Rohde** saw this firsthand, watching essential shipments from the Red Cross and the United States Agency for International Development pile up on airport runways in Dacca while the agencies refrained from even the mildest criticism of Yahya. The agencies were caught in a kind of prisoner's dilemma, knowing that if they publicly shamed Yahya, he'd ban them. They reasoned that it would be better to express concern behind closed doors through "official channels" than in the press. It's a gut-wrenching choice that agencies continue to be faced with in conflict zones today. But in East Pakistan, the choice to keep their heads down allowed the Pakistan Army to repurpose USAID and UNICEF trucks as military jeeps. It allowed the military to steal aid shipments and trade them for sex or money, and allowed Yahya to shut down all aid in the country anyway, including HELP. Had the international aid community taken a more aggressive stance, Yahya may have been forced to help the Bengalis even though he loathed them.

Third, malevolent political leaders can use disasters as excuses for suppression and violence, but the results can be counterproductive. Often, outsiders initially see the chaos and look the other way, like most of the world did after the Great Bhola Cyclone. Alternately, outside groups offer relief that ends up supporting a government's law-and-order crackdown like the United States did. **Yahya Khan** anticipated this response and used a climate disaster as an excuse for suppression and war. The same thing happened in 1985 in Ethiopia and in Syria in 2012. But these actions also trigger rebellion. **Mohammad Hai** had no initial intention of being a freedom fighter, but he picked up a gun and was willing to give his own life due to several factors: Mujib using the Bhola response to show how Bengalis were being discriminated against, his personal loss and subsequent experiences of societal destitution after the cyclone, and the horror of Operation Searchlight's fallout. Hai's story, in some way, is the story of the other ninety thousand people who took up arms across East Pakistan in early 1971.

Fourth, institutionalized discrimination against minority groups is the single biggest predictor for future conflict. The experiences of **Hafiz Uddin Ahmad** showed how persecution of ethnic minorities can trigger even apolitical people to take violent action. As a football star and army officer, Hafiz was in an upper echelon of Bengalis who were the most insulated from discrimination, and yet even he felt the stings and barbs. Many know the baggage inherent in statements from well-meaning people who say things like "But not you, you're one of the good ones." Those experiences, combined with the needless brutality of Operation Searchlight, made what would otherwise have been an unfathomable decision—to mutiny—inevitable. The fact that every single Bengali army regiment mutinied in late March of their own devices shows the power of pervasive discrimination on the human psyche.

Fifth, climate-conflict connections contain so many meteorological and political variables that causal chains are never clear enough to make causal predictions. The question of, for example, whether Bangladesh would be an independent country today if the Great Bhola Cyclone hadn't hit would certainly help us order the world and focus on fixing what harms us the most. But we cannot answer that definitively, even with the most sophisticated conflict data modeling. However, we do know that persecution of one group by another creates the conditions under which a large disaster can be the trigger for war. But even then, horrific disaster responses can fail to move the needle to action before the conflict starts. We hope that as we continue to build correlations of where it has happened elsewhere, we can better understand how future climate wars are most likely to play out.

Sixth, the Concert for Bangladesh gave birth to a new global player: the celebrity activist. The 1971 concert marked a high point of the world's interest in the plight of Bangladesh. Piggybacking off of

Beatlemania, the album of the concert sold a million copies and won a Grammy, raising nearly $10 million. It became the model for dozens of other aid concerts that followed. Ever since, celebrity activists have tried to use their brand to amplify worthy causes. To name just two, Bono and Bob Geldof called the concert an inspiration for Live Aid, the world's second major aid concert aimed at raising money for the 1985 Ethiopian famine victims.

But the aftermath of the Concert for Bangladesh had a darker side. Money that was supposed to go to UNICEF sat in a lawyer's bank account for twelve years awaiting an IRS audit into tax evasion and improper nonprofit registration. George Harrison's manager Allen Klein was indicted for tax evasion and "allegedly selling thousands of promotional copies of the Bangladesh album and pocketing the proceeds." In a pattern often repeated by well-meaning benefit concerts in the decades since, very little money actually made it from New York to Bangladesh, and none made it at all until 1983. Be it to help starving people or climate change, performative do-gooding is no substitute for the hard work of aid delivery. Back in 1971, a *Village Voice* columnist said of the audience at the Concert for Bangladesh: "How glorious—to be able to launder one's conscience by laying out a few tax-deductible dollars to hear the biggies." In the present day, social media aid campaigns after disasters are just the most recent iteration of the same phenomenon.

Seventh, and most important, these events can trigger a domino effect that leads to global conflict. Our examples should not breed a false sense of complacency that these are just problems of poor developing countries that were already on the brink of failure. **Richard Nixon** cared little about East Pakistan in February 1971, and it was about as low on the American geostrategic agenda as humanly possible. After all, that was a big reason why Candy and John Rohde elected to move there in the first place. Ten months later, Nixon was ready to start a nuclear war with the USSR to protect it. Today, if a megastorm hits Mozambique, the South China Sea, or Yemen, it's unlikely to be front-page news. But we ignore possible black-swan effects to our peril. The Great Bhola Cyclone didn't directly liberate Bangladesh; it only flicked the first domino over. It's the placement of the other dominoes—and the reasons why they are there—that determine if a storm leads to war. By understanding these chain reactions, we're better positioned to take a few dominoes out of the chain when we need to. Our survival as a human race may depend on it.

On the positive side, Bangladesh is better equipped to deal with cyclones than ever before. New satellites track storms, and warning systems and defensive concrete structures dot the delta, including on the islands of Manpura, Hatiya, and Bhola. Citizens are well-versed in warning messages, and know when to seek high ground in the event of another catastrophic cyclone. But as is typical of disaster management in the developing world, where preventative resources are scarce, humans tend to fortify previous disaster zones while ignoring nearby areas that are equally as vulnerable. To wit, cyclone Nargis formed in the Bay of Bengal in 2008, in the same patch of water that Bhola did. But instead of going north to Bangladesh it took a right turn toward neighboring Myanmar. More than a hundred thousand people were killed when it made landfall in a low-lying area that was unprepared for the surge. The devastation played a role in exacerbating the political upheaval that continues in Myanmar to this day.

One thing that we can be confident of is that increasingly powerful storms will hit increasingly fragile places. Bhola won't remain just a lesson from the distant past; it's a harbinger of our future. It's only a matter of time until a new storm knocks over a domino that requires more than humanitarian aid to resolve. Every new vortex represents nothing less than a low-probability gamble against the future of humanity.

WHERE THEY ARE NOW

Hafiz Uddin Ahmad continued his career as a footballer and military man in an independent Bangladesh. In 1975, after Mujib's assassination, Hafiz participated in a coup-d'état to establish the future political direction of the country. He was arrested, put in jail, escaped, and then took command of eight hundred soldiers he'd fought with during the Liberation War who were willing to rebel with him once again. Later, he became a high-ranking member of the Awami League's primary opposition party, the Bangladesh National Party (BNP). These two parties have traded power ever since. Hafiz continued to play with the Mohammedan Sporting Club until 1978. His father never attended a single game.

Mohammad Hai saw his country's political promise hijacked by authoritarians. He earned a bachelor's and then a master's degree in political science from Dacca University. Hai went into hiding for five years due to his refusal to renounce the Awami League after Mujib was assassinated. He retired in 2011 from his post as chief inspector at the Ministry of Shipping, dedicating his career to maritime safety throughout the delta. His freedom-fighting exploits are unknown even by his neighbors and former cubicle mates. Hai remains good friends with **Malik Mahmud** even though Malik supports the rival BNP political party, something they relentlessly tease each other about. Hai dotes on his three children and many grandchildren at every opportunity.

Candy Rohde continued her activism after she and Jon returned to the States from Calcutta in 1972. The stay was short: Candy spent the next two decades working around the world with various education agencies wherever a new crisis called. She brought her expertise and endless enthusiasm to hundreds of thousands of people. Candy took early retirement in the 1990s and switched to a life as a poet, spending her winters riding out hurricanes at the same little beach house she had visited in the Bahamas when she was four years old. She passed away in 2020. Her memoir, *Catalyst: In the Wake of the Great Bhola Cyclone*, describes her experiences founding HELP and her personal account of the terrible days of Operation Searchlight.

Jon Rohde went with Candy around the globe, working in various stints as a cholera doctor, children's pediatrician, research fellow, and international consultant for organizations like UNICEF India and the South Africa EQUITY rural health project. He and Candy returned to Bangladesh nearly every year and maintained a deep love for the country. Jon splits his time between Cape Town and Cape Cod.

Agha Muhammad Yahya Khan earned a brief bout of infamy as one of the worst leaders in world history for starting a genocide that broke his own country in two. He died in 1980 as a disgraced drunk still under house arrest. He is largely forgotten today, even in his native Pakistan. When his name does come up, it is a symbol of a shameful national period that most would rather not relive.

Zulfiqar Ali Bhutto wasn't around for Yahya's funeral. Bhutto was Pakistan's prime minister from 1971 until 1977, when he was overthrown in a coup d'état by a general who had just replaced **Tikka Khan** as head of the army. Bhutto was then tried, convicted, and hung for plotting to kill a political opponent in 1979. Pakistan has a complicated relationship with Bhutto's memory. Today he is often seen as a deeply flawed but well-meaning nationalist who fought for the country's glory. Bhutto's daughter, Benazir, became prime minister twice, before her assassination in 2007.

Neil Frank, after a career at the National Hurricane Center, took a job as a weatherman. He became one of America's most popular hurricane experts on national TV in the 1980s. But around then, he grew concerned about how climatologists like James Hansen presented connections between climate change and weather. In short, he didn't see the evidence the same way. Frank questioned the veracity of man-made climate change claims, in the process captivating conservative politicians and activists eager to find respected scientists who agreed with their beliefs. Permanently shaken by his experiences in East Pakistan, Frank has never been back to a free Bangladesh. He became a born-again Christian a few years after returning to Miami, and remains unconvinced that enough scientific data supports the conclusion that man-made global warming is a threat.

Acknowledgments

This book began as a conversation five years ago when we (the authors) came across a passing reference to the deadliest storm in history—the Great Bhola Cyclone. Despite working in and on South Asia for nearly a decade each at that point, it was something that we'd heard little of before, and we wanted to know why.

As we dug deeper into the sources, we realized that this wasn't just a story that people needed to know about because of its history or scale, but because of what it means for our world of climate crisis today. We discovered a clear connection between the cyclone and a war that led to global nuclear brinkmanship. This was both encouraging—because we knew we could write something meaningful—and terrifying: because who were we to be the ones to tell it. More so than any project either of us has worked on, *The Vortex* could never have come together without the legion of experts, historians, researchers, eyewitnesses, colleagues, editors, and interlocuters who guided us along the way. The following people were integral to the book in your hands right now. We could not have done it without them.

First and foremost were our primary sources who spent hours, days, and in a few cases weeks telling us their memories of this time. Hafiz Uddin Ahmad generously met us many times over tea and snacks in his office in Dhaka and then corresponded over text and e-mail for years. Mohammad Abdul Hai and Malik Mahmud had tears in their eyes as they recounted the days of the cyclone. Jon Rohde and Candy Rohde were equally generous with their time, and Candy's book *Catalyst* is one of the most important accounts of the cyclone and relief efforts that exists. Neil Frank even carved out time to discuss his years at the NHC in the days after a massive hurricane battered his own home in Texas.

There is also no book without Rezaur Rahman Lenin. Reza has worked with us on every project that we've embarked on in Bangladesh since 2007. He is an exceptional lawyer, researcher, and human rights activist who makes everything he touches just a little bit better. He's achieved the impossible time and again throughout this project, everything from finding dusty fifty-year-old Bengali books in obscure markets, to listening patiently for hours to kindly old souls who heard that he was on the lookout for cyclone stories, to teaching us about the rich Bengali culture and how to sidestep minefields within today's political scene in Bangladesh. Without him we would have been lost. Thank you, Reza, from the bottom of our hearts.

The following people also contributed their own eyewitness accounts and helped us tell a much fuller story overall: Abdul Gafur, Abdul Hakim, Abdul Latif, Abdus Salam, Abul Hashim (T.J.), Ahmed Fuad, Ali Ahmed Ziauddin (concierge at the InterContinental), Dil Mohammad Faruk, Eakub Ali Chowdhury, Hanna Chowdhury, Julian Francis, Koysor Ahmed Dulal, Lincoln Chen, Mahye Alam Kuti, Martha Chen, Mir Abdur Rab Mintu, Mohammad Ali, Mohammad Habib Miah, Mohammad Mostafizur Rahman, Mohammad Nur Alam, Mohammad Shahjahan, Mustafij Rahman, Pattie Boyd, Lieutenant Colonel (Ret'd) Quazi Sajjad Ali Zahir Bir Protik, Ripon Chaudhury, Runi Khan, Shuja Nawaz, Simone Sultana, Stephen Baldwin, Zahirul Haq Master.

Primary sources could take us only so far. In addition, scholars, archivists, experts, and historians shared with us their valuable expertise and added necessary context to our mission. These include Abdul Gafur, Alexander Rozin, Billy Haisley, David Stone at the US Naval War College, Dimitri Zelensky, Gary Bass, Gonzalo Chacon at the US State Department Archives, Jeff Vahrenwald, John Gaddis, John O'Brien at the British Library Army Archives, Katherine Mollan at the Center for Legislative Archives, Kristian Hoelscher, Mahadi Malik, Maren Aase, Md Nazrul Islam Khan, Michael Greco at the Miller Center, Michael Gross, Muntassir Mamoon, Musa Sadik, Naomi Hossain, Nayeem Wahra, Niladri Chatterjee, Rajat Kanti Sur, Rohin Francis, Ryan Pettigrew at the Richard Nixon Presidential Library and Museum, Samuel Jaffe, Simon Reid-Henry, Md Sarwar Ali and staff of the Bangladesh Liberation War Museum, Shahidul Alam and staff of the Drik Picture Library, staff of eTranslators, staff of the Rahman Memorial Museum, staff of the Magnum Photos archives, staff of World Translator, Captain T. Rajkumar, Tim Tacl.

We are especially grateful to Laura Nolan at Aevitas Creative Management, Wendy Strothman at the Strothman Agency, and Geri Thoma at Writer's House who stewarded the idea from infancy into maturity. We were also incredibly fortunate that Denise Oswald at Ecco realized how relevant this forgotten part of history was to the present day. Her precise and generous review of the manuscript, along with Norma Barksdale, was essential to delivering the essence of our vision. The manuscript also benefited significantly from Alicia Lipinski's close editorial insight.

Writing acknowledgments is difficult because the last people whom authors traditionally credit are really the most important in the world: our family members who have listened to our musings about long-forgotten cyclones and unspeakable tragedies, and stood by our sides through the most challenging writing times. For Scott, this is his wife and partner in all things, Laura Krantz; his family Wilfred Carney, Linda Carney, and Joan Carney; as well his sisters, Allison Carney and Laura Erny.

For Jason, this is the love of his life, Åshild Falch, who somehow listened to half a decade of esoteric cyclone and war factoids without once losing her enthusiasm, along with his parents Wayne and Linda for their unwavering support. Jason hopes that *The Vortex* can be a lodestar for their boys, Orion and Elliot, as they grow up navigating a more dangerous world of perpetual climate crises.

Note on Sources

References, interviews, and sources for *The Vortex* are presented here in chronological order of their appearance, noting the relevant sentence or paragraph. An exception is in the material gathered from Hafiz Uddin Ahmad, Candy Rohde, Malik Mahmud, and Mohammad Hai. To avoid citing every sentence in places, we state that the entirety of Hai's experiences came from our interviews. Unless otherwise referenced, the entirety of Hafiz's section comes from interviews or his memoir, and Candy's from interviews and her memoir. We cross-checked these experiences by interviewing others who were at the same events or had shared experiences and we cite those accordingly. We feel confident that these narratives are truthful and consistent, to the best of their recollective abilities and our abilities as writers. We cite additional sources used in their corresponding chapters in our references.

That said, compiling events from primary and secondary sources as well as the recollection of various witnesses can make it hard to tell history in a coherent way. This is the difficult terrain of any work of narrative nonfiction. Therefore, we mark the places where we truncated timelines that took place over longer periods and instead condensed them into a matter of hours or days.

Further, in a handful of places we used composite scenes to draw out the essence of someone's experience and character more quickly instead of narrating a series of different events that occurred over several months in bits and pieces. The first and most extensive example of this occurs in Hafiz's opening chapter. The match against the Soviets that we narrate derives from two different games (him scoring and the locker-room scene were actually from different games), and Hafiz's meeting with the army major didn't occur as a single moment at Madhusudan Dey's canteen. In fact, Hafiz can't remember a single aha moment where the major won him over. Instead, he was convinced slowly over a matter of many months. We placed it at the canteen because of its importance to Hafiz (he was indeed a regular) and as the spiritual center of Bengali student politics. This site is critical to the larger story of Operation Searchlight and Madhusudan Dey's execution by the Pakistani military. This reworking allowed us to show several different important elements of Bangladesh's history instead of writing out a long series of poorly connected vignettes. In other words, we condensed some of our witnesses' decision-making processes into their key moments. We chose to present those stories in a way not dissimilar to how we often remember the key decisions we make in our own lives. These sorts of composite scenes are rare but important in this book. We cite each instance in the endnotes so that the reader can follow our decision process along the way.

There are also inherent challenges of discovering any singular "truth" from events that happened fifty years ago between people who each have their own interpretation of what happened. For example, on Kissinger's clandestine car ride from President House to the airport on his way to China, Kissinger wrote in his memoirs that he took a blue Datsun. But the driver of the car, Pakistan foreign minister Sultan Khan, said that he took him in a red VW Beetle. For both men, the event itself was exceptionally memorable. Yet they disagreed on a detail that neither man would presumably have any reason to fabricate. In short, memories are fallible.

Of course, *The Vortex* contains more consequential details than the make and color of a car. Many had reason to give a rosy version of the past. Kissinger and Nixon each wrote memoirs, and facts in those books didn't always align with the White House Tapes or with eye-witnesses. For example, Kissinger insisted that Yahya helped unite the United States and China out of the goodness of his heart, asking for nothing in return. This was not the case per eyewitness accounts, official documents, or other evidence, including Pakistan ambassador to the United States Agha Hilaly's talks with Kissinger. And one can assume that Kissinger and Nixon didn't "forget" the sole demand from the man responsible for their greatest foreign policy achievement. Instead, we read these memoirs with a critical eye as both Nixon and Kissinger were known for taking liberties with facts, and they stood to benefit from whitewashing a likely quid pro quo. Make no mistake, US arms and support to fight East Pakistan came in exchange for Yahya's matchmaking services. In such instances, we attempted to decipher the reasons *why* individuals might give conflicting accounts of key moments. Most times, third-party accounts corroborated one side of the story. Otherwise, we placed more faith in actors who had less to gain personally by embellishing their accounts. We note major discrepancies of relevance as appropriate in the references.

Bhutto and Niazi also wrote memoirs of 1971, and Yahya Khan's fifty-page affidavit for the Hamoodur Rahman Commission functioned as a de facto autobiography. These three documents are, as expected, quite kind to their authors at the expense of other players in the drama. All three had much to gain by blaming the other two for Pakistan's dismemberment. In order to determine the factual accuracy of their statements therein, we triangulated claims from other eye-witness accounts and memoirs written during the 1970s and 1980s by military officers in West Pakistan, also making note of each of these authors' alignments and possible prejudices. Perhaps surprisingly, Bhutto, Niazi, Tikka, and Yahya freely admitted committing egregious war crimes. Those weren't the scandalous bits as far as they were concerned. Instead, they were more preoccupied with airing dirty laundry about the personal proclivities of the others. Bhutto, Niazi, Tikka, and Yahya all called each other an incompetent drunk who was responsible for the fall of Pakistan. In many ways, they're all correct.

Regarding Mujib, eyewitness accounts, including those by his close friend, the veteran journalist Anthony Mascarenhas, painted the portrait of a man trying to straddle two worlds. Like many politicians, he was prone to telling everyone what they wanted to hear. This created inconsistencies about what Mujib actually stood for. For example, there is considerable confusion over when he sought independence for Bangladesh: before the elections, after Operation Searchlight, or somewhere in between. This is complicated by the fact that he is now celebrated as the country's George Washington, and the government has passed laws forbidding questioning the official (and occasionally sanitized) version of Mujib's beliefs and actions during the period between 1966 and 1971. Indeed, in October 2018, Bangladesh adopted a new law that makes it illegal to defame "the Liberation War, the spirit of the Liberation War, the father of the nation, national anthem, or national flag," punishable with up to life in prison. Despite this, enough eyewitness accounts exist, through memoirs and survivors that we interviewed, that we are confident that the Mujib presented here strikes close to the heart of this complex and revered individual.

We also drew upon video and audio recordings and transcripts to better triangulate the "truth" of key events. We drew upon archival data from many audiovisual outlets, including the BBC, Associated Press, Agence France Presse, Radio Pakistan, and US State Department. We thank the Nixon Library in particular for their prodigious help with obscure audio, video, and photographic materials. Such material helped us better determine which accounts were truest to the mannerisms, temperaments, and personal styles of Nixon, Yahya, and Mujib.

Reiterating that all events in the preceding pages happened, we wanted to capture the emotional spirit of certain events and confer the dramatic experiences of what people thought and felt in the moment. For example, the Bengali language is incredibly rich, lyrical, and poetic. But in practical terms, direct translations often result in odd turns of phrase that don't make any sense to non-Bengali speakers. Therefore, while each dialogue in *The Vortex* represents a real discussion that took place, and is usually expressed verbatim (for example, between Yahya and Nixon), we employed a limited degree of paraphrase in places or made educated guesses about what might have been said in simple conversations between main characters in settings where the characters themselves did not remember the exact dialogue. Some conversations between Hai and Malik and Jon and Candy have been extrapolated where there are no concrete recordings. In such situations we used our research, interviews, and secondary accounts to build a profile of the most likely actions and words that each character would employ. The same principles guide the way we described physical gestures and descriptions where no good records exist.

In addition, we asked interviewees about their feelings during events. Recall of such memories can be hard, and people often dissociate what they did with how they felt. We were mindful when discussing thoughts and feelings, and to the best of our abilities conveyed the essence of these moments. In support, we conducted multiple interviews, asking some of the same questions, not only to help our sources articulate thoughts and feelings but also to build trust so that they felt comfortable enough to tell difficult, painful, or perhaps even embarrassing details about their own lives.

We also recognize our own positionality and worked to counteract power imbalances and address ethical concerns during our interviews. We have conducted hundreds of interviews of vulnerable people around the world over the previous decade, and building a legitimate rapport means employing empathy and patience. Our role as white male American researchers entering Bangladeshi households constituted a visible power imbalance. We took care to discuss up front the purpose of our project and address expectations, did not pay for interviews or information, allowed interviewees to end the interview at any time, and operated under standard principles of informed consent. For our major informants, conducting interviews repeatedly over a three-year period allowed us to achieve a depth of understanding of their experiences, and showed interviewees our intentions and motivations to get the details right.

Lest it go without saying, we have done our best to navigate this incredibly complex material and present it in an intelligible way, but that does not mean that our best is perfect or without errors. Any decision to interpret interviews, research materials, fifty-year-old memories, and timelines necessarily inserts our own biases into the manuscript. We hope that future historians will read this work in its appropriate context and realize that we are just one of many voices presenting an account of this troubled period.

A deeper ethical challenge lay in discussing and presenting Mukti Bahini activities. Bangladesh has no statute of limitations on murder. The *razakar* Tonir's murder can still be prosecuted, and other *razakars* have risen to positions of political prominence in the years since the conflict. A long-delayed truth and reconciliation committee is still not operational, making it difficult for villages to move beyond crimes committed fifty years ago. Thus, to protect our sources but still deliver material that is true to the spirit of the events of the war, we changed two details so as to guard against possible incrimination of our sources. These details do not alter the essence of the events as presented in *The Vortex* whatsoever.

Notes

PROLOGUE: BLACKOUT

xix **It was November 11** Captain T. Rajlkumar of the Indian Merchant Navy described the navigational challenges in the 1970s as well as his memories of the *Mahajagmitra* and its crew. Further information on the disappearance of the ship appeared in the Lok Sabha proceedings of November 20, 1970 (219.6), as well as from an assessment of the disaster, the timeline, and radio messages as reported in H. N. Sen, "Missing of MV *'Mahajagmitra'*: Report of Court on Formal Investigation," *Oceanite* (1971): 34–44.

xix **Barring radio contact** Buys Ballot's law, and the process of turning your back to the wind, was first described to us by Captain T. Rajkumar. See also Training Division U.S. Navy, Bureau of Aeronautics, *Aerology for Pilots* (New York: McGraw-Hill, 1943), 43.

xx **Das also noted that** Sen, "Missing of MV *'Mahajagmitra,'*" 39.

xx **Perhaps he told her** It is not possible to know exactly what Machado said to his wife when the *Mahajagmitra* was in its final hours, as only a few official radio transmissions survive. But he would likely have attempted to comfort her in their last moments. We also calculated that Nesari would have ordered his crew to secure the ship under storm conditions. We filled out these details with the help of interviews with Captain T. Rajkumar, who served in the Indian Merchant Navy at the time, to understand typical protocols, orders, and actions likely taken or mandated in such situations.

xxi **The forty-eight-member crew** The discussion of what to do when abandoning a ship stems from Rajkumar and the instructional sailing manual by C. H. Cooter, *Master and His Ship* (London: Maritime Press Limited, 1962), 222–27.

1: HAFIZ UDDIN AHMAD

3 **Thirty thousand fans erupted** We reconstructed plays from Hafiz's accounts of two different matches: one where he scored against the Soviets,

the other a game against another Bengali team, which he recounted during author interviews on August 31, 2019, and February 2, 2020. Unfortunately, no official records exist of these matches aside from the scores. Most facts in this chapter come from a series of interviews with Hafiz. To convey important information about the history of Pakistan and Hafiz's career before the war, we condensed the timeline.

6 **"Why don't they"** In author interview, February 24, 2020, Hafiz described how the crowd did not cheer the West Pakistani players and their bafflement that the crowd only reacted to Hafiz as being a star.

7 **Back on Hafiz's home** Karen C. McNamara, Laura Olson, and Md. Ashiqur Rahman, "Insecure hope: the challenges faced by urban slum dwellers in Bhola Slum, Bangladesh. Migration and Development," *Migration and Development* 5, no. 1 (2016): 1–15.

9 **"Madhur Café"** Hafiz's meetings with the major occurred over the course of two years in multiple locations around Dacca. The content of the discussion between the major and Hafiz is a faithful re-creation of their dialogues based on Hafiz's memories. However, as far as we are aware, they didn't hold any meetings at Madhur Café. We located the scene at the café because Hafiz was a frequent patron. Still, Hafiz noted to us that it would be very unlikely that an officer in uniform would ever show up there since it was so notoriously political. The café was a central hub for the student movement. We chose to write this composite scene at this site because it, and its patron, played an important role in Operation Searchlight. See Authors' Note for additional discussion.

10 **Hafiz caught sight** The banyan tree at Dacca University continues to be a central location for political gatherings, and scenes like this were common since the university's founding in 1921. While Hafiz would have seen events like this frequently, and he expressed the sentiments we describe in this chapter toward the student leaders at the time, this particular scene is a composite of multiple events that occurred over years.

10 **It didn't take a PhD** There is no one canonical source for the history of Bangladesh specifically or South Asia in general. However, a good overview can be found in Willem van Schendel, *A History of Bangladesh* (Cambridge: Cambridge University Press, 2009).

12 **The *New York Times*** Sydney Shanberg, "The Bengalis and the Punjabis: Nation Split by Geography, Hate," *New York Times*, December 4, 1970: A10.

2: AGHA MUHAMMAD YAHYA KHAN

17 **Agha Muhammad Yahya Khan** This opening scene is a composite based on facts at hand from the period. To note what we mean by "composite" in our

citations, here we have evidence that the call happened, and the details are evidence-based (for example, his favorite cigarette brand, the things on his desk, and the decor of the room), and we made educated assumptions about other parts of this night. For example, we are confident—but not completely positive—that he was alone, and we assume that he smoked and had a drink at that particular time, given that he was a chain-smoker and drank Black Dog most every night. Key sources include Dewan Berindranath, *Private Life of Yahya Khan* (New Delhi: Sterling, 1974); G. W. Choudhury, *The Last Days of United Pakistan* (London: Hurst, 1974); Marie Gillespie, "Bangladesh, 1971 and the BBC World Service: Witness Seminar" (London: Open University and BBC, 2009); and author interview in 2019 with the scholar and Yahya's personal acquaintance Shuja Nawaz, as well as archival photographs of the President House interior under Ayub Khan, Yahya Khan, and Z. Ali Bhutto, among others.

18 **He could accomplish** Berindranath, *Private Life of Yahya Khan*, 19–22; Archer Blood, *The Cruel Birth of Bangladesh: Memoirs of an American Diplomat* (Dhaka: University Press Limited, 2002), 42–44.

18 *Let them come* Robert Payne, *Massacre* (New York: Macmillan, 1973), 148; and author interview with Shuja Nawaz.

19 **So he made Yahya** "Man in the News: Martial Pakistani Chief Agha Muhammad Khan," *New York Times*, May 25, 1971.

19 **The window of opportunity** Details and quotes from this scene from A. H. Amin, "The Anatomy of Indo-Pak Wars: A Strategic and Operational Analysis," *Defence Journal* (August 2011); Shuja Nawaz, *Crossed Swords: Pakistan, Its Army, and the Wars Within* (Karachi: Oxford University Press, 2008), 207–14; author interview with Shuja Nawaz; B. A. R. Siddiqi, *General Agha Mohammad Yahya Khan: The Rise and Fall of a Soldier, 1947–1971* (Karachi: Oxford University Press, 2020).

20 **India got even cozier** See Robert H. Donaldson, *Soviet Policy Toward India: Ideology and Strategy* (Cambridge, MA: Harvard University Press, 1974).

20 **He handpicked eighty thousand** Shaikh Aziz, "Autocracy: Absolute Power," *Dawn*, October 23, 2011.

20 **Yahya never wanted** General (Ret'd) Agha Muhammad Yahya Khan, affidavit to the Lahore High Court at Lahore, re: Writ Petition No. 1649 of 1978 (Lahore: Lahore High Court, 1974), Point 7.

21 *My prime duty* Choudhury, *The Last Days of United Pakistan*, 55.

21 **Bengali-speaking East Pakistan** Musa Sadik, ed., *Bangladesh Wins Freedom* (Dhaka: Mowla, 2009), 198. See also Shaikh Maqsood Ali, *From East Bengal to Bangladesh: Dynamics and Perspective* (Dhaka: University Press Limited, 2nd edition, 2017); A. M. A. Muhith, *Bangladesh: Emergence*

of a Nation (Dhaka: University Press Limited, 3rd edition, 2014) 106–7, 120–30.

21 **Yahya said that** Choudhury, *The Last Days of United Pakistan*, 95–97.

21 **The convincing display** Siddiqi, *General Agha Mohammad Yahya Khan*, 18–19.

22 **Yahya's heavy British** See Blood, *The Cruel Birth of Bangladesh*, 41–42; Gary Bass, *The Blood Telegram: Nixon, Kissinger, and a Forgotten Genocide* (New York: Vintage, 2014), 7.

22 **His critics called it** Nawaz, *Crossed Swords*.

23 **Historian Gary Bass** Bass, *The Blood Telegram*, 7.

23 **He felt they were** "Good Soldier Yahya Khan," *Time*, August 2, 1971; and Blood, *The Cruel Birth of Bangladesh*, 41.

23 **So he twisted** Author interview with Shuja Nawaz, October 2019.

3: CANDY ROHDE

24 **Candy Rohde squeezed** In the chapters with Candy Rohde, we draw extensively from her self-published memoir, Cornelia Rohde, *Catalyst: In the Wake of the Great Bhola Cyclone* (Scotts Valley, CA: CreateSpace Independent Publishing Platform, 2014), in addition to interviews with her husband, Jon Rohde, and friends from the period. We cite such additional sources accordingly, and note that *Catalyst* is the primary source for Candy's chapters unless otherwise specified.

24 *It had to be* This is a composite scene that aims to portray what Old Dacca was like in 1968, and how Candy experienced it. We know that she loved going to this market and saw most of these scenes in the market, but we cannot confirm if she saw these exact things on this day. For example, she did not offer a detailed story about the time she got lost in a market while seeking a particular jeweler; we crafted this scene by incorporating details from author interviews with Candy, Jon Rohde (July 2020), Martha Chen (January 2020), Runi Khan (January 2020), Stephen Baldwin (December 2019), and others who frequented Shankar Bazaar during that time. Our aim was to bring out the essence of those trips as dutifully as possible. Another educated guess was that the hawkers in an old bazaar would find watching her as amusing in 1970 as many do in 2000 or even in 2020. Color from eyewitness account was found in Nadeem F. Paracha, "The Pakistan Zeitgeists: A Nation Through the Ages," *Dawn*, May 29, 2014. Old Dacca images are drawn from, among others, "Old Photos Bring Back Sweet Memories of Dhaka," *Complete World News* (2016).

26 **She made a mental note** Rohde, *Catalyst*, and author interview with Jon
Rohde.

26 **Candy made her way** Author interview with Jon Rohde.

26 **Her sinewy driver slapped** Robert Payne, *Massacre* (New York: Macmillan, 1973), 7. Likewise with the bazaar scene, we don't know exactly which
rickshaw Candy took on this particular day, she'd likely taken dozens, if not
hundreds, during her time in the city. We picked a representative model (per
Payne), and what many considered representative artwork of the time on
such rickshaws.

27 **As she gazed out** Rohde, *Catalyst*, and author interview with Jon Rohde.

27 **Raised in the middle** Rohde, *Catalyst*, and Cornelia Rohde *Pleached Poetry*,
available at thepoetryplatform.wordpress.com.

28 **She'd even started designing** Author interview with Jon Rohde.

29 **Candy's mind snapped back** Color from this scene from Rohde, *Catalyst*;
Stephen C. Baldwin, *Shadows Over Sundials: Dark and Light Life in a Large
Outside World* (Online: iUniverse, 2009), 210; and author interview with
Stephen Baldwin.

29 **Children with protruding bellies** Siddiq Salik, *Witness to Surrender* (Karachi: Oxford University Press, 1977), 3.

29 **The price included** Payne, *Massacre*, 7.

30 **Their sparse home had** Author interview with Jon Rohde.

4: YAHYA KHAN

31 **on the airport tarmac** Details in the following scenes of Nixon's visit come
from archival Associated Press film footage, as collated by Footage Farm,
documentary file footage numbers 221733, 221094, and 221362.

31 **Pakistan was the final stop** F. S. Aijazuddin, *From a Head, Through a Head,
to a Head: The Secret Channel Between the US and China Through Pakistan* (Karachi: Oxford University Press Pakistan, 2000), 2.

32 **Nixon and Yahya sat together** Images of the event provided by the Richard
Nixon Presidential Library and Museum and ibid., image #3.

32 **Inside was something precious** Author interview with Shuja Nawaz.

32 **Twenty years had passed** Richard Nixon, *RN: The Memoirs of Richard Nixon*
(New York: Simon and Schuster, 2nd edition, 1990), 341, 369–70.

33 **In exchange, Nixon promised** Henry Kissinger, *White House Years* (New
York: Simon and Schuster, 2nd edition, 2011), 333–34.

33 **He said yes immediately** Aijazuddin, *From a Head, Through a Head, to a
Head*, 3.

33 **Crystal candelabras, giant bowls** Dinner details from Footage Farm and Associated Press, and file photos courtesy of the Nixon Library and White House Correspondents Association.

33 **After some speechwriter-induced** Quotes from the Yahya and Nixon speeches taken from White House Correspondents' Association, "Yahya speech to Richard Nixon, gala dinner," 1969, file number SR P 690804–R.

35 **Ali was Yahya's ultimate** Author interview with Shuja Nawaz.

35 **He wrote in his diary** H. R. Haldeman, *The Haldeman Diaries: Inside the Nixon White House* (Santa Monica: Sony, 1994).

35 **yellow lilies were** Srinath Raghavan, *1971: A Global History of the Creation of Bangladesh* (Cambridge, MA: Harvard University Press, 2013), 14.

35 **He wrote CHINESE CONNECTION** Aijazuddin, *From a Head, Through a Head, to a Head*, xvi.

5: NEIL FRANK

37 **Each image covered** Data on ESSA-8 in this paragraph taken from NASA, "ESSA: Environmental Science Services Administration Satellite Program," informational flyer (2013).

37 **Frank unspooled a finger's** Author interview with Neil Frank.

38 **The NHC was a strange** Biographical information in this chapter from author interviews with Neil Frank, and William Kellar, "Houston History Profile, Dr. Neil Frank," *Houston History* 5, no. 3 (2008): 40–41; Kansas Historical Society, "Dr. Neil Frank," *Kansapedia* (2016).

39 **Everyone in Miami knew** Robert C. Sheets, "The National Hurricane Center: Past, Present, and Future," *Weather and Forecasting* 5, no. 2 (1990): 185–231.

39 **The deadliest hurricane to hit** Eric Larson, *Isaac's Storm* (New York: Vintage, 2011).

40 **In 1737 and again** Death tolls and dates taken from the India National Cyclone Mitigation Project available at http://ncrmp.gov.in/ncrmp/AnnIIb.html, and Lt. Col. J. E. Gastrell and Henry F. Blanford, *Report on the Calcutta Cyclone of 1864* (Calcutta: Cutter Orphan Military Press, 1866).

41 **Dunn directed them to** For details of the development of the warning system, see Gordon Dunn, "The Tropical Cyclone Problem in East Pakistan," *Monthly Weather Review* (March 1962): 83–86; Neil Frank and S. A. Husain, "The Deadliest Tropical Cyclone in History?," *Bulletin American Meteorological Society* 52, no. 6 (1971): 438–45.

41 **The potential military applications** Jack Schafer, "Schooling Ross Douthat in Conspiracy Theory," *Slate*, March 22, 2010.

6: YAHYA KHAN AND GENERAL RANI

43 **And right now General Rani** Details on General Rani's life are sparse; our primary two sources for this scene are Ayesha Nasir, *Night of the General* (Karachi: Newsline, 2002); and Dewan Berindranath, *Private Life of Yahya Khan* (New Delhi: Sterling, 1974).

43 **She knew above all** Nasir, *Night of the General.*

43 **But halfway to her** This scene of Rani, the Shah, and Yahya derives from the memoir of former police superintendent Muhamad Chaudry in Sardar Muhammad Chaudry, *The Ultimate Crime: Eyewitness to Power Games* (Karachi: Quami, 1997).

44 **Rani herself put it** Nasir, *Night of the General.*

44 **By 1965, Rani was** Ibid.

45 **Yahya started to import** Berindranath, *Private Life of Yahya Khan*, 64.

45 **Rani played matron** Ibid., 82.

45 **As she explained** Nasir, *Night of the General.*

46 **When Ayub first hired** Stephen C. Baldwin, *Shadows Over Sundials: Dark and Light Life in a Large Outside World* (Online: iUniverse, 2009), 208.

46 **Like other planned capitals** Markus Daechsel, *Islamabad and the Politics of International Development in Pakistan* (Cambridge: Cambridge University Press, 2015), 169–75, 197, 235; and Orestes Yakas, *Islamabad: The Birth of a Capital* (Karachi: Oxford University Press, 2001).

46 **The true miracle was** Daechsel, *Islamabad and the Politics of International Development in Pakistan*; Yakas, *Islamabad*; and Berindranath, *Private Life of Yahya Khan*, 22–23.

46 **This doubled or even** Robert Payne, *Massacre* (New York: Macmillan, 1973), 41.

47 **Here, cloaked and bearded men** Baldwin, *Shadows Over Sundials*, 208–9.

47 **One peg of whiskey** We note that our sourcing is limited on several personal Yahya moments where we reference Berindranath as a primary source, given that there is limited or at times no other information available. We add a caveat that while Berindranath's analysis carries authoritative weight from his employment of dozens of archival sources from West Pakistan, there may be discrepancies in historical records based on the exact details of such events. Berindranath was a prolific Indian journalist who covered the Islamic world and worked extensively in Pakistan. As an Indian writing just after the war, his writings may be biased. Still, while we have been unable to secure several of his Pakistani primary sources, those we have located align with his analyses. We also note that Yahya never publicly disputed the events

depicted in Berindranath's account. We have done our best to adhere to the most likely interpretations of these events. On his progression and timeline of Yahya's increased drinking habits, see Berindranath, *Private Life of Yahya Khan*, 24.

47 **In Karachi, he was** Sherbaz Khan Mazari, *A Journey to Disillusionment* (Karachi: Oxford University Press, 1999), 34–36.

47 **It was a great** Baldwin, *Shadows Over Sundials*, 209.

49 **By now, everyone knew** Payne, *Massacre*, 32.

7: HAFIZ UDDIN AHMAD

51 **Hafiz lofted Pakistan's** This chapter comes entirely from Hafiz's personal accounts of his time in Tehran but is a composite of two different times that he went to Iran to play football—once in April 1969, when he met Ravi Shankar, and then again September 1970.

8: MOHAMMAD HAI

56 **Mohammad Abdul Hai's** All of the primary information about Hai comes from multiple author interviews with him over three years. In addition to his firsthand account, we triangulated and/or fact-checked his accounts where possible to ensure that his narrative was truthful and consistent. We cite other sources in support (marked in his chapters where relevant, both other interviews and archival or secondary material). This supplementary research also helped fill gaps where Hai did not remember specific details on events from fifty years ago, in particular colors, food, conversations, activities, and so forth.

57 **Fishermen told stories** Author interview with Hai, 2019. See also "Species Profile: Wallago Attu," *Seriously Fish*, available at https://www.seriouslyfish.com/species/wallago-attu/, and on the Animal Planet show *River Monsters*, on the episodes "Asian Slayer" and "Malaysian Lake Monster."

58 **At Manpura High School** We have opted to use the pseudonym Malik. The next two paragraphs are from author interview with Malik, November 2019.

62 **Nobody knew what that** From Hai and also author interview Mostafizur, September 2019.

62 **A second warning** See also "East Pakistan: The Politics of Catastrophe," *Time*, December 7, 1970; "A warning—*moha bipod shonket* (big danger coming)—was broadcast, but someone forgot to include a code number indicating the force of the expected storm."

63 **This hodgepodge of systems** World Bank, *Note on the Experience of a World*

Bank Mission During the Recent Cyclone in East Pakistan (Washington, DC: World Bank, 1971).

9: CANDY ROHDE

64 **One day before landfall** We have condensed the timeline of this chapter. The consulate event happened about six months before Bhola. It has been placed here instead to better present Candy's transition, and better describe and present her frustrations, to maintain chronological continuity. Author interview with Jon Rohde, July 2020.

64 **Even after living** Author interview with Runi Khan, January 2020.

64 **They'd weave past** Stephen C. Baldwin, *Shadows Over Sundials: Dark and Light Life in a Large Outside World* (Online: iUniverse, 2009), 213.

65 **There was even** Author interview with Ali Ahmed Ziauddin, February 26, 2020.

65 **In an attempt to** Typical photos of the period can be seen at https://twitter.com/LandOfBengal/status/580440277451669504.

66 **Expats gave their kids** Baldwin, *Shadows Over Sundials*, 211.

66 **Then he motioned to** Author interview with Jon Rohde.

66 **The British were jealous** Ibid. This scene represents the type of conversations that happened at these kinds of parties. In author interviews with Jon Rohde and Stephen Baldwin (another regular at such events) they didn't remember the entirety of any specific conversation but did remember the details as supplied in this scene. Supplemental material includes memoirs by individuals such as then–deputy consul Archer Blood, *The Cruel Birth of Bangladesh: Memoirs of an American Diplomat* (Dhaka: University Press Limited, 2002).

68 **In the last year** Author interview with Jon Rohde, and Cornelia Rohde, *Catalyst: In the Wake of the Great Bhola Cyclone* (Scotts Valley, CA: CreateSpace Independent Publishing Platform, 2014), 26–27.

68 **These people welcomed** Author interview with Martha Chen, January 2020, and Runi Khan, January 2020.

68 **Candy and Jon earned** Author interviews with Martha Chen, Runi Khan, and Stephen C. Baldwin, January 2020.

68 **Candy loved flying kites** Author interview with Jon Rohde, January 2020.

68 **They played endless games** Rohde, *Catalyst*, 46.

10: MOHAMMAD HAI

70 **Hai jumped out of bed** All details in this chapter taken from author interviews with Hai unless otherwise stated.

76 **In the span of** Additional cyclone landfall and weather details on the

following two pages come from eyewitness survivor accounts on Monpura: author interviews with Mohammad Mostafizur Rahman, October 2019, and Mohammad Shahjahan, October 2019.

11: CANDY ROHDE

79 **A newly planted tree** Faruq Aziz Khan, *Spring 1971* (Dhaka: Agamee Prakashani, 2014), 36.

79 **The few Bengalis who** Stephen C. Baldwin, *Shadows Over Sundials: Dark and Light Life in a Large Outside World* (Online: iUniverse, 2009), 217.

80 **Marty was right behind** Author interview with Martha Chen.

80 **She read it out loud** Details of this meeting and day's events from Cornelia Rohde, *Catalyst: In the Wake of the Great Bhola Cyclone* (Scotts Valley, CA: CreateSpace Independent Publishing Platform), 2014; and author interviews with Jon Rohde, Martha Chen, and Runi Khan.

12: MOHAMMAD HAI

83 **Bodies of animals and** "Pakistan: When the Demon Struck," *Time*, November 30, 1970.

84 **A dead woman hung** Author interview with Mostafizur Rahman, October 2019.

85 **They ate tree roots** Author interview with Abdul Latif, October 2019.

86 **Some raved with madness** "Pakistan: When the Demon Struck."

13: HAFIZ UDDIN AHMAD

89 **Hafiz motioned to the boatman** The description of the journey from Jessore to Bhola comes from several author interviews with Hafiz, supplemented by details added from other eyewitnesses, including Nayeem Wada and Mohammad Hai. Most cyclone survivors we spoke with on Bhola and Manpura recounted similar scenes. Few press images exist of the direct aftermath of the cyclone, but the photo archives of the Liberation War Museum, Getty Images, and Drik Picture Library in Dhaka have limited examples.

14: YAHYA KHAN

92 **"It doesn't look so bad"** Yahya was overheard to make these comments in passing; see Archer K. Blood, *The Cruel Birth of Bangladesh: Memoirs of an American Diplomat* (New Delhi: University Press Limited, 2002). See also

Khadim Hussain Raja, *A Stranger in My Own Country: East Pakistan 1969–1971* (Karachi: Oxford University Press, 2012), 38.

92 **Gripping an ice-cold beer** Blood, *The Cruel Birth of Bangladesh*, 77. On the in-flight drinking, Yahya's lack of empathy, and the airplane model, see Raja, *A Stranger in My Own Country*, 38, and B. A. R. Siddiqi, *General Agha Mohammad Yahya Khan: The Rise and Fall of a Soldier, 1947–1971* (Karachi: Oxford University Press, 2020), 46.

92 **He drew the aluminum** Brian Barron, "Age of Dictators: Lessons of the Past," *BBC News*, November 21, 1998. Barron was on the helicopter with Yahya that day.

92 **He'd arrived in Dacca** Blood, *The Cruel Birth of Bangladesh*, 77.

92 **After landing, a boozy** Ibid., and Nuran Nabi and Mush Nabi, *Bullets of '71: A Freedom Fighter's Story* (Dhaka: Shahitya Prakash, 2012), 127.

93 **He threw an impossibly** Details of this scene from, among others, *Peking Review* 13, no. 47 (November 20, 1970): 4–9; and William Barnds, "China's Relations with Pakistan: Durability Amidst Discontinuity." *China Quarterly* 63 (1975): 463–89.

94 **He missed, slamming into** "Key Polish Official Is Killed by Truck at Karachi Airport," *New York Times*, November 2, 1970, A1.

95 **He waved a telegram** No official sources indicate exactly how Yahya received the news on that day; this was our best approximation based on typical usage of communications to him at that time. Siddiqi, *General Agha Mohammad Yahya Khan*, 46, confirms the timing of Yahya's notification.

95 **The press knew that** Blood, *The Cruel Birth of Bangladesh*, 77.

96 **He refused to declare** David Loshak, *Pakistan Crisis* (London: Heinemann, 1971).

96 **Abandoned by Yahya** Blood, *The Cruel Birth of Bangladesh*, 89–90.

15: CANDY ROHDE

97 **"But it's the only one"** This conversation was reconstructed based on memories of the scene. Neither Jon Rohde nor Martha Chen remembered the exact language (and Candy's book, *Catalyst*, does not go into detail on the event), but they did remember a quick conversation taking place.

97 **Too much of a hassle** On this being East Pakistan's only helicopter and officials refusing to use it for anything other than moving officials around, see Archer K. Blood, *The Cruel Birth of Bangladesh: Memoirs of an American Diplomat* (New Delhi: University Press Limited, 2002), 80.

98 **Camaraderie with any woman** "Pakistan: HELP for Manpura," *Newsweek*, January 4, 1971: 25.

99 **"What do you need?"** Author interview with Martha Chen.

99 **In addition to their** "Pakistan: HELP for Manpura."

99 **The officials set up** Details of the meeting with the Pakistani and USAID officials on the following pages were as recounted in author interview with Martha Chen.

16: NEIL FRANK

102 **Seven days after** Information in this chapter is from author interviews with Neil Frank unless otherwise noted.

103 **A day earlier** Frank does not remember how exactly he heard the news, but he was an avid reader of the *New York Times*, and the most relevant story of that week was about Manpura.

104 **Economists estimated that** Neil Frank and S. A. Husain, "The Deadliest Tropical Cyclone in History?," *Bulletin American Meteorological Society* 52, no. 6 (1971): 438–45.

104 **In what must pass** Details of the service life of the ITOS 1 and ESSA-8 satellites are on the NASA website at https://nssdc.gsfc.nasa.gov/nmc/space craft/display.action?id=1970–008A.

17: MOHAMMAD HAI

106 **"Come, come quickly!"** This is a reconstructed conversation as neither Hai nor Malik remember their exact dialogue leading up to the visit. Hai was doing this sort of work but did not remember if he was doing it on this morning. His memories of the day were understandably filled completely by what came after Mujib arrived, not before.

106 **He smiled for the first** Hai said it was the first time he remembered something positive after Bhola.

107 **After all, when the** "Pakistan: When the Demon Struck," *Time*, November 30, 1970.

107 **Scanning the horizon** This was the only line that Hai remembered verbatim from Mujib's speech.

107 **Hundreds of people surrounded** Author interview with Mostafizur Rahman.

108 **It was nothing much** Author interview with Malik Mahmud.

108 **Mujib grabbed his tailored** Ibid.

108 **A couple shopkeepers** Author interview with Hai, and details from author interview with Ahmed Fuad, January 2019.

109 **One father peered into** "Pakistan: When the Demon Struck."

109 **The crowd was so thick** Author interview with Mostafizur Rahman; see also photos and documentation of airdrops at "Bhola Cyclone (1970)—

International Aid" (London: Worldwide, 2021), available at http://www.londoni
.co/index.php/history/25-history-of-bangladesh/1970-bhola-cyclone/317
-bhola-cyclone-1970-international-aid-history-of-bangladesh.

109 **Malik thought it looked** Author interview with Malik; event corroborated
in author interview with Rahman.

109 **The fifty-pound rice bags** Additional information in Rehman Sohban,
Milestones to Bangladesh (Collected Works of Rehman Sobhan, Volume 2)
(Dhaka: Centre for Policy Dialogue, 2007).

109 **Ignoring the bodies** Author interview with Rahman.

109 **The pilot whisked him** "East Pakistan: The Politics of Catastrophe," *Time*,
December 7, 1971.

18: HAFIZ UDDIN AHMAD AND YAHYA KHAN

110 **Hafiz stood on a large** This story appears in Munawar Hafiz, ed., *Bangladesh
1971: Dreadful Experiences* (Dhaka: Shahitya Prakash, 2017), and in Hafiz's
recollections to the authors in 2019 by e-mail and in several telephone conversations. In the cases where there were some discrepancies between his
writings and his personal recounting, we chose to favor what he told us in interviews. Pieces of dialogue are quoted here verbatim, except for minor cor-
rections to syntax.

112 **In accordance with** All details in this paragraph on communications derived
from F. S. Aijazuddin, *From a Head, Through a Head, to a Head: The Secret
Channel Between the US and China Through Pakistan* (Karachi: Oxford University Press, 2000), 29–49.

113 **He had his public** Ibid., 44; B. A. R. Siddiqi, *East Pakistan: The Endgame.
An Onlooker's Journal, 1969–1971* (Karachi: Oxford University Press, 2005),
44–49.

113 **Stripped naked by the cyclone** Footage of the meeting between Yahya and
Hafiz exists in the BBC archives and on YouTube at the 1:30 mark, available
at https://www.youtube.com/watch?v=DHWjrulnAao. While Hafiz is not
visible in this clip, someone who is likely Jalil appears in a group shot behind
Yahya.

19: CANDY ROHDE

117 **"Hello?"** This conversation is reconstructed, as the exact discussion is lost to
time. Candy remembered being incredulous. Details from the day's events
in this chapter are as recounted by author interviews with Candy Rohde and
Jon Rohde, unless otherwise noted.

119 **She even managed** Author interview with Martha Chen.

120 **He ordered Dacca's consul** Archer Blood, *The Cruel Birth of Bangladesh: Memoirs of an American Diplomat* (Dhaka: University Press Limited, 2002), 90–92.

122 **Somewhere out on the delta** Additional details on the boat trip from Hatiya to Manpura from author interview with Stephen C. Baldwin.

20: MOHAMMAD HAI

123 **On Bhola island** "East Pakistan: The Politics of Catastrophe," *Time*, December 7, 1970.

123 **When reporters asked Yahya** "Good Soldier Yahya Khan," *Time*, August 2, 1971.

124 **Mujib said that there** "Mujibur Rahman Warns Against Bid to Frustrate Elections: Remarks Made at a Press Conference at Dacca on November 26, 1970," *Morning News*, November 27, 1970.

124 **Designed to be simple** The government of Bangladesh provides an overview at "Six-point Programme," in Banglapedia, 2021, available at: http://en.banglapedia.org/index.php/Six-point_Programme.

125 **He was about to drop** David Ludden, "Forgotten Heroes," *Frontline* 20, no. 15 (July 19–August 1, 2003).

125 **He said the relief efforts** "President Yahya Khan Touring Flood Relief Operation," Associated Press, November 26, 1970, available on YouTube. See also Sydney Schanberg, "Yahya Concedes 'Slips' in Relief but He Defends Government Against Charges," *New York Times*, November 28, 1970.

21: JON ROHDE, MOHAMMAD HAI, AND CANDY ROHDE

127 **In the other direction** Details from Jon Rohde and Hai's meeting and other events in this chapter come from author interviews with Hai and Jon Rohde, with additional details from Cornelia Rohde, *Catalyst: In the Wake of the Great Bhola Cyclone* (Scotts Valley, CA: CreateSpace Independent Publishing Platform, 2014); "Pakistan: HELP for Manpura," *Newsweek*, January 4, 1971; and Stephen C. Baldwin, *Shadows Over Sundials: Dark and Light Life in a Large Outside World* (Online: iUniverse, 2009), 218–20.

131 **"How's the smell today?"** This note is a composit of two letters that Candy sent Jon; see Rohde, *Catalyst*, pp. 107–110.

131 **The Americans dumped bacon** Author interview with Mostafizur Rahman.

133 **corrupt landowners** Rodhe, *Catalyst*, pp. 328–34; author interview with Malik, author interview with Hai, author interview with Latif; Father Timm, *Forty Years in Bangladesh, Memoirs of Father Timm*. Dhaka: UDA, 1995, 141–42.

134 **Finally, the Germans arrived** Details about this meeting from author interviews with Martha Chen, Jon Rohde, and Runi Khan, and in Rohde, *Catalyst.*

22: NEIL FRANK

136 **The concierge saluted** The make and model of the vehicle is an educated guess, based on the predominance of chauffeur-driven vehicles for foreigners that were used at the time.

136 **Everyone in the country** Author interview with Neil Frank.

138 **Preliminary estimates showed** Neil Frank and S. A. Husain, "The Deadliest Tropical Cyclone in History?," *Bulletin American Meteorological Society* 52, no. 6 (1971): 438–45.

138 **The general led** Frank recounted this scene during several author interviews. He recalled the general specifically saying, "This cyclone solved about half a million of our problems," and asking repeatedly for C-130 aircraft. He remembers the overall tone and topics of the conversation but did not recall exact language. Minor details are based on his memories and common mannerisms of various Pakistani generals we and others have met in similar circumstances.

23: YAHYA KHAN AND ZULFIKAR ALI BHUTTO

141 **"After these elections"** Yahya interview taken from "An Interview with Pakistani President Khan," Associated Press, December 1, 1970; available on YouTube.

141 **Some of his generals** Muntasir Mamoon, *The Vanquished Generals and the Liberation War of Bangladesh* (Dhaka: Somoy, 2000), 56.

142 **Or better yet** M. A. Khan, *Generals in Politics: Pakistan 1958–1982* (New Delhi: Vikas, 1983), 28.

142 **Why couldn't they be** Oriana Fallaci, *Interview with History* (Rome: Rizzoli/Liveright, 1976), 15.

142 **He thought that a** G. W. Choudhury, *The Last Days of United Pakistan* (London: Hurst, 1974), 77.

142 **He thought that reading** Fallaci, *Interview with History*, 2–3.

143 **He organized against** Ibid., 12; and Archer Blood, *The Cruel Birth of Bangladesh: Memoirs of an American Diplomat* (Dhaka: University Press Limited, 2002), 42.

143 **He married his first** Fallaci, *Interview with History*, 12.

143 **As an Italian journalist** Ibid., 2–3.

144 **Three weeks before** Siddiq Salik, *Witness to Surrender* (Karachi: Oxford University Press, 2nd edition, 1997), 28–29.

24: MOHAMMAD HAI AND YAHYA KHAN

145 **A golden dawn broke** All details from Hai's portions of this chapter are taken from author interviews with Hai, unless otherwise noted.

146 **Malik wasn't upset** Author interview with Malik, November 2019.

147 **Yahya's advisers claimed** Shuja Nawaz, *Crossed Swords: Pakistan, Its Army, and the Wars Within* (Karachi: Oxford University Press, 2008), 260.

147 **"Pakistan is saved!"** G. W. Choudhury, *The Last Days of United Pakistan* (London: Hurst, 1974), 102.

147 **His own thumb still** Ralph Blumenthal, "Bengali and Leftist Parties Lead in Pakistani Election," *New York Times*, December 8, 1970.

147 **Just after breakfast** Nuran Nabi and Mush Nabi, *Bullets of '71: A Freedom Fighter's Story* (Dhaka: Shahitya Prakash, 2012), 137.

148 **He read through it** Author interview with Shuja Nawaz.

149 **Foreign reporters rushed** Ibid.

150 **Malik thought it was** Author interview with Malik, November 2019.

150 **To get his mind off** Henry Kissinger, *White House Years* (New York: Simon and Schuster, 2nd edition, 2011), 1248–49.

150 **"What in the devil's name"** Arshad Sami Khan, *Three Presidents and an Aide* (New Delhi: Pentagon Press, 2008), 130–31.

151 **With General Rani** Choudhury, *The Last Days of United Pakistan*, 149.

151 **Rani came up with** Dewan Berindranath, *Private Life of Yahya Khan* (New Delhi: Sterling, 1974), 79.

151 **"I don't see what"** General (Ret'd) Agha Muhammad Yahya Khan, affidavit to the Lahore High Court at Lahore, re: Writ Petition No. 1649 (Lahore: Lahore High Court, 1974), Point 41.

151 **"Don't think I'm a"** The exact exchange is lost to time, but longtime acquaintance Nawaz surmised that he would make such a comment with the British-English aphorism in reply. Author interview with Shuja Nawaz.

151 **"You are simply"** Yahya Khan, affidavit to the Lahore High Court, Point 9. He also had a habit of calling Bhutto a "power-hungry devil" on occasion.

151 **Despite all the promises** Siddiq Salik, *Witness to Surrender* (Karachi: Oxford University Press, 2nd edition, 1997), 29; see also Zufikar Ali Bhutto, *The Great Tragedy* (Islamabad: PPP Publications, 1971), 49.

152 **Even Yahya's advisers did** Muntassir Mamoon, *The Vanquished Generals and the Liberation War of Bangladesh* (Dhaka: Somoy, 2000), 56.

INTERMISSION: YAHYA KHAN AND TIKKA KHAN

153 **A fit and trim Lieutenant** Many details of Yahya's military record during this period are lost. We have done our best to estimate particular details like the

make and model of the tanks used, weather, precise location of operations, and others from time-appropriate sources, which include Satyen Basu, *A Doctor in the Army*, self-published memoir, 1960; M. G. Syed Ali Hamid, "Prisoners of Aversa," *Friday Times*, February 9, 2019; B. A. R. Siddiqi, *General Agha Mohammad Yahya Khan: The Rise and Fall of a Soldier, 1947–1971* (Karachi: Oxford University Press, 2020); Shuja Nawaz, "The Sage of Yahya Khan," *Friday Times*, January 24, 2021. Additional details of the battle where Yahya was captured are available at https://en.wikipedia.org/wiki/Battle_of_Gazala/.

153 **Yahya's tank** Agha Humayun Amin, *Pakistan Army Since 1965* (Lahore: Defence Journal Publications, 2000).

154 **Yahya already stood out** Dewan Berindranath, *Private Life of Yahya Khan* (New Delhi: Sterling, 1974), 19–34.

154 **The Nazis imprisoned Yahya** Details of Yahya's POW camp are primarily from fellow POW Satyen Basu in his self-published memoir, *A Doctor in the Army*, 34–55.

155 **As it turned out** Yasmin Khan, *India at War: The Subcontinent and the Second World War* (Oxford: Oxford University Press, 2015), 76–78.

155 **Yahya met a fellow** See K. C. Sagar, *The War of the Twins* (New Delhi: Northern Book Centre, 1997), 57–62.

155 **Given their officer status** Hamid, "Prisoners of Aversa."

155 **He especially loved pulping** *Sainik Samachar: The Pictorial Weekly of the Armed Forces* 25 (1978): 23.

156 **Where Yahya was a** Archer Blood, *The Cruel Birth of Bangladesh: Memoirs of an American Diplomat* (Dhaka: University Press Limited, 2002), 159–60, 179.

156 **So Tikka hatched an** Hamid, "Prisoners of Aversa."

156 **The camp commandant told** Shaukat Riza, *The Pakistan Army War of 1965* (Karachi: Natraj, 2018).

156 **Eventually, Yahya and Tikka** The exact location of Yahya's interment and where they crossed over to the front lines is a matter of some dispute. While most sources place him in camp PG 63 in Aversa for the entire period, including eyewitness sources (Basu, *A Doctor in the Army*; Hamid, "Prisoners of Aversa"), one reputable source (Nawaz, "The Sage of Yahya Khan") believes that his first escape attempt was in Libya, just before they were sent to Italy. All sources, however, agree on the circumstances that led to his capture and journey by foot back to the Allied lines in southern Italy.

157 **So he raced to** Sagar, *The War of the Twins*, 57.

157 **The heavy-handed tactics** S. Sareen, *Balochistan: Forgotten War, Forsaken*

People (New Delhi: Vivekananda Foundation, 2017), 36. See also Robert Payne, *Massacre* (New York: Macmillan, 1973), 44–45.

25: YAHYA KHAN

161 **He told Mujib** Robert Payne, *Massacre* (New York: Macmillan, 1973), 12.

161 **He wrote Yahya that** G. W. Choudhury, *The Last Days of United Pakistan* (London: Hurst, 1974), 85.

162 **He tried convincing** Anthony Mascarenhas, *Bangladesh: A Legacy of Blood* (London: Hodder and Stoughton, 1986), 5.

162 **They hammered out** Choudhury, *The Last Days of United Pakistan*, 151.

162 **"It's going to be"** Ibid.

162 **He told his counterpart** Ibid., 89.

162 **Yahya left for Islamabad** Khadim Hussain Raja, *A Stranger in My Own Country: East Pakistan 1969–1971* (Karachi: Oxford University Press, 2012), 41.

163 **Safely tucked away** Several scholars and eyewitness accounts are combined for the Larkarna scene: Siddiq Salik, *Witness to Surrender* (Karachi: Oxford University Press, 2nd edition, 1997), 34; Zufikar Ali Bhutto, *The Great Tragedy* (Islamabad: PPP Publications, 1971), 20–23; Muntassir Mamoon, *The Vanquished Generals and the Liberation War of Bangladesh* (Dhaka: Somoy, 2000), 160; Choudhury, *The Last Days of United Pakistan*, 152; B. A. R. Siddiqi, *General Agha Mohammad Yahya Khan: The Rise and Fall of a Soldier, 1947–1971* (Karachi: Oxford University Press, 2020), 54–55. See also S. A. Karim, *Triumph and Tragedy* (New Delhi: University Press Limited, 2009), 172–76; Mohammed Asghar Khan, *Generals in Politics: Pakistan 1958–1982* (New Delhi: Vikas, 1983), 28; Inam Ahmed and Shakhawat Liton, "Genocide Plot Conceived at Duck Shooting Trip," *Daily Star*, December 4, 2015; R. Chowdhury, "Bangladesh: The Road to 1971: Birth Pangs of a Nation," *South Asia Journal*, March 27, 2019. Much of the exact language derives from events as depicted by these sources.

163 **"Yahya, what if we"** General (Ret'd) Agha Muhammad Yahya Khan, affidavit to the Lahore High Court at Lahore, re: Writ Petition No. 1649 (Lahore: Lahore High Court, 1974), Point 1, Point 22.

164 **The name didn't mean** Raja, *A Stranger in My Own Country*, 73.

164 **He gave Tikka a special** Archer Blood, *The Cruel Birth of Bangladesh: Memoirs of an American Diplomat* (Dhaka: University Press Limited, 2002), 216; author interview with Lieutenant Colonel Quazi Sajjad Ali Zahir Bir Protik, February 2020.

164 **The soldiers first received** Blood, *The Cruel Birth of Bangladesh*, 179.

165 **The imams said that** Ibid., 179, 216; author interview with Lieutenant Colonel Quazi Sajjad Ali Zahir Bir Protik.

165 **Tikka and the imams** See Haskar Papers, Subject File 168, B. R. Patel to I. G. Patel, June 18, 1971, in Gary J. Bass, *The Blood Telegram: Nixon, Kissinger, and a Forgotten Genocide* (New York: Vintage, 2014), 363–64n60; Siddiqi, *General Agha Mohammad Yahya Khan*, 67; Choudhury *The Last Days of United Pakistan*, 155; author interview with Lieutenant Colonel Quazi Sajjad Ali Zahir Bir Protik.

166 **"Kill three million"** Payne, *Massacre*, 50; Philip Hensher, "The War Bangladesh Can Never Forget," *The Independent*, February 19, 2013.

166 **Then, to eliminate any** Blood, *The Cruel Birth of Bangladesh*, 150.

26: MOHAMMAD HAI AND SHEIKH MUJIBUR RAHMAN

167 **Like a hive mind** On the story of the rat infestation, see Cornelia Rohde, *Catalyst: In the Wake of the Great Bhola Cyclone* (Scotts Valley, CA: CreateSpace Independent Publishing Platform, 2014), 283–85.

168 **The army gave almost** Author interview with Jon Rohde. The BBC no longer has the video in their archives, and Jon accidentally give the master tape to Goodwill when cleaning out some old junk, along with other keepsakes. If anyone in the Boston area finds it, he'd love to have it back.

169 **Bhutto refused to return** On the escalating tensions, see Kamal Hossain, *Bangladesh: Quest for Freedom and Justice* (Dhaka: University Press Limited, 2016), 73–87, and Keesing's Contemporary Archives research report 9 (1971), 108, for Bhutto's February 17 statement.

169 **In response to the** "Mujib strongly condemns firing—Bangladesh cannot be suppressed as colony any more"; see Mujibur Rahman, press statement, March 2, 1971, in Musa Sadik, ed., *Bangladesh Wins Freedom* (Dhaka: Mowla, 2009), 115–17.

169 **In Dacca, one million** Estimates of the crowd size reach as high as two million. See Asif Muztaba Hassan, "What makes the 7th March speech one of the best?," *Daily Star*, March 7, 2021.

170 **"My brothers"** The full text of Mujib's March 7 speech is available from UNESCO's Memory of the World International Register, and audio is available on YouTube at https://www.youtube.com/watch?v=ZsQfqlkayJ4.

27: HAFIZ UDDIN AHMAD

172 **As far as the West Pakistan** The entirety of this chapter comes from author interviews with Hafiz, August 2019, with clarifications made to the text over the following years.

28: TIKKA KHAN

175 **As choruses of *Joi Bangla!*** Khadim Hussain Raja, *A Stranger in My Own Country: East Pakistan 1969–1971* (Karachi: Oxford University Press, 2012), 64.

175 **Unaware of the passenger's** Siddiq Salik, *Witness to Surrender* (Karachi: Oxford University Press, 2nd edition, 1997), 46.

176 **He begged Yahya not** Raja, *A Stranger in My Own Country*, 56–57.

176 **For the sake of appearances** Ibid.; Salik, *Witness to Surrender*, 50–51.

176 **The governor penned** Muntassir Mamoon, *The Vanquished Generals and the Liberation War of Bangladesh* (Dhaka: Somoy, 2000), 66.

176 **"We cannot let it"** "Press Conference," *Pakistan Observer*, March 2, 1971.

176 **Tikka rushed from the Dacca airport** Details of Tikka's arrival and first full day of quotes in Salik, *Witness to Surrender*, 50–56, unless otherwise noted.

177 **"The Awami League has"** Mamoon, *The Vanquished Generals*, 67, 154.

178 **"I want the land"** International Crimes Tribunal, ICT-BD Case No. 06 OF 2011 ICT-1 (Dhaka: International Crimes Tribunal, Old High Court Building, Government of Bangladesh, 2011), 48, Point 78.

178 **The ecstatic president ordered** Salik, *Witness to Surrender*, 59–60, notes that Yahya tells Tikka twice to prepare, once on March 7 and again on March 17.

29: HAFIZ UDDIN AHMAD

179 **His team's loss** All events in this chapter come from Hafiz Uddin Ahmed, *Bloodshed '71* (Dhaka: Shahitto Prokash Books, 1997), and author interviews with Hafiz and T.J. (Abul Hasmem).

183 **That brutal sixteen-day** Higgins, David R., *M48 Patton vs Centurion: Indo-Pakistan War 1965* (Oxford: Osprey Publishing, 2016).

30: YAHYA KHAN, TIKKA KHAN, SHEIKH MUJIBUR RAHMAN, AND ZULFIKAR ALI BHUTTO

185 **"YAYHA IS WELCOME"** Siddiq Salik, *Witness to Surrender* (Karachi: Oxford University Press, 2nd edition, 1997), 60.

185 **He twisted the paper** This particular action is based on Yahya's customary reaction to similar slights.

185 **And in the car behind** Khadim Hussain Raja, *A Stranger in My Own Country: East Pakistan 1969–1971* (Karachi: Oxford University Press, 2012), 22–23.

185 **"The abuses hurled"** General (Ret'd) Agha Muhammad Yahya Khan, affidavit to the Lahore High Court at Lahore, re: Writ Petition No. 1649 (Lahore: Lahore High Court, 1974), Point 26.

186 **It was the flag** Archer Blood, *The Cruel Birth of Bangladesh: Memoirs of an American Diplomat* (Dhaka: University Press Limited, 2002), 189.

186 **Yahya thought it looked** Malcolm W. Browne, "New Separatist Demands Threaten Ailing Pakistan," *New York Times*, February 27, 1972. See also Gary J. Bass, *The Blood Telegram: Nixon, Kissinger, and a Forgotten Genocide* (New York: Vintage, 2014), 33–35.

186 **The motorcade lurched down** Muntassir Mamoon, *The Vanquished Generals and the Liberation War of Bangladesh* (Dhaka: Somoy, 2000), 133.

186 **Even when they pulled** Nuran Nabi and Mush Nabi, *Bullets of '71: A Freedom Fighter's Story* (Dhaka: Shahitya Prakash, 2012), 160.

186 **One perplexed adviser said** Siddiq Salik, *Witness to Surrender* (Karachi: Oxford University Press, 2nd edition, 1997), 60.

186 **That night at headquarters** Several details of this meeting taken from Khan, affidavit to the Lahore High Court, Point 27.

186 **"The bastard is not"** Salik, *Witness to Surrender*, 62.

186 **He drew a map** Khan, affidavit to the Lahore High Court, 46, Points 27 and 28.

186 **He circled the entrance** Blood, *The Cruel Birth of Bangladesh*, 199.

187 **"You can get ready"** Salik, *Witness to Surrender*, 62.

187 **Yahya fired the commander** Faruq Aziz Khan, *Spring 1971* (Dhaka: Agamee Prakashani, 2014), 69.

187 **He briefed the command** Kamal Hossain, *Bangladesh: Quest for Freedom and Justice* (Dhaka: University Press Limited, 2013), 100–101.

187 **Bhutto told Mujib that** Zufikar Ali Bhutto, *The Great Tragedy* (Islamabad: PPP Publications, 1971), 31.

187 **Bhutto politely declined Mujib's** Raja, *A Stranger in My Own Country*, 72.

187 **Bhutto's plane made** Bhutto, *The Great Tragedy*, 35.

188 **But unlike Tikka and Yahya** Khan, affidavit to the Lahore High Court, Point 13.

188 **Yahya would later yell** Ibid.

188 **Employees and guests jeered** Bhutto, *The Great Tragedy*, 35–36.

188 **It vanished once Bhutto** Nabi and Nabi, *Bullets of '71*, 160.

188 **Up in the room** Henry Bradsher, "East Pakistan in Agony after the Storm," *Evening Star* (March 1971): 28–29.

188 **There would be no** Salik, *Witness to Surrender*, 63.

188 **The next day** Ibid., 68.

189 **"I'm here to reach"** Oriana Fallaci, *Interview with History* (Rome: Rizzoli/Liveright, 1976), 9.

189 **Bhutto interjected, annoyed** Ibid., 9.

189 **"If you refuse"** Salik, *Witness to Surrender*, 39.

189 **Yahya ran through** Hossain, *Bangladesh*, 91–102.

189 **Mujib bit the tip** Pierre Bois, "Interview with Yahya Khan," *Le Figaro*, September 8, 1971.

189 **He needed to get** G. W. Chaudhary, *The Last Days of United Pakistan* (London: Hurst, 1974), 165.

189 **"Mujib, my friend!"** About the details and conversation of this meeting, Bhutto and Yahya mostly align in their own written accounts; see Bhutto, *The Great Tragedy*, 36–39, and Khan, affidavit to the Lahore High Court, Point 17.

190 **He agreed to keep** Hamoodur Rahman Commission, "Hamoodur Rahman Commission Report," Government of Pakistan, unpublished report, 1972, 63.

190 **He complained that** Fallaci, *Interview with History*, 10.

190 **Kept waiting for so long** All details from this paragraph are from Salik, *Witness to Surrender*, 67, unless otherwise noted.

190 **The Soviet consulate** Blood, *The Cruel Birth of Bangladesh*, 192.

190 **Mujib awoke on the** B. A. R. Siddiqi, *East Pakistan: Endgame*, 69–71.

191 **"It is tonight"** Salik, *Witness to Surrender*, 71.

191 **"Let's give them"** Siddiqi, *East Pakistan: Endgame*, 40.

191 **"Very well!"** Bois, "Interview with Yahya Khan."

192 **As the sun set** Salik, *Witness to Surrender*, 72.

192 **Months of secret planning** Raja, *A Stranger in My Own Country*, 80.

192 **He rounded up the** Khan, *Spring 1971*, 33.

192 **Mujib was still** Hossain, *Bangladesh*, 103.

192 **A single unmarked plane** Khan, *Spring 1971*, 46.

192 **He called Mujib** Robert Payne, *Massacre* (New York: Macmillan, 1973), 25.

192 **The spy said Yahya** Salik, *Witness to Surrender*, 69–70.

192 **Bhutto feigned surprise** Payne, *Massacre*, 26; Khan, *Spring 1971*, 47.

193 **"The 75 million people"** For the full text of Mujib's radio address, along with an analysis, see Mashuqur Rahman and Mahbubur Rahman Jalal, "Swadhin Bangla Betar Kendro and Bangladesh's Declaration of Independence," *Daily Star*, November 25, 2014. Also see Chaudhury, *The Last Days of United Pakistan*, 186.

193 **Then he turned off** Sadik Musa, "I Arrested Sheikh Mujibur Rahman for His Declaration of Independence," in *Bangladesh Wins Freedom* (Dhaka: Agamee Prakashani, 2000), 44.

31: CANDY ROHDE AND JON ROHDE

194 **It felt like a giant** The Operation Searchlight scene and conversations in this chapter are from details given in Cornelia Rohde, *Catalyst: In the Wake of the*

Great Bhola Cyclone (Scotts Valley, CA: CreateSpace Independent Publishing Platform, 2014), 292–300, and author interview with Jon Rohde, unless otherwise noted.

195 **It was too anguished** This is a partial composite as Jon didn't remember this specific scream, but others who lived in the neighborhood recounted similar events (for example, author interview with Stephen C. Baldwin).

197 **The moon and stars** Siddiq Salik, *Witness to Surrender* (Karachi: Oxford University Press, 2nd edition, 1997), 76.

32: YAHYA KHAN AND TIKKA KHAN

198 **On their way out** Muntassir Mamoon, *2002. Media and the Liberation War of Bangladesh*, Vol. 2 (Dhaka: Centre for Bangladesh Studies), 149.

198 **As field general** Robert Payne, *Massacre* (New York: Macmillan, 1973), 45.

198 **An Awami League spy** As in Musa Sadik, ed., *Bangladesh Wins Freedom* (Dhaka: Agamee Prakashani, 2000), 150–54. The military communication that follows is abridged and edited for clarity from the longer verbatim transcript. In addition, code words and some military slang have been replaced with more specific and direct language for clarity.

199 **He even sent up** Archer Blood, *The Cruel Birth of Bangladesh: Memoirs of an American Diplomat* (Dhaka: University Press Limited, 2002), 283–84.

199 **Mujib was just so** General (Ret'd) Agha Muhammad Yahya Khan, affidavit to the Lahore High Court at Lahore, re: Writ Petition No. 1649 (Lahore: Lahore High Court, 1974), Point 18.

200 **It took army rocket** Siddiq Salik, *Witness to Surrender* (Karachi: Oxford University Press, 2nd edition, 1997), 75.

200 **Even Yahya's press secretary** B. A. R. Siddiqi, *East Pakistan: The Endgame*), 111.

200 **Yahya was pretty sure** Salik, *Witness to Surrender*, 75–76.

200 **Four soldiers handcuffed Mujib** Payne, *Massacre*, 26.

201 **An American Chaffee tank** Simon Dring, "How Dacca Paid for a United Pakistan," *Daily Telegraph*, March 30, 1971. Also Payne, *Massacre*, 16.

201 **They gunned him down** Payne, *Massacre*, 17.

201 **Throughout the executions** Willem van Schendel, *A History of Bangladesh* (Cambridge: Cambridge University Press, 2009), 162; Gary J. Bass, *The Blood Telegram: Nixon, Kissinger, and a Forgotten Genocide* (New York: Vintage, 2014), 135.

202 **Tikka emptied out the** Anthony Mascarenhas, "Genocide," *Sunday Times*, Special Edition, June 13, 1971.

202 **Another unit raided** Musa, ed., "Genocide in Dhaka: A Tragic Episode in Human History," in *Bangladesh Wins Freedom*, 160.

202 **Tanks surrounded the hotel** Oriana Fallaci, *Interview with History* (Rome: Rizzoli/Liveright, 1976), 4, 11.

202 **The captain in charge** Payne, *Massacre*, 21.

202 **Snacking on room-service** Details of the scene of Bhutto at the InterContinental are from Fallaci, *Interview with History*; Zufikar Ali Bhutto, *The Great Tragedy* (Islamabad: PPP Publications, 1971), 42; Mamoon, *Media and the Liberation War of Bangladesh*, 26; and author interview with Ali Ahmed Ziauddin.

203 **A couple hours** Salik, *Witness to Surrender*, 77.

203 **A colonel confided that** Siddiqi, *East Pakistan: The Endgame*, 91, 110.

203 **Much of the rank and file** Ibid., 97.

203 **One officer announced** Salik, *Witness to Surrender*, 78.

203 **One man bragged** Schendel, *A History of Bangladesh*, 163.

203 **Platoons of heavily armed** Blood, *The Cruel Birth of Bangladesh*, 198.

204 **In the first twelve hours** Hamoodur Rahman Commission, "Hamoodur Rahman Commission Report," Government of Pakistan, unpublished report, 1972, 33.

204 **Bhutto's own calculations** Fallaci, *Interview with History*, 6–7.

204 **The president had slept** Srinath Raghavan, *1971: A Global History of the Creation of Bangladesh* (Cambridge, MA: Harvard University Press, 2013), 186.

204 **Ever the admirer** Khan, affidavit to the Lahore High Court, 47, Point 29B.

204 **Just three** Blood, *The Cruel Birth of Bangladesh*, 199.

204 **The official story was** Siddiqi, *East Pakistan: The Endgame*, 101–3.

204 **Nixon wished Yahya well** Transcript of phone conversation between Nixon and Kissinger, March 29, 1971, US Department of State, Foreign Relations of the United States, FRUS E-7 Doc 1971, 35–36.

33: CANDY ROHDE AND JON ROHDE

205 **That same morning** All scenes in this chapter are from Cornelia Rohde, *Catalyst: In the Wake of the Great Bhola Cyclone* (Scotts Valley, CA: CreateSpace Independent Publishing Platform, 2014), 292–302, and author interview with Jon Rohde, unless otherwise specified.

205 **They traced the military's** See also Nuran Nabi and Mush Nabi, *Bullets of '71: A Freedom Fighter's Story* (Dhaka: Shahitya Prakash, 2012), 171.

206 **The couple dashed behind** Additional detail of street scenes from ibid., 173–74, which gives a similar eyewitness account of the razing of Shankar Bazaar, and from B. A. R. Siddiqi, *East Pakistan: The Endgame. An Onlooker's Journal, 1969–1971* (Karachi: Oxford University Press, 2005), 91–94.

207 **Down the road** David Loshak, *Pakistan Crisis* (London: Heinemann, 1971).

207 **He then heard** Archer Blood, *The Cruel Birth of Bangladesh: Memoirs of an American Diplomat* (Dhaka: University Press Limited, 2002), 205–6.

209 **"Any door that wasn't"** Rohde, *Catalyst*, 299.

209 **The faculty housing hosted** Stephen C. Baldwin, *Shadows Over Sundials: Dark and Light Life in a Large Outside World* (Online: iUniverse, 2009), 231–32.

210 **She insisted that they** This is a partial reconstruction, as Jon couldn't remember where exactly the needle was on the gauge but he did recollect that they didn't have much fuel left.

210 **But it was strongest** Baldwin, *Shadows Over Sundials*, 230.

210 **They fired indiscriminately** G. W. Chaudhary, *The Last Days of United Pakistan* (London: Hurst, 1974), 186, 184.

210 **By the time Candy and Jon** Author interview with Martha Chen.

210 **Then they poured gasoline** Dan Coggin, "Dacca: City of the Dead," *Time*, May 3, 1971.

210 **Bodies and half bodies** Author interview with Martha Chen.

213 **Pundits marveled at how** Siddiqi, *East Pakistan*, 114.

213 **As his voice rose** Syed Badrul Ahsan, "March 26, 1971 . . . and After," bcnews24.com, March 26, 2015.

213 **He scrambled jets to** Siddiqi, *East Pakistan*, 107, 118.

34: HAFIZ UDDIN AHMAD

214 **Hafiz and his men** Events in this chapter are from author interviews with Hafiz in 2018, as well as his memoir, *Bloodshed '71* (Dhaka: Shahitto Prokash Books, 1997), in which he relates the events in Jessore and which was translated from Bengali by the authors. Where there are discrepancies, the authors erred on the side of using the in-person transcripts. Most of the dialogue comes directly from *Bloodshed '71*, with only minor changes for clarity or to correct grammar. T.J. sat in on one of these interviews and helped fill in details from his own actions that day, supplemented by follow-up communications with the authors' research assistant Md. Reza Lenin.

219 **Today, whether he survived** T.J. offered a terse description of his tactics while firing from the culvert in author interview with T.J.

227 **"This is Swadhin Bangla"** Zia's declaration is technically the second of two radio broadcasts announcing Bangladesh's independence. "Bangabondhu Mujibur Rahman" is an honorific for Sheikh Mujib. See https://www.virtual bangladesh.com/the-basics/history-of-bangladesh/independence/history -war-independence/the-declaration-of-independence/.

35: CANDY ROHDE, JON ROHDE, AND RICHARD NIXON

228 **"Goddamnit, Henry!"** Archer Blood, *The Cruel Birth of Bangladesh: Memoirs of an American Diplomat* (Dhaka: University Press Limited, 2002), 213. See also Gary J. Bass, *The Blood Telegram: Nixon, Kissinger, and a Forgotten Genocide* (New York: Vintage, 2014).

228 **Kissinger reminded Nixon** details from the following two paragraphs from Henry Kissinger, *White House Years* (New York: Simon and Schuster, 2nd edition, 2011), 1513–514. Archer Blood, *The Cruel Birth of Bangladesh: Memoirs of an American Diplomat* (Dhaka: University Press Limited, 2002), 211–15. Also see Gary J. Bass, *The Blood Telegram: Nixon, Kissinger, and a Forgotten Genocide* (New York: Vintage, 2014), Chapter 4, "Selective Genocide" subheading for further discussion.

228 **they'd pretend** Gary J. Bass, *The Blood Telegram*, 83–87, 103–112.

228 **Then they'd find some** Henry Kissinger, *White House Years* (New York: Simon and Schuster, 2nd edition, 2011), 1513–514.

228 **For his part** Letter from Zhou Enlai to Yahya Khan, in *Pakistan Horizon* no. 2 (1971): 153–54. See also M. Ali, "China's Diplomacy During the Indo-Pakistan Par, 1971–72," *Pakistan Horizon* 25 no. 1 (1972): 53–62.

229 **Yeager thought it was** Blood, *The Cruel Birth of Bangladesh*, 288.

229 **Jon watched from his** All details about the Rohdes in this chapter are from Cornelia Rohde, *Catalyst: In the Wake of the Great Bhola Cyclone* (Scotts Valley, CA: CreateSpace Independent Publishing Platform, 2014), 292–302, and author interview with Jon Rohde, unless otherwise specified.

230 **Nobody was willing to risk** Blood, *The Cruel Birth of Bangladesh*, 201.

231 **He crumpled up the** Stephen C. Baldwin, *Shadows Over Sundials: Dark and Light Life in a Large Outside World* (Online: iUniverse, 2009), 232.

231 **No one got to leave** Author interview with Martha Chen.

232 **A massive lightning storm** Ibid.

232 **Guards rushed them into** Blood, *The Cruel Birth of Bangladesh*, 234–35.

232 **Jon, Candy, Marty, and** Ibid., 234–41, and author interview with Martha Chen.

233 **When they landed six** Author interview with Martha Chen.

233 **The ambassador and his wife** Ibid.

233 **"It's too late now"** Jon Rohde, "Women in the Bangladesh Liberation Struggle," in A. M. A. Muhith, ed., *American Response to Bangladesh Liberation War* (Dhaka: University Press Limited, 1996), 453.

234 **All around the pool** Author interview with Martha Chen.

234 **"The law of the jungle"** The letter was read on May 11, 1971, into the Record of the U.S Senate, and titled "Recent Events in East Pakistan."

234 **Disturbed, Kissinger told** Bass, *The Blood Telegram*, 117.

234 **She packed the letter** Jon Rohde, "Women in the Bangladesh Liberation Struggle."

36: MOHAMMAD HAI

236 **Nine men grunted softly** Details in this chapter are from author interviews with Hai, unless otherwise noted.

237 **Malik had an uncle** Author interview with Abdul Latif.

237 **Eventually, Malik convinced his** Author interview with Malik, November 2019.

238 **and the chairman's son** For an extensive discussion of the graft committed by him and his cronies (and HELP's eventual recognition of this), see Cornelia Rohde, *Catalyst*, 328–40.

238 **The city was a pastiche** Author interview with Ziauddin.

240 **Then he heard something** This conversation is reconstructed from author interview with Hai. Details of the fund-raising and planning come from author interview with Malik, who remembered the details of this time better than Hai did.

240 **With more troops landing** Shamsul Bari, "News from Inside Bangladesh," in Bari (ed), *Bangladesh War of Independence: Documents (Part IV)–Mujibnagar: Activities of Expatriate Bengalis*. Dhaka: Government of Bangladesh 22.

243 **The teen posse sat** Hai recalls singing the anthem. Anthem lyrics as translated in B. A. R. Siddiqi, *East Pakistan: The Endgame. An Onlooker's Journal, 1969–1971* (Karachi: Oxford University Press, 2005), 146.

37: YAHYA KHAN, TIKKA KHAN, AND A. A. K. NIAZI

244 **Muddy tire tracks** Archer Blood, *The Cruel Birth of Bangladesh: Memoirs of an American Diplomat* (Dhaka: University Press Limited, 2002), 282–83; and Associated Press file footage of Tikka's swearing-in available at https://www.youtube.com/watch?v=_p6ivAV6HGo.

244 **It made him feel** Robert Payne, *Massacre* (New York: Macmillan, 1973), 44.

244 **Only the Chinese delegation** Blood, *The Cruel Birth of Bangladesh*, 283.

245 **The judge signed the handover** "Bangladesh Leader Says 15,000 Pak Soldiers Killed Since March 25," *Statesman*, May 16, 1971.

245 **The dozen drivers** Blood, *The Cruel Birth of Bangladesh*, 283.

245 **The policy said that** Malcolm Browne, "Pakistanis Will Impose Collective Fines in East," *New York Times*, November 10, 1971.

245 **In a speech to promote** "Tikka Kahn's Appeal," *Dawn*, April 19, 1971.

246 **The Associated Press reported** "West Pakistan Hits Rebels," Associated Press, April 11, 1971.

246 **But the *New York Times*** Benjamin Welles, "U.S. Continues Aid to Pakistan Army," *New York Times*, April 10 1971, A1.

246 **Bhutto remained a loyal** Zufikar Ali Bhutto, *The Great Tragedy* (Islamabad: PPP Publications, 1971), 43.

246 **They told *Time* magazine** Dan Coggin, "Pakistan: Round 1 to the West," *Time*, April 12, 1971, pp. 23–24.

246 **Tikka joined in** Muntassir Mamoon, *Media and the Liberation War of Bangladesh*, 158.

246 **Yahya and Bhutto started** Oriana Fallaci, *Interview with History* (Rome: Rizzoli/Liveright, 1976), 8.

246 **"All Normal in the East"** Coggin, "Pakistan: Round 1 to the West."

246 **"LIQUIDATED"** Willem van Schendel, *A History of Bangladesh* (Cambridge: Cambridge University Press, 2009), 168.

246 **Yahya promised that he** "Interview with Yahya Khan," Associated Press, 1971 [exact date unknown], available at https://www.youtube.com/watch?v= GjNEaH-bYQ0.

247 **Yahya preached about how** Mamoon, *Media and the Liberation War of Bangladesh*, 25, 27.

247 **If he could make** F. S. Aijazuddin, *From a Head, Through a Head, to a Head: The Secret Channel Between the US and China Through Pakistan* (Karachi: Oxford University Press, 2000), 61.

247 **Mao thanked Yahya** Henry Kissinger, *White House Years* (New York: Simon and Schuster, 2nd edition, 2011), 1270, 1278.

247 **Nixon even told Yahya** Aijazuddin, *From a Head, Through a Head, to a Head*, 58.

248 **Yahya liked Tikka** Faruq Aziz Khan, *Spring 1971* (Dhaka: Agamee Prakashani, 2014), 95.

248 **Only a few weeks** Author interview with Shuja Nawaz.

248 **Yahya ran through the** Mamoon, *The Vanquished Generals and the Liberation War of Bangladesh* (Dhaka: Somoy, 2000), 59.

248 **He was a real** B. Samir Bhattacharya, *Nothing But!* (New Delhi: Partridge, 2014).

248 **Everyone called him** A. A. K. Niazi, *The Betrayal of East Pakistan* (Karachi: Oxford University Press, 1988); see also "Lieutenant-General A. A. K. Niazi" (obituary), *Times* (London), March 11, 2004.

248 **He had a reputation** Mamoon, *The Vanquished Generals*, 59.

249 **Niazi, sharply dressed** B. A. R.Siddiqi, *East Pakistan: The Endgame*, 126–

27. Other details in Hassan Abbas, *Pakistan's Drift into Extremism: Allah, the Army, and America's War on Terror* (New York: Routledge, 2004), 67–75.

249 **"Hey, don't worry"** Khadim Hussain Raja, *A Stranger in My Own Country: East Pakistan 1969–1971* (Karachi: Oxford University Press, 2012), 97–99, and other details from Siddiqi, *East Pakistan* and Abbas, *Pakistan's Drift into Extremism*.

249 **I am here to change"** Mamoon, *The Vanquished Generals*, 86–87; Rao Farman Ali Khan, *How Pakistan Got Divided* (Karachi: Oxford University Press, 2017); and Raja, *A Stranger in My Own Country*, 98.

249 **"You have made the"** Ian Cardozo, ed., *In Quest of Freedom: The War of 1971* (New Delhi: Bloomsbury, 2016), 53–55.

249 **Niazi stood in one** Blood, *The Cruel Birth of Bangladesh*, 309, 328.

249 **"What have I been"** The quote and details in this paragraph from Hamoodur Rahman Commission, "Hamoodur Rahman Commission Report," Government of Pakistan, unpublished report, 1972, 13–14.

250 **The Tiger glared back** Raja, *A Stranger in My Own Country*, 98.

250 **He said it was** Ian Cardozo, ed., *In Quest of Freedom: The War of 1971* (New Delhi: Bloomsbury, 2016), 56.

250 **"What was your score"** Siddiqi, *East Pakistan: The Endgame*, 167.

250 **He wrote orders to** Hamoodur Rahman Commission, 27.

250 **Nor could anyone else** Siddiq Salik, *Witness to Surrender* (Karachi: Oxford University Press, 2nd edition, 1997), 92.

250 **The army rarely found** Ibid., 94–95.

250 **"You do not go"** Malcolm Browne, "Bengalis Depict How a Priest Died," *New York Times*, May 9, 1971.

251 **Some girls were as** Bangladesh Liberation War Museum. See also Musa Sadik, ed., *Bangladesh Wins Freedom* (Dhaka: Agamee Prakashani, 2000), 168–69; Muntassir Mamoon, *Birangona 1971: Saga of the Violated Women* (Dhaka: Journeyman, 2019).

251 **He claimed it was** Shamsul Bari, "Death and Terror Reign in Bangladesh," *Daily Star*, March 27, 2001, 90–91.

251 **Bhutto told the Italian** Fallaci, *Interview with History*, 5.

251 **Niazi said that the** Mamoon, *Birangona 1971*, 70.

251 **Later studies estimated that** See Ahmed Ziauddin, "The Case of Bangladesh: Bringing to Trial the Perpetrators of the 1971 Genocide," in *Contemporary Genocides: Causes, Cases, Consequences*, ed. Albert J. Longman (Leiden: PIOOM, 1996), 99, 100. The researcher Sarmila Bose, in "Losing the Victims: Problems of Using Women as Weapons in Recounting the Bangladesh War," *Economic and Political Weekly* 42, no. 38 (2007): 3864–871, disputes

higher-end figures given the number of Pakistani troops in the country and the possible desire of the Bangladesh government to inflate figures.

251 **Tikka opened an extermination** Payne, *Massacre*, 55.

252 **They all shared the** Anthony Mascarenhas, "Genocide," *Sunday Times*, Special Edition, June 13, 1971; International Commission of Jurists, "The Events in East Pakistan, 1971 (1972): A Legal Study by the Secretariat of the International Commission of Jurists" (Geneva: ICJ, 1972).

252 **Yahya gave a few** Payne, *Massacre*, 57.

252 **For example, the trains** Ibid., 56.

38: HAFIZ UDDIN AHMAD AND MOHAMMAD HAI

253 **Call it mutiny** Hafiz's accounts in this chapter from Hafiz Uddin Ahmad, *Bloodshed '71* (Dhaka: Shahitto Prokash Books, 1997) and from author interviews with Hafiz.

253 **The Bengalis didn't last** Muhammad Nurul Huda, "Bangladesh Police in Liberation War," *Daily Star*, December 16, 2019.

254 **Word eventually leaked out** It wouldn't be until after the Liberation War that Hafiz would learn that the Pakistanis spared some officers' lives at Jessore. Jalil was arrested during the war, but survived.

256 **About two hundred miles** Accounts in this chapter come from author interviews with Hai, Malik, and Abdul Latif.

261 **"What is this?"** Neither Hai nor Latif remember much about the exact details of this exchange, though they remember the gist of what they talked about.

39: CANDY ROHDE

263 **"Why are they so"** Material about the Rohdes in this chapter is from Jon Rohde, "Women in the Bangladesh Liberation Struggle," in A. M. A. Muhith, ed., *American Response to Bangladesh Liberation War* (Dhaka: University Press Limited, 1996), 453–55; Kaiser Zaman, "The Bangladesh Information Center in Washington: Reminiscence of a Refugee," also in Muhith, 428–30; David Nalin, "Twenty-Five Years After the Emergence of Bangladesh: An American Reminiscence," also in Muhith, 446–49; Cornelia Rohde, "View of US Citizen Action in Support of the Bangladesh Liberation War," also in Muhith, 449–53, and Samuel Jaffe, "An Internal Matter," in *The United States, Grassroots Activism, and the Creation of Bangladesh* (Dhaka: University Press Limited, 2021); and author interview with Jon Rohde, unless otherwise cited.

265 **With Nixon preventing** Author interview with Samuel Jaffe, August 2020.

267 **Candy overlooked the slight** Archer Blood, *The Cruel Birth of Bangladesh: Memoirs of an American Diplomat* (Dhaka: University Press Limited, 2002), 329–31.

268 **The horrified team wrote** Editors, "Chronology: June–August 1971," *Pakistan Horizon* 24, no. 3 (1971): 70–110.

269 **Hilaly managed the details** U.S. State Department "Foreign Relations of the United States 1969–1976 (E-7), Washington, June 17, 1970, 7:30 p.m. Also see F. S. Aijazuddin, *From a Head, Through a Head, to a Head: The Secret Channel Between the US and China Through Pakistan* (Karachi: Oxford University Press, 2000), and Arif Yousuf, "BLOCKADE: A Guide to Nonviolent Intervention (based on a book by Richard Taylor), Dhaka, DW Productions, 2016.

269 **The story ran the** Tad Szule, "U.S. Military Goods Sent to Pakistan Despite Ban," *New York Times*, June 22, 1971, A1.

269 **Kennedy yelled at everyone** Tad Szule, "Kennedy Reports on Pakistan Arms," *New York Times*, June 23, 1971, A8.

270 **Minutes passed before Kissinger** Richard M. Nixon, *In the Arena: A Memoir of Victory, Defeat, and Renewal* (New York: Simon and Schuster, 1990), 16; Gary J. Bass, *The Blood Telegram: Nixon, Kissinger, and a Forgotten Genocide* (New York: Vintage, 2014), 159. Additional details extrapolated from Nixon's and Kissinger's recounting of the event.

270 **They tried not to** Details about the room are from ABC News, "A Look Inside the Nixon Oval Office," available at https://abcnews.go.com/Politics /video/inside-nixon-oval-office-42789931.

270 **A Pakistani foreign service** Aijazuddin, *From a Head, Through a Head, to a Head*, 78, note 38.

270 **Nixon made one demand** Ibid., 69, and Henry Kissinger, *White House Years* (New York: Simon and Schuster, 2nd edition, 2011), 1290–291.

270 **"This is the most important"** Richard Nixon, *RN: The Memoirs of Richard Nixon* (New York: Simon and Schuster, 2nd edition, 1990), 551–52, and ibid., 727.

271 **Jon never felt more** Author interview with Jon Rohde, July 2020.

272 **They trudged past babies** Dan Coggin, "The Bengali Refugees: A Surfeit of Woe," *Time*, June 21, 1971.

40: YAHYA KHAN AND HENRY KISSINGER

273 **Squatting on a luxurious** Henry Kissinger, *White House Years* (New York: Simon and Schuster, 2nd edition, 2011), 1312–313.

273 **"That Bitch."** Gary J. Bass, *The Blood Telegram: Nixon, Kissinger, and a For-*

gotten Genocide (New York: Vintage, 2014), 252, 255. Gandhi's state dinner was the most likely, although not guaranteed, source of the bug.

274 **"The heat of Islamabad"** Henry Kissinger, *White House Years* (New York: Simon and Schuster, 2nd edition, 2011), 1315. See 'Note on Sources' with regards to the veracity of Kissinger's memory and memoirs.

275 **"I don't know"** Ibid., 1526–527.

275 **He excused himself** Additional details from this scene provided in ibid.

275 **A red VW Beetle** F. S. Aijzuddin, *From a Head, Through a Head, to a Head: The Secret Channel Between the US and China Through Pakistan* (Karachi: Oxford University Press, 2000), 111. The driver, Sultan Khan, says it was a red VW Beetle, confirmed by a crew member of the 707; see Abdul Hayee, "A Secret VVIP Flight: 48 Hours That Changed the World," original publication unknown, but available at https://historyofpia.com/forums/viewtopic.php?t=19137. Kissinger, in *White House Years*, 1315, said it was a blue Datsun, but in another book he said that it was a military convoy.

275 **He contorted himself** Aijazuddin, *From a Head, Through a Head, to a Head*, 96.

275 **All radio traffic** Ibid., 111. Additional airport details from Kissinger, *White House Years*, 1314–317.

276 **The car rolled** Hayee, "A Secret VVIP Flight."

276 **Once inside the plane** Aijazuddin, *From a Head, Through a Head, to a Head*, 85.

276 **They whipped out their** Ibid., 108; see also see John H. Holdridge, *Crossing the Divide: An Insider's Account of Normalization of U.S.-China Relations.* The ADST-DACOR Diplomats and Diplomacy series. Lanham, MD: Rowman and Littlefield, 1997, 53.

276 **He had never touched** Aijazuddin, *From a Head, Through a Head, to a Head*, 90.

277 **The cranes and swans** Dan Coggin, "Pakistan: The Ravaging of Golden Bengal," *Time*, August 2, 1971.

277 **Without an opposition party** Salik, Siddiq, *Witness to Surrender.* Karachi: Oxford University Press, 1977, 107.

277 **Half the guests were** Details of this event are abridged and consolidated from accounts of typical Yahya parties from this period, as detailed most extensively in Dewan Berindranath, *Private Life of Yahya Khan* (New Delhi: Sterling, 1974), 60–68; Salik, ibid., 107; Abbas, *Pakistan's Drift Into Extremism: Allah, then Army, and America's War Terror*, 66–69 (Abbas uses the nickname "Black Pearl" instead, calling her as Shamim), Government of Pakistan, "The Report of the Commission of Inquiry-1971 War as Declassified by the Government of Pakistan" (Karachi: Dawn, 2003), and Muntas-

sir Mamoon, *The Vanquished Generals and the Liberation War of Bangladesh* (Dhaka: Somoy, 2000), 119. Details on Mrs. Hussain are sparse and occasionally conflicting, but all sources describe a similar narrative. It is a matter of dispute how much Yahya was indeed in love with Mrs. Hussain, a fact that Yahya's supporters and detractors had clear reason to promote or downplay. Some reports say they first met in 1969, others in 1970, others in 1971. Regardless, Yahya's own actions and documented physical time with her indicate that he was at the very least deeply infatuated with her during this time period.

278   **The only hiccup that** Aijazuddin, *From a Head, Through a Head, to a Head*, 112.

278   **He was grinning from** Kissinger, *White House Years*, 1341–343.

279   **Kissinger called it one** Ibid., 1323.

279   **And Yahya got his** US Department of State, Foreign Relations of the United States, Volume XVII (China) document #143, undated.

279   **"I shall always remember"** Aijazuddin, *From a Head, Through a Head, to a Head*, 119.

280   **Kissinger later said it** Kissinger, *White House Years*, 1313.

41: HAFIZ UDDIN AHMAD

281   **Hafiz flexed his bare** This chapter combines scenes in Hafiz Uddin Ahmad's memoir, *Bloodshed '71* (Dhaka: Shahitto Prokash Books, 1997), with his recollections in author interview in 2019.

281   **Hafiz and a handful** Force strength and the battle chronology also appears in the Wikipedia article "Defense of Kamlapur" and in an exhibit at the Liberation War Museum in Dhaka.

MUSICAL INTERLUDE: RAVI SHANKAR, GEORGE HARRISON, RICHARD NIXON, AND HENRY KISSINGER

287   **Surrounded by marigolds** Color in this section from the video release of *The Concert for Bangladesh*, Apple Records, 1971; Don Heckman, "The Event Wound Up as a Love Feast," *Village Voice*, August 5, 1971; Editors, "The George Harrison Bangla Desh Benefit," *Rolling Stone*, September 2, 1971. There were actually two shows on August 1. Most of the material in this chapter refers to the first show, in the afternoon.

287   **He smirked like he** Randy Lewis, "Ravi Shankar Got by with a Little Help from His Friends," *Los Angeles Times*, December 12, 2012.

287   **"If you appreciate the"** *Concert for Bangladesh*.

288   **Two months earlier** Steve Van Zandt, "With a Little Help from His Friends:

George Harrison and the Concert for Bangla-Desh," *TeachRock*, May 2011.

288 **But Harrison was different** Details in this paragraph from Gary Tillery, *Working Class Mystic: A Spiritual Biography of George Harrison* (Wheaton, IL: Quest, 2011).

289 **The moment Harrison heard** Belmo (Scott Belmer), *George Harrison: His Words, Wit & Wisdom* (New York: Belmo Publishing, 2002), 24.

289 **When Shankar listened to** Al Weisel, "Ravi Shankar on His Pal George Harrison and 'Chants of India,'" *Rolling Stone*, May 15, 1997.

289 **"George, this is the situation"** Jann Wenner, "George Harrison's Bangladesh Concert," *Rolling Stone*, September 2, 1971, and Ravi Shankar, *Raga Mala* (New York: Genesis, 1997).

289 **Shankar mailed Harrison** Shankar, *Raga Mala*, 220.

289 **Harrison sat back** Details of this exchange in Tillery, *Working Class Mystic*, chapter 9.

290 **Bob Dylan was Harrison's** Harvey Kubernik, "Celebrating the 100th Birthday of Indian Music Legend Ravi Shankar," *Music Connection*, March 2, 2020.

290 **And Eric Clapton was** Tillery, *Working Class Mystic*, chapter 8, and Eric Clapton, *Clapton: The Autobiography* (New York: Broadway, 2008), 135.

290 **Harrison hired an Indian** Pattie Boyd, *Wonderful Tonight: George Harrison, Eric Clapton, and Me* (New York: Crown, 2008), 174.

290 **Behind them, 19,500** Heckman, "The Event Wound Up as a Love Feast."

290 **Thousands of screaming fans** Editors, "The George Harrison Bangla Desh Benefit"; ibid.

290 **The cord got wrapped** Kubernik, "Celebrating the 100th Birthday of Indian Music Legend Ravi Shankar."

291 **Clapton wedged his lit** *Concert for Bangladesh.*

291 **Clapton later said he** Clapton, *Clapton: The Autobiography*, 137.

291 **He'd just biked into** Van Zandt, "With a Little Help from His Friends."

291 **West Pakistan imprisoned** The initiative was called Operation Omega; see more at https://en.wikipedia.org/wiki/Operation_Omega.

291 **A Dutch man stole** "Vermeer Thefts: 1971—The Love Letter," *Daily Star*, 2015.

291 **Children in thirty thousand** Shamsul Bari, "Fast a Day to Save a People," *Bangladesh Newsletter* (1972): 121.

292 **Activists built a refugee** Shamsul Bari, "Bangladesh Refugee Camp at the United Nations," *Bangladesh Newsletter* (1972): 134–35.

292 **Nevertheless, the French Red Cross** Sajjad "Salute to John Kay," In Sajjad (ed.), *Liberation*, 32–35.

292 **"This will always be"** *The Concert for Bangladesh Revisited with George Harrison and Friends*, directed by Claire Ferguson (Apple Corps, 2005).

292 **Shankar agreed** Ibid.

292 **At the after party** Graeme Thomson, "How George Harrison Staged One of the Most Influential Concerts in History," *GQ*, February 25, 2021.

292 **Transcripts of their conversations** This conversation is abridged and condensed from three different conversations that Nixon and Kissinger had on the topic over two days in August 1971, beginning at 9:20 a.m. on August 2 at the Oval Office. The men famously wandered from topic to topic in their long talks (as anyone who has spent hours listening to the Nixon tapes can attest), so they are combined here for clarity. For additional details on the transcripts, see Gary J. Bass, *The Blood Telegram: Nixon, Kissinger, and a Forgotten Genocide* (New York: Vintage, 2014), 290, and Douglas Brinkley and Luke Nichter, *The Nixon Tapes: 1971–1972* (New York: Mariner, 2015), 381–87.

42: HAFIZ UDDIN AHMAD

297 **Hafiz blinked through** Details of Hafiz's recovery and trip to Calcutta are recounted in his memoir, Hafiz Uddin Ahmad, *Bloodshed '71* (Dhaka: Shahitto Prokash Books, 1997), as well as in author interviews.

299 **Now Zaker used his** Zaker is mentioned in Ahmad, *Bloodshed '71*. See also Ershad Kamol, "I read the last news announcing the victory on the eve of December 16, 1971—Aly Zaker," *Daily Star*, December 14, 2008.

300 **In the previous months** Rao Farman Ali Khan, *How Pakistan Got Divided* (Karachi: Oxford University Press, 2017), 100; and M. Rafiqul Islam, *A Tale of Millions: Bangladesh Liberation War, 1971* (Dhaka: Bangladesh Books International, 1981).

300 **India was building up** Gary J. Bass, *The Blood Telegram: Nixon, Kissinger, and a Forgotten Genocide* (New York: Vintage, 2014), 98–101.

300 **One man died** A. T. M. Abdul Wahab, *Mukti Bahini Wins Victory: Pak Military Oligarchy Divides Pakistan in 1971* (Dhaka: Columbia Prokashani, 2004), 352.

301 **Indira Gandhi warned Nixon** Oriana Fallaci, "Interview with Indira Gandhi," in *Interviews with History and Conversations with Power* (New York: Rizzoli, 2011), 262–86.

43: MOHAMMAD HAI

303 **"On the ground"** All material in this chapter is from author interviews with Hai, unless otherwise noted, and is cross-referenced with interviews with other eyewitnesses.

304 **He was one of ten teens** Author interview with Malik.

304 **Now Malik imparted** Ibid.

304 **On the way to town** Ibid.

305 **The next morning he** Author interview with Latif.

306 **It might have started** Author interview with Malik.

44: CANDY ROHDE AND JON ROHDE

309 **One errant jerk of** Several former refugees and doctors working in the camps described lines of refugees holding their deceased babies and the ration-card exchange in author interviews, including Nayeem Wada and the then-head of OxFam Julian Francis, among others.

309 **Salt Lake, an impromptu** Julian Francis, "Remembering the 1971 Refugees," *Dhaka Tribune*, June 20, 2016.

309 **For months now** Dan Coggin, "Pakistan: The Ravaging of Golden Bengal," *Time*, August 2, 1971.

309 **Most all were barefoot** Ibid.

310 **Vultures and wild dogs** Dan Coggin, "The Bengali Refugees: A Surfeit of Woe," *Time*, June 21, 1971.

311 **Once she made it** Details from this paragraph provided by author interview with Julian Francis.

311 **Women who didn't have** Coggin, "The Bengali Refugees" and "Pakistan: The Ravaging of Golden Bengal."

311 **It rolled past** Julian Francis, "Dhaka Memories of 20 Years Ago and My Heart and Soul Touched by a Saint—Mother Teresa," bdnews24.com, September 5, 2017.

312 **He worked with American** Along with Jon's work and that of his colleagues, one comprehensive history of South Asian contributions to ORT is S. K. Bhattacharya, "History of Development of Oral Rehydration Therapy," *Indian Journal of Public Health* 38, no. 2 (1994): 39–43.

312 **Jon's task was to** Details in this and the following two paragraphs from author interview with Jon Rohde, July 2020.

313 **He made sure that** Cornelia Rohde, "View," in A. M. A. Muhith, *American Response to Bangladesh Liberation War* (Dhaka: University Press Limited, 1996), 454.

313 **He offered them** Details here and in the following two paragraphs from author interview with Jon Rohde, July 2020.

314 **She gave them curriculum** Cornelia Rohde, "View," 454; and ibid.

314 **With stories of the** Archer Blood, *The Cruel Birth of Bangladesh: Memoirs of an American Diplomat* (Dhaka: University Press Limited, 2002), 301–2.

315 **To fix that inconvenient** Malcolm W. Browne, "Horrors of East Pakistan Turning Hope into Despair," *New York Times*, October 14, 1971, A1.

315 **They burned anything** Malcolm W. Browne, "East Pakistan Town After Raid by Army: Fire and Destruction," *New York Times*, November 17, 1971, A1.

315 **Letters from whistleblowers** Coggin, "Pakistan: The Ravaging of Golden Bengal."

315 **Fresh off his legislative** Sydney Schanberg, "Kennedy, In India, Terms Pakistani Drive Genocide," *New York Times*, August 17, 1971.

45: A. A. K. NIAZI AND TIKKA KHAN

316 *"Ay Behanchod chod!"* This scene adapted from David Loshak, "A Savage Occupation Army," *Daily Telegraph*, October 27, 1971. See also *Der Spigel*'s account of the girl from October 11, 1971, as translated in Shamsul Bari, "Fast a Day to Save a People," *Bangladesh Newsletter* (1972): 121, and David Loshak, *Pakistan Crisis* (London: Heinemann, 1971).

316 **More than forty thousand** A. M. A. Muhith, *Bangladesh: Emergence of a Nation* (Dhaka: University Press Limited, 3rd edition, 2014), 315.

317 **As one diplomat put** Peter Kann, "Determined Course: Pakistan Seems Likely to Push Its Repression of Bengalis in the East," *Wall Street Journal*, September 20, 1971.

317 **He ordered troops** Sidney Schaumberg, "Hindus Are Targets of Army Terror," *New York Times*, July 4, 1971; and Schaumberg, "West Pakistan Pursues Subjugation of Bengalis," *New York Times*, July 14, 1971.

317 **After his men finished** Robert Payne, *Massacre* (New York: Macmillan, 1973), 58.

317 **"I am in their"** Muntassir Mamoon, ed., *Media and the Liberation War of Bangladesh*, vol. 1 (Dhaka: Centre for Bangladesh Studies, 2002), 163.

317 **Niazi wished he was** Details in this paragraph from Hamoodur Rahman Commission, "Hamoodur Rahman Commission Report," Government of Pakistan, unpublished report, 1972, 15–17.

318 **Most every rooftop** Dan Coggin, "Dacca: City of the Dead," *Time*, May 3, 1971.

318 **When the Mukti Bahini** Sydney Shaumberg, "Power in Dacca Reported Cut Off," *New York Times*, July 6, 1971.

318 **When World Bank and** Malcolm Browne, "Bomb Blasts Welcome World Bank Team to 'Normal Dacca,'" *New York Times*, June 10, 1971; and Shamsul Bari, "What Pakistan Wants," *New Republic*, October 16, 1971, 106–7.

318 **But the InterContinental held** Details of the information campaign at the

InterContinental are taken from Marie Gillespie, "Bangladesh, 1971 and the BBC World Service: Witness Seminar" (London: Open University and BBC, 2009); Peter Kann, "Dacca Diary," *Wall Street Journal*, December 17 and 20, 1971; and author interview with Rahman, who was a concierge at the Intercontinental in 1971 (2020).

319 **Broke vagabonds carried bags** Siddiq Salik, *Witness to Surrender* (Karachi: Oxford University Press, 2nd edition, 1997), 103.

46: MOHAMMAD HAI AND MALIK MAHMUD

321 **They, along with about** Author interview with Malik, November 2019.

322 **Then they'd gun down** Arnaud de Borchgrave, "The Subcontinent: A Losing Battle," *Newsweek*, November 15, 1971.

323 **"Hai, I've got to tell"** Malik remembers telling this story and Hai remembers hearing it, but neither could quite pinpoint the exact words of the conversation or exact place where it happened. Still, both remember clearly how they felt about it. Additional details on this scene and Tonir's activities during the dinner slaughters come from additional author interviews with Malik's and Hai's collaborators at the time, primarily Mintu (2019).

324 **"He kills all our"** The official encyclopedia of Bangladesh offers further corroboration of the surprise attack at Tonir Hat, indicating eighty freedom fighters were killed on October 27, 1971. See additional information at the Bangladesh Official State Encyclopedia at http://en.banglapedia.org/index.php?title=Bhola_District.

324 **"He terrorizes the whole"** While the accounts of Tonir come mostly from interviews with Malik and Hai, oblique references to the locations and people mentioned in their accounts are also included in ibid.

47: YAHYA KHAN AND RICHARD NIXON

326 **Yahya stood on a wobbly** This scene is based on documentation of Yahya's nightmares during the time as mentioned in Dewan Berindranath, *Private Life of Yahya Khan* (New Delhi: Sterling, 1974), 12; Amir Tahiri, "Yahya Khan," *Kayhan International*, February 27, 1972; and from eyewitnesses like Yahya's former press secretary, who defined these weeks as a time where "pimps and prostitutes ruled" the country in B. A. R. Saddiqi, *General Agha Mohammad Yahya Khan: The Rise and Fall of a Soldier, 1947–1971* (Karachi: Oxford University Press, 2020), 189.

327 **After one call Nixon** "Nixon Asks Congress to Authorize $250 Million for East Pakistan," *Washington Post*, October 2, 1971.

327 **Nixon was rambling on** Henry Kissinger, *White House Years* (New York: Simon and Schuster, 2nd edition, 2011), 1543–544, 1552–554.

328 **"We aren't going to"** Abridged from Douglas Brinkley and Luke Nichter, *The Nixon Tapes: 1971–1972* (New York: Mariner, 2015), 584–86.

328 **Kissinger egged him on** Ibid.

328 **What if they turned** Srinath Raghavan, *1971: A Global History of the Creation of Bangladesh* (Cambridge, MA: Harvard University Press, 201), 233.

329 **A little while later** Details from Berindranath, *Private Life of Yahya Khan*, 68–70; "Yahya Khan and Black Beauty," *Nawa-e-Waqt*, March 1972. We have not been able to obtain additional details corroborating this exact sequence of events, although to our knowledge neither Yahya, Mrs. Hussain, nor Yahya's son, Ali, ever publicly disputed the events as presented by Berindranath and *Nawa-e-Waqt*.

331 **Yahya picked up** Archer Blood, *The Cruel Birth of Bangladesh: Memoirs of an American Diplomat* (Dhaka: University Press Limited, 2002), 334–35.

48: A. A. K. NIAZI AND YAYHA KHAN

332 **The Pakistani strike force** Gary J. Bass, *The Blood Telegram: Nixon, Kissinger, and a Forgotten Genocide* (New York: Vintage, 2014), 268–69.

333 **After her safe landing** Ibid., 269.

333 **"We meet as a"** Indira Gandhi, "Speech to Lok Sabha," India Ministry of Home Affairs, HI/121/25/71, December 4, 1971. Also in ibid.

333 **The dentist-turned-governor** Siddiq Salik, *Witness to Surrender* (Karachi: Oxford University Press, 2nd edition, 1997), 194.

334 **"for PRESIDENT OF PAKISTAN"** Hamoodur Rahman Commission, "Hamoodur Rahman Commission Report," Government of Pakistan, unpublished report, 1972, 100. We have lightly abridged the source here for clarity.

335 **"full scale and bitter"** Ibid.

49: HAFIZ UDDIN AHMAD

336 **Hafiz sensed victory** Hafiz's accounts at Chargram and Atgram appear in his memoir, Hafiz Uddin Ahmad, *Bloodshed '71* (Dhaka: Shahitto Prokash Books, 1997). Additional details from author interviews with Hafiz.

336 **Just a few hours** Additional information on the battle at Atgram from Brigadier Rattan Kaul, "Battle of Atgram—20th/21st November 1971 (Sylhet District—East Pakistan) Khukri Assault by 4/5 Gorkha Rifles," *Bharat Rakshak* (New Delhi: Bharat Rakshak, 2015).

50: YAHYA KHAN AND RICHARD NIXON

343 **Some villagers used** Anthony Mascarenhas, "Genocide," *Sunday Times*, Special Edition, June 13, 1971, and International Commission of Jurists, "The Events in East Pakistan, 1971 (1972): A Legal Study by the Secretariat of the International Commission of Jurists" (Geneva: ICJ, 1972).

343 **In his first act** Siddiq Salik, *Witness to Surrender* (Karachi: Oxford University Press, 2nd edition, 1997), 194–96.

343 **The governor asked Yahya** Hamoodur Rahman Commission, "Hamoodur Rahman Commission Report," Government of Pakistan, unpublished report, 1972, 102–6.

344 **As Bhutto's plane taxied** Shamsul Bari, "Reality of Bangladesh—at a Glance," *Bangladesh Newsletter*, 1971, 158–59. See also original reporting that bought Yahya's initial claim, for example, "Bombs Raze an Orphanage There," *New York Times*, December 10, 1971, A1.

344 **"Mr. President, this is"** Srinath Raghavan, *1971: A Global History of the Creation of Bangladesh* (Cambridge, MA: Harvard University Press, 2013), 243.

344 **Nixon had a bad habit** Anthony Summers and Robbyn Swan, "Drunk in Charge (Part Two)," *Guardian*, September 2, 2000.

344 **"Get tougher, goddamnit!"** Details from next six paragraphs from Henry Kissinger, *White House Years* (New York: Simon and Schuster, 2nd edition, 2011), 1585–1601. Also Raghavan, *1971*, 240.

345 **"It's a typical Nixon"** Raghavan, *1971*, 255–56; and Nixon-Kissinger conversation, December 12, 1971, Foreign Relations of the United States Office of the Historian, E7, 769.

346 **"for GOVERNOR from PRESIDENT"** Hamoodur Rahman Commission, 110–112. Abridged for clarity.

346 **Bhutto wired Yahya** Dewan Berindranath, *Private Life of Yahya Khan* (New Delhi: Sterling, 1974), 125–27.

346 **So he threw a** Ibid., 129, and Abbas, *Pakistan's Drift into Extremism*, 66–68.

51: CAPTAIN ERNEST TISSOT AND REAR ADMIRAL VLADIMIR KRUGLYAKOV

347 **Since then, it had** Willard J, Webb and Walter Poole, *The Joint Chiefs of Staff and the War in Vietnam* (Washington, DC: Office of Joint History, 2007), 114.

347 **At the helm was** "Ernest Eugene Tissot," Naval History and Heritage Command, entry of 2015.

348 **Flight crews could load** "USS Enterprise," US Navy, 2019, archived at

https://web.archive.org/web/*/https://www.navy.mil/navydata/ships
/carriers/powerhouse/powerhouse.asp.

348 **The *Enterprise* carried enough** Hans Kristensen, "Declassified: US Nuclear Weapons at Sea," Federation of American Scientists Report #1, 2016.

348 **Flanked by two quick-strike** Naval History and Heritage Command, "Enterprise VIII (CVAN-65) 1971–1975," US Navy Publication, 2015.

348 **An American nuclear-attack** Raghavendra Mishra, "Revisiting the 1971 'USS Enterprise Incident': Rhetoric, Reality and Pointers for the Contemporary Era," *Journal of Defence Studies* 9, no. 2 (2015): 49–80.

348 **Military radios crackled** Robert Payne, *Massacre* (New York: Macmillan, 1973), 124.

348 **Nixon authorized Tissot** Srinath Raghavan, *1971: A Global History of the Creation of Bangladesh* (Cambridge, MA: Harvard University Press, 2013), 254.

348 **The *Enterprise* would** Henry Kissinger, *White House Years* (New York: Simon and Schuster, 2nd edition, 2011), 1505–506.

348 **Five hundred miles south** Alexander Rozin, "Mission of the Soviet Navy During the War between India and Pakistan in 1971," self-published manuscript, July 7, 2011, and personal communication with author. Soviet accounts of this incident remain limited to those of a select few eyewitnesses including most prominently those of Admiral Kruglyakov in several TV interviews in Russian media. Official Soviet naval records of the period remain classified. Rozin's writings in the Soviet sections are the best cited and most extensive historical accounts of the Soviet side of the encounter.

348 **The Soviet fleet included** Ibid.

349 **Candy held him tight** Author interview with Julian Francis, January 2020.

349 **The Soviet naval commander** Interview with Admiral Kruglyakov, Russia TV, 2012, available at https://www.youtube.com/watch?v=O8S8KPjmIGA.

350 **"We're going to war"** Rozin, "Mission of the Soviet Navy."

350 **She was dumbstruck** Mishra, "Revisiting the 1971 'USS Enterprise Incident'"; Gary J. Bass, *The Blood Telegram: Nixon, Kissinger, and a Forgotten Genocide* (New York: Vintage, 2014), 299–301.

350 **She worried that** Raghavan, *1971*, 254.

350 **"They must have gone"** Payne, *Massacre*, 123.

52: ZULFIKAR ALI BHUTTO, YAHYA KHAN, AND HENRY KISSINGER

352 **Half a world away** The breakfast scene and details are from Henry Kissinger, *White House Years* (New York: Simon and Schuster, 2nd edition, 2011), 1607–616.

353 **Big E would chug** Gary J. Bass, *Blood Telegram*, 314–18.

353 **Bhutto decided to walk** See, for example, Kemal A. Faruki, "The Indo-Pakistan War, 1971 and the United Nations," *Pakistan Horizon* 25, no. 1 (1972): 10–20.

354 **Out of nowhere** General (Ret'd) Agha Muhammad Yahya Khan, affidavit to the Lahore High Court at Lahore, re: Writ Petition No. 1649 (Lahore: Lahore High Court, 1974), Point 49.

354 **Worse, the Indians realized** Faruq Aziz Khan, *Spring 1971* (Dhaka: Agamee Prakashani, 2014), 150.

354 **Bhutto didn't tell Yahya** Srinath Raghavan, *1971: A Global History of the Creation of Bangladesh* (Cambridge, MA: Harvard University Press, 2013), 267.

354 **"Soon. Soon."** Siddiq Salik, *Witness to Surrender* (Karachi: Oxford University Press, 2nd edition, 1997), 199–200.

53: RICHARD NIXON

355 **Just a few months** Jozef Goldblat, *Arms Control: The New Guide to Negotiations and Agreements* (London: SAGE Publications Ltd, 2002), 301–2.

355 **"We have waited"** Henry Kissinger, *White House Years* (New York: Simon and Schuster, 2nd edition, 2011), 1609.

355 **"It became urgent to"** Ibid., 1613.

355 **Nixon would employ** Faruq Aziz Khan, *Spring 1971* (Dhaka: Agamee Prakashani, 2014), 149; see also Kissinger, *White House Years*, 1609, 1505–506.

356 **"After this is over"** This conversation is abridged and edited from "Conversation Among President Nixon, the President's Assistant (Haldeman), and the President's Assistant for National Security Affairs (Kissinger)," Foreign Relations of the United States, 1969–1976, Volume E-7, December 15, 1971, 8:45–11:30 a.m., US Department of State, Nixon Presidential Materials, White House Tapes, Office of the Historian, National Archives, Recording of conversation between Nixon, Haldeman, and Kissinger, Oval Office, Conversation No. 638–4; and an earlier conversation with Kissinger, Nixon, and Alexander Haig, as noted in *Foreign Relations of the United States: Diplomatic Papers*, US Department of State, Volume XIV, 74. See also Gary J. Bass, *The Blood Telegram: Nixon, Kissinger, and a Forgotten Genocide* (New York: Vintage, 2014), 267–79, for an extensive discussion of this period and additional supporting quotations.

54: A. A. K. NIAZI AND YAHYA KHAN

357 **"They will have to"** Siddiq Salik, *Witness to Surrender* (Karachi: Oxford University Press, 2nd edition, 1997), 202.

357   **"You must hold out"** Robert Payne, *Massacre* (New York: Macmillan, 1973), 122.

357   **They barricaded themselves** Salik, *Witness to Surrender*, 206–7.

357   **A rumor circulated** Dan Coggin, "We Know How the Parisians Felt," *Time*, December 27, 1971.

357   **The Dentist and his** Peter R. Kaan, "Dacca Diary," *Wall Street Journal*, December 14, 1971.

358   **They held an all-night poker** Ibid.; Coggin, "We Know How the Parisians Felt."

358   **Photographers sat in folding** Kaan, "Dacca Diary."

358   **Every few hours** Coggin, "We Know How the Parisians Felt."

358   **The InterContinental was** L. G. S. Singh, "An Army Surrenders," in Dhruv C. Katoch and Q. S. A. Zahir, eds., *Liberation Bangladesh—1971* (New Delhi: Bloomsbury, 2015), 239–40.

358   **The guards outside** Coggin, "We Know How the Parisians Felt."

358   **Their new objective** K. M. Safiullah, *Bangladesh at War* (Dhaka: Agamee Prakashani, 2005), 235–45.

358   **Yahya hadn't slept** Salik, *Witness to Surrender*, 208; Dewan Berindranath, *Private Life of Yahya Khan* (New Delhi: Sterling, 1974), 131.

358   **The Indian Navy lobbed** Gary J. Bass, *The Blood Telegram: Nixon, Kissinger, and a Forgotten Genocide* (New York: Vintage, 2014), 280.

359   **"What? I can't hear you."** The details of this conversation are from an interview with Yahya Khan in 1979, in Richard Sisson and Leo E. Rose, *War and Secession: Pakistan, India, and the Creation of Bangladesh* (Berkeley: University of California Press, 1991), 306–7, note 28.

360   **"for GOVERNOR and GENERAL"** Hamoodur Rahman Commission, "Hamoodur Rahman Commission Report," Government of Pakistan, unpublished report, 1972, 116–20.

361   **Niazi had to accomplish** Payne, *Massacre*, 125.

361   **"They cut out"** "Dacca Dispatch," *Evening Star*, December 19, 1971.

361   **His men threw** Rakesh Krishnan Simha, "Sweeping Mines, Salvaging Looted Gold After the 1971 War," *Russia Beyond*, August 31, 2013.

55: REAR ADMIRAL KRUGLYAKOV AND RICHARD NIXON

362   **A few hundred feet beneath the surface** The exact location of the so-called red line in the sea is a matter of debate with authors cited in this chapter positing various locations inside the Bay of Bengal. Most authors agree that it occurred in the vicinity of India's Andaman and Nicobar islands, though no official report has ever confirmed the Seventh Fleet's coordinates at that time.

362 **Kruglyakov's fleet stalked** Sebastien Roblin, "In 1971, the U.S. Navy Almost Fought the Soviets Over Bangladesh," *War Is Boring*, July 19, 2016.

363 **"A city is coming"** Arsney Korolev, "The Americans Stood and Left," (Simbirsky) *Courier*, no. 28 (March 18, 2006).

364 **"We are constantly being"** Alexander Rozin, "Mission of the Soviet Navy During the War Between India and Pakistan in 1971," self-published manuscript, July 7, 2011.

364 **When the US ambassador** Dewan Berindranath, *Private Life of Yahya Khan* (New Delhi: Sterling, 1974), 16.

364 **"I consider this"** This conversation condensed and abridged from Gary J. Bass, *The Blood Telegram: Nixon, Kissinger, and a Forgotten Genocide* (New York: Vintage, 2014), 298–303. See also *Foreign Relations of the United States: Diplomatic Papers*, US Department of State, Volume XIV, E-7. "Conversation Among President Nixon, the President's Assistant (Haldeman), and the President's Assistant for National Security Affairs (Kissinger)," Foreign Relations of the United States, 1969–1976, Volume E-7, December 15, 1971, 8:45–11:30 a.m., US Department of State, Nixon Presidential Materials, White House Tapes, Office of the Historian, National Archives, Recording of conversation between Nixon, Haldeman, and Kissinger, Oval Office, Conversation No. 638–4.

365 **"If the Soviets move"** Ibid., 637–43.

365 **The men stood on** Rozin, "Mission of the Soviet Navy."

365 **Except in this case** Interview with Admiral Kruglyakov, Russia TV, 2012, available at https://www.youtube.com/watch?v=O8S8KPjmIGA.

365 **Both men prayed** Korolev, "The Americans Stood and Left."

365 **"I have targeted"** Interview with Kruglyakov, Russia TV.

56: A. A. K. NIAZI, RICHARD NIXON, ZULFIKAR ALI BHUTTO, AND HAFIZ UDDIN AHMAD

367 **He set up a fancy** J. F. R. Jacob, *An Odyssey in War and Peace: An Autobiography* (New Delhi: Roli, 2015), excerpted in Jacob, "How Lt. General JFR Jacob Secured Pakistan's Surrender in 1971," *Scroll.in* (2016).

367 **The Indians even promised** Ibid., and Siddiq Salik, *Witness to Surrender* (Karachi: Oxford University Press, 2nd edition, 1997), 210–12.

368 **Then Aurora sent Niazi** Jacob, *An Odyssey in War and Peace*, 136–37.

368 **He'd been wearing** Dewan Berindranath, *Private Life of Yahya Khan* (New Delhi: Sterling, 1974), 12.

368 **Not knowing what else** Nawaz was the television announcer; author interview with Shuja Nawaz.

368 **News of the surrender** Author interview with Hafiz.

369 **"Mr. President?"** This conversation is an abridgement and combination of two conversations of the time period: Transcript of Telephone Conversation Between President Nixon and Kissinger, Library of Congress, Kissinger Papers, Box 370, 315. The president traveled to Key Biscayne, Florida, on the afternoon of December 15 and remained there through December 16; Kissinger was in Washington, December 15, 1971, 324. Transcript of Telephone Conversation Between President Nixon and Kissinger, Library of Congress, Manuscript Division, Kissinger Papers, Box 370, Telephone Conversations, Washington, December 17, 1971.

370 **He hoped that India** This conversation abridged and edited for clarity from President Richard M. Nixon, Zulfikar Ali Bhutto, Nawabzada Am Raza, Alexander M. Haig Jr., Manolo Sanchez, White House from 1:36 p.m. to 2:06 p.m., Conversation 639–011, December 18, 1971.

371 **"The people of Pakistan"** Bhutto interview with British TV (channel unknown), available at https://www.youtube.com/watch?v=Xu4MTv5wgys.

57: MOHAMMAD HAI AND MALIK MAHMUD

372 **Hai inspected the** All details from this chapter come from author interviews with Hai and Malik.

58: CANDY ROHDE AND JON ROHDE

378 **Jon pinched the large** All details in this chapter from author interviews with Jon Rohde; Jon Rohde, "Women in the Bangladesh Liberation Struggle," in A. M. A. Muhith, ed., *American Response to Bangladesh Liberation War* (Dhaka: University Press Limited, 1996); and Cornelia Rohde, *Catalyst: In the Wake of the Great Bhola Cyclone* (Scotts Valley, CA: CreateSpace Independent Publishing Platform, 2014).

59: YAHYA KHAN AND ZULFIKAR ALI BHUTTO

380 **Three days after Dacca** The birthday party scene is from Dewan Berindranath, *Private Life of Yahya Khan* (New Delhi: Sterling, 1974), 13–14.

380 **To prove his love** Author interview with Nawaz. The exact day of his making up with Ali is uncertain but was most likely before his house arrest later that week. Other sources say that Ali was let back into President House as early as December 15, where he drank with Ambassador Farland while they watched Pakistan's fall from Yahya's parlor.

381 **"Death to Yahya Khan!"** Feroz Hassan Khan, *Eating Grass: The Making*

of the Pakistani Bomb (Stanford, CA: Stanford Security Studies, 2012), 78–79.

381 **Wives of fallen soliders** Dan Coggin, "Ali Bhutto Begins to Pick Up the Pieces," *Time,* January 3, 1972.

381 **Too drunk to speak** *The Bangladesh Papers: The Recorded Statements of Politicians of United Pakistan, 1969–1971* (Dhaka: Vanguard, 1978), 288–94, and Berindranath, *Private Life of Yahya Khan,* 13–14.

381 **Keeping Yahya there** General (Ret'd) Agha Muhammad Yahya Khan, affidavit to the Lahore High Court at Lahore, re: Writ Petition No. 1649 (Lahore: Lahore High Court, 1974), Point 35.

381 **That night, Bhutto drank** Berindranath, *Private Life of Yahya Khan,* 14.

382 **"My dear countrymen"** "President Addresses Nation," *Pakistan Affairs* 38, nos. 23–25 (December 28, 1971): 1.

382 **"Your Excellency"** US Department of State, Nixon Presidential Materials, Office of the Historian, National Archives, NSC Files, Box 760, Presidential Correspondence File, Telegram 233015, December 30, 1971, and NSC Files, Box 573, Indo-Pak War, South Asia, 12/17/71–12/31/71.

382 **They decided that their** Anthony Lewis, "At Home Abroad," *New York Times,* December 20, 1971.

383 **"Congratulations Mr. President"** FRUS 1969–73, Document 191, December 15. See also Srinath Raghavan, *1971: A Global History of the Creation of Bangladesh* (Cambridge, MA: Harvard University Press, 2013), 262.

383 **First, he ordered** Berindranath, *Private Life of Yahya Khan,* 35.

383 **Bhutto arrested General Rani** Ibid., 81, 75.

384 **Bhutto told Tikka** Khushwant Singh, "Foreign Affairs: Pakistan, India and the Bomb," *New York Times,* July 1, 1979.

384 **Bhutto named Tikka** Attar Chand, *Nuclear Policy and National Security* (New Delhi: Mittal, 1993), 59.

384 **Having nukes** Steve Weissman and Herbert Crossney, *The Islamic Bomb* (New Delhi: Vision, 1983).

60: SHEIKH MUJIBUR RAHMAN AND ZULFIKAR ALI BHUTTO

385 **Mujib sat on the** Robert Payne, *Massacre* (New York: Macmillan, 1973), 88.

385 **Since the Pakistan Army** "Mujib's Statement and Excerpts from News Session," *New York Times,* January 9, 1972.

385 **They were digging** Anthony Mascarenhas, *Bangladesh: A Legacy of Blood* (London: Hodder and Stoughton, 1986), 15–17.

386 *I am ready* Payne, *Massacre,* 90; edited for grammar.

386 **"No, Mujib, I am"** Kamal Hossain, *Bangladesh: Quest for Freedom and Jus-*

tice (Dhaka: University Press Limited, 2013), 114; see also Kuldip Nayar, "In Their Words: Bhutto and Mujib, December 1971," *Daily Star*, November 15, 2006.

386 **"I am a good"** Nayar, "In Their Words."

386 **"No Mujib, I'm here"** Kuldip Nayar, *Scoop! Inside Stories from the Partition to the Present* (New York: HarperCollins, 2007), 398–99.

386 **Mujib staggered toward it** Payne, *Massacre*, 131.

386 **Bhutto told him** Details of this scene from ibid., 132–37; and Nayar, *Scoop!*, 397–400.

387 **He threw Mujib** Hossain, *Bangladesh*, 115–16.

388 **"The Pakistani people"** Payne, *Massacre*, 137.

388 **Mujib blinked in bewilderment** Dan Coggin, "Bangladesh: A Hero Returns Home," *Time*, January 24, 1972.

388 **He didn't even know** Mascarenhas, *Bangladesh*, 6.

389 **At the press conference** A clip of the press conference is available courtesy of the Bangladesh Awami League at https://www.youtube.com/watch?v=2Gi5VkMxLsA.

389 **Advisers tried to brief him** Hossain, *Bangladesh*, 118.

389 **"Switzerland of Asia"** Coggin, "Bangladesh: A Hero Returns Home."

389 **His famous thick black hair** Clip of press conference; Faruq Aziz Khan, *Spring 1971* (Dhaka: Agamee Prakashani, 2014), 188–89; and Mascarenhas, *Bangladesh*, 7.

389 **He wished Bhutto** "Mujib's Statement and Excerpts from News Session"; Payne, *Massacre*, 138.

389 **Mujib's mind had been** Khan, *Spring 1971*, 191.

61: HAFIZ UDDIN AHMAD

391 **Mujib's right-hand man** Kamal Hossain, *Bangladesh: Quest for Freedom and Justice* (Dhaka: University Press Limited, 2013), 121.

391 **The blue-and-silver British** Dan Coggin, "Bangladesh: A Hero Returns Home," *Time*, January 24, 1972.

391 **With tears in his eyes** Robert Payne, *Massacre* (New York: Macmillan, 1973), 140–41.

391 **Mujib climbed atop** Archival news footage of the crowd and events of the day is available at https://www.youtube.com/watch?v=poPZ_hqACxk (Bangladesh News) and https://www.youtube.com/watch?v=PsTOIiJr7so (NBC News).

392 **The military tradition** Author interview with Hafiz.

393 **Smiling, he breezed through** Peter Jennings, "Report from Dacca," *ABC*

News, January 13, 1972, available at https://www.youtube.com/watch?v=d0 QWIXSXjGE.

62: MOHAMMAD HAI AND MALIK MAHMUD

394 **Hai sat cross-legged** All details from this section are from author interviews with Hai and Malik , unless otherwise noted.

395 **Students were beginning** "Dacca University Slowly Returns to Life," *Bangladesh Bulletin* (January 14, 1972): 2.

397 **"I could not give"** Nuran Nabi and Mush Nabi, *Bullets of '71: A Freedom Fighter's Story* (Dhaka: Shahitya Prakash, 2012), 402–3.

63: NEIL FRANK

399 **He adapted storm-surge** Robert Sheets, "The National Hurricane Center: Past, Present and Future," *Weather and Forecasting* 5, no. 2 (1990): 185–231.

399 **He helped the country** Author interview with Neil Frank.

399 **After he filed** World Bank, "Bangladesh: Cyclone Protection and Coastal Area Rehabilitation Project" (Washington DC: World Bank, 1972).

64: RICHARD NIXON AND ZHOU ENLAI

401 **Nixon then teased Kissinger** This conversation is abridged from a long discussion on February 23, 1972, in US Department of State, Nixon Presidential Materials, White House Tapes, Office of the Historian, National Archives, White House Special Files, President's Office Files, Box 87, Memoranda for the President, Top Secret, Sensitive, Exclusively Eyes Only; and Nixon Archives, Memorandum of Conversation No. 3, February 23, 1972, National Security Archive, Washington DC. See also F. S. Aijazuddin, *From a Head, Through a Head, to a Head: The Secret Channel Between the US and China Through Pakistan* (Karachi: Oxford University Press, 2000), 142–45.

402 **"President Yahya was probably"** Aijazuddin, *From a Head, Through a Head, to a Head*, xxii, and Nixon, Memorandum of Conversation No. 3, February 23, 1972, National Security Archive, Washington DC.

403 **They left the residence** Richard Nixon Presidental Library, China Highlights, Part 2, February 23–25, 1972, available at https://www.youtube.com/watch?v=W6EkWX5NT_U.

403 **Later that week** Aijazuddin, *From a Head, Through a Head, to a Head*, 144.

AFTERWORD: THE GATHERING STORM

406 **Analysis from peace research** These connections are a matter of intense scholarly debate regarding their intensity, causality, and peripheral relationships to other climate and conflict phenomena. Good overviews and assessments in this rapidly growing field include, for example, T. Knutson et al., "Tropical Cyclones and Climate Change Assessment: Part II: Projected Response to Anthropogenic Warming," *Bulletin of the American Meteorological Society* 101, no. 3 (2021): E303–E322; Solomon Hsiang, Marshall Burke, and Edward Miguel, "Quantifying the Influence of Climate on Human Conflict," *Science* 341, no. 6151 (2013): 1235367; Guy Abel et al., "Climate, Conflict and Forced Migration," *Global Environmental Change* 54 (2019): 239–49; Katherine Mach et al., "Climate as a Risk Factor for Armed Conflict," *Nature* 571 (2019): 193–97; Vally Koubi, "Climate Change and Conflict," *Annual Review of Political Science* 22 (2019): 343–60; and Carl-Frederich Schleussner, Jonathan Donges, Reik Donner, and Hans Joachim Schnell, "Armed-Conflict Risks Enhanced by Climate-Related Disasters in Ethnically Fractionalized Countries," *Proceedings of the National Academy of Sciences* 113, no. 33 (2016): 9216–221. We expect that additional research over the coming decade will continue to refine the conditions and associations between climate disasters and conflict.

410 **Money that was supposed** See, for example, Graeme Thomson, "How George Harrison Staged One of the Most Influential Concerts in History," *GQ*, February 25, 2021, Peter Doggett, *You Never Give Me Your Money: The Beatles After the Breakup* (New York: It Books, 2011), 211–13, and David Johnston, "Bangladesh: The Benefit that Almost Wasn't." *Los Angeles Times*, June 2, 1985.

Selected Bibliography

Abbas, Hassan. *Pakistan's Drift into Extremism: Allah, the Army, and America's War on Terror.* New York: Routledge, 2004.

Ahmad, Hafiz Uddin. *Bloodshed '71.* Dhaka: Shahitto Prokash Books, 1997.

Aijazuddin, F. S. *From a Head, Through a Head, to a Head: The Secret Channel Between the US and China Through Pakistan.* Karachi: Oxford University Press, 2000.

Ali, Shaikh Maqsood. *From East Bengal to Bangladesh: Dynamics and Perspectives.* Dhaka: University Press Limited, 2nd edition, 2017.

Amin, Agha Humayun. *Pakistan Army Since 1965.* Lahore: Defence Journal Publications, 2000.

Baldwin, Stephen C. *Shadows Over Sundials: Dark and Light Life in a Large Outside World.* Online: iUniverse, 2009.

Bass, Gary. *The Blood Telegram: Nixon, Kissinger, and a Forgotten Genocide.* New York: Vintage, 2014.

Berindranath, Dewan. *Private Life of Yahya Khan.* New Delhi: Sterling, 1974.

Bhutto, Zufikar Ali. *The Great Tragedy.* Islamabad: PPP Publications, 1971.

Blood, Archer. *The Cruel Birth of Bangladesh: Memoirs of an American Diplomat.* Dhaka: University Press Limited, 2002.

Boyd, Pattie. *Wonderful Tonight: George Harrison, Eric Clapton, and Me.* New York: Crown, 2008.

Brinkley, Douglas, and Luke Nichter. *The Nixon Tapes: 1971–1972.* New York: Mariner, 2015.

Cardozo, Ian, ed. *In Quest of Freedom: The War of 1971.* New Delhi: Bloomsbury, 2016.

Choudhury, G. W. *The Last Days of United Pakistan.* London: Hurst, 1974.

Fallaci, Oriana. *Interview with History.* Rome: Rizzoli/Liveright, 1976.

Guhathakurta, Megna, and Willem van Schendel, eds. *The Bangladesh*

Reader: History, Culture, Politics. Durham, NC: Duke University Press, 2013.

Hafiz, Munawar, ed. *Bangladesh 1971: Dreadful Experiences*. Dhaka: Shahitya Prakash, 2017.

Hamoodur Rahman Commission. "Hamoodur Rahman Commission Report." Government of Pakistan, unpublished report, 1972.

Hossain, Kamal. *Bangladesh: Quest for Freedom and Justice*. Dhaka: University Press Limited, 2013.

Imam, Jahanara. *Of Blood and Fire: The Untold Story of Bangladesh's War of Independence*. New Delhi: Sterling, 1990.

International Commission of Jurists. "The Events in East Pakistan, 1971 (1972): A Legal Study by the Secretariat of the International Commission of Jurists." Geneva: ICJ, 1972.

International Crimes Tribunal. ICT-BD Case No. 06 OF 2011 ICT-1. Dhaka: International Crimes Tribunal, Old High Court Building, Government of Bangladesh, 2011.

Islam, M. Rafiqul. *A Tale of Millions: Bangladesh Liberation War, 1971*. Dhaka: Bangladesh Books International, 1981.

Jacob, J. F. R. *An Odyssey in War and Peace: An Autobiography*. New Delhi: Roli, 2015.

———. *Surrender at Dacca: Birth of a Nation*. Dhaka: University Press Limited, 1981.

Jala, Ayesha. *The Struggle for Pakistan: A Muslim Homeland and Global Politics*. Cambridge, MA: Harvard University Press, 2014.

Karim, S. A. *Triumph and Tragedy*. New Delhi: University Press Limited, 2009.

Katoch, Dhruv C., and Q. S. A. Zahir, eds. *Liberation: Bangladesh—1971*. New Delhi: Bloomsbury, 2015.

Khan, A. Qayyum. *Bittersweet Victory: A Freedom Fighter's Tale*. Dhaka: University Press Limited, 2nd edition, 2016.

Khan, Arshad Sami. *Three Presidents and an Aide*. New Delhi: Pentagon Press, 2008.

Khan, Faruq Aziz. *Spring 1971*. Dhaka: Agamee Prakashani, 2014.

Khan, General (Ret'd) Agha Muhammad Yahya, affidavit to the Lahore High Court at Lahore, re: Writ Petition No. 1649. Lahore: Lahore High Court, 1974.

Khan, Mohammed Asghar. *Generals in Politics: Pakistan 1958–1982*. New Delhi: Vikas, 1983.

Khan, Rao Farman Ali. *How Pakistan Got Divided*. Karachi: Oxford University Press, 2017.

Khan, Yasmin. *India at War: The Subcontinent and the Second World War*. Karachi: Oxford University Press, 2015.

Kissinger, Henry. *White House Years*. New York: Simon and Schuster, 2nd edition, 2011.

Lewis, David. *Bangladesh: Politics, Economy and Civil Society*. Cambridge: Cambridge University Press, 2011.

Loshak, David. *Pakistan Crisis*. London: Heinemann, 1971.

Mamoon, Muntassir. *Birangona 1971: Saga of the Violated Women*. Dhaka: Journeyman, 2017.

———. *The Vanquished Generals and the Liberation War of Bangladesh*. Dhaka: Somoy, 2000.

Mamoon, Muntassir, ed. *Media and the Liberation War of Bangladesh*, vols. 1 & 2. Dhaka: Centre for Bangladesh Studies, 2002.

———. *1971: Chuknagar Genocide*. Dhaka: University Press Limited, 2011.

Mascarenhas, Anthony. *Bangladesh: A Legacy of Blood*. London: Hodder and Stoughton, 1986.

———. "Genocide." *Sunday Times*, Special Edition, June 13, 1971.

Mazari, Sherbaz Khan. *A Journey to Disillusionment*. Karachi: Oxford University Press, 1999.

Mowla, Enayet. *Birth of a Nation: Story of the Liberation War of Bangladesh*. Dhaka: Shahitya Prakash, 2010.

Muhith, A. M. A. *Bangladesh: Emergence of a Nation*. Dhaka: University Press Limited, 3rd edition, 2014.

Muhith, A. M. A., ed. *American Response to Bangladesh Liberation War*. Dhaka: University Press Limited, 1996.

Mukerjee, Dilip. *Yahya Khan's "Final War": India Meets Pakistan's Threat*. London: Bennet, Coleman, 1972.

Nabi, Nuran, and Mush Nabi. *Bullets of '71: A Freedom Fighter's Story*. Dhaka: Shahitya Prakash, 2012.

Nasir, Ayesha. *Night of the General*. Karachi: Newsline, 2002.

Nawaz, Shuja. *Crossed Swords: Pakistan, Its Army, and the Wars Within*. Karachi: Oxford University Press, 2008.

Nayar, Kuldip. *Scoop!: Inside Stories from the Partition to the Present*. New York: HarperCollins, 2007.

Niazi, A. A. K. *The Betrayal of East Pakistan*. Karachi: Oxford University Press, 1998.

Nixon, Richard M. *In the Arena: A Memoir of Victory, Defeat, and Renewal*. New York: Simon and Schuster, 1990.

———. *RN: The Memoirs of Richard Nixon*. New York: Simon and Schuster, 2nd edition, 1990.

Payne, Robert. *Massacre*. New York: Macmillan, 1973.

Raghavan, Srinath. *1971: A Global History of the Creation of Bangladesh*. Cambridge, MA: Harvard University Press, 2013.

Raja, Khadim Hussain. *A Stranger in My Own Country: East Pakistan 1969–1971*. Karachi: Oxford University Press, 2012.

Rohde, Cornelia. *Catalyst: In the Wake of the Great Bhola Cyclone*. Scotts Valley, CA: CreateSpace Independent Publishing Platform, 2014.

Sadik, Musa, ed. *Bangladesh Wins Freedom*. Dhaka: Agamee Prakashani, 2000.

Safiullah, K. M. *Bangladesh at War*. Dhaka: Agamee Prakashani, 2005.

———. *Bangladesh at War*. Dhaka: Academic Press and Publishers Library, revised edition, 2015.

Salik, Siddiq. *Witness to Surrender*. Karachi: Oxford University Press, 2nd edition, 1997.

Schendel, Willem van. *A History of Bangladesh*. Cambridge: Cambridge University Press, 2009.

Sen, H. N. "Missing of MV '*Mahajagmitra*': Report of Court on Formal Investigation." *Oceanite* (1971): 34–44.

Shamsuddin, Abul Kalam M. *Confession of a Terrorist!: Musings on Bangladesh Liberation War*. Baltimore, MD: IP-6 Research Inc., 2010.

Shankar, Ravi. *Raga Mala*. New York: Genesis, 1997.

Siddiqi, B. A. R. *East Pakistan: The Endgame. An Onlooker's Journal, 1969–1971*. Karachi: Oxford University Press, 2005.

———. *General Agha Mohammad Yahya Khan: The Rise and Fall of a Soldier, 1947–1971*. Karachi: Oxford University Press, 2020.

Sisson, Richard, and Leo E. Rose. *War and Succession: Pakistan, India and the Creation of Bangladesh*. Berkeley: University of California Press, 1990.

Sohban, Rehman. *Milestones to Bangladesh* (Collected Works of Rehman Sobhan, volume 2). Dhaka: Centre for Policy Dialogue, 2007.

Summers, Anthony. *Arrogance of Power: The Secret World of Richard Nixon*. New York: Penguin, 2001.

Tillery, Gary. *Working Class Mystic: A Spiritual Biography of George Harrison*. Wheaton, IL: Quest, 2011.

Tripathi, Salil. *The Colonel Who Would Not Repent: The Bangladesh War and Its Unquiet Legacy*. New Haven, CT: Yale University Press, 2016.

US Department of State. Foreign Relations of the United States, volume XVII (China) document #143, undated.

———. Nixon Presidential Materials, White House Tapes, Office of the Historian, National Archives, undated.

Vanguard Publications. *The Bangla Desh Papers: The Recorded Statements and*

Speeches of Z. A. Bhutto, Mujeeb-ur-Rahman, Gen. Yahya Khan, and Other Politicians of United Pakistan, 1969–1971. Lahore: Vanguard, 1978.

Wahab, A. T. M. Abdul. *Mukti Bahini Wins Victory: Pak Military Oligarchy Divides Pakistan in 1971.* Dhaka: Columbia Prokashani, 2004.

Weissman, Steve, and Herbert Crossney. *The Islamic Bomb.* New Delhi: Vision, 1983.

World Bank. *Note on the Experience of a World Bank Mission During the Recent Cyclone in East Pakistan.* Washington, DC: World Bank, 1971.

Zahir, Quazi Sajjad Ali. *Fearless Falcon.* Dhaka: Shudhui Muktijuddho, 2017.

———. *The Return of a Hero.* Dhaka: Self-published memoir, 2009.

Zaman, Niaz, and Asif Farrukhi, eds. *Fault Lines: Stories of 1971.* Dhaka: University Press Limited, 2nd edition, 2017.

Index